£30.40

John Wilkes

A Friend to Liberty

John Wilkes

A Friend to Liberty

Peter D. G. Thomas

CLARENDON PRESS · OXFORD

1996

Oxford University Press, Walton Street, Oxford OX2 6DP

Oxford New York
Athens Auckland Bangkok Bombay
Calcutta Cape Town Dar es Salaam Delhi
Florence Hong Kong Istanbul Karachi
Kuala Lumpur Madras Madrid Melbourne
Mexico City Nairobi Paris Singapore
Taipei Tokyo Toronto

and associated companies in
Berlin Ibadan

Oxford is a trade mark of Oxford University Press

Published in the United States
by Oxford University Press Inc., New York

British Library Cataloguing in Publication Data
Data available

Library of Congress Cataloging-in-Publication Data
Thomas, Peter David Garner.
John Wilkes, a friend to liberty / Peter D. G. Thomas.
p. cm.
Includes bibliographical references (p.   ) and index.
1. Wilkes, John, 1727–1797. 2. Great Britain—Politics and government—1760–1789. 3. Radicalism—
Great Britain—History—18th century. 4. Politicians—Great Britain—Biography. 5. Liberty. I. Title.
DA512.W6T55 1996
941.07'3'092—dc20   [B]   95-36715
ISBN 0–19–820544–9

10 9 8 7 6 5 4 3 2 1

Typeset by Alliance Phototypesetters
Printed in Great Britain
on acid-free paper by
Bookcraft Ltd., Midsomer Norton
Nr. Bath, Avon

Preface

JOHN WILKES is a well-known personality of modern British history, albeit for reasons of prurience as well as political significance. Yet no researched biography of him has appeared since the thorough but now dated study by Horace Bleackley in 1917. My debt to that book and to other accounts of Wilkes and of radicalism will be obvious. This biography, while primarily a political study, seeks to present a rounded view of Wilkes by consideration also of his social and sexual life, financial problems, administrative skills, and cultural interests.

News that I was writing a biography of John Wilkes led to various offers of help, not all of which I was able to utilize, for there was a danger of being inundated with information, such was the interest that Wilkes generated among his contemporaries. I am nevertheless grateful for all of this assistance, and especially to Martin Fitzpatrick, Graham Gibbs, Clare Wilkinson, and David Wilkinson; and, above all, to Nicola Jones (née Davies) for a copy of her unpublished thesis on the Bill of Rights Society. Useful advice has come from anonymous readers for the Clarendon Press.

Research and writing is expensive and time consuming. I am grateful to the British Academy for a grant that enabled me to purchase microfilms of Wilkes MSS and to do research in London manuscript repositories and libraries; to the Leverhulme Trust, for an award that enabled the University of Wales, Aberystwyth, to grant me a term's study leave, and also financed research in Winchester and London; and to that University for permitting that leave and for providing a grant from its Research Fund. Claire Swatheridge converted my holograph into a text fit for the printer.

For help with my research I am indebted to the staffs of the Hampshire County Record Office; the British Library; the Guildhall Library; the National Maritime Museum; the Public Record Office; the W. L. Clements Library, University of Michigan, especially for the loan of microfilms; the National Library of Wales; the Institute of Historical Research; the History of Parliament Trust; and the Library of the University of Wales, Aberystwyth.

For permission to use manuscripts I owe thanks to the Earl of Malmesbury, and to the Trustees of both the National Maritime Museum and the British Library. I am grateful to the editors of *Parliamentary History* and

Historical Research for permission to reproduce substantial portions of articles that originally appeared in the former periodical and in the *Bulletin of the Institute of Historical Research*.

P. D. G. T

Contents

List of Plates

1

Youth and Pleasure
1725–1761

JOHN WILKES, a jester to the end, perpetrated a posthumous joke on posterity by instructing that a wrong year of birth should be inscribed on his tombstone. By his direction the tablet read 'A Friend to Liberty: Born at London, Oct. 17, 1727'.[1] Some historians, including several of his biographers, have thereby been deceived:[2] but few of his contemporaries were fooled. After all, his younger brother Heaton, born on 9 February 1727, was still alive at the time.[3] The claim may not, indeed, have been altogether a prank, but some kind of vanity.[4] Certainly it was a long-standing one, traceable back to about 1770. In 1769 there was public celebration of his forty-fourth birthday, as marking the entry into his forty-fifth year; but by 1771 he was openly saying he had been born in 1727, and that remained his story thereafter.[5]

Another claim made by John Wilkes was that he was a gentleman, and contemporaries often commented how perfectly he behaved like one. But he was a self-made one: his family roots were indubitably plebeian. His father Israel was a distiller, living in Clerkenwell in the City of London. His mother Sarah was also a Londoner, a tanner's daughter from Bermondsey. The family was prosperous, with its own coach, but this background was not one that would normally encourage social pretensions, let alone political aspirations. John, born on 17 October 1725, was the second of three sons. Israel, three years older, was apprenticed into the family business at the age of 16, but when 19 announced that he was unsuited to 'trade'.[6] Thereafter he drifted through life, sometimes seeking patronage through John, and mostly residing abroad. When their father died in 1761 the family business was taken over by the third son, Heaton: for the clever and charming John, evidently the parental favourite, was the focus of the family's social ambitions, and early destined for better things. There were three sisters also, but only Mary enjoyed good health and played a role in John's public life.[7]

The children were brought up strictly by their Presbyterian mother, clearly a more dominant figure in the Wilkes household than their easy-going, Anglican, father. In 1734 all three brothers were sent away to a school at Hertford, kept by a John Worsley, much celebrated among Presbyterians for inculcation of morality and learning. There, between the ages of 9 and 14, John received such a thorough grounding in Latin and Greek that he re-mained a classical scholar all his life.[8] John was a star pupil, and Worsley com-plimented him when he left on 'the increase of those generous sentiments and that love of letters, which I myself beheld the first dawnings of . . . Go on, dear youth, and prosper in your noble pursuits'.[9] John was next placed at a small private school of an eccentric Presbyterian minister, Matthew Leeson, which after a brief sojourn in Oxfordshire moved in 1741 to Ayles-bury in Buckinghamshire, where for a nominal rent Leeson was provided with a house by a wealthy widow Mrs Mary Mead, a close friend of John's mother.[10] Early in 1744 Leeson agreed to accompany John to the University of Leiden in Holland, his letter of acceptance making fulsome references to 'those fine parts and excellent natural endowments he is possessed of'.[11]

About sixty years later another British student at Leiden, Scotsman Alexander Carlyle, wrote up this recollection of Wilkes there from notes made at the time, beginning with his introduction by fellow Scot John Gregory.

When we came to John Wilkes, whose ugly countenance in early youth was very striking, I asked earnestly who he was; his answer was that he was the son of a London distiller or brewer, who wanted to be a fine gentleman and man of taste, which he could never be, for God and nature had been against him. I came to know Wilkes very well afterwards and found him to be a sprightly entertaining fellow, too much so for his years, as he was but 18—for even then he showed something of [the] daring profligacy for which he was afterwards notorious. Though he was fond of learning, and passionately desirous of being thought something extra-ordinary, he was unlucky in having an old ignorant pedant of a dissenting parson for his tutor. This man, a Mr Leeson or Lyson, had been singled out by the father as the best tutor in the world for his most promising son.

According to Carlyle's account Leeson had quitted his Church at the age of 60 because he had adopted the Arian creed, a denial of the full divinity of Christ, a doctrine that enjoyed a revival in eighteenth-century Britain.

His chief object seemed to be to make Wilkes an Arian also, and teased him so much about it, that he was obliged to declare, that he did not believe the Bible at all, which produced a quarrel between them—and Wilkes for refuge went frequently to Utrecht, where he met with Immateriallity Baxter, as he was called . . . This gentleman [Andrew Baxter] was more to Wilkes's taste than his own tutor for though he was a profound philosopher and a hard student, he was at the same time a man of the world ... Baxter was so much pleased with Wilkes, that he dedicated one of his pieces to him ... Wilkes was very fond of shining in conversation very prematurely, for at that time he had but little knowledge, except what he derived from Baxter.[12]

If one reason Leeson accompanied Wilkes to Leiden was to safeguard John's virtue, this precaution proved unavailing. Twenty years later he recounted to James Boswell that he was 'always among women at Leyden. My father gave me as much money as I pleased. Three or four whores; drunk every night. Sore head morning, then read. I'm capable to sit thirty hours over a table to study.'[13] Leiden was a favourite alma mater of Dissenters, debarred from a university education in England, and more generally for others of a Whig tradition. Among the fellow students of Wilkes were two future Chancellors of the Exchequer, Charles Townshend, who outshone him in wit, and duller William Dowdeswell, who was always to say that Wilkes was never as wicked as his reputation made him out to be, and who, when John left in 1746, urged him to 'enjoy all the blessings Heaven can shower down upon you'.[14] Certainly, for all his boasting to Boswell, Wilkes while at Leiden polished both his education, attaining a good knowledge of French, and his manners: he acquired the habits of a gentleman, and not merely in an aptitude for loose living and a careless generosity.[15]

His formal education complete, Wilkes returned home to an arranged marriage aimed to secure the status in society coveted for him by his parents. On 23 May 1747 he wed a bride some ten years older than himself, Mary, sole heiress of Mrs Mead, becoming as he later commented 'a sacrifice to Plutius not to Venus'.[16] Israel Wilkes settled on his son an estate of £330 a year, while Mrs Mead gave her daughter the Manor of Aylesbury. The marriage settlement specified that the other Mead estates, in Bedfordshire, Buckinghamshire, Cambridgeshire, and Norfolk, should be entailed on any children.[17] The plan was for the couple to live in Aylesbury during the summer, and reside in London during the winter with Mrs Mead.

In the next few years John Wilkes played the dual role of rural squire and man about town. In 1752 he persuaded Mary to settle the Aylesbury estate on him. He became a magistrate, and his zealous and efficient performance of his duties; his support of the local Church, for he was now an Anglican; his generosity to charities; all this made him a man of influence in Aylesbury. Wilkes was leading a Jekyll and Hyde existence, respectable in the country and disreputable in town. It was the London side of his life that portended his future, and underlined the mismatch of a marriage that even the birth of their daughter Polly on 5 August 1750 could not salvage.[18] Mary was a simple, devout woman with no taste for pleasure and the cultivated life of metropolitan society.[19] That John loved sophisticated company is evidenced by his election in 1749 as a Fellow of the Royal Society, then a social honour as much as anything, and as a member of that famous dining society the Beef Steak Club, in 1754. John's wit, charm, and generosity gave him an entrée to high society. It may have been in London that he met his evil genius Thomas Potter, seven years his senior, who had begun his life of dissipation at Lambeth Palace when his father was Archbishop of Canterbury. When Potter and Wilkes became acquainted is unknown, but their mutual encouragement to vice was well advanced by 1752; for in a letter of 19 October Potter urged his friend 'if you prefer young women and whores to old women and wives . . . hasten to town'.[20] Wilkes had presumably by then joined the Hell Fire Club, as local Buckinghamshire folk called the society styled 'The Monks of St. Francis', headed by Sir Francis Dashwood of West Wycombe Park. The club met at a house on the site of former Medmenham Abbey, and its activities comprised sexual orgies spiced with copious drinking and black magic.[21] Prominent in the membership was Lord Sandwich, a past and future cabinet minister, and the Hell Fire Club was the probable venue for a famous piece of repartee: Sandwich prophesied that Wilkes would die of venereal disease or on the scaffold, to meet this retort: 'That depends, My Lord, whether I embrace your mistress or your principles.'[22]

During the 1750s the proceedings of the society were doubtless enlivened by occasional readings from the *Essay on Woman*. The original version of this obscene parody of Alexander Pope's *Essay on Man* was written by Wilkes in 1754, for on 27 October of that year Thomas Potter wrote to him. 'I have read your parody for the ninety-ninth time, and have laughed as heartily as I did at the first . . . In my conscience I think you exceed yourself.'[23] The *Essay* was intended only for private circulation, and various alterations were to be made in it, some by Potter, before it achieved public notoriety in 1763, when it was used as the basis of a character assassination of Wilkes for attacking the King's government.

Whether or not it was Thomas Potter who introduced Wilkes into the Hell Fire Club, he was certainly responsible for his election to Parliament. In the middle of the eighteenth century the British political world was as quiescent as it would ever be. There was no real contest for power. No great issues of policy divided politicians. Only death in 1754 was to end the rule of Prime Minister Henry Pelham, who presided over a ministry embodying the political dominance established in 1714 by a Whig Party reaping its reward for support of the Hanoverian Succession to the throne. Unchallenged supremacy in subsequent decades had led to Whig schisms, and the growth of factions that would make mischief if not bought off. But by the early 1750s the conciliatory tactics of Pelham had contrived to ensure that only one such group, that headed by the Duke of Bedford, was in overt opposition. Among the factions won over by office in the 1740s was one centred on the Grenville family in Buckinghamshire. Lord Temple, wealthy master of Stowe, was head of the family. His abler brother George served on the Treasury Board with Pelham, and their alliance with William Pitt, the most formidable Parliamentarian of the age, was cemented in 1754 by his marriage to their sister Hester.* Potter, MP for the Cornish borough of St Germans since 1747, was an adherent of the Grenvilles and introduced their neighbour Wilkes into the faction. But Potter had an ulterior motive in thus acting as his political mentor. At the next general election, due by 1754, he was faced with the loss of his Cornish seat, and intended to exploit his friendship with Wilkes by obtaining one of the two seats for Aylesbury.

Any candidate for Aylesbury needed a deep purse. The electorate of some 500 inhabitant voters was notoriously venal. John Wilkes, as Lord of the Manor and with an efficient political agent in local farmer John Dell, was a man with considerable influence in the town, as Potter acknowledged when he made an early announcement of his candidature in a letter of 15 March 1753. He claimed that he had 'for many years been known to the principal inhabitants and respected by them . . . That Mr Wilkes is likewise talked of who lives in the town and has great property and in his own power the nomination of the returning officers.'[25]

Wilkes took up this hint of a joint candidature and until the end of the year cherished the hope that he and Potter might be elected together.[26] But there was another candidate in barrister John Willes, whose brother Edward was now retiring as one of the borough's MPs. Wilkes found himself squeezed out, since he was not prepared to fight an expensive contest. Thomas Potter, perceiving his frustration and as one who would seem to have exploited his friendship and naivety, contrived to flatter his vanity by obtaining for Wilkes the office of sheriff, and thereby returning officer, for the county of Buckinghamshire in 1754.[27]

Wilkes was nevertheless to be a candidate at the general election. His new-found political ambition had been noted by the Duke of Newcastle, who had succeeded his recently deceased brother Henry Pelham as Prime Minister. The Duke sent Wilkes to fight, at his own expense, the Delaval family in distant Berwick-upon-Tweed, in retaliation for their attack on Pelham control of the Nottinghamshire borough of Newark. Off Wilkes

---

* Potter expressed vehement disgust to Wilkes on hearing of the betrothal. 'All that wit and fire and spirit is to be matrimonially soaked in the cold, slimy aquatick c— of Lady H. Gr. What can so unnatural a mixture produce? The seed of heaven will congeal into frogspawn.' Not a good forecast, for the second son of the marriage was to be the Younger William Pitt.[24]

went, at the behest of Lord Temple, and deaf to the entreaties of his own family, who dreaded the cost.[28] In an address of 16 April to the Berwick Town Guild Wilkes spoke of virtue and patriotism, declaring that 'as he would never take a bribe so he would never offer one'.[29] An unknown outsider professedly unwilling to spend money would seem to have little chance, but there was a strong government interest in this borough on the Scottish border, through the presence of an army garrison, and of many officials employed in the customs and excise services and in the post office; and Wilkes went armed with a letter of recommendation from George Grenville in his role as a Lord of the Treasury.[30] Berwick was deemed an open borough, many of whose 500 freeman voters were non-resident, and Newcastle sent there a shipload of them from London. The Duke told George II on 24 April 'that Mr W. has a very good chance at Berwick, if the voters who went by sea can arrive'. But later he had to report to the King: 'I am very sorry that the Berwick election is lost. The ship with a great many voters was not arrived when the poll was closed.'[31] The Duke's reference was to John Delaval's defeat of Wilkes for the second seat by 307 votes to 192, for Thomas Watson, a local man with government support, had topped the poll with 374 votes. Potter commiserated with Wilkes on his failure, the more so because he believed his friend could have secured a seat elsewhere. 'Had it not been for that damned Berwick, you might now have been Member for Bristol with Nugent. There was an opening once, and I could have brought it about that you should have joined him.'[32]

This Berwick venture doubtless cost Wilkes more than the 'trifling expense' he had at first envisaged.[33] Displaying the pertinacy that was to characterize his political career, he visited Berwick again in September to seek evidence of bribery, and then submitted a petition to the House of Commons alleging that his opponents had engaged in such malpractice.[34] It came before the House on 25 November, when Delaval ridiculed the complaint. Pitt, acquainted with Wilkes through the Grenville connection, came to his rescue, lambasting levity on such a serious subject as corruption. Wilkes later recalled his own alarm at the ferocity of this denunciation, until he realized Pitt was on his side, comparing it to the terror of Mr Worsley's birch at school.[35] Not until 6 February 1756, after Watson had made repeated complaints to Newcastle about the trouble and expense the petition was causing him, did Wilkes agree to withdraw it.[36]

Later that year the Wilkes marriage began to break up. Mary, a thrifty Puritan, much under the malign influence of her mother, disapproved alike of John's fashionable life and political adventures. In September 1756 John gave up all pretence of living with his wife, and the next year this trial separation became permanent.[37] Their daughter Polly, then aged 6, fell ill with smallpox, but while her father haunted her bedside her mother did not visit the sick child. 'I wrote to Mrs. Wilkes, recommending Miss Wilkes to her mother's care, but she has never once come near her', Wilkes wrote indignantly to Dell on 26 April 1757.[38] His resentment at such behaviour led to a formal deed of separation, by which he paid his wife £200 a year out of the estates she had given him. Polly, who spent the summer of 1757 convalescing at Aylesbury, thereafter lived with her father, and the most hostile of his critics always concurred in the opinion that John's loving relationship with his daughter, who never married, was a redeeming feature of his life. A year or so later he ostensibly sought a reconciliation with his wife, issuing a writ to compel her to appear before the Court of King's Bench to answer his claim for restoration of conjugal rights. Cynical contemporaries deemed the real motive was the future inheritance due to his wife. Wilkes found himself warned by the judge that since his wife wished to abide by the separation agreement any pressure on her would be construed as contempt of court.[39]

By that time John Wilkes was an MP. Far from being discouraged by his first ventures into politics he had resolved to exploit his electoral interest at Aylesbury at the first opportunity. The chance came soon because of a crisis in national politics, a struggle for power at home coinciding with problems of foreign policy. Newcastle's attempt to head the ministry from the House of Lords had aroused resentment in a House of Commons that had become accustomed during the previous three decades to having the Prime Minister in their midst. The Duke had therefore deemed it expedient to ally with a prominent Commons spokesman, and instead of William Pitt had chosen his debating rival Henry Fox to be Commons Leader and Secretary of State. Pitt remained in the minor post of Paymaster of the Forces that he had held since 1746. Newcastle's decision had been made because Pitt would have been a difficult cabinet colleague, overbearing in personality and known to hold opinions on the conduct of foreign policy that differed from those of the Duke. Their disagreement was over how best to conduct the international rivalry with France. Newcastle followed the traditional Whig strategy of war in Europe. Pitt envisaged the imminent conflict more as an overseas contest over colonies and commerce. By the autumn of 1755 public criticism fuelled by private resentment had led to the dismissal from office of Pitt and his Grenville allies. During the consequent ministerial reshuffle there was gossip that John Willes might obtain a minor post. MPs appointed to office were at this time compelled to seek re-election to Parliament, and on 24 November 1755 Wilkes told Dell that he would fight any consequent Aylesbury by-election. 'I am determined to oppose him, and will attack him with the utmost spirit in every way, particularly the true Aylesbury way of *palmistry*. Be assured I will at any expense carry my point. It is of importance to the situation of my friends, as well as my own.' Wilkes seems to have persuaded himself that he might strike a blow not only for the Pitt–Grenville group but also against undue government influence on Parliament, albeit by bribery of the electorate, for he wrote again to Dell a week later. 'I will sink Willes by weight of metal, and we shall be thought heroes to turn a man out the moment he has kissed hands for a place.'[40]

The story about Willes proved false, and so did one in May 1756 that Potter had only a month to live: on that occasion Wilkes asked Dell to spread a 'general rumour' that he would then be a candidate for the vacancy.[41] But when Potter had to seek re-election Wilkes did not oppose his friend. A change of ministry resulted from a disastrous start to the Seven Years War against France. During October 1756 Pitt and his friends, with the Duke of Devonshire as nominal Prime Minister, replaced Newcastle and Fox. Potter, appointed to a minor post, had to face the Aylesbury electorate, and he kept an eye open for an opportunity for Wilkes, assuring him on 19 November that 'I have tried in the scramble to get you into *the* House. At present there is no opening.' In his by-election he intended to distribute £500 among the Aylesbury voters, but only after his safe return.[42] That idea evidently did not appeal to the electors, for Potter was defeated, by 267 votes to 248, by an unidentified Frederick Halsey, possibly a candidate introduced to put up the price: but Potter was promptly conceded the seat when he demanded a scrutiny of the poll.

Within months Wilkes was himself elected for Aylesbury, as another flood of by-elections was triggered off by a renewed political crisis consequent on the dismissal of the Pitt–Devonshire ministry in April 1757. Pitt and his friends had only been accepted as his government by George II with reluctance, and were dependent in Parliament on Newcastle's unwillingness to deploy his voting strength against them. They risked unpopularity, moreover, by their sympathy with Admiral John Byng, executed after his court-martial conviction for failing to do his utmost the previous summer to save Minorca, Britain's Mediterranean naval base, from capture by France.* Defenceless against royal dismissal, Pitt guaranteed himself power by a coalition with Newcastle. The Duke would manage Parliament, while Pitt ran and won the war as Secretary of State for the South. Numerous Parliamentary seats were

---

* Wilkes had himself shared this feeling, writing to George Grenville on 16 Oct. 1756. 'Byng has now everywhere some warm advocates, from an idea I hope of his innocence, at least a less degree of guilt . . . *Poor Byng* is the phrase in every mouth' (Wilkes MSS (Clements), iv, unnumbered). But 10 years later he was telling this story as proof that Byng had been deemed a coward even before the Minorca episode. 'I remember Byng would not take a country house near Finchley, because he must sometimes traverse a common where now and then robberies were committed. An English admiral afraid of being robbed. I declared he was a coward, and from this circumstance before he was sent into the Mediterranean.'[43]

vacated on appointments to office, among them that of Thomas Potter. He at first thought of standing again for Aylesbury, but Wilkes warned him off, as he told Dell in a letter of 24 May 1757: 'I have been explicit with him, that he can never be elected again at Aylesbury, but if he stands I will not oppose him.'[44] The problem was resolved when Pitt accepted an offer of a seat at Bath, for Potter replaced him as MP for Okehampton. On 22 June Wilkes informed Dell that he would be standing for Aylesbury. He was prepared to give two guineas a man, or three or even five, to ensure his election. 'I am secure of no opposition to me either from Fox or Newcastle.'[45] Potter did his utmost to ensure Wilkes that 'safe and cheap election' he wished him on 28 June. Pitt prevented Newcastle raising any opposition, and Potter himself deterred Halsey and another prospective candidate.[46]

Wilkes was elected without a contest on 6 July. Potter advised him to call at Pitt's house 'and by letter signify to him your election and your disposition to enter into his connection. Forgive these hints from one hackneyed on the stage you are now mounting.'[47] Wilkes promptly did so, assuring Pitt that 'my ambition will ever be to have my Parliamentary conduct approved by the ablest minister, as well as the first character of the age. I live in the hope of doing my country some small services at least, and I am sure the only certain way of doing any is by a steady support of your measures.'[48]

Pitt sent a flattering reply on 20 July, congratulating Wilkes 'on your being placed in a publick situation of displaying more generally to the world those great and shining talents which your friends have the pleasure to be so well acquainted with'.[49] Another prompt to congratulate Wilkes was George Grenville, now Treasurer of the Navy.[50] He did not prove to be a valuable Parliamentary recruit to the Pitt group. Although a sparkling conversationalist, and adept with his pen, he was never to be a fluent public speaker, and as yet he was not prepared to make the careful preparation he always needed for effective Parliamentary orations. There is no record of any speech by him in these years, and that he did not catch the public eye is shown by the absence of any reference to him in the detailed memoirs of the 1750s written by that great gossip Horace Walpole. John Wilkes remained anonymous and silent, his only active public role being service in the militia. The reorganization and expansion of this voluntary home defence force was a cherished scheme of Pitt and part of his overall war strategy, since it released soldiers to serve overseas. Wilkes joined the Buckinghamshire militia, commanded by his old Hell Fire Club friend Sir Francis Dashwood.

On 25 October 1760 the accession of the young King George III changed the British political scene overnight. He intended to play a more active role than his predecessor, and to install his favourite and former tutor Lord Bute as his Prime Minister as soon as he could decently rid himself of the

successful wartime coalition of Pitt and Newcastle. An immediate consequence of the change of sovereign was the need to have a general election
within six months, and that was a matter of concern to Wilkes more than
most MPs. Aylesbury was a constituency shunned by prudent or ambitious
men, for its avaricious voters demanded recompense on every possible occasion, even formal by-elections consequent on appointment to office. Wilkes
therefore explicitly timed his first known patronage request for the interval
between the two Parliaments when he wrote to Pitt on 27 February 1761.

I am very desirous of business, in which I might, usefully I hope to the public, employ my time and attention. The small share of talents I have from nature are such
as to fit me, I believe for active life; and, if I know myself, I should be entirely
devoted to the scene of business I was engaged in. I wish the Board of Trade might
be thought a place in which I could be of any service. Whatever the scene is, I shall
endeavour to have the reputation of acting in a manner worthy of the connection
I have the honour to be in, and, among all the chances and changes of a political
world, I will never have an obligation in a Parliamentary way but to Mr Pitt and his
friends.

Wilkes added the specific request that such a post should be given him 'between the two Parliaments', so as to avoid 'very disagreeable circumstances'
at Aylesbury.[51] In seeking appointment as a Lord of Trade Wilkes was asking
too much for a new MP who had never spoken in debate. Nothing came of
the request. At about the same time Wilkes also apparently applied for the
vacant post of British ambassador to Constantinople. That post, in the gift of
Pitt as Southern Secretary, went to his own brother-in-law Henry Grenville,
youngest brother of Lord Temple.[52]

John Wilkes had meanwhile long been employed in securing his re-
election for Aylesbury. He had at first intended to represent that troublesome and expensive town only once.[53] But by early 1760 he announced his
candidature, having heard that county MP Sir William Stanhope would be
sponsoring a challenger to the sitting members: this proved to be his son-in-
law Welbore Ellis, currently MP for Weymouth and a junior office-holder, a
man expected therefore to have Treasury support. Wilkes decided to stand
alone, without joining either Ellis or Willes, commenting to Dell on 19 February, 'I make no doubt of the affection of my townsmen'.[54] In the autumn
Wilkes carried out a lively canvass, at a cost of at least £200, writing to Dell
on 4 November: 'After all the uproars and riots of that noisy Wilkes I hear
that you are all subsided into the calm and quiet of a county town.' The
Willes family had sought Grenville family support in return for joining Pitt's
party in Parliament, 'but found no encouragement from Lord Temple, who
declared for me alone in terms which do me the highest honour'.[55] Wilkes
preferred the tactic of bribery to alliance with another candidate, informing

Dell on 27 December that he would buy 300 'trees' at five guineas each.[56] On 3 January 1761 he observed jokingly, 'I am told this poll is to be taken in golden letters. To be serious, as I wrote last post, I think I am fixed for five pounders ... Select 300, bid the others do their worst.'[57] The contest confirmed Wilkes in his low opinion of the Aylesbury electorate. 'I have reason both to despise the baseness of the vulgar, and their astonishing fickleness', he wrote to Dell on 24 January. 'But I am a philosopher, and I will sooner sell my estate among such wretches, and represent better men, worse I cannot, than be trampled upon.'[58] Ellis also offered £5 a man, Willes withdrew, and no poll took place.

Before the new Parliament met in the autumn of 1761 the political career of John Wilkes had taken a new turn. Pitt and Temple resigned office in October, and Wilkes chose to follow them into opposition, without being put under any pressure to do so according to Lord Temple, who penned this comment on 7 October 1762 with reference to Wilkes. 'I have, indeed, frequently recommended to him, as well as to others of my friends, to sail with the new current, which, however, I would not do, and avail themselves of the tide of court favour before it was spent: how I have prevailed with him you know.'[59]

It was during the next two decades that Wilkes established his historical reputation as an opponent of government. His radical career stemmed from this decision of 1761, although he could not then have anticipated how far events would carry him. It is even possible to question whether his role as popular agitator and critic of authority was the only path open to him; to ask whether in other circumstances he might have become an efficient 'man of business' on behalf of the King's government. There is evidence enough to suggest that such a concept is not entirely fanciful, that when given the opportunity Wilkes demonstrated a capacity to be a successful administrator, conscientious in judgement and industrious in application.

Praise, albeit not always impartial or disinterested, but extending to his obituary notices, was to be heaped on him for his early role as a Buckinghamshire magistrate and militia officer, and subsequently for the various ways in which he served the City of London as Alderman and magistrate, sheriff, Lord Mayor, and City Chamberlain. Wilkes seemingly performed all these tasks not only competently but to high acclaim. That he did not have the opportunity to serve the King's government was not necessarily a decision of his own making. His 1761 application for appointment to the Board of Trade emphasized his desire for useful employment, and so implicitly did his request then to be appointed envoy to Constantinople, one he renewed in 1765. Above all there is the curious tale of the Governorship of Canada.

John Almon subsequently recounted how, if peace negotiations with France had been successfully concluded in the summer of 1761, Wilkes would have been appointed to that post. He had asked it of Lord Temple and received 'the most flattering assurances' from Temple and Pitt. According to Almon Wilkes recalled 'that his ambition was to have gone to Quebec the first governor; to have reconciled the new subjects to the English; and to have shown the French the advantages of the mild rule of laws, over that of lawless power and despotism.'[60] When the actual appointment came to be made early in 1763 Lord Bute was Prime Minister, and Wilkes the chief protagonist in a vitriolic press campaign against him. Yet in January 1765 Richard Rigby regaled a dinner party of ministerial office-holders with the story of how in January 1763 Wilkes had invited himself to breakfast: 'That then he declared against opposition, said he was tired of writing, and would willingly make his peace with government, and accept an office. That what he desired was to be Governor of Canada.'[61] Although Rigby held only minor office, Wilkes had approached him as a close friend of Henry Fox, then Leader of the House of Commons. Diarist Horace Walpole picked up the story. 'Wilkes had, early in his warfare on the Court, told Rigby that he liked the ministers better than their opponents (no great compliment to the first) and desired him to apply to Fox to make him (Wilkes) Governor of Canada —a proposal Fox rejected.'[62] Indirect but more contemporary confirmation of the incident is to be found in a cartoon of April 1763 that showed Bute offering Wilkes the choice of the Tower or the Governorship of Canada.[63] Wilkes himself later referred to the subject in a marginal note to a pamphlet published in 1766. He neither confirmed nor denied whether he had requested the office, merely describing the alleged consternation such a rumour had caused among the opposition leadership. 'The Duke of Devonshire, though the least heated of the party, came to Lord Temple upon the report of Mr Wilkes's accepting the government of Canada, and declared if he went to America, the opposition would be undone, for Wilkes was the life and soul of it.'[64]

During the next decade political opponents of Wilkes occasionally revived the stories of his applications for the Constantinople embassy and the Governorship of Canada. Such smear campaigns did Wilkes as little harm among his supporters as the frequent aspersions on his sexual immorality and financial failings. The sacrifices of freedom and property Wilkes manifestly suffered were for them evidence enough of his devotion to the cause of 'liberty'. To the mob, if not polite society, Wilkes was to be fireproof against rumour and innuendo.

2

Gadfly of Government
1761–1763

IF John Wilkes had not existed he would have had to be invented. That is the impression conveyed by several analyses of the concordance of circumstances that produced the political environment in which he flourished. That interpretation of his career does scant justice to the charismatic personality, genius for propaganda, and political skills of the man. But that Wilkes did fulfil a political need was perceived by contemporaries who had no motive to welcome his success. After his first election for Middlesex in 1768, Edmund Burke, by then a leading Parliamentary spokesman of the main opposition party of Lord Rockingham, reflected on that surprising event: 'The crowd always want to draw themselves, from abstract principles to personal attachments, and since the fall of Lord Chatham, there has been no hero of the mob but Wilkes.'[1] Four years later, Lord Mansfield, Lord Chief Justice of the Court of King's Bench before which Wilkes so often appeared, made the private observation 'that if Wilkes were dead, it would avail little, another demagogue would arise'.[2]

What were these 'abstract principles', and who comprised 'the mob'? Some historians have been at pains to argue that much of the radicalism of the 1760s and 1770s was simply a refurbishment of old political ideas long part of the traditional 'country party' programme proffered by opponents of government since the seventeenth century. So much stress has been placed on this continuity that an important change of emphasis has often been overlooked.[3] That ideology had had two broad aims: to reduce the influence of the executive over the legislature, and to increase the dependence of the legislature on the electorate. In the reign of George III the former objective largely became a campaign pursued in Parliament by the Rockinghamite party, to reduce the number of MPs under ministerial influence and to disfranchise voters on the government payroll. An early shot was a proposal in 1770 to disqualify revenue officers from voting at Parliamentary elections, but it became a more consistent and sustained programme when the Parliamentary politicians took over a popular movement for so-called Economical Reform in the years from 1778. Although some appropriate legislation was enacted when the Rockingham party briefly returned to office in 1782, the campaign was patently self-interested, an evident attempt to seek a more level playing-field in the Parliamentary contest between administration and opposition.[4]

The early radical movements displayed little interest in such attempts to reduce the direct power of the King's government over Parliament. It was the other part of the old country programme, that concerned with the representative nature of Parliament, which formed a main plank of radicalism, together with defence of the liberty of the subject. The rights of electors was the central theme of both the Middlesex Elections controversy and the struggle to secure press reporting of Parliamentary debates. Responsibility of MPs to their constituents was the argument also for more frequent elections and for electoral reform. The earlier occasional motions for Shorter Parliaments, whether annual or triennial was seldom clear, formed a regular part of the political calendar in the 1770s. Ideas of electoral reform, by extending voting qualifications and by transferring seats from decayed boroughs to counties and new unenfranchised towns, now became a permanent feature of the political landscape. Parliamentary reform, in a spasmodic way, had a history dating back to the middle of the seventeenth century.[5] It is the continuous advocacy of such ideas thereafter that explains why British radicalism is generally held to begin with the Wilkite period.

This change of emphasis reflected a distinctive characteristic of the radical movement: that, in contrast with the old Court–Country or Whig–Tory alignments of past generations, it was an attack on 'establishment politics'. As early as the popular excitement in 1763 over the *North Briton* case, George Grenville, then Prime Minister, perceived that 'the clamour of the people' was not a demand for a change of ministry, as opposition politicians claimed: it was directed against all Parliamentary politicians.[6] A new phenomenon in British politics had appeared, and the press became a major player in the political game.[7] By 1761 there were in London four daily and six thrice-weekly newspapers.[8] But the press also took a multiplicity of other forms: monthly magazines, weekly essay papers, occasional pamphlets, and one-sheet handbills, these last being produced in thousands at times of high excitement. Cartoons were at this time published separately: expensive to purchase, especially in colour, they could be hired in portfolios from the specialist print-shops, in whose windows they might be seen for free. Circulation figures mislead as to the readership of controversial or newsworthy items: they range from 10,000 for the monthly *Gentleman's Magazine* down to print runs of 500 for most pamphlets and cartoons, with newspapers usually selling between 1,500 and 3,000 copies per issue. But copying between rival publications was endemic, and pamphlets were summarized in newspapers and magazines, for dissemination throughout the country as well as in London. Provincial newspapers would then recycle news and extracts. In London hundreds of coffee-houses and countless taverns purchased newspapers for their customers to peruse, and also provided meeting-places for both informal discussions and organized clubs and societies. Contemporary observers often noted how highly politicized London society was at all levels, foreign correspondents marvelling at such a state of affairs.

This was fertile soil for those who wished to arouse intense political feelings: but, apart from the ease with which popular violence could thereby be instigated, this circumstance would have availed Wilkes little had it not been for the political structure of the City of London, and, more generally, the representative system as embodied in Parliament. The City proper comprised only a part of the urban sprawl which had already swallowed up Westminster and, across the river Thames, Southwark, as well as much of the county of Middlesex and part of Surrey. But it was the City's political institutions that were to make it the power base of the Wilkite movement. Ultimate power lay with the 7,000 or so liverymen of the City Companies. This was a lower middle-class electorate, of artisans, shopkeepers, small traders, and the like, the very class from which Wilkes himself had sprung. The working class was not enfranchised, and its participation in the Wilkite movement was largely vicarious, though numbers of poor men illegally attended meetings of the Livery and many took part in street mobs. It was the Livery that, as the Common Hall of London, at Michaelmas chose two candidates for the Lord Mayoralty each year, and at Midsummer elected the two sheriffs who served for Middlesex as well as London: other officials were also chosen then, notably the Chamberlain who was in charge of the City's finances. A stumbling-block to any Wilkite take-over was the Court of Aldermen, one being elected for life for each of the City's twenty-six wards, and vacancies therefore occurred fortuitously. The Court of Aldermen had the ultimate decision on the Mayoralty. Aldermen were the City's magistrates, and otherwise responsible for the government of London, and tended to be wealthy supporters of government. During the Wilkite period the Court of Aldermen was often in dispute with the Court of Common Council, the institution intended to be the City's representative body, and composed of the Aldermen themselves and 236 representatives of the Livery elected annually. When even Common Council failed the Wilkite cause the Common Hall of Livery would, contrary to received practice, be convened to voice the alleged opinion of London.

A Parliamentary dimension Radicals could seldom attain elsewhere was provided by the metropolitan area constituencies. Ten seats were at stake, four for the City where the Livery constituted the Parliamentary electorate, and two each for Middlesex, Westminster, and Southwark. Over half the 3,500 freeholders of Middlesex lived in the urbanized part of the county. Westminster lacked the political framework of London, but possessed the largest constituency electorate in Britain apart from the vast county of Yorkshire, for in this urban area the franchise was vested in the resident ratepayers, some 12,000 of them. But whereas the City of London had a long-standing tradition of opposition to the King's government, in Westminster that same government exercised considerable power: for the borough included two royal palaces, numerous government offices in the Whitehall area, as well as Parliament. Many voters were employed by the Treasury, or the Court itself. This prestigious constituency, divided as it was between a large popular vote and a powerful government interest, therefore had a history of turbulent elections. Southwark also had a ratepayer electorate, of some 2,000 voters. These metropolitan constituencies provided opportunities for electoral initiatives by London Radicals. In 1761 their systematic exploitation of this situation lay in the future, but earlier popular candidates had made their mark in London and Westminster. Already a City MP since 1754 was William Beckford, a man whose political influence among the Livery anticipated that of Wilkes. The Beckford family drew its wealth from West Indies sugar plantations, and Beckford's opponents sometimes contrasted this exploitation of slavery with the radical opinions he professed in politics. In 1761 this early populist leader had been re-elected for the City, and, like Wilkes, was a follower of Pitt.

Pitt's resignation from the ministry, on 5 October 1761, was over a major issue of policy. The cabinet refused to accept his demand for an immediate pre-emptive strike against Spain, although that country was evidently planning to join France in the war. Lord Temple, who had served alongside Pitt in the cabinet as Lord Privy Seal, resigned with him, but George Grenville refused to do so. Resentful of their failure to advance him to a cabinet post, for he was still only Treasurer of the Navy, he now broke with his relatives, and was even persuaded by George III and Bute to replace Pitt as Leader of the Commons. Reluctant to risk undue comparison with his able and popular brother-in-law, Grenville declined to succeed Pitt also as Secretary of State. But he did now enter the cabinet, and ensured that the vacant Secretaryship was given to his wife's brother, Lord Egremont.

John Wilkes knew where his duty lay. On 16 October Lord Temple took the trouble to send him this account of Pitt's fall from power: 'The cause of his quitting the Ministry was from a difference of opinion in a capital measure relating to Spain; as you know, the favourite united with the Minister of numbers, bore down the Minister of measures . . . A time will come, I trust, when these measures will be fully explained to both Houses of Parliament.'[9] The reply by Wilkes was evidently one of appropriate indignation, for Temple wrote again, on 22 October, to 'my good, though wicked friend . . . Your generous and discerning spirit felt as it ought the indignity done to a man who had deserved far other treatment from the public.'[10] The Parliamentary response of Wilkes was immediate. In the opening Commons debate, that of 13 November on the Address of Thanks for the King's Speech, he launched into what was probably his maiden speech. Diarist James Harris, a new MP, noted that Wilkes was the first to rise after the Address had been proposed and seconded: 'a friend of Lord Temple's and spoke much on that Lord's model in the House of Lords', when that House had debated the Address on 6 November. Adopting the convention that the King's Speech was that of his minister, Wilkes joked, 'of what minister he could not tell', according to Horace Walpole. Both diarists recorded Wilkes as taking up two Pittite points against the ministry, the lack of any mention of the militia, and its assertion that Spain did not intend war. That claim Wilkes sought to refute by saying that he himself possessed evidence of Spanish collusion with France. But Wilkes failed to move any formal amendment, even when William Beckford later gave him a hint by offering to second any motion he might make for Spanish papers. When the debate grew warm, the ministry therefore had the tactical advantage of reminding the House that Spain was not the subject of discussion. Pitt characteristically ignored this when he argued the need not only to fight Spain but also to continue the main European war alongside Britain's ally Prussia: 'America had been conquered in Germany.' Although no vote was forced on the Address, a clear divide on war policy had become apparent, with Pitt and his friends wishing to maintain hostilities.[11]

Wilkes spoke twice more on foreign policy that session. On 11 December George Cooke, a Pittite MP for Middlesex, put forward the motion Wilkes had failed to make on 13 November, that the correspondence with Spain be laid before the House. Wilkes was one of the first speakers to support it, declaring that 'Spain ought to be considered as hostile'.[12] That Pittite forecast was duly fulfilled. War with Spain commenced early in 1762, and on 12 May the ministry had to propose a vote of credit for a new campaign in Portugal. Diarist Harris noted Wilkes as 'an advocate for the German war', and Horace Walpole recorded him as making a more general attack on the administration.

'Wilkes censured the weakness and irresolution of the ministry, . . . neglecting to send over the officers to Germany. It was even said, he affirmed, that they had been humiliating themselves at the Court of Vienna', capital of France's other major ally, Austria.[13] Only one other speech by Wilkes is known for that session, an early example of his anti-Scottish stance. On 26 March a Scottish MP moved for £4,000 of public money to build a bridge over the river Tweed, using the argument of its military advantage. Diarist Harris noted that Wilkes 'well observed the same thing might as well be asked for the River Trent'.[14]

Wilkes must soon have realized that he would never make a name as a Parliamentary speaker. Horace Walpole had early come to that conclusion. 'His appearance as an orator had by no means conspired to make him more noticed. He spoke coldly and insipidly, though with impertinence; his manner was poor, and his countenance horrid.'[15] His real political talent lay in his pen rather than his tongue, and a foretaste of this was his anonymous pamphlet published on 9 March, *Observations on the Spanish Papers*.[16] This tract was a eulogy of Pitt. He had correctly anticipated Spain's intention to make war on Britain. He had wished to deny her time to prepare for it. He would have triumphed in the conflict. 'I am persuaded, had the direction of British counsels been suffered to continue in the same hands, the name of Pitt had soon been as dreaded at Madrid as it is at Paris.' Wilkes pointed the contrast by voicing scorn of Bute and Egremont, the incumbent Secretaries of State: 'We have as little experience of them as they of business.'[17]

Wilkes was soon to turn from defence of Pitt to attacks on Bute, after he became openly Prime Minister two months later. The Duke of Newcastle resigned on 26 May, when the cabinet refused to support his demand for the continuation of the alliance with Prussia. Bute succeeded as First Lord of the Treasury, Grenville replacing him as Northern Secretary of State. The most bizarre appointment was that of Sir Francis Dashwood as Chancellor of the Exchequer, one later made a public jest by Wilkes when he depicted his old friend as a man 'puzzling all his life over tavern bills'.[18] Dashwood himself saw the joke, for he promptly told Wilkes about his post with the comment that the news would 'make him wonder and that very justly'.[19] Sir John now informed the Buckinghamshire militia that he would be obliged to resign as their Colonel, and recommended his second-in-command as his successor, 'a man of spirit, good sense, and civil deportment, who has shown resolution and industry'.[20] This paragon was John Wilkes, who, with Lord Temple as still Lord Lieutenant of the county, promptly became Colonel Wilkes. He took his militia duties seriously that summer, spending much of the time in camp near Winchester, guarding French prisoners. Here he met the historian Edward Gibbon, who after a convivial occasion wrote this pen-portrait:

I scarce even met with a better companion. He has inexhaustible spirits, infinite wit, and humour, and a great deal of knowledge; but a thorough profligate in principle as in practice; his character is infamous, his life stained with every vice, and his conversation full of blasphemy and bawdy. These morals he glories in—for shame is a weakness he has long since surmounted. He told us himself, that in this time of public dissension he was resolved to make his fortune.[21]

It was a busy period for Wilkes, albeit enlivened by a visit or two to Medmenham Abbey; for he now found his true metier as a political journalist. Wilkes had the perception to realize that vehement invective was best calculated to win the popular audience he was seeking. Seven years later, perhaps conscious that his robust, unsubtle style did not bear comparison in the eyes of sophisticated friends with the polished writing of Junius, he explained his method to a French correspondent: 'The taste of a nation must be consulted. Be so good as to apply this to words of the manufacture of the press. Delicacy is not the thing. Strength and force are requisite.'[22]

It was an irony that Lord Bute, already angry and anxious about press attacks on the King's government, should in his endeavours to counter them have provoked a more devastating onslaught from Wilkes. Lord Bute's especial concern was the damaging and incessant criticism in the leading weekly essay paper, the *Monitor*, founded in 1755 by the now deceased Richard Beckford, brother of William. The *Monitor* reflected the more old-fashioned side of the 'country programme', advocating the independence of Parliament from the government rather than its dependence on the electorate.[23] On becoming Prime Minister, Bute established a political weekly to defend his administration, the *Briton*, launched with a Scottish editor Tobias Smollett. Wilkes had followed up his first venture into political journalism by an article on royal favourites in the *Monitor* of 22 May, and was to make seven more contributions to that paper between 12 June and 30 October. But he was also provoked by Bute's action into founding the weekly *North Briton* on 5 June. On the ministerial side the feeble *Briton* was joined by the *Auditor*, written by Arthur Murphy.[24] There followed in these weeklies a lively controversy that spread to the newspapers.

Foremost in this war of words was the *North Briton*. The first issue voiced a principle Wilkes was always to champion. 'The *liberty of the press* is the birthright of a BRITON, and is justly esteemed the firmest bulwark of the liberties of this country. It has been the terror of all bad ministers.' Wilkes had named his paper not so much in derision of the *Briton* but so as to adopt the satirical guise of Scottish approval of Lord Bute's political take-over of England, to the prospective benefit of his own nation. The second issue purported to boast of this achievement, urging that the new free bridge over the Tweed should be completed so that more Scots could have easy access to

English wealth. Wilkes intended to write only a few issues, to scarify the Scots, not to establish a weekly paper. For, as he later commented, it was started at a 'very bad season', the end of a Parliamentary session when public interest in politics was temporarily satiated.[25] The paper's success ensured its permanence. The weekly sale was nearly 2,000, whereas that of the *Briton* did not reach 250.[26]

Wilkes, out of London for the early months of the *North Briton*, soon regularized production arrangements with a partner, Charles Churchill. An ordained clergyman, Churchill served in country parishes before succeeding his father in 1758 as curate and lecturer at St John's Church, Westminster. Poetry and politics soon engrossed his attention. In 1760 he made £2,000 within two months by publishing his poems, and his political zeal in the cause of liberty equalled that of Wilkes himself. Wilkes waived any share in the profits as Churchill took charge in London, where publisher George Kearsley received the copy and passed it on to printer Dryden Leach. Both agreed to be involved only after assurances that every issue would have the legal opinion of counsel that it was not libel, and that if nevertheless prosecuted they could reveal the author.[27] Charles Sayer of the Inner Temple, a personal friend, was the legal adviser used by Wilkes, who on 15 June urged Churchill to consult him, 'for fear I have got too near the pillory. You will be pleased to know him and he will give you a fair and fee-less opinion in everything.'[28]

The *North Briton* campaign against Bute was so scurrilous as to annoy and embarrass Pitt, on whose behalf many deemed it to be fought. He soon visited Lord Temple at Stowe, and 'expressed himself warmly against all kinds of political writing, as productive of great mischief'. Wilkes tartly commented, when Temple passed on this reprimand, 'that such a declaration was in character from Mr Pitt, who ought to fear the shadow of a pen, that he was undoubtedly the best speaker and the worst writer of his age, that he would do well to harangue the 500 deputies of the people in the cause of liberty, and the *North Briton* would endeavour to animate the nation at large'.[29] This rather contemptuous dismissal of the claim of a mere Parliamentarian to be a popular leader reflected the belief of Wilkes that the political arena extended beyond the Palace of Westminster. The *North Briton* soon surpassed its previous audacity as Wilkes ignored the rebuke. The fifth issue, on 3 July, had originally been planned for the *Monitor* on 19 June, but Wilkes dropped that idea at the behest of Lord Temple, who did not want to give the ministry an excuse to prosecute that more prestigious journal.[30] Its topic was the series of national misfortunes suffered in the early years of Edward III's reign when England had been ruled by that young King's mother and her lover Roger Mortimer. Readers did not need any allusion to Bute:

the inferences were obvious. A week later the next number waxed sarcastic on George Grenville's desertion of his family and friends, to the amusement of his brother Lord Temple. It concluded with the implication, drawn from history, that since Bute was a Scotsman he must be a friend of France. Wilkes insisted on publication even though Kearsley thought this a libel.[31] Diarist Horace Walpole pondered the remarkable immunity of the *North Briton* from prosecution, and provided his own explanation:

The *North Briton* proceeded with an acrimony, a spirit, and a licentiousness unheard of before even in this country. The highest names, whether of statesmen or magistrates, were printed at length and the insinuations went still higher. In general favouritism was the topic, and the partiality of the Court to the Scots. Every obsolete anecdote, every illiberal invective, was raked up and set forth in strong and witty colours against Scotland. One of the first numbers was one of the most outrageous, the theme taken from the loves of Queen Isabella and Mortimer. No doubt but it lay open enough to prosecution, and the intention was to seize the author. But . . . as the daring audaciousness of the writer promised little decorum, it was held prudent to wait till he should furnish a less delicate handle to vengeance.[32]

Shrewd political calculation and legal advice saved the *North Briton* from prosecution, and of more concern to Wilkes than the libel law was the problem of keeping the paper afloat until the next session of Parliament revived a more general interest in politics, a problem exacerbated by Churchill's unreliability and laziness. The regular production of copy, and its weekly publication, became something of a treadmill operation, and occasional recourse was had to outside contributors. The author of the definitive study of the paper assigns twenty-six of the forty-five numbers to Wilkes, five to Churchill, four to other authors, and assumes without direct evidence that Wilkes wrote most of the other ten.[33] A more recent study attributes at least ten issues to Churchill, and claims that he also edited and altered much of what Wilkes had written. Wilkes himself was certainly at pains to disclaim the assumption of journalist John Almon that he was the sole author.[34]

Sometimes the paper was filled up with poor quality material. It was just such an emergency production that led Wilkes into his first duel. The edition of 21 August offended the Lord Steward of the Royal Household, Lord Talbot. In preparation for the coronation of George III in 1761 he had so well trained his horse to walk backwards away from his sovereign that the animal instead backed towards the King, to the general ridicule of the Lord Steward. The *North Briton* coupled a reminder of this ignominy with derision of his economy measures in the Royal Household, dismissing some of its employees only to put them on a pension list. A pistol duel eventually resulted on 6 October in which honour was satisfied and neither man was injured. The Wilkes squint probably made it difficult for him to fire straight![35]

By that time Wilkes had clashed with the veteran cartoonist William Hogarth. Hitherto Hogarth had eschewed cartoons of an overtly partisan nature, but now, at the end of his life, he enrolled under the banner of government. Wilkes, for some years his personal friend, was told that Hogarth intended to publish a print attacking Pitt, Temple, Churchill, and himself. 'Mr Wilkes, on this notice', Almon recalled, 'remonstrated by two of their common friends to Mr Hogarth, that such a proceeding would not only be unfriendly in the highest degree, but extremely injudicious; for such a pencil ought to be universal and moral, to speak to all ages and all nations, not to be dipt in the dirt of the faction of the day.' This appeal to Hogarth not to prostitute his talent fell on deaf ears. He was short of money, and supported Bute's peace policy. He informed Wilkes that a cartoon attacking Lord Temple and Mr Pitt, though not himself, would be published. Wilkes warned his erstwhile friend that he would respond in the *North Briton*.[36]

When Hogarth's print *The Times* duly appeared on 7 September Wilkes drafted a vigorous reply which he submitted to Temple for approval and amendment.[37] It was published on 25 September, a personal attack that commented on Hogarth's 'rancour and malevolence', impugned his allegedly failing technique, and ascribed money and malice as his motivation. This powerful piece of writing was all the more effective for being couched in a spirit of regret for Hogarth's alleged fall from grace.[38] Soon, however, Wilkes expressed genuine remorse for what he had written, in a letter of 23 November to Temple: 'Mr Hogarth is said to be dying, and of a broken heart. It grieves me much. He says that he believes I wrote that paper, but he forgives me, for he must own I am a thorough good-humoured fellow, only *Pitt-bitten*.'[39] Hogarth was not dying, and neither had he forgiven Wilkes. He had the last word in this quarrel, for his savage cartoon *John Wilkes Esquire*, a representation of an impudent demagogue with a hideous squint, was the visual image of Wilkes conveyed to both contemporaries and posterity.[40]

By the autumn of 1762 political argument in Britain was dominated by the peace treaty negotiated in Paris by the Duke of Bedford. Seven of the eleven numbers of the *North Briton* published from 2 October onwards were taken up with this topic, all of them written by Wilkes. The two themes of his attack were the claim that the peace was made by a Scottish minister to the detriment of England's interests, and the contrast of the recent conduct of the war with Pitt's success. Wilkes went out of his way to laud Pitt and defend him from ministerial innuendoes, as in the issue of 20 November. There, to the delight of Lord Temple,[41] he pointed out that the Secretary of State who in 1756 had signed the treaty of alliance with Prussia was the same Henry Fox who had just replaced Grenville as Commons Leader in order to carry the peace. Why, Wilkes asked, should blame for the now unpopular German war be thrown on Pitt? In Parliament Wilkes proved more moderate in his criticism of the peace terms than he had been in the *North Briton*. In the main Commons debate of 9 December on that subject, he spoke 'neither with the abuse nor bitterness, that twas reasonable to expect': so noted diarist James Harris, who had himself put the motion for approval of the peace terms. Wilkes of course opposed it, and was a teller for the minority of 65 against the ministry's 319.[42] Later Wilkes even privately admitted to a supporter of the Duke of Bedford that 'it was the damn'dest peace for the Opposition that ever was made'.[43]

The Bute ministry moved to silence opposition criticism in the press simultaneously with this success in Parliament. On 6 November Lord Halifax, who had just replaced Grenville as Secretary of State, issued a warrant for the arrest of attorney Arthur Beardmore as 'the author of several weekly very seditious papers', these being eight specified issues of the *Monitor*.[44] Beardmore was arrested on 11 November, the same day when Nathan Carrington, a King's Messenger, seized papers of the Reverend John Entinck, a leading contributor to the *Monitor*: it was to be this event, not as is often stated the famous *North Briton* affair, that led to the well-known legal case of 1765 in which Lord Chief Justice Camden condemned as 'contrary to law' the use of a warrant to search for and seize papers in charges of seditious libel.[45] Wilkes characteristically launched a counter-attack, visiting Beardmore in prison in a vain attempt to persuade him to sue Halifax for false arrest.[46] Next the Secretary of State issued on 18 November a general warrant for the arrest of 'the Authors, Printers and Publishers of a seditious and scandalous weekly paper, entitled *The North Britain*', specifying issues one to twenty-five printed by 'G. Kearsley'.[47] Halifax had had to resort to this device, which did not name those who were to be arrested, because the *North Briton* was ostensibly anonymous. This general warrant was never executed, but it frightened the paper's printer, now William Richardson, into refusing to continue its publication, so Wilkes told Churchill on 24 November.[48] Wilkes found another printer, but he too refused to continue when a revised version of the general warrant was drafted to include his one issue.[49] On 2 December Wilkes, whose own handwriting is admirably legible, wrote a laconic letter to Churchill on this latest development.

My Dear Churchill, I wish you would learn to write——a good hand. Nature's chief masterpiece is writing well, and you are microscopical . . . I have seen Leach, whose printer, Peter Cock, had the terrors of the Lord of the Isle, so strong before him, that he has fallen ill to avoid printing the paper. Kearsley however has got it done. I passed 3 hours today in Pitt's bed-chamber at Hayes. He talks as you write. As no other man ever did or could.[50]

Kearsley's new printer was Richard Balfe, who was to produce all the sub-sequent issues, Wilkes having assured Balfe that there was no legal danger because three counsel examined each paper before it was printed.[51] Wilkes had already told Kearsley on 1 December that Charles Sayer was still ap-proving each text.[52] The issue of 4 December was a vigorous defence of the freedom of the press by Churchill, who claimed that the action against the *Monitor* had been taken to silence press criticism of the peace terms. The *North Briton* had not been intimidated, and no prosecution was ever launched against the *Monitor*.[53]

This first attempt to curb the *North Briton*, although unsuccessful in that aim, did serve indirectly to stop another publication plan of Wilkes. When in his militia camp at Winchester, Wilkes, as if the *North Briton* was not enough to occupy him, conceived the idea of printing the *Essay on Woman*, for private circulation only. He obviously took the opportunity to make some changes, for the ribald reference to Lord Bute is unlikely to have been in earlier ver-sions.* By the autumn he had sent a copy to Kearsley to be set up in type: that a manuscript text seized among his papers in 1763 was in his own hand seemed convincing evidence of his authorship to contemporaries. On 18 October Wilkes wrote to Kearsley: 'I am impatient for my *Essay on Woman*. Let it be on very good paper. Two proofs.' Three days later he ordered six copies of an engraved illustration.[55] The project was abandoned, presumably because Kearsley took fright at the threatened prosecution of the *North Briton*.

During the ensuing winter the *North Briton* maintained an unrelenting attack on Lord Bute and his supporters, while carefully avoiding any asper-sions on George III himself. Perusal of the paper reveals Wilkes to be a devas-tatingly effective propagandist, who knew just how far he could go within the law. He was a master of irony, insinuation, and innuendo: sample high-lights can suffice to convey the flavour of the campaign, for it has been fully described elsewhere.[56] *Number Thirty*, published on 25 December 1762, pointed out how none of the ministers who had won the Seven Years War was left in the cabinet. Wilkes mentioned not only Pitt and Temple but also Newcastle, the political proscription of whose followers then in progress being encapsulated in the famous witticism that 'it is generally believed that every person *brought in* by the Duke of Newcastle is by the present minister, to be *turned out*—except the *King*'. That the old Duke appreciated such a jibe is shown by a message he sent on 25 January 1763 to Lord Middleton, one of his followers evidently in touch with Wilkes. 'I am sure, you will take care, not to discourage Mr Wilkes; if your lordship should, in discourse, have occasion to mention my name, I beg, you would make my best compliments

---

* 'Then in the scale of various Pricks, 'tis plain, Godlike erect, Bute stands the foremost Man.' This reference is reputed to have caused the 1763 search for the poem.[54]

to him.'[57] In the next issue, that of 1 January 1763, Wilkes satirized Richard Rigby, Bedford's Commons spokesman, for having been amply rewarded for his part in making a peace that had 'saved England from the certain ruin of success'.

The importance of Wilkes in these months to the fading cause of opposition was emphasized by Horace Walpole in a letter of 25 March: 'Wilkes shows most spirit. The last *North Briton* is a masterpiece of mischief. He has writ a dedication too to an old play, *The Fall of Mortimer.*' That was a dedication of Ben Jonson's play to Lord Bute, reviving the old innuendo about his relationship with George III's mother by a mocking contrast between his reign and that of Edward III. Wilkes, according to Walpole, had had the impudence to ask Treasury Secretary Jeremiah Dyson to remind Lord Bute that it was customary for dedicators to be rewarded.[58] The issue of the *North Briton* that so delighted Walpole, *Number Forty-Two* published on 19 March, had anticipated modern investigative journalism. It named those ministerial supporters who had profited from a recent government loan, to a total of £350,000 altogether, by gaining from an immediate rise in the value of their stock. One of those listed, MP Peregrine Cust, stated to be a stockjobber who had made £20,000 in this way, initiated a libel prosecution in the Court of King's Bench, claiming that he had been 'prejudiced and injured in his character and credit', because he had not anticipated such a capital gain. Realization of the ridicule that such a contention would incur soon led Cust to abandon it. Wilkes had again displayed shrewd judgement in what he could say.

In the early months of 1763 the journalistic talent of Wilkes seemed to have become almost the sole recourse of Bute's opponents; but then his ministry offered a hostage to fortune by proposing a new tax on cider. Highly unpopular in the cider counties of western England, the tax was to be levied by an excise duty; that method was historically associated with Stuart tyranny, and viewed as a threat to individual rights because of the powers of search bestowed on excisemen. In the *North Briton* Wilkes reinforced opposition attacks in Parliament by denouncing the tax as 'odious and partial' and a threat to liberty. Moreover, he added, it would have been unnecessary but for the corrupt management of the government loan. The publicity Wilkes now enjoyed was such that Horace Walpole could write jestingly on 6 April that 'in the western counties the discontent is so great, that if Mr Wilkes will turn patriot-hero, or patriot-incendiary in earnest, and put himself at their head, he may obtain a rope of martyrdom before the summer is over'.[59] That was a prescient observation, albeit for the wrong reason.

Wilkes had meanwhile gone to France for a brief visit, to place his daughter Polly, now 12, under the care of a Madame Carpentier. He left London on

26 March, arrived at Dover the next day, was entertained three times to dinner by the Duke of Bedford when in Paris, and was back in Calais on his return journey by 9 April.[60] The governor of that port, according to Walpole, 'asked him how far the liberty of the press extended in England. He replied, "I cannot tell, but I am trying to know." '[61]

Before he left Wilkes had instructed Churchill to write a *North Briton* about ministerial interference in the East India Company, now not only Britain's largest trading organization but also territorial ruler of parts of India, notably much of Bengal. The first major power struggle within the Company had commenced, and Wilkes sided with Lord Clive, who was supported by the Parliamentary opposition, against his rival Laurence Sulivan, who enjoyed ministerial backing. Early in March Wilkes had received a request for support from his old friend Lord Sandwich, busy organizing the ministerial interest: and had replied on 9 March that 'I have for some time formed warm wishes, and taken a part for Lord Clive, and his friends of the India Company'.[62] In letters of 25 and 27 March to Churchill Wilkes enclosed materials from Thomas Rous, Chairman of the Company, and asked him to discuss the subject with Clive's friend, MP John Walsh.[63] After this interview Churchill prepared a paper that would have been 'North Briton Number Forty-Five' on 9 April, but it was never published.[64] Nor was there one the next Saturday. The reason was that Lord Bute had resigned on 8 April; for on 13 April Wilkes, in the name of the *North Briton*, published a handbill, reprinted widely in the newspapers, explaining that the paper had been opposed to Lord Bute and was now holding fire to see whether his malign hand guided the new ministry under George Grenville. The pretext that it did so prompted the next, fateful, issue of the paper.

3

The Case of *North Briton, Number Forty-Five*

> Nothing is at present talked of here, but the affair of a very impudent
> worthless man named Wilkes, a member of Parliament, who was
> lately taken up by the Secretaries of State for writing a most seditious
> libel personally attacking the King . . . The mob are as usual for the
> Libeller, and he is a kind of Sacheverell, but I think I never knew all
> persons above the degree of mob more united than at present in
> lamenting the insolence with which Government is attacked.

So reported Lord Barrington, that exemplary supporter of the King's government at all times, to the British envoy in Berlin on 13 May 1763. The libel
was *Number Forty-Five* of the *North Briton*, provoked by the King's Speech at
the end of the Parliamentary session on 19 April, commending the Peace of
Paris.[1] Prime Minister George Grenville, as a courtesy, sent a copy to his
brother Lord Temple the previous day. Pitt and Temple were discussing it
when Wilkes walked in, and the controversial issue was born out of this conversation.[2] *Number Forty-Five* was published on 23 April.[3] Wilkes, who wrote
it all himself, began by pointing out that whereas the King's Speech at the
beginning of each session usually gave rise to a debate, the one at the close
of a session was a piece of ministerial propaganda on which MPs had no
opportunity to comment. Having been careful to emphasize that all such
orations were known to be the composition of the ministry, he declared that
both monarch and country had been the victims of 'the most abandoned instance of ministerial effrontery ever attempted to be imposed on mankind'.
There followed this feigned regret:

Every friend of his country must lament that a prince of so many great and amiable qualities, whom England truly revere, can be brought to give the sanction of

his sacred name to the most odious measures, and to the most unjustifiable, public declarations, from a throne ever renowned for truth, honour, and unsullied virtue.

That incidental side-swipe at royal morality, implicitly reminding readers that only Queen Anne of the six previous sovereigns since the Restoration of the monarchy in 1660 could have been accounted virtuous, may have compounded the priggish young King's fury at being portrayed as a dupe. George III's personal indignation may be the explanation for the prompt ministerial reaction to a paper not conspicuously more outrageous than some of its predecessors. Lord Bute had maintained a dignified refusal to respond to press provocations. But Grenville and his colleagues, less confident of the King's favour, were more susceptible to royal pressure. Mrs Grenville later recalled that 'in Mr Wilkes's affair' the ministry acted 'by his Majesty's commands'.[4] The day after the offending *North Briton* was published the Prime Minister arranged to see Treasury Solicitor Philip Carteret Webb the next morning, and Treasury Secretary Charles Jenkinson followed up with an afternoon appointment.[5] The ministry perceived that the prosecution of Wilkes was the path to royal favour, and that was one motive for the vigorous conduct of the case even after fear of Bute's backstairs influence had faded, as the Duke of Newcastle wryly commented in December: 'They will keep up this affair of Wilkes, as long as they can, in order to hold the King's Favour by it. For that seems to affect the King more than any point of much greater consequence.'[6]

The events of the next few days are among the best documented in British history.[7] *Number Forty-Five*, comprising eight pages instead of the customary six, had been published as usual on a Saturday. On the Monday, 25 April, Secretary of State Lord Halifax, acting expressly by the King's command, sought legal advice about the paper from Attorney-General Charles Yorke and Solicitor-General Sir Fletcher Norton, but when he took action he could have received only a verbal opinion.[8] The veil of ostensible anonymity had first to be penetrated before action could be taken against Wilkes. On 26 April Lord Halifax therefore signed a general warrant, as he had done on 18 November 1762, for the arrest of 'the authors, printers and publishers of a seditious and treasonable paper, entitled the North Briton, Number 45'.[9] The word 'treasonable', a variant from the usual terminology, was doubtless inserted to defeat any resort by Wilkes to Parliamentary privilege, which conferred immunity from arrest except for treason, felony, and breach of the peace. Those deputed to carry out the warrant were the King's Messengers, senior among them Nathan Carrington.[10] The first action taken under the warrant, early on 29 April, was an astonishing blunder. Messengers arrested the wrong printers, Dryden Leach and over a dozen of his journeymen. This remarkable mistake Attorney-General Yorke privately attributed to the incompetence of Webb.[11] It was made because Wilkes had been observed to visit Leach frequently. *Number Twenty-Six* was the sole issue Leach had printed, and he was released a few days later, without any interrogation. Lawsuits were to make the error an expensive one for the Treasury.

The ministry, however, struck gold with the almost simultaneous arrest of George Kearsley, the bookseller who had allowed his name to appear as publisher of every issue of the *North Briton* in return for a share of the profits. He had been little more than the middle man between the author and the printers, and not always that. Wilkes at once visited Kearsley and promised to obtain for him a writ of habeas corpus from Lord Chief Justice Pratt at the Court of Common Pleas. But that Court had adjourned, and within a few hours the panic-stricken Kearsley had revealed all he knew in an interrogation conducted by the two Secretaries of State themselves, Halifax and Egremont. He named Richard Balfe as the printer, and stated that Wilkes had been the author of most issues of the *North Briton* and Charles Churchill of some others. Part of *Number Forty-Five* he had received from Wilkes in his own hand.[12] Balfe was thereupon arrested, and the Secretaries of State sought further advice from the Crown's two law officers as to whether Wilkes, being an MP, could be arrested as author. When Balfe was examined that evening he stated that he had printed *Number Forty-Five* from a copy given to him by Wilkes in his own handwriting. Papers seized from both Kearsley and Balfe provided further confirmation that Wilkes was the author.[13] His arrest was now decided upon, even though none of the evidence had been taken on oath, and only a verbal reply had been received from the Crown lawyers.[14] The two Secretaries of State both wanted to draw up a new warrant specifically naming Wilkes, but Treasury Solicitor Webb dissuaded them from a needless departure from the usual practice.[15] Bad legal advice led to the use of the general warrant against Wilkes and the consequent political storm over the alleged attack on liberty.[16]

Wilkes was arrested the next morning, on Saturday, 30 April, mocking the general warrant as 'a ridiculous warrant against the whole English nation', since no suspects were named. Charles Churchill, whose arrest had also been ordered, chanced to intrude on this event, but was not recognized and took the hint when Wilkes addressed him as 'Mr Thompson', leaving immediately for the country.[17] It was over two hours before Wilkes, insisting on his status as an MP, agreed to leave his house, and in the meantime it filled with his friends, including Lord Temple, printer John Almon, wine-merchant Humphrey Cotes, solicitor Alexander Philipps, MP John Walsh, and Richard Hopkins, a follower of the Duke of Grafton. Some of them Wilkes dispatched to the Court of Common Pleas for a writ of habeas corpus. When Wilkes did consent to go to Halifax's house, only a few doors along Great

George Street, he refused to answer any questions put to him by the two Secretaries of State. Walsh and Hopkins then arrived to inform Wilkes that Chief Justice Pratt had granted him a writ of habeas corpus, but Webb overheard their conversation.[18] The two Secretaries of State thereupon invalidated that writ by a new warrant consigning Wilkes by name to the Tower of London.[19] That afternoon his house was searched under the direction of Lord Egremont's Under-Secretary Robert Wood, with Webb also present, and a large quantity of papers was removed.[20] The ministry was so confident of its evidence against Wilkes that Halifax's Under-Secretary Edward Weston was sent to inform the Speaker of the House of Commons, Sir John Cust, of the arrest. 'Full proof had been made that Mr Wilkes, a Member of the House of Commons, was author of a libel called the North Briton, published on Saturday, April 23rd.' The offence was 'a breach of the peace to which privilege did not extend', so Cust was told, and the House of Commons would be informed when it next met.[21] Since that would not be until the autumn, the ministry envisaged the permanent detention of Wilkes in custody.

The Tower officials, through a misunderstanding, were ordered to keep Wilkes in close confinement,[22] denying access even to his solicitor Arthur Beardmore. News of the arrest of Wilkes and forty-eight others under the general warrant aroused concern among Parliamentary politicians, and consternation in London. Newcastle commented to Hardwicke the next day, 'I always feared that the *North Briton* of Saturday last would bring on some examination and persecution. To be sure, it was wrote with very little consideration or caution, and in times like these people should be cautious, when they know, that the Crown will be stretched to the utmost.' As he was writing George Onslow and two other MPs arrived from London. 'They all agree that the City and Suburbs, are in the utmost alarm, at these proceedings, which they call illegal and oppressive.' Lord Temple, anxious to demonstrate solidarity, 'wants us all to go and see Mr Wilkes in the Tower'.[23] Newcastle did not respond to this suggestion, for it was Temple, the Dukes of Bolton and Grafton, and John's brother Heaton who vainly sought access to the prisoner. That ban was lifted on Monday, 2 May, and Judge Pratt issued a new writ of habeas corpus, in consequence of which Wilkes appeared at the Court of Common Pleas the next day.[24]

His counsel, Sergeant John Glynn, then moved for his discharge from custody on three grounds: that he was not charged in the warrant of commitment by any evidence given on oath; that the warrant did not accurately describe the offending paper; and that Wilkes enjoyed Parliamentary immunity from arrest on such a charge. Counsel for the Crown contended that libel tended to breach of the peace, one of the exceptions to Parliamentary

privilege. The Court adjourned the case for three days to consider the arguments, and Wilkes was remanded back to the Tower without a bail option.[25]
Westminster Hall echoed to cries of 'Liberty, Liberty, Wilkes for ever', and
Attorney-General Charles Yorke told his father Lord Hardwicke that 'there
were such shouts in the Hall and in the Court of Common Pleas that you
would have thought the Seven Bishops had been acquitted'.[26] While Wilkes
was in the Tower he was dismissed from his much-prized Colonelcy of the
Buckinghamshire militia, Egremont directing Temple as the county's Lord
Lieutenant to take this step.[27]

When Wilkes returned to Court on Friday, 6 May, he portrayed his plight
in the widest possible terms. 'The liberty of all peers and gentlemen—and
(what touches me more sensibly) that of all the middling and inferior set of
people, who stand most in need of protection—is, in my case, this day to be
finally decided upon; a question of such importance, as to determine at once
whether English liberty be a reality or a shadow.'[28] That put the case on too
high a plane, for the validity of general warrants was not the question at
issue. In his judgment Chief Justice Pratt rejected Glynn's first two points,
but ruled that the arrest of Wilkes had been an infringement of Parliamentary privilege, since libel was not a breach of the peace, and ordered his
discharge.[29] This verdict was a shock to the ministry. Lord Chancellor
Henley, presiding that day at another Court in Westminster Hall, whispered
to another judge, 'By God! Pratt is mad', and Newcastle's old friend Lord
Grantham informed the Duke two days later that 'the judgement in the
Common Pleas on Friday seems to have been unexpected, and has surprised
most people'.[30]

The elated Wilkes claimed this technical success as a triumph for liberty.
The crowd, ignorant of legal niceties, and misled by his rhetoric, saw only
their hero being released, and Westminster Hall reverberated to shouts of
'Wilkes and Liberty'.[31] The public jubilation was widely reported in the
press, which estimated that a crowd of 10,000 accompanied Wilkes back to
Great George Street.[32] George Onslow, in his report of the day's events to
Newcastle, mentioned that 'the many thousands that escorted Wilkes home
[were] of a far higher rank than common mob'. But Onslow, like other
Parliamentary politicians, failed as yet to perceive that this incipient Wilkite
movement was a novel factor in the political scene, believing it would be a
tide to carry the Newcastle party back to power:

Nor can I help feeling a joy at my heart at hearing the common cry of the multitude
be 'Whigs for ever. No Jacobites'. On that noble principle, a spirit is certainly gone
forth beyond what has been known since Sacheverell's time. In my opinion, the
liberty of the subject, and the dignity of the House of Commons, which is the support of it, has this day received a glorious support. The acclamations of the people

in the Hall are beyond what you can imagine, and on the whole showed what I have long been convinced of, that the genius of this country is Whiggism, and that the People will never be satisfied but on the re-establishment of the Old System, under which this country has of late years flourished under this family.[33]

The same day Wilkes, with the approval of Glynn and Lord Temple, wrote an impudent epistle to Secretaries of State Egremont and Halifax: 'I find that my house has been robbed, and am informed that the stolen goods are in the possession of one or both of your Lordships. I therefore insist that you forthwith return them.'[34] Copies of this letter were distributed as hand-bills and sent to the newspapers.[35] Wilkes himself was later to describe this letter as 'flippant and ludicrous, very unbecoming the dignity of the cause'.[36] But at the time, still on a high, he next day visited Bow Street police station for a warrant to search the houses of the two Secretaries of State for his stolen property. Lord Grantham heard the story that when Sir John Fielding refused Wilkes said to him, 'Then you too shall hear from me.'[37] To his surprise and delight the two Secretaries were provoked into a reply by his letter, stating that papers had been seized as evidence for an impending libel prosecution: 'We are at a loss to guess what you mean by stolen goods, but such of your papers as do not lead to a proof of your guilt, shall be restored to you.'[38] Wilkes could not resist a riposte: 'I fear neither your prosecution nor your persecution, and I will assert the security of my own house, the liberty of my person, and every right of the people, not so much for my own sake, as for the sake of every one of my English fellow subjects.'[39] Both these letters were also sent to the newspapers. It was unwise to bandy words with Wilkes.

More significant legal battles lay ahead. It had always been the intention of the ministry to prosecute Wilkes for seditious libel, and evidence against him was steadily being accumulated. Lovell Stanhope examined a Kearsley apprentice Charles Shaw on 7 May, re-examined George Kearsley himself and Richard Balfe on 9 May, and the next day John Williams, a former employee of Balfe.[40] The Pratt judgment now presented a barrier. Wilkes would first have to be deprived of his Parliamentary immunity, either by expulsion or by a resolution of the House of Commons, and that could not be done until Parliament reassembled at the end of the year. Nevertheless, on 9 May, Secretary of State Halifax ordered Attorney-General Yorke to prosecute Wilkes for libel in the Court of King's Bench, and Yorke duly filed a charge that day.[41] Wilkes countered by a whole series of actions: for trespass against Robert Wood and Philip Webb, claiming £5,000 damages from each; for trespass also against those lesser officials, a Constable and three Messengers, who had arrested him and seized his papers; while various claims were lodged against the two Secretaries of State for having authorized the proceedings.[42] His case against Halifax had been prepared by 1 June; it claimed

£440 for damage to doors, locks, and cabinets, £1,000 for loss of goods and chattels, and made unspecified claims concerning noise, disturbance, assault, and imprisonment.[43] The legality of the general warrant would be brought into question by such cases, but not by the simultaneous series of actions brought by the printers who had been mistakenly arrested. Wilkes spent much of June in preparing for these legal confrontations. On 11 June he assured Temple, who was providing the finance for his legal campaign, that 'I have never lost sight of the great object of the liberty of the subject at large. All my researches are directed to that great point'; and on 30 June he complained that 'I am so deeply engaged with Serjeants, Counsellors, Attorneys, etc. that I shall not be able to eat a single strawberry out of my own garden'. After numerous consultations with John Glynn, John Dunning, and other lawyers he was confident of success. 'There is but one opinion respecting all those actions', he assured Temple on 18 June.[44]

There were political as well as legal ramifications of the *North Briton* case. However low an opinion many MPs and peers had of the character of Wilkes, there was widespread concern about the wholesale arrests made under the general warrant. The mob cry of 'Wilkes and Liberty' met a response in many Parliamentary hearts. Particular anxiety as to what might be the political consequences was felt by Yorke's father Lord Hardwicke. The former Lord Chancellor was in an ambivalent position, because although he was privately advising his son in the Wilkes case he had accompanied his long-term friend Newcastle into opposition in 1762. In a letter of 8 June to the Duke he discussed the role that William Pitt might adopt; for the Marquess of Rockingham, a young follower of Newcastle, had returned from a conversation with the great man to report his opinions to be not merely that Wilkes was entitled to Parliamentary privilege, but also that 'he doubted much whether the *North Briton No. 45*, is a libel and whether the holding it to be so would not in a high degree infringe the liberty of the press, as to censuring the transactions or advice of ministers'.[45] This news convinced Newcastle that 'the affair of Wilkes is a very unfortunate one', as he commented to the Duke of Devonshire on 23 June. 'It has not only drawn Addresses from almost every county, and borough in the Kingdom, *upon us*. But I am afraid may produce differences as to proceedings upon this point, amongst some of our most material friends. I mean my Lord Hardwicke and his family, Lord Temple and Mr Pitt.' Irreconcilable viewpoints would make a united opposition impossible, and there was the further disadvantage, so Newcastle had been informed by Lord Lyttelton, that 'the King was so exasperated against my Lord Temple and Mr Pitt, and that we were so connected with them, that nothing could be done'.[46] These fears of the Duke that the *North Briton* case had destroyed all chance of an early return to office were to prove unfounded, for within two months George III was negotiating with the opposition leadership.

The Parliamentary battle anticipated in the winter was preceded by one in the press during the summer, as both opponents and supporters of Wilkes filled newspaper columns with arguments and propaganda.[47] The ministry made a prompt and sustained effort to counter the tide of popular opinion. The *London Chronicle* of 7 May reported that paragraphs had been sent 'by authority' to that day's *Public Advertiser* and *Gazetteer*, stating that the general warrant for the arrest of Wilkes had conformed to precedent and that no law court had condemned the practice. 'No Member' in the *St. James's Chronicle* for 10 May sourly pointed out that Wilkes had been discharged only because of his Parliamentary privilege. The same point, that 'common people' were not protected by Pratt's judgment, was made in the *London Chronicle* on 2 June, and that Parliamentary privilege might in fact threaten popular liberty had been argued in the same paper five days earlier. The campaign against Wilkes soon turned into a personal vendetta. Identical paragraphs in the *London Chronicle* and *St. James's Chronicle* for 28 May accused him of being out for pecuniary gain in the numerous court actions he had initiated. He had cases pending against Egremont, Halifax, Webb, Wood, and six others, while fourteen printers had sued for wrongful arrest. Forty-six writs had been served on 24 May alone. An article by 'a quondam friend of John Wilkes' in the *London Chronicle* of 25 June attacked 'his juvenile vanity which will not suffer him to be quiet, till he has told all the world that he laughs at those things which they consider as the most sacred and inviolable'. The dissolute character of Wilkes was always to be a liability to any political cause he championed, and an attempted mocking defence of him by 'Philagathas' in the *London Chronicle* for 2 July rather misfired by first repeating the comprehensive accusation that 'Mr Wilkes is a man of abandoned and profligate character, a buffoon, whose common conversation is blasphemy and baudry, that he is likewise an ugly fellow, insults justice, has abused his wife and strives to rob her of her alimony'. More effective was the assertion from 'Tacitus Britannicus' in the same paper on 7 July that the attacks on Wilkes for his private character arose less from 'a love of virtue' than from 'an aversion to his political conduct, and a spirit of revenge'.

John Wilkes was not a man to let grass grow under his feet. While awaiting the commencement of the various lawsuits, he set up a printing press at his Great George Street house, defying all Lord Temple's effort to deter him.[48] He ran off twelve copies of the *Essay on Woman* out of fifty apparently intended, but they were not for publication. As a commercial venture he decided to print a collected edition of the *North Briton*, 2,000 two-volume sets to be sold at half a guinea. But even Wilkes did not dare to advertise this project, and on 9 July he told Lord Temple he had 'not 120 subscribers'.[49] He did not at first intend to include the controversial *Number Forty-Five*, but on 7 July changed his mind, presumably to boost sales.[50] That was a fateful decision, exposing Wilkes to legal retribution, but the reprint became a financial success, with Wilkes and printer Leach clearing £800 by 23 August. This profitability, however, seemingly owed much to harsh treatment of the journeymen printers. According to a hostile account Wilkes 'refused giving them the wages agreed for, and applied to Leach to value their labour, which he did greatly to the prejudice of the engagement which they had made with Wilkes, who turned them out of doors as soon as his purpose was served with usual ignominy'.[51]

The first case arising out of the arrests under the general warrant had meanwhile been heard on 6 July. The plaintiff, William Huckwell, was one of Leach's journeymen who had been arrested by mistake on 29 April. The issue was simply one of false imprisonment, not the legality of the warrant. Lord Chief Justice Pratt heard the case for eleven hours, and, despite the endeavours of both Yorke and Norton, the jury awarded Huckwell £300 in damages, plus costs.[52] This award was seen by the ministry as outrageously excessive, inflicted by a biased jury as a punishment, not as reparation to the injured party, who had merely suffered confinement for six hours. None of the friends of government on the jury panel had dared to appear at the Court. Attorney-General Yorke, who thought a shilling would have been sufficient, said privately that the jury had been egged on by Judge Pratt, who had 'talked of their finding damages like an English jury, that it was a matter of liberty'.[53]

The next day a similar case involving journeyman printer James Lindsay came before Judge Pratt. Counsel on both sides now agreed that the verdict given by the jury should decide the twelve similar actions depending on the same offence; for the Treasury, facing a potential bill of about £4,000, was anxious to keep the cost down.[54] When the jury found for Lindsay with £200 damages, the other plaintiffs were allowed the same damages and costs.[55]

John Wilkes attended the trials, receiving frequent public acclaim.[56] He was naturally delighted at the outcome. 'The merchants are firm in the cause of liberty', he told Lord Temple on 9 July. 'The City are warmly my friends and talk of £20,000 damages to me. The Administration are stunned, and poor Webb is really an object of compassion. In the course of the proceedings the Chief Justice was amazingly great.'[57] Temple was the instigator and financial backer of the legal action directed against the enforcement of the general warrant. It was his deep purse that made possible the expensive and sustained legal challenge.[58] He now suggested to Wilkes that the printers should initiate provisional actions for damages against the Secretaries of State themselves, who could otherwise invoke an immunity after six months.[59]

These early trials had been of no legal significance. A newspaper squib by 'Justiciarus' pointed out that there had been no condemnation of general warrants as illegal, merely retribution exacted for their improper use.[60] Wilkes himself commented to Temple that 'the cause only determines that a warrant of that nature, *illegally executed*, entitles to damages'. But he also stated that Judge Pratt had in fact raised a doubt as to the right of the Secretaries of State to issue general warrants: 'The origin of their power, he said, was uncertain. He believed it rested on prescription.' Wilkes assured Lord Temple that he had cast aside indolence and pleasure: 'I know that next winter I shall be *wholly* the man of business, and indefatigable in it. Many things I formerly found very difficult are now quite easy, and I can for a day together pore over journals and votes, as well as hear trials in Guildhall from 9 to 9.'[61]

Before that he would visit his daughter in Paris. After a brief stay at Aylesbury, where on 14 July he failed to prevent a loyal Buckinghamshire Address on the Peace of Paris proposed by the new Lord Lieutenant, Lord Le Despencer,[62] he returned to the metropolis, whence he assured Lord Temple on 23 July that 'the City of London and County of Surrey are almost unanimous in the great cause of Liberty. The noble spirit and animation of the people is beyond description.'[63] He left on 26 July for France, where he would spend two months with his beloved Polly, but intent also, so he told Churchill, on seducing her chaperone, Madame Carpentier.[64]

The legal ramifications of the *North Briton* case were to continue for several years, before all the cases brought by aggrieved parties were resolved. The ministry, for its part, was determined to prosecute Wilkes for seditious libel, and by mid-July had obtained the opinions of a whole galaxy of legal luminaries that he could not shelter behind Parliamentary privilege. Those who had expressed such a view included Lord Chancellor Henley, Lord Chief Justice Mansfield of the Court of King's Bench, Attorney-General Yorke, Solicitor-General Norton, and Yorke's father Lord Hardwicke, an eminent former Lord Chancellor. Even that staunch guardian of the honour of the House of Commons, former Speaker Arthur Onslow, confessed that the precedents were against such a claim; yet his political connections were with the opposition party of Newcastle, and his son George was a keen Wilkes partisan. No action was taken, however, for Chief Justice Pratt had pronounced to the contrary in the Court of Common Pleas, and Attorney-General Yorke was convinced that Lord Mansfield, if an action was commenced in his Court of King's Bench, would prudently postpone the point of privilege until after Parliament met to decide the matter.[65]

If the Parliamentary recess therefore caused a postponement of ministerial action, the political crisis of August 1763 provided a practical explanation of why nothing was done. Not until the end of that month could Grenville be sure that he would continue as Prime Minister. He could insist on George III's full confidence only after giving the King the opportunity to find out, through negotiation with Pitt, that he had no realistic alternative minister.[66] But the fortuitous death of Egremont through apoplexy on 21 August made necessary a cabinet reshuffle.* Halifax moved to be Southern Secretary, being replaced as Northern Secretary by Lord Sandwich, a follower of the Duke of Bedford, who himself became Lord President of the Council. Another consequence of these political discussions was the clear polarization that had developed between government and opposition. Both Newcastle and Pitt, and their various connections, were now permanently estranged from a ministry founded on the Grenville and Bedford groups. This cost the ministry its Attorney-General, who found himself on the wrong side of the political divide. Charles Yorke told Grenville that he could not take a public role against his family and their political allies, and wished to resign before the next Parliamentary session. Grenville took the view that Yorke, as a point of honour, should defend as Attorney-General the advice he had given as holder of that office, and he was astounded when Yorke requested that this advice should be kept secret; as if, Grenville commented, though not to Yorke, the Secretaries of State would have acted as they did without prior consultation with the law officers of the Crown. He could not prevent Yorke's resignation, which formally took place on 2 November.[68]

During the autumn the ministry formulated its campaign against Wilkes, with the intention of meeting Parliament on 15 November. The session would begin with a message from the King to the House of Commons describing the sequence of events. That would be followed by two resolutions, that *Number Forty-Five* was a seditious libel and that Parliamentary privilege did not cover seditious libel, thereby exposing Wilkes to the mercy of the lawcourts. Finally there would follow the expulsion of Wilkes from the Commons, not as a punishment but as the removal of an unworthy member. Although that might seem an unfairly premature step, before Wilkes had even been found guilty in a court of law, Grenville ascertained that there were precedents for such expulsions prior to legal prosecution as well as after conviction.[69] He made clear to his colleagues that the Parliamentary success

---

* When Wilkes heard the news, he wrote to Churchill: 'What a scoundrell trick has Lord Egremont played me? I had formed a fond wish to send him to the Devil; but he is gone without my passport.' Egremont's death put an end to the legal action against him. It was in this letter that Wilkes made the oft-quoted comment that 'the French are on the eve of some great revolution'. This was not, however, percipience, merely a report of contemporary opinion.[67]

of this strategy would be regarded as a vote of confidence in his ministry, his friend James Harris noting this conversation with Grenville on 29 October:

He then turned to Wilkes affair, to the resolution intended of a libel, no privilege and expulsion. Here (he said) that if this question were lost he must immediately quit administration. That this would be a test, whether government could support itself or not.[70]

This attitude was not such a hostage to fortune as it might appear. The policy would have the support of large majorities in both Houses of Parliament, partly because any challenge to it would appear to be a defence of what seemed to most MPs to be indefensible, the character and behaviour of Wilkes. Grenville was not avowedly staking his future on the validity of general warrants, a much more contentious and difficult issue, one certain to be raised by the Parliamentary opposition and one that would prove to be the real battleground of the session.

If the ministry's Parliamentary strategy was centred on the *North Briton* a separate smear campaign against Wilkes would be based on the *Essay on Woman*. Exactly how the ministry obtained a copy of this notorious poem, which in these less censorious times would hardly cause a raised eyebrow, was itself a matter of heated controversy. The key figure was Michael Curry, a printer employed by Wilkes at his house during the summer of 1763. Wilkes for long publicly maintained that the ministry had bribed Curry to steal a copy from his home. That was a good propaganda line, but whether Wilkes thought it the truth must be uncertain. The accusation was made, for example, in his *Letter to the Electors of Aylesbury*, published on 22 October 1764. Yet at his trial on 21 February there had been no attempt to prove these charges of robbery and bribery, which government sources always dismissed as 'mere fictions'.[71] Curry himself made at least three statements to the Grenville ministry, and much later, on 3 August 1768, a sworn affidavit at the behest of Wilkes.[72] From these, and a mass of other evidence, much of it erroneous or misleading, a simple story can be sketched.[73] Curry's story is consistent, and much of it is confirmed from other sources. He had printed off for himself an extra copy of the *Essay on Woman*. This circumstance was accidentally discovered by friends of the Grenville ministry, which was known to be eager for any weapon to use against Wilkes. Curry came under increasing pressure, both monetary inducements and threats of prosecution, to hand it over. Although one of the printers dismissed by Wilkes in July, and offered a bribe when Wilkes was absent in France, he refused to do so. But when Wilkes returned on 27 September he seemingly accused Curry of betraying him, and ministerial agents may even have misled the printer into thinking he faced prosecution for theft. Curry's own statement was that 'some expressions dropping from him which affected my private character I voluntarily' handed over the copy, which was passed on to Webb.[74]

The new Secretary of State, Lord Sandwich, an old acquaintance of Wilkes as a fellow member of both the Beef-Steak Society and the Hell Fire Club, meanwhile had sought a reconciliation on the basis that both Wilkes and the ministry would drop all legal actions. Whether this offer was personal or official, it was one that Wilkes rejected with scorn.[75] Sandwich, who may well have known the manuscript version of the *Essay on Woman*, now proposed to exploit the blunder of Wilkes in printing a few private copies, even though there was no proof either of his authorship or of its publication. Apart from the obvious political motives of pleasing his sovereign and winning his ministerial spurs, there was the personal incentive of the discovery among the Wilkes papers seized at his house on 30 April of a ribald lampoon on himself that contrived to impugn his courage and his morality in a single sentence.* Sandwich intended a character assassination of Wilkes in the House of Lords, by the dubious device of a complaint that a peer, William Warburton, now Bishop of Gloucester, had been libelled by the attribution to him of the notes on the poem. Sandwich suggested this tactic after Lord Chancellor Henley had disapproved of the cabinet's initial plan of denouncing the *Essay on Woman* as a blasphemous and impious work.[77] Sandwich took personal charge of the whole operation, informing Webb on 1 November that 'Mr Grenville much approves my idea of taking up the second charge singly in the House of Lords and beginning with it while they are taken up with the main point' of the *North Briton* in the House of Commons. He therefore asked what had been obtained from an examination of Curry the previous day, since 'the whole in my opinion depends upon him'. On 13 November Sandwich requested Webb to bring him 'the original papers of the *Essay on Woman*'; and on 14 November informed him that the tactic next day, when Parliament met, would be for the messenger who had seized the papers to produce them at the Bar of the House of Lords.[78] During the last few days before Parliament met Curry and other witnesses were sent out of town, in a surprisingly successful attempt to ensure secrecy about what was planned for the House of Lords. Wilkes remained blissfully ignorant of the blow that was to fall there.[79]

Throughout the autumn the ministry was aware that it might be at a tactical disadvantage in the clash with Wilkes. Although Lord Mansfield's attitude prevented any immediate prosecution of Wilkes for seditious libel

---

* The paper comprised mock instructions to Sandwich on his proposed appointment as ambassador to Madrid, and included this jibe: 'It is beneath your lordship to measure swords with the men, and we do most expressly restrain you to make all your thrusts at the women.'[76]

there was nothing to stop Wilkes and other complainants about government action under the general warrant having recourse to legal redress. On 26 September Lord Sandwich told Lord Holland, the former Henry Fox, that 'we think the attack upon Wilkes, which is our strong and popular point, will be greatly weakened, if there should be a verdict of a London Jury in his favour before his case is discussed in Parliament'.[80] For his part Wilkes was confident that this would happen, writing to Lord Temple on 18 October:

I have seen Mr Dunning twice . . . and have the satisfaction of finding him very sanguine in the law causes, both from the fullness of the evidence, and the general
opinion of mankind, which is highly favourable . . . Mr Beardmore . . . says that I
cannot fail of success, and that the action against Wood and Webb for the seizure
of papers will be certainly tried on the 11th of November, and the actions against
the messengers on the 16th. I feel the importance of one of these actions being
tried before the Parliament meets.[81]

His hopes were to be disappointed, for the court cases were postponed by what would seem to have been deliberate government obstruction,[82] whereas Parliament duly met on 15 November. That the ministry would take action concerning *Number Forty-Five* was evident to all political observers. What was uncertain was how much resistance there would be to the administration's Parliamentary measures. Grenville found it difficult to believe that the outrageous behaviour of Wilkes would be countenanced by such respectable opposition leaders as the Dukes of Devonshire and Newcastle, and especially by Lord Hardwicke, lifelong champion of law and order.[83] He nevertheless prepared for a Parliamentary campaign with the attention to detail that characterized his ministry. The MP chosen to lead the Commons attack was the able young Lord North, then a junior Lord of the Treasury. His initial diffidence, caused in part because he had 'personally rather received civilities from Wilkes', had been overcome by the time Grenville assembled on 5 November a meeting of a dozen Commons office-holders who all agreed to take part in the debates on Wilkes, with North moving the resolutions and the legal evidence being managed by Solicitor-General Norton, who was to succeed Yorke as Attorney-General in December.[84] A characteristic piece of cheek by Wilkes added a bizarre touch to the ministry's final preparation at the traditional eve-of-session meeting of government supporters at the Cockpit. Grenville reported to the King that 'Mr Wilkes thought fit to make his appearance there, and was, as I am informed, universally avoided'.[85]

On his return to Britain Wilkes had not only refused to make any bargain with the ministry: he had also reassured the Parliamentary opposition about his intentions. George Onslow visited him on 29 September, 'being desirous to know his sentiments', and reported to Newcastle:

They are exactly what I could wish them. . . . He desires to be understood as being devoted to the service of the Opposition, in any plan of uniting that may be thought right. He is in great spirits and, if thought right, . . . intends to begin his weekly entertainment of us, about a fortnight before the Parliament meets.[86]

Apart from his legal actions over the seizure of his person and property, Wilkes also intended to make a formal complaint in the House of Commons about the violation of Parliamentary privilege involved in his arrest: but, unknown to the ministry, he was willing to waive his privilege in the libel actions brought against him, perhaps confident that his authorship could not be proved in the case of either *Number Forty-Five* or the *Essay on Woman*. Battle would therefore be joined on all fronts. On 9 November, six days before the Parliamentary session, Wilkes called on Speaker Cust, declaring that 'he was not very well versed in Parliamentary proceedings'. His purpose was to ascertain how to obtain priority for his complaint of breach of privilege, but Cust replied that while 'this was certainly the rule of the House, a message from the Crown respecting the privileges of Parliament must be the first object of the consideration of the House'.[87] Wilkes would thus have had a shrewd idea of what was likely to happen on 15 November.

When business began that day in the House of Commons Wilkes and Grenville rose simultaneously, the former to raise a matter of privilege, the latter with a message from the Crown. Speaker Cust ruled both out of order, insisting that it was the invariable practice of the House to commence each session with the formal reading of a Bill, to establish its right to decide its own order of business. After this was moved Pitt denounced the procedure as a piece of nonsense, adding an amendment that it would be in preference to a matter of privilege raised by Wilkes. Lord North countered this by a prior amendment, that it would be in preference to a message from the King. The House rejected both amendments by 300 votes to 111. Such a large majority for government was a bad omen for Wilkes. Preference was then given to Grenville. The purpose of the royal message was to inform the House that Parliamentary privilege had been used by Wilkes to obstruct the course of justice. Copies were read out not only of *North Briton, Number Forty-Five* but also of the examinations of George Kearsley and Richard Balfe taken on 29 April. North then put to the House this ministerial resolution:

That the Paper, entitled 'The North Briton, No. 45' is a false, scandalous and seditious Libel, containing expressions of the most unexampled Insolence and contumely towards His Majesty, the grossest Aspersions upon both Houses of Parliament, and the most audacious Defiance of the Authority of the whole Legislature; and most manifestly tending to alienate the Affections of the People from His Majesty, to withdraw them from their Obedience to the Laws of the Realm, and to excite them to traitorous Insurrections against His Majesty's Government.

Wilkes promptly challenged the imputation of 'false'. Pitt began, so diarist James Harris noted, as if he was a prosecutor of Wilkes, denouncing the *North Briton* as licentious and indecent, but 'artfully came round to take exception' to the assertion that it tended to incite 'traitorous insurrections' and moved an amendment to omit that wording. A long debate ended in its rejection by 273 to 111. North's motion was then passed, the libel was voted to be burnt by the public hangman, and, long after midnight, Wilkes was at last permitted to make his complaint; but the whole issue of privilege was postponed. Pitt declared that the King had been ill-advised by his ministers and lawyers, an assertion which an angry Norton deemed a personal insult and was quietly resented by the Yorke family. More heat than light had been generated by the debates and altercations of the day, during which eighty-two speeches were made, fifteen of them by Pitt. Harris on the Treasury Bench thought that Pitt had demeaned himself by defending 'the most abandoned of men', and ended: ''Twas a rough day. The Tempest was acted at St Stephens, as well as at Drury Lane.'[88]

Simultaneously with this expected attack on Wilkes in the Commons the ministry exploded the *Essay on Woman* bombshell in the House of Lords. Raising the matter as a breach of privilege, since the notes had been attributed to the man now Bishop of Gloucester, Sandwich announced that Wilkes had published an obscene and impious poem, parts of which he read out to the House. That such a reprobate as Sandwich should adopt this role struck contemporaries as rank hypocrisy. According to Horace Walpole, his old Hell Fire Club colleague Lord Le Despencer commented that he had never heard the Devil preach before: and soon afterwards, at a performance of the *Beggar's Opera* at Covent Garden, the audience made an immediate identification when Macheath complained of betrayal by a member of his gang: 'That Jemmy Twitcher should peach me, I own surprises me.' Delighted laughter fixed the nickname of Jemmy Twitcher to Sandwich for ever more.[89] But in the Lords debate such reflections were outweighed by the offence. The Bishop of Gloucester gave intemperate vent to his feelings by denouncing Wilkes as worse than Satan. Lord Temple could make no defence, but criticized the underhand methods used to obtain the poem. The House voted it to be a 'scandalous, obscene and impious libel'. Nine witnesses, including Lovell Stanhope and Michael Curry, were examined to prove that Wilkes was the author. But before the Lords voted a resolution to that effect Lord Mansfield said that he ought to be heard in his defence, and the matter was postponed until 17 November.[90]

In all 15 November had been a bad day for John Wilkes. He had been held up to ridicule in the Lords, and prevented from pursuing his privilege complaint in the Commons, where his personal courage had been impugned.

For Samuel Martin, who had been maligned in the *North Briton* of 5 March, now belatedly chose to denounce the anonymous author as 'a cowardly rascal', staring at Wilkes. The latter ignored this outburst then, but wrote to Martin the next morning acknowledging his authorship. There followed a challenge to an immediate duel with pistols. This took place in Hyde Park, at noon, and Wilkes was badly hurt, Martin's second shot lodging in his stomach. There was a whiff of suspicion about the episode. Martin, an adherent of Bute, had been busy at target practice for much of the summer, and Horace Walpole was not alone in deeming it a plot against the life of Wilkes.[91] Whatever the truth of the matter, the injury to Wilkes placed him at a disadvantage by preventing his attendance at either House of Parliament.

An illness of the Speaker caused the postponement of the Wilkes case in the Commons until 23 November.[92] Lord North moved then that the House should consider the King's message about privilege, and there ensued a long wrangle as opposition members argued that this should not be done in the absence of Wilkes. North contended that the extent of privilege was a matter of general principle, and Grenville said that there had been a legal impasse for six months. Warming to this theme, the Prime Minister declared not only that Judge Pratt's ruling had been precipitate and wrong, but even that he should not have made it at all in his Court of Common Pleas. Ministerial speakers made the general point that delay might mean a decision on privilege in a court of law, an argument countered by the opposition contention that the legal cases pending could be unfairly influenced by a Parliamentary decision against Wilkes. Charles Yorke spoke for postponement. Norton answered that Wilkes might not be present until February. Pitt attacked both of them by asserting that the law officers should be brought to account by the House for their opinion on privilege. He believed libel to be covered by it, and deemed Wilkes 'unfortunate'. The vote at the end of the debate was 243 to 166 in favour of proceeding, but it was late and Speaker Cust was tired. The House adjourned after the ministry had revealed its intention by the formal proposing of the motion, 'That Privilege of Parliament does not extend to the case of writing, and publishing seditious Libels'. Diarist Harris attributed the sharp fall in the ministerial majority to the influence of Yorke, who, however, privately informed Grenville that on the issue of privilege he and other lawyers would be voting with the ministry.[93]

Business in the Commons next day began with a letter and a petition from Wilkes, asking that the motion be postponed, a request rejected on the ground that the House had already decided to proceed. Lord North then made the distinction that was to be the main ministerial argument throughout the ensuing debates, that between criminal offences and civil ones.

Although only treason, felony, and breach of the peace were named as exceptions to the privilege that MPs enjoyed of immunity from arrest, 'all crimes' were meant, and there were some precedents to that effect. MPs had no 'license of misdemeanour for themselves and their servants. That would be fatal to the liberty of the people.' The opposition response to this powerful line of argument, voiced first by George Onslow, was to suggest a Committee to examine precedents. Charles Yorke, torn between his political allegiance and his legal opinion, made a tortuous speech of two hours. He disagreed with Judge Pratt's ruling, he told MPs, but respect for the judiciary had led him to avoid a legal clash. Libel and some other offences, Yorke said, were breaches of the peace. He had fulfilled his promise to Grenville, who told the King that the speech was 'the greatest performance that could be made'. Pitt feared that a simple issue might be confused by a variety of precedents. Parliamentary privilege existed to preserve liberty, not to screen crimes, he said, an argument neatly turned against him later by James Harris, who deduced from this premiss that therefore privilege must apply only to civil cases. Pitt now denounced Wilkes as 'an impious criminal, that sets at defiance his God, his King, and his country'.[94] Having made it clear that he was not defending the behaviour of Wilkes, he warned that MPs might be at the mercy of a Secretary of State or an Attorney-General. 'He spoke two hours', Harris noted, 'leaning on two crutches, with both his legs and both his arms in flannel, and seemed to suffer much fatigue and pain.'

Solicitor-General Norton informed the House that there was no record of any privilege being granted in any criminal case, only in civil suits, and that common law depended on precedent. He dreaded the idea that Parliamentary privilege might interfere with the operation of the criminal law. Norton concluded by defending the advice he had given, claiming that 'he was above the favour of a minister or the foul tongue of faction'. The waspish Horace Walpole recorded with delight an altercation that occurred next, after Richard Rigby, Bedford's chief lieutenant in the House, denounced Lord Temple, who was as usual listening to the debate, as 'an incendiary peer, encouraging mobs from windows of coffee-houses'. Temple's brother James Grenville responded with such a bitter attack on Rigby that the Speaker had to insist on their promises that the dispute would not end in a duel. Another Grenville brother, the Prime Minister himself, wound up the debate by reiterating the point that 'criminal matters were never understood to be privileged', and he scorned the idea, implied by Pitt, that bad ministers would use the excuse of libel to strike at opposition MPs, for non-bailable offences like treason and felony already provided ample opportunity. The resolution was carried, long after midnight, by 258 votes to 133, many MPs having already left.[95] It is an ironic part of the Wilkes story that the main argument put forward on behalf of this Commons resolution, which was intended to clear the obstacle to punitive legal action against him, was one for 'liberty', in this instance the right of the ordinary subject not to suffer from crimes protected by Parliamentary privilege.

On the following day the Commons formally communicated this resolution, and those of 15 November, to the House of Lords, which agreed with them after a debate on 29 November by 114 votes to 35. The Duke of Newcastle, though voting in the minority, defended the use of the general warrant, presumably because he had issued many such when Secretary of State himself for thirty years. Lord Temple, who publicly disclaimed any connection with the *North Briton*, afterwards organized an official *Protest*, signed by sixteen peers.[96] On 1 December the Lords accepted a Commons proposal that *North Briton, Number Forty-Five* should be publicly burnt by the common hangman on 3 December at the Royal Exchange in the City of London.[97] Whether that decision was unthinkingly obtuse or deliberately provocative, the result was predictable. 'A great riot ensued', as Horace Walpole laconically put it, 'the cry was "Wilkes and Liberty" ', as a crowd prevented the order from being carried out: but nothing more lethal than mud was used as missiles.[98] Grenville went next day to consult the King, and although George III was 'much disturbed and exasperated' both men agreed not to do anything that might provoke the City.[99] But the irascible Duke of Bedford was not disposed to let the matter rest. On 6 December the House of Lords interrogated the two sheriffs of London, who had supervised the proceedings, and heard that the crowd had been incited by gentlemen watching from coffee-houses and balconies. The Duke's anger was directed against Lord Mayor William Bridgen and other City officials, who had made no attempt to quell the mob, but the ministry persuaded both Houses to express their annoyance merely by a resolution condemning the rioters as 'perturbators of the public peace, dangerous to the liberties of this country', followed by an Address, voted on 8 December, asking the King to bring the offenders to justice.[100]

The popular support for Wilkes in London was openly demonstrated on 9 December, when the Common Council of the City refused to thank the sheriffs or order any retributive action against the rioters, thereby retrospectively justifying Bedford's strictures.[101] Later in the month, when George III visited Drury Lane Theatre, he must have been mortified to hear the galleries call out 'Wilkes and Liberty'.[102] This popular enthusiasm foreshadowed the Wilkite control of the City in the next decade. Prime Minister George Grenville was one Parliamentarian who perceived the emergence of a new political phenomenon, as in a rejoinder to Charles Yorke on 17 December. Yorke had gone to urge Grenville to strengthen his ministry by recruiting from the Parliamentary opposition, and 'laid great stress upon the clamour of the people'. Grenville replied that any such ministerial reshuffle would be irrelevant, 'since it was no longer a cry for the Duke of Newcastle, Lord Hardwicke, or even Mr Pitt, but for Pratt and Wilkes'.[103]

That was the popular cry because Wilkes had just won a major legal triumph, when Judge Pratt made the first condemnation of general warrants. The action by Wilkes against Under-Secretary Wood for trespass and seizure of papers was heard in the Court of Common Pleas on 6 December, before Pratt and a Middlesex jury at Westminster Hall. His counsel, Serjeant Glynn, argued that the case was of general significance, affecting the liberty of every subject, and asked for £5,000 damages. The defence was able to produce many examples of the use of general warrants, but Judge Pratt scorned this line of argument in his summing-up, when he declared that 'the office precedents are . . . no justification of a practice in itself illegal, and contrary to the fundamental principles of the constitution'. Pratt did concede that past evidence of such practice could lead to mitigation of damages, but he had already voiced the opinion that 'damages are designed not only as a satisfaction to the injured party, but likewise as a punishment of the guilty', and the jury awarded Wilkes £1,000.[104] He wrote in delight to his daughter two days later: 'I expect the same damages against Mr Webb and ten times as much against Lord Halifax.'[105] Lord Chief Justice Mansfield told the King in private that 'no man had ever behaved so shamefully as Pratt',[106] but the decision was not as partisan as government men would have had it appear. On 22 December William Guthrie, a veteran journalist who was a ministerial supporter, informed Treasury Secretary Charles Jenkinson that 'the illegality of the forms of the warrants from the Secretary of State's office for apprehending printers, etc has been long suspected under former Administrations.'[107] It had simply been that Wilkes, backed by Lord Temple's money, had now challenged this dubious practice. The Pratt judgment, moreover, was not a universal condemnation of general warrants, merely of their use as general search-warrants of unspecified houses and other buildings. The contemporary press celebrated this precise point. 'By this important decision, every Englishman has the satisfaction of seeing that "his house is his castle".'[108]

It had been altogether a bad day for the ministry, for during the trial Solicitor-General Norton attempted and failed to prove that Wilkes was the author of *North Briton, Number Forty-Five*.[109] The prosecution charge against Wilkes concerning that paper was therefore now altered to one of republishing it in his collected edition.[110] The humiliation of the government on 8 December was completed by the popular rejoicing. A delighted crowd rushed from Westminster Hall to convey the news to their house-bound hero in Great George Street, 'and stayed there an hour, playing with French Horns, and crying out "Pratt, Wilkes, and Liberty, for ever" '.[111]

The ministry would retaliate against Wilkes in Parliament and the Court of King's Bench, and on 16 November, the day of his duel with Martin, Secretary of State Halifax had assured George III that precautions were being taken 'to prevent the criminal's escape from justice'.[112] His house was kept under observation, probably from that date, and suspicions grew as to how far Wilkes was malingering, with good reason; for in his letter of 8 December to Polly he told his daughter, 'I hope to eat my Christmas dinner with you in Paris'.[113] On 1 December the House of Common ordered his attendance for 7 December, to answer the charge of being author and publisher of *North Briton, Number Forty-Five*. His physician, Dr Richard Brockesly, and a Dr Graves, then gave the House information on his health, and his attendance was postponed until 16 December. They made another report that day, and the attendance was postponed to 19 January 1764; but the House voted that one of the King's doctors, Caesar Hawkins, and a Dr Heberden, should visit Wilkes regularly to check on his progress.[114] Wilkes refused to admit them, and contrived to defeat the surveillance on him. Although the *St. James's Chronicle* of 24 December reported that Charles Churchill and Samuel Martin were awaiting Wilkes at Calais, he was able to leave that day for Dover while feigning a visit to his friend Humphrey Cotes.[115] Next day he sailed to Calais, enduring a stormy Channel crossing, and arrived in Paris on 29 December.[116]

The Grenville ministry, no wiser than anybody else as to whether or not Wilkes would return, finalized arrangements for the Parliamentary campaign against him after the Christmas break. At a meeting of a dozen office-holders at Grenville's house, 10 Downing Street, on 5 January 1764, Sir Fletcher Norton, now Attorney-General, recounted the evidence showing Wilkes to be the author of the *North Briton* in general, and more specifically of *Number Forty-Five*. Still smarting at Pratt's conduct of Wood's case, he stated that the judge then had been biased and that none of a score of general warrants brought before the Court of King's Bench had been condemned there. The meeting decided to proceed against Wilkes whether or not he appeared in the Commons, and to reject any motion for postponement.[117] Five days later a second meeting, this time of some twenty MPs who were office-holders or lawyers, received a legal briefing from Norton. Although Wilkes had been deprived of his Parliamentary privilege concerning his libels, his own claim of breach of privilege against those who had seized him and his papers was due to come before the Commons. They should be voted not guilty, Norton suggested, and if opposition MPs raised the question of the illegality of the general warrant any decision should be avoided by a resolution to postpone consideration for six months. 'He wished the warrant might be as little discussed as possible', noted James Harris, 'intimating that he thought it would not bear it.'[118]

There was much contemporary speculation in Britain as to whether Wilkes intended to return to London for the meeting of Parliament. That he should do so was the general advice of his friends, and on 4 January the British ambassador to France, Lord Hertford, reported to Grenville that he would.[119] The worst the House of Commons could do to him would be expulsion, and his attorney Alexander Philipps assured Wilkes that no jury would convict him; whereas avoidance of confrontation would cost him popular support.[120] Wilkes seemed to have accepted these arguments, for on Monday, 9 January, he wrote this assurance to George Onslow:

I burn with impatience for the 19th January, because I shall then have an opportunity of vindicating myself [from] the many unjust and cruel attacks made upon me, and I doubt not the House of Commons will do the nation and me the most signal justice, and that I shall meet with a satisfaction adequate to the unparalleled injuries which English liberty suffered in my person, from a wicked and corrupt administration. I have ordered my post-chaise for Friday morning at four, and hope to embark on Sunday. I hope my passage will rather be longer than it was to Calais, for I was half killed in coming over in two hour and three quarters.[121]

But that travel ordeal had reopened his wound and worsened his condition. Two days later Wilkes wrote to inform Onslow, 'I am now too ill to undertake the journey'.[122] From his sick bed he wrote also to the Speaker of the House of Commons, stating that he was unfit to travel and enclosing a medical certificate to that effect signed by two French doctors, one of the King's physicians and an army surgeon. On 17 January Sir John Cust wrote back to acknowledge receipt of these documents: 'I am very sorry, Sir, for the account which you give of your health.'[123] This evidence would seem to be convincing, were it not for a letter written by Wilkes to Humphrey Cotes on 20 January, wherein he said that he was following a plan agreed in London with Lord Temple and Cotes, who had confirmed it by repeated hints to return '*only if your health permits*'. Wilkes frankly told Cotes that the two doctors 'from friendship gave me the certificate in the handsomest manner. I have, to keep up appearances, been in my room sick and complaining ever since.'[124]

Although MPs could not have known it, there was thus good reason for the evident suspicion of the House of Commons when Speaker Cust produced the letter and certificate from Wilkes on 19 January.[125] Much was made of the technical point that no Public Notary had authenticated the certificate.[126] Grenville even opposed its being read out, but that was done, in French! The two doctors appointed by the House reported that Wilkes had refused them admission. His own doctors said that they had urged him not to go out at all, and opined that he would be unable to travel from Paris. A first adjournment motion, put by William Beckford, was rejected by 239 votes to 102. Opposition speakers protested that relevant legal cases were pending. Both Norton and Yorke, facing each other across the House, replied that the Commons should not leave its dignity at the mercy of Crown lawyers, and a resolution to proceed was carried by 275 votes to 70. It was prefaced by a statement that the behaviour of Wilkes in refusing admission to the House's doctors and withdrawing to a foreign country amounted to 'contempt of the authority of this House'. MPs from the dwindling minority then argued vainly that all proposed witnesses should be examined on oath, another adjournment motion failing by 225 votes to 64.

Damning evidence against Wilkes was provided by Michael Curry, who stated that the reprinting of the *North Briton* had taken place at his house, and that most of the copy was in his own writing.[127] After a last adjournment motion failed by 227 votes to 57, letters from Wilkes to George Kearsley about various issues of the *North Briton* were read out.[128] Richard Balfe was heard as to *Number Forty-Five*. Diarist James Harris noted with satisfaction that he provided 'clear, consistent and conclusive' evidence about the involvement of Wilkes. There had been ministerial alarms that this key witness, from fear of self-incrimination, would not give evidence, 'having been tampered with by Wilkes's people', and Norton had told the meeting of 5 January that he had a private pardon ready to overcome any such objection, a precaution that proved unnecessary. Lord North then put two motions, that Wilkes was guilty of writing and publishing *North Briton, Number Forty-Five*, already voted to be a false, scandalous, and seditious libel, and that he be expelled. 'There was a remarkable silence when the last questions were put', recorded diarist Harris, 'and a very loud affirmative succeeded by the single negative' of Colonel George Onslow, cousin of the late Speaker's son. The House then rose at 3.30 a.m.

James Harris thought the opposition had been badly managed, both in the general organization of the debates and in the questions to witnesses, which tended to condemn rather than acquit Wilkes. The reason was that this activity had been the response of young or partisan MPs like the Onslow cousins and Beckford. The opposition leadership had shunned Wilkes, with both William Pitt and Newcastle's chief Commons spokesman Henry Legge conspicuous among the deliberate absentees. The old Duke of Newcastle had forecast that behaviour in a letter to the Duke of Devonshire on 21 December:

The expulsion . . . appears to me, the most unjust thing, that ever was attempted, and therefore I hope Mr Pitt will vigorously oppose it. Though, as I hear some pretend to justify this proceeding, by former precedents. I own, I am fearful how far Mr Pitt will engage in it. For he has always had a backwardness, in what relates to Wilkes, except it carries with it (as, indeed, I think this would do) some constitutional point, upon which Mr Pitt is always ready.[129]

The ministry could not expect such an easy time of it when questions of constitutional principle were at stake, over general warrants. Many would defend the cause of 'liberty' who shunned its unworthy champion. What lay ahead was one of the great Parliamentary battles of the century, the first of two sparked off by the catalystic career of John Wilkes. The opposition counter-attack began the next day, 20 January, when one of Newcastle's most respected followers Sir George Savile, together with Sir William Meredith, a man whom the Wilkes case seemingly converted from government to opposition, raised the matter of the complaint of breach of privilege brought by Wilkes over the seizure of his personal papers when an MP. Those accused were Under-Secretary Robert Wood and Treasury Solicitor Philip Webb, both MPs themselves, together with three messengers. The hearing was fixed for 26 January, but later postponed until 13 February in order to allow time for witnesses to attend, notably Matthew Brown, a servant of Wilkes now in Paris.[130]

There meanwhile occurred in the House of Lords on 24 January an incident that revealed the ministerial animosity towards Wilkes. Although the *Essay on Woman* case had not yet come before a lawcourt, Lord Sandwich put a resolution that anticipated a conviction, to vote Wilkes the author and order him into custody of Black Rod, the House's executive officer. The Duke of Devonshire was among those who opposed such a precipitate proceeding, and Lord Temple responded hotly to mention of his association with Wilkes. Their protests proved successful. A preface 'it appearing to the House' modified the motion, and the second part was dropped in favour of a resolution to establish a Committee to decide on how to proceed in the absence of the culprit.[131]

Nor was the opposition above Parliamentary sharp practice. On 3 February, just as the House of Commons was rising after a long finance debate and many MPs had actually left, Meredith launched a preliminary attack on the issue of general warrants. He proposed an Address to the King for the various warrants, examinations, and other papers relevant to the Wilkes case, 'keeping up to the Temple and Pitt style of great indignation *in words* against Wilkes and his behaviour', as Harris laconically noted. The ministry, caught by surprise in a thin House, carried an adjournment motion only by 73 votes to 60, and the debate was resumed on 6 February. Meredith then defended Parliamentary privilege as a safeguard against the Crown, though he agreed it should not shelter MPs from the law. It was a bad omen for the ministry when Sir John Philipps, one of Grenville's foremost independent supporters, condemned the use of warrants by Secretaries of State without evidence taken on oath, precisely what Halifax and Egremont had done with respect to *North Briton, Number Forty-Five*. Attorney-General Norton argued that the documents requested were not secret, since they had been printed in the press and filed in court, and he warned against the dangerous precedent of asking the Crown for such papers. After a long debate that anticipated the one on general warrants the ministry rejected the motion by 217 votes to 122.[132]

A week later, on 13 February, the hearing of the breach-of-privilege complaint by Wilkes opened with a letter from him, dated 5 February in Paris, expressing the hope that he would be instrumental in establishing the liberty of the subject. The Speaker read it out, and, after Savile had talked of giving the devil his due and Pitt had dismissed the letter as irrelevant, the House got down to business. A number of prosecution witnesses were heard, first among them Wilkes's servant Brown, over from Paris, who recounted how the papers had been seized. James Harris on the Treasury Bench scornfully noted how 'Pitt and his friends in the course of the above evidence were in two points for transgressing the rules of all evidence: one was, they were for admitting hearsay evidence; the other was they were against cross-examination', even though the Speaker had said that this facility would be allowed to those accused, whether MPs or not. When all the prosecution witnesses had been heard, it was eleven o'clock at night, but Pitt opposed a motion to adjourn, declaring that 'he could not sleep while the cause of liberty was in such jeopardy', or, as Harris derisively noted, 'whether we were to go home bondsmen or free'. Grenville also spoke for proceeding, and the House decided to do so by 379 votes to 31; but MPs then voted with their feet instead, streaming out of the chamber, and the House rose at midnight.[133]

The next day began with examination of messenger Nathan Carrington, who produced a series of general warrants since 1662, signed by various Secretaries of State, including Pitt, who commented that his warrants had been expedients of wartime and not used against libels.[134] This evidence of official practice was presented until long past midnight, for not until one o'clock did Meredith put this motion: 'That a general warrant for apprehending and seizing the authors, printers and publishers of a seditious libel, together with their papers, is not warranted by law.' This was a much broader condemnation than that made by Judge Pratt, for it concerned the arrest of persons and not merely the sanctity of private residences. The five accused, Meredith declared, should be found guilty of acting under an illegal warrant. When Grenville expressed the hope that they would be acquitted, Pitt replied that a decision on general warrants must take priority. But the ministry was resolved to clear the officials before the House rose, and defeated an adjournment motion by only ten votes, 207 to 197. There followed a long altercation between Pitt and Grenville. Pitt dramatically declared that liberty was at its last stand. He deliberately distinguished between that cause and Wilkes himself, expressing pleasure that the House had purged itself of such an unworthy member, and stating that he had always been an enemy of that seditious paper, the *North Briton*. But a general warrant was a symptom of arbitrary government, and Webb and Wood were violators of justice and liberty. Grenville answered that he was as much a friend to liberty as anybody, and asked why Pitt had used warrants if he thought such power wrong. Grenville then launched into a personal attack on Wilkes as a man who had sought to divide Scotland from England, the people from Parliament, and the Parliament from the King. Pitt recalled the age of Pym and Hamden. Grenville scorned any comparison of them with Wilkes, and claimed that ministerial forbearance in overlooking so many libels was not the hallmark of arbitrary government. At half-past seven in the morning the ministry defeated another adjournment motion by 208 votes to 184, and then secured the acquittal of the five accused before the debate on Meredith's motion was adjourned until 17 February. Horace Walpole thought it had been 'the longest sitting on record' of the House of Commons.[135]

The resumed debate began with ministerial amendments designed to render Meredith's motion more unacceptable. 'Treasonable' was inserted to describe libel, while additional clauses were to assert that such warrants had been frequently used and had never been challenged in the Court of King's Bench. Charles Yorke thought it proper to adopt these changes, and soon afterward Pitt sent word round the opposition benches not to force a vote on them. Meredith, who described Wilkes as 'profligate', put a good face on the situation by declaring the question to be one of liberty not law. Even now the ministry did not risk a direct vote on the motion. After a long debate Attorney-General Norton moved to postpone the question for four months, lest it interfere with legal cases then pending. 'That were he a judge below, he should no more regard a resolution of the House of Commons upon this subject, than that of so many drunken porters. This an unlucky sample of nisi prius eloquence', thought Harris, and one that was to be long remembered against Norton. The ministry was here adopting a line of argument it had brushed aside itself when in November the Commons had condemned *North Briton, Number Forty-Five* as a libel. It was the tactic Norton had suggested on 10 January, and the ministry's reluctance to seek a direct negative on Meredith's motion had been strengthened by debating evidence that some of its independent supporters favoured a Bill. An offer by Sir John Philipps to introduce one may even have saved the day for the administration.[136] The debate had run strongly against the ministry. Charles Yorke now at last declared that the general warrant was illegal, claiming that he had not been consulted on it before the arrest of Wilkes. Also down off the political fence was the brilliant and erratic Charles Townshend, the most sparkling speaker in Parliament. 'He abhorred Wilkes, he said, and drew a severe picture of him', according to Horace Walpole, before commending his achievement. 'One advantage had been derived from Wilkes; he had stopped a growing evil. Nobody could think what thirty years more in abler hands would have done. This warrant without any description of person might take up any man under any description of a libel.'

Diarist Harris recorded the tense atmosphere when the adjournment motion was put just before six in the morning: 'On giving the Ayes and Noes, the Speaker declared for the Noes, which so invigorated the opposition, that they were so indecent as to clap. When we went out, twas quite dubious where the majority lay. Many friends had deserted us, on an idea that privilege and liberty were concerned. . . . Others of the more wary sort left us, as rats on certain occasions quit the ship.'[137] But the tellers recorded a ministerial majority of fourteen, 232 to 218. 'The House adjourned at 25 minutes past seven, a fine sunshine morning, and the longest day they had been known within memory to sit.' A ministerial defeat had been widely anticipated, and the Common Council of London had prepared bonfires and illuminations.[138]

This Parliamentary confrontation of February 1764 was one of the famous political contests of the eighteenth century, and the episode has usually been seen as the story of how John Wilkes nearly toppled the King's government. That is a complete misreading of the political situation. Grenville had already completed the Parliamentary campaign on which he had staked his political reputation, writing in triumph to the British ambassador in Paris on 28 January: 'We have got rid of Mr Wilkes, who was expelled with only one negative voice, and who will find, too late, how much too far he has gone.'[139] Grenville strained every nerve to avoid defeat on 17 February, but before that debate the King had sent him this assurance: 'The Opposition might, for what he knew, carry the question of the warrants on Friday . . . but that would make no change in him in regard to his present Administration, which he meant to support to the utmost.' When on 19 February the Duke of Bedford informed George III how elated the opposition was and 'how sure they thought themselves of a change in the Ministry, the King told him if that was their hope they would find themselves deceived'. Grenville and George III had already agreed not to dismiss any office-holders who had rebelled over such a popular question.[140] Both men knew that few of their deserters over general warrants, whether placemen or independents, had intended to bring down the ministry. One of the court party, Gilbert Elliot, explained to his father about 'the alarm having been recently spread of the danger of seizing papers, and delegating so great a discretionary power to messengers. Many friends to government had got so far engaged on this general ground that they could not disentangle themselves, even upon our state of the question.'[141]

Hardly had this Parliamentary excitement died down when the trial of Wilkes for libel took place, before Lord Chief Justice Mansfield in his Court of King's Bench on 21 February. There was no attempt to prove his authorship of either *North Briton, Number Forty-Five* or the *Essay on Woman*. The charge was simply one of publication. Wilkes now paid the price for establishing his printing press in the previous May. It was the inclusion of *Number Forty-Five* in the collected edition of the *North Briton*, not its original publication, that provided the ground for a charge of publishing 'a seditious and scandalous libel', and the private printing of the *Essay on Woman* for one of publishing an 'obscene and impious libel'. This careful wording meant that the verdict of a respectable Middlesex jury was not in doubt, even though two jurors expected to be hostile to Wilkes did not attend because they received letters falsely stating that the trial had been postponed.[142] The jury was asked to decide only the facts of publication, not the issue of libel, and found Wilkes guilty on both counts after hearing the evidence of such key witnesses as Michael Curry, Richard Balfe, and George Kearsley, all promised immunity from prosecution themselves.[143] No sentence was passed in the absence of Wilkes, but after he failed to answer five summonses to attend he was outlawed on 1 November: all legal actions in which he was involved were automatically suspended, notably his case against Lord Halifax. Wilkes was incensed about his conviction over the *Essay on Woman*, for delivering a paper to the printer had been deemed publication, with his counsel not being allowed to challenge what his solicitor Alexander Philipps deemed a 'curious' interpretation of the law.[144] His indignation was still manifest in his speech to the same court on his surrender to justice on 20 April 1768:

Twelve copies of a small part of it had been printed in my house at my own private press. I had carefully locked them up and I never gave one to the most intimate friend . . . I pray God to forgive, as I do, the jury who have found me guilty of publishing a poem I concealed with care, and which is not even yet published if any precise meaning can be affixed to any word in our language.[145]

Wilkes believed that the promptness of his outlawry was a 'ministerial scheme, . . . to prevent the great cause against Lord Halifax (on which the first warrant must be formally condemned) being ever decided'.[146] Whether or not this suspicion was justified, that circumstance did not prevent general warrants receiving condemnation in both the lawcourts and in Parliament. A case for false imprisonment by printer Dryden Leach against John Money and other messengers led to a condemnation by Lord Mansfield in the Court of King's Bench on 18 June 1764, and more positively on 8 November 1765, that had the practical effect of ending the use of general warrants for the arrest of persons.[147] This complemented Pratt's judgment of 6 December 1763 over trespass and seizure of papers.[148]

The Parliamentary postscripts to the general warrant story took place in 1766. In July 1765 George III dismissed Grenville and appointed the Marquess of Rockingham to head a ministry composed out of the old Newcastle party. Since the verdicts by Mansfield had not been formal and unequivocal, the new administration decided on a Parliamentary resolution. That was muddled thinking, because no such motion would have any legal validity. The Stamp Act Crisis concerning the American colonies delayed the introduction of any motion until 22 April 1766, when Meredith and Savile virtually repeated the one defeated in 1764 and again on 29 January 1765, when the Grenville ministry carried a wrecking amendment by 224 votes to 185.[149] The 1766 motion was 'That a general warrant to apprehend the Author, Printer or Publisher, of a libel, is illegal; and if executed on the Person of a Member of this House, is also a Breach of the Privilege of this House.' This, however unexceptionable in principle, was an easy target for criticism. George Grenville, now leader of the main opposition party, explained his earlier opposition to such a motion on the ground that it would have been improper for his ministry to have passed resolutions on matters then before the lawcourts. He now condemned the motion as too narrow, since it implied the validity of warrants in other cases. Norton, also in opposition, objected to the joining together of two propositions concerning law and privilege. The ministry's own Solicitor-General William De Grey objected that one House of Parliament alone could not declare the law. Pitt, by then increasingly hostile to the ministry, thought that the court rulings obviated the need for the motion and supported Grenville's idea of widening its scope. The motion was carried by 173 votes to 71, but that was not the end of the matter.[150] Grenville and Pitt obviously both intended to take what credit they could for themselves, and Pitt on 25 April put forward a motion that virtually repeated the one of three days before, as several speakers pointed out. Grenville took the opportunity to declare that an Act of Parliament would be preferable. During these debates both Yorke and Norton condemned the legality of general warrants, and Pitt asked why they had not done so in 1763 as the Crown's law officers. Diarist Harris dryly noted the reason: they had not been consulted in time![151] Grenville followed up his idea of legislation by proposing two Bills on 29 April. One, condemning warrants for arresting people, was defeated at once after opposition from both the ministry and Pitt. The other, banning warrants for seizing papers except for treason and felony, progressed through the Commons in thin Houses, but was rejected in the House of Lords.[152] The *North Briton* case ended not with a bang but a whimper.

4

French Leave

1763–1768

'PARIS seems very fatal to Wilkes's courage', wrote Horace Walpole when he knew that the popular hero would not be returning to face Parliament. 'We may do what we will with him, now we can do nothing, expel him, send his writings to gaol, and execute his excuses.'[1] Wilkes was wise to deem discretion the better part of valour. Expulsion from the House of Commons deprived him of Parliamentary immunity from his financial creditors. No useful purpose would be served by returning to Britain to be sentenced for libel by Lord Mansfield. Nor, as he told Humphrey Cotes in a letter of 20 January 1764, did he feel political martyrdom to be a duty after the way in which he had been treated:

With all the fine things said and wrote of me, have not the public to this moment left me in the lurch, as to the expense of so great a variety of lawsuits? . . . Can I trust likewise a rascally Court, who bribe my own servants to steal out of my house? Which of the opposition, likewise, can call on me, and expect my services? I hold no obligation to any of them, but to Lord Temple. . . . I believe, both parties will rejoice at my being here. . . . If I stay in Paris, I will not be forgot in England; for I will feed the papers, from time to time, with gall and vinegar against the administration.[2]

Within a month, on 17 February, Wilkes was contemplating a long sojourn abroad. 'I am too proud ever to ask pardon. . . . I think myself an exile for life, and I flatter myself, my dear Cotes, with no foolish hopes, not even on the restoration of Mr. Pitt and the Whigs.'[3] Eight days later, on news of his convictions for libel, he admitted to Lord Temple his folly that previous May in setting up his printing press 'in disregard of your Lordship's advice. . . . I foresee all the consequences of being so entirely at the mercy of an abandoned Administration and vindictive judge, and intend never to put myself in their power, though I leave my native country, and all the charms it ever had for me.'[4]

Financial problems were soon of more concern to Wilkes than his long-term predicament. Before leaving Britain he had entrusted the conduct of his affairs to Humphrey Cotes, a man more willing than able to cope with such a task. Wilkes was wont to blame his monetary difficulties on the expenditure incurred by his various Parliamentary elections and the cost of his daughter's education.[5] It might have suited his public image to emphasize such matters, but Wilkes, careless and generous equally with his own and other people's money, always lived beyond his means. In Paris, although he did leave the expensive Hôtel de Saxe after a few weeks, the economies he told Cotes he was making proved to be minimal, verbal emollients for the £1,067 he drew on Cotes between January and July, an amount that belied his early claim that he could live in Paris for half the cost in London.[6]

Wilkes also took steps to counter the danger of legal proceedings against his property in Britain, either from actions for debt or in consequence of his anticipated outlawry. On 17 February he therefore suggested the sale of the Manor of Aylesbury, in order to raise a French annuity.[7] By midsummer it had been purchased by a Sir William Lee for £4,000.[8] Everything else went too, including his plate and, to his particular regret, his books for a total of £504. The lease on his Great George Street house was taken over by Sir Edward Astley, soon to be an opposition MP. Cotes, however, seems to have mismanaged his affairs from the start. He at first told Wilkes to expect an assured income of £500, after all debts had been cleared. Lord Temple cancelled those due to him, and others Wilkes denounced as false and exaggerated.[9] Yet soon Cotes claimed to be unable to send Wilkes any more money at all, a statement Wilkes refused to accept in a letter of 16 August: 'You told me, in a former letter, that I should have £500 per annum clear, Mrs Wilkes and everybody paid. Since that, you tell me that the Aylesbury estate sold for £1,000 more than you could possibly imagine; yet, in your last, you mention my affairs as desperate. . . . All this is beyond my poor abilities to reconcile.'[10] Four days later Wilkes belatedly and vainly requested Cotes to remit all his assets to France:

My affairs draw to a crisis. By the outlawry I shall be cut off from the body of English subjects. Yet I will ever remain a warm friend to my country. I believe an outlaw can neither sue nor be sued. . . . It therefore becomes me to have all my private affairs settled as soon as possible . . . *I had rather everything was sold for my life, and the amount sent me to manage here,* for I can have no legal connection with England very soon.[11]

This attempt by Wilkes to regain from Cotes control of his finances came to nothing, and shortly before his outlawry in November Wilkes signed over to him 'full powers . . . for the arrangement of my private affairs', so he was to inform Lord Temple in 1767. Cotes betrayed this trust by sending Wilkes no more money and no accounts.[12] Wilkes, however, was not a man to allow financial embarrassment to diminish his zest for life, and later commented to a Paris correspondent that he 'was never so happy' as in his French exile.[13] He had early launched himself into the dazzling intellectual society of contemporary Paris, through the salon of Baron D'Holbach, a former fellow student at Leiden. Here he met such famous critics of the ancien régime as Denis Diderot. The tale Wilkes told of his ill-treatment in Britain was music to their ears, and he boasted to Cotes on 1 March that 'all Europe has sufficiently condemned the mean, base and unworthy arts' deployed to obtain a copy of the *Essay on Woman*.[14] The genuine champion of 'liberty' was lionized by those who merely spoke and wrote about the cause.

During the summer of 1764 the quality of his life was presumably enhanced, and his expenses certainly increased, by the acquisition of a tempestuous Italian mistress Gertrude Corradini, a 19-year-old opera dancer. She was still being financed by Wilkes when she departed for Italy in October.[15] The same month he went to meet Humphrey Cotes and Charles Churchill at Boulogne, having published in Paris on 22 October *A Letter to the Worthy Electors of the Borough of Aylesbury*, a pamphlet defence of the libels for which he had been convicted. Wilkes pointed out that *North Briton, Number Forty-Five* had not included any 'disrespect' to the King, and denied that it was 'false, scandalous or seditious', but a remark that the *Essay on Woman* was merely ludicrous and harmless conveyed the impression that he had been the author.[16] Lawyer John Dunning had read the tract in Paris, and Cotes and Churchill did so at Boulogne, so John Wilkes told brother Heaton on 2 November: 'It is a flaming libel, and merits well the hangman's torch. Churchill says it is the best thing I have done, and clear English in every part.'[17] The pamphlet was subsequently sold in Britain and reprinted extensively in the London press, but it proved a rather damp squib, making little impact on a political world increasingly attentive to the nascent crisis in the American colonies.

The happy reunion at Boulogne dissolved into tragedy. Churchill fell ill on 29 October and died a week later. It was to take Wilkes some time to recover from this sudden blow.[18] But at Boulogne he nevertheless concerted his future plans with Cotes. His daughter Polly, now aged 14, would go and live with his brother Heaton in London, while he himself would leave for an Italian tour, passing on to actor David Garrick the last few months of his Paris lease.[19] Wilkes also intended to embark on two publishing enterprises, an edition of Churchill's work as a memorial to a man whose literary executor he was, and a two-volume 'History of England' since 1688, 'for my fame and my purse'.[20]

Wilkes took his daughter to Calais by 4 December, and she left for London next day with a French maid and his sole remaining servant Matthew Brown, who was to return with Churchill's papers. John instructed Heaton by letter that Polly could visit her mother for meals at any time but was never to stay overnight: 'I know the demerit of the Mead family, and I am implacable as to my injuries.'[21] Heaton promptly dismissed the maid as an extravagance, to the impotent fury of his brother. 'Heaton is a barbarian', he wrote to Cotes on 12 December. 'He has done the most cruel thing in the world by Miss Wilkes; and he held a language to her about me, which is false, insolent and infamous. . . . I have cried ever since I read her letter.'[22]

Delayed longer than he had expected in Calais, Wilkes finally left Paris for Italy on 25 December. By mid-January he had joined Gertrude Corradini in Bologna. They left on 28 January for the south of Italy, arriving in Naples on 26 February. It was a triumphant progress, with Wilkes being much feted by his fellow countrymen, although he was careful to avoid embarrassing the British envoys in Florence and Naples by making the customary visits of British travellers. But the food, roads, and people excited his scorn, and the contentment of Naples proved illusory, albeit enlivened by a visit from young James Boswell and an ascent of Vesuvius on 16 March. Wilkes was unable to write his 'History of England' without documents. Nor did he make much progress with his edition of Churchill's poems. Life with his mistress was anything but peaceful, the more so as she often quarrelled with Matthew Brown. At the end of May she decamped with everything of value she could carry. Wilkes magnanimously not only eschewed legal redress, but even sent her £200 as a parting gift, or so he claimed in his autobiography.[23] After hearing rumours of a change of ministry in Britain Wilkes ended his Italian adventure by taking ship for Toulon on 27 June, arriving there ten days later. Subsequently, he stayed at Geneva from 29 July to 22 September, writing to Heaton on 12 August that 'Voltaire caresses me enough to turn my head'.[24]

While in Geneva Wilkes heard that there had now certainly been a change of administration in Britain, Grenville being replaced as Prime Minister by Lord Rockingham, at the head of Newcastle's old party.[25] He hastened back to Paris in order to negotiate, so he hoped, a return to Britain, staying at the Hôtel de Saxe again from 29 September. When the new ministry's ambassador, the Duke of Richmond, arrived in Paris Wilkes, though an outlaw, went to pay his respects and was honoured with a return visit.[26] It was at this time that Wilkes met the Reverend John Horne, that eccentric and exuberant clergyman who was to become in turn a valuable political ally and a bitter foe.[27] Another new acquaintance was diarist Horace Walpole, already an avid narrator of his deeds and misdeeds. Here is Walpole's initial impression of Wilkes: 'He was very civil, but I cannot say entertained me much. I saw no wit; his conversation shows how little he has lived in good company, and the chief turn of it is the grossest bawdy. He has certainly one merit, notwithstanding the bitterness of his pen, that is, he has no rancour—not even against Sandwich, of whom he talked with the utmost temper.'[28] So unimpressed was Walpole that on 13 November he commented to his old friend Sir Horace Mann that 'Wilkes's day is over', not the most prescient of his political observations.[29]

In Paris Wilkes made no secret of what he wanted from the new ministry. He still hankered after the British embassy to Constantinople, so Horace Walpole wrote on 6 October to inform his friend Henry Conway, who as Southern Secretary of State held that post in his gift.[30] Private letters to Cotes and brother Heaton reaffirmed this wish, citing the dismissal of Lord Bute's brother from a Scottish post as an example of how the ministry could override George III's objections. In a letter of 26 August to Heaton John had explained why he wanted such an appointment: 'As to my return to England, I cannot with honour and dignity till my seat in Parliament is restored to me. That cannot be till the next General Election.' He intended the Constantinople embassy to be the opportunity of reconciliation. 'If I go to Turkey . . . I will immediately try to heal all breaches, and not hazard the least offensive thing in future.'[31]

Wilkes was denied this opportunity to mend fences, for the ministry was unwilling to seek a pardon for him, let alone an office. Negotiations with Wilkes were entrusted to two MPs who had enjoyed a close personal relationship with him and who now held junior office, George Onslow at the Treasury Board and William Fitzherbert at the Board of Trade. On 21 September Onslow wrote a most friendly letter to Wilkes, expressing goodwill and voicing the hope that he would support the principles of the new ministry.[32] Next there followed a positive but indirect offer, conveyed by Cotes in a letter to Wilkes on 18 October:

As to the outlawry, it is under consideration, and the event uncertain. So that, the agreeable news I can convey to you is that Mr Fitzherbert has assured me, that an annual sum of one thousand pounds shall be paid you, but upon what establishment or fund I cannot learn. . . . I will likewise do the justice to many in the present ministry to say their wishes are to serve you but I really think they want the power of doing you the essential service they wish.[33]

Five days later Fitzherbert also told Heaton Wilkes that his brother would be offered £1,000 a year, adding the assurance that 'many considerable persons are willing to show him every act of friendship in their power'.[34] Wilkes was not enamoured of this offer. 'The idea does not captivate my imagination', he replied to Cotes on 27 October. 'You avoid, my dear friend, the word *pension*, with great care: yet I believe the world would rather consider such a grant only in that light.' Wilkes then resorted to threats. 'I have digested my thoughts very carefully, and I intend to give them to the public the first day of the meeting of Parliament. How the ministry will like it, I very little care.' To make crystal clear the message Cotes was to give the ministers Wilkes went on to say that 'it depends . . . on them, whether Mr Wilkes is their friend or their enemy', again mentioning that the Constantinople post was what he had in mind.[35] This riposte was ignored by the Rockingham administration, and on 4 December Wilkes wrote directly to Fitzherbert a letter conveyed to London by his friend Lauchlin Macleane: 'I ought at the entrance into power of the present gentlemen to have had a pardon under the Great Seal without my asking it, and to have been indemnified as far as it could be for two years' sufferings and the cruel anxiety of near four.' The request Wilkes now made was for the vacant Governorship of Jamaica, and he characteristically ended with another menace:

I love and honour many of the present Ministers, and would serve the cause of liberty in conjunction with them as well as my poor faculties permitted me. I am at their service for every good word and work, and I wish they never bring things to the alternative either of their finding employment for me, or of my finding enough for them. One set of Ministers I occupied a year and a half.[36]

This letter crossed in the post with one from Fitzherbert explaining that the ministry's offer of £1,000 a year was one to be paid privately by individuals out of their salaries.[37] Wilkes promptly rejected this on 8 December, as 'precarious, eleemosynary, and clandestine. I claim from the present Ministry a full pardon under the Great Seal for having successfully served my country.'[38] Four days later he repeated this demand in a letter to George Onslow, requesting an answer by 1 January 1766.[39] But the ministry was unable to meet his demands. Edmund Burke, then Rockingham's private secretary, wrote to his brother Richard, currently in Paris, advice intended to be conveyed to Wilkes:

He ought to be sensible that though the true *motives* for all his prosecutions were political, the prosecution he actually labours most under, is not at all political, but for an offence against the ordinary laws; for Blasphemy, for which it would be rather awkward to desire his pardon. . . . It is true he is capable, as an incendiary of doing some mischief, but it would fall ten fold on his own head whilst it would not conciliate the affection of his former enemies and would be sure to exasperate his former friends. Between ourselves; Lord Rockingham is extremely averse from asking anything for him from the King at the same time that he is willing to do almost any thing for him from his private pocket, and to avow it to the King or to any person. If Wilkes has the least knowledge of the nature of popularity and the smallest degree of attention to his own interest he will wait the convenience of his friends who do not forget him. But this to be insinuated more or less, or not at all according to your discretion.[40]

Wilkes soon had to swallow his pride and take the money, after Fitzherbert explained the ministry's predicament to him in a letter of 3 January 1766. 'The difficulty which arises is from one having two pardons to get—one public—another private. I do verily believe there is a disposition to get you home with credit. So the temporary offer is not precarious, nor is it clandestine. . . . We both know that more than politics has mixed in your case.'[41] Wilkes received this letter on 7 January, together with one from Macleane explaining the ministry's inability to help further: 'That they could defend all your political principles, but that the personal invectives were not so easily justified.' The allowance to Wilkes would be increased by £500, since Fitzherbert had argued that it was 'too scanty'. But Macleane warned that Prime Minister Rockingham had scorned his threats, telling Fitzherbert that 'everything designed to be done was from friendship and not from fear. . . . He loved you as a friend but did not dread you as an enemy.'[42] Wilkes sought to save face by announcing that he would accept the money because it came from 'private hands' and was not a government pension, a circumstance he had already known. He at once attempted, in vain, to draw bills for £1,000 instead of the £500 Fitzherbert had authorized as a first payment.[43]

The defiance of Wilkes had been a bluff. In a letter of 4 December to Cotes Wilkes, who had again moved out of the expensive Hôtel de Saxe into lodgings, made it clear he had been sorely tempted by the ministerial offer, and why: 'I have waited to hear from you on the subject of my private affairs, and to know if you could send me a letter of credit. . . . Living here not in a *hotel garnie* and privately, £1,000 a year would soon make me easy and independent, as well as pay my debts in time, and you may imagine I have some here, which I should be very glad to settle. Such is the state of my exile and outlawry.'[44] On 1 January Wilkes made a more direct request: 'I beg you to send me immediately some kind of remittance . . . What am I to do otherwise. I have not received, my dear Cotes, one shilling the whole year 1765.'[45] Even the good-natured Wilkes issued a mild reproof when this appeal also fell on deaf ears, writing again to Cotes on 15 February: 'I am in debt here, and you know that the whole of last year and this you have not sent me anything out of the management of my private estates.' He had been obliged to borrow sixty guineas from banker Thomas Walpole, then in Paris, 'who lent them with a good grace'.[46] Let down in this manner by Cotes, Wilkes had had little choice but to accept the ministerial offer. How much he actually received is almost as unclear as the general state of his finances. John Horne, in a hostile public letter to Junius on 31 July 1771, was to claim that there had been a planned annual total of £1,040, of which Rockingham was to pay £500, the other five Treasury Lords £60 each, and the eight Lords of Trade £40 each, all payments to cease on loss of office.[47]

Payment of such danegeld did not end the ministry's Wilkes problem. In his letter of 4 December to Cotes he had raised the possibility of a visit to Britain with or without official cognizance. 'Suppose I return immediately, will the ministry dare to let the law take place? . . . Would it be allowed, if I asked it, to steal over privately. . . . Nothing would alarm the present ministers so much as the idea of my coming to London; nothing perhaps would so much advance my affairs.'[48] He did not carry out his idea until 12 May 1766, when he secretly lodged in London with Lauchlin Macleane, having told no one of his intention.[49] It was now that Cotes confessed to Wilkes that to avoid bankruptcy he had put all his money into his own account, including the £1,000 damages awarded against Under-Secretary Wood, handing over a mere twenty guineas as pocket money. Cotes did promise Wilkes, however, 'that he would soon replace it', and account for everything he had received on his behalf.[50] During the next two or three weeks those who negotiated with Wilkes included Onslow, Fitzherbert, Edmund Burke, and London merchant Sir William Baker. His reputed demands were too outrageous to be met: a pardon, £5,000 in cash, and a pension of £1,500 on the Irish civil list. Rockingham refused to meet them, or to see Wilkes himself. Wilkes, fearing arrest if he stayed too long, left London on 31 May, taking Polly back to Paris with him.[51] According to a later derisive account by John Horne, 'Mr Wilkes declared that he could not leave England without money; and the Duke of Portland and Lord Rockingham purchased his absence with one hundred pounds apiece.'[52]

Failing to recognize his visit as the débâcle it had been, Wilkes continued to put his faith in the goodwill professed by the ministry. Macleane wrote on 6 June to tell him that he had seen 'our common, I mean our uncommon friend Burke. He says the handsomest things possible of you, and bids me assure you of his entire regard. He thinks your matters will be made. very easy in a few days.'[53] Wilkes thereupon wrote a fulsome letter to Burke on 12 June: 'The great object of my hopes is a pardon, which I wish to owe to his Majesty's goodness and to the favour of our friends.'[54] Burke's reply was cautious and noncommittal.[55]

A month later the Rockingham ministry was dismissed, but the hopes of Wilkes soared when he heard the news. For if the new Prime Minister, albeit as Lord Privy Seal, was William Pitt, now Earl of Chatham, the Treasury was held by a man who had visited him in prison in 1763, the Duke of Grafton. 'I am sure I shall now have justice done to myself, as well as to the great cause in which I have been so deeply embarked', he wrote to Cotes on 20 July. 'I hope a full and free pardon will immediately be granted me, and that I shall have leave to return to England by the first post.'[56] After three months passed without any such intimation he landed at Dover on 28 October. This time Wilkes could not stay with Macleane, for he was now Under-Secretary of State to the Southern Secretary, Lord Shelburne. He lodged therefore with Horne's brother-in-law William Wildman, who had been proprietor of a famous political club opposed to the Grenville ministry.[57] Wilkes at once contacted Grafton, indirectly through Fitzherbert and then by a letter of 1 November humbly requesting the Duke to ask George III for a pardon. In his subsequent memoirs Grafton stated that he did show the letter to the King,

who, as well as I recollect, read it with attention; but made no observation upon it. Lord Chatham, on reading it remarked on the awkwardness of the business, with which it was so difficult to meddle; and on my pressing to know what was to be done, he answered: 'the better way, I believe at present is to take no notice of it'. And his advice I followed.

Thereafter such important business as America and India engrossed ministerial attention, and whenever friends of Wilkes pressed his case Grafton took the line that 'the weight of Lord Chatham's name could alone effect it'.[58] The account of this episode by Wilkes differs from this bland retrospect. He claimed that Grafton told him to apply to Chatham, a course of action the Duke must have known to be impossible, since Chatham and Temple had just had a bitter quarrel. To Temple's delight Wilkes disdained to do so, and his behaviour met with popular approval: 'my friends in the City greatly applaud my firmness', he told brother Heaton.[59]

Wilkes promptly left London for Paris on 7 November, seething with fury at his treatment. Abandoning all hope of a pardon he now burnt his boats. He published his letter of 1 November,[60] and then gave vent to his feelings in a *Letter to the Duke of Grafton*, dated 12 December from Paris, and published as a pamphlet both there and in London.[61] It was an attack on Chatham rather than Grafton, a scathing account of how 'a proud, insolent, over-bearing, ambitious man' with a 'flinty heart' had sacrificed his popularity and prestige for 'the poor consolation of a place, a pension, and a peerage'. But the real significance of the tract was the detailed and dramatic account of his treatment in the *North Briton* case. Reproduced widely in the British press, it re-established his reputation as a champion of, and martyr for, the cause of liberty, providing the springboard for his future career.

Heaton Wilkes was at first uneasy over 'the part where you confess yourself the author of the Essay on Woman. It can in no way raise your fame in friends' eyes and with enemies must give them an advantage over you.'[62] Wilkes in reply reminded his brother that his authorship had been proved in the House of Lords: 'My defence is solid. I never *published*. I never gave copies. . . . Even as a juvenile performance I claim only candour and indulgence. No man has the right to inquire into my private amusements if they are not prejudicial to society.'[63] Continuing indignation at the unfair way in which he had been treated over the *Essay on Woman* had led Wilkes to an admirable principle of toleration.

Soon Heaton was enthusiastic about the impact of the pamphlet, informing John on 11 May 1767 that 'your letter to Grafton has done you infinite service in the City and on the Exchange, and it is deservedly spoken of as by much the best publication that has appeared with the name of J. W.' Dryden Leach had published a version with all names undisguised, and John Almon a mutilated one that the ministry had intended to prosecute if Onslow's namesake cousin Colonel George Onslow had not threatened to oppose such a move in Parliament. 'The little reputation Pitt had left, you have totally destroyed. . . . I hear Chatham is so provoked and storms so much his friends talk of its having had the effect on him of driving him mad.'[64] But what Grafton had called 'a very impudent letter' would adversely affect the private payments still being made to Wilkes by some members of the former Rockingham ministry. Fitzherbert had agreed to pay some of his debts before Wilkes left Britain, and remained the channel through which any payments should be forwarded to him.[65] Grafton, so Heaton thought, would now 'withdraw the paltry pittance which stood against his name'. George Onslow had already told Fitzherbert that he would pay nothing more, and another Treasury Lord Thomas Townshend was expected to follow suit.[66]

Failure to obtain a direct pardon led Wilkes to fall back on an alternative tactic he had already had in mind. In the autumn of 1766 John Dunning, when visiting him in Paris, offered the legal opinion that Wilkes would be able to reverse his outlawry. In November he therefore asked Dunning and John Glynn to have it set aside, and in January 1767 instructed them to commence the action that spring.[67] Wilkes wanted reversal of the outlawry so as to facilitate his election to Parliament, as he confided to Heaton on 8 January 1767: 'The law is tedious, and the time of the new election approaches. Though it is decided that an outlaw can be chosen, but it would not go so smooth.'[68]

The plan to challenge the outlawry was soon abandoned, perhaps because news came of the bankruptcy of Humphrey Cotes, a financial catastrophe for Wilkes, who thereby lost all the assets entrusted to his care. Wilkes did not at first realize the totality of the disaster, expressing sympathy for Cotes to Heaton on 11 February: 'All that remains for a friend whom one cannot assist, is concern and pity. I feel those in a lively manner, and with all his imprudence I will ever love him.' But he asked his brother to find out 'how my affairs are circumstanced with him', and compassion soon turned to in-dignation.[69] Wilkes was shocked to find that Cotes had charged him £31. 10s. for the 1765 visit to Boulogne, 'the meanest thing I ever knew', and commented to Heaton that 'he is inexcusable' after finding out that the bankruptcy certificate signed by Cotes on 11 April made no provision for any payment to creditors.[70] Wilkes was nevertheless still hoping to salvage something from the wreck, for he mentioned to Lord Temple in a letter of 11 May that Cotes admitted nominal liability to Wilkes of only £488, whereas solicitor Thomas Life thought Wilkes was owed £1,300.[71] All such calculations would seem to have been academic, for in a letter of 16 June Cotes asked Wilkes to forget all their financial transactions, without offering any payment.[72] It says much for the sanguine temperament of John Wilkes that he did not allow this episode to destroy his friendship with Cotes.

He had now to cast around desperately for other means of support. Lord Temple had given him no money since his departure for France.[73] By the end of March he had received nothing more from Fitzherbert, and on 8 April commented to Heaton that on that point 'I have experienced more baseness and treachery than any man of this age'. Two months later, on 8 June, announcing that he was tired of promises, he asked his brother both to press Fitzherbert and to sound Lord Temple, who had ignored the hint Wilkes had given him on 11 May that 'Mr Cotes has left me in the most cruel embarras'.[74] Fitzherbert thereupon told Heaton that he had approached the Duke of Portland as well as the office-holders who had previously contributed, the men who, as John bitterly remarked to Heaton on 22 June, 'came in without me, have received great emoluments, and offered me £1,000 a year till I was better provided for. . . . I am universally deserted, as much as James II was, with one small difference, that I have not merited it. I never deserted a friend.'[75] Fitzherbert was able to tell Heaton in July that he had had promises of money from Rockingham, Portland, and Lord John Cavendish, all now back in opposition, but had been discouraged from proceeding further by refusals from six office-holders.[76] By 13 August John Wilkes had received £200 and expected another £100.[77]

Simultaneously Wilkes sought to raise money by negotiating a contract with John Almon for publication of his 'History of England', which he assured the printer on 7 April was making good progress. The terms he asked on 25 May were an immediate advance of £300, and £300 on delivery in January 1768 of the text of Volume One, covering the period 1688 to 1714. Almon balked at this arrangement in a letter of 12 June, but did subsequently offer the £600, to be paid in instalments of £200 on 1 September, £100 on 1 October, and £300 on completion of the text by 2 January 1768. Wilkes signed an agreement accepting these terms on 13 July, when he told Almon, 'I have a little house near Paris, in a sweet situation, and I give five days a week to my History.'[78] That was patently untrue. Wilkes was to write only an introduction of thirty-nine pages. That was a political polemic, surveying the Stuart period and ending with the assertion that 'other nations can bear slavery, but liberty is the characteristic of Englishmen'.[79]

Neglect of his literary endeavours can be attributed to the increasing attention Wilkes gave in 1767 to planning his return to Britain. The money from Fitzherbert and Almon served only to alleviate, not solve his financial problems. New debts were piling up in Paris, not least on account of his daughter and another expensive mistress. This situation reinforced his determination to return to Britain and seek a Parliamentary seat, a decision captured in this admittedly apocryphal statement. 'What the devil have I to do with prudence? I owe money in France, am an outlaw in England, hated by the King, the Parliament, and the bench of bishops . . . I must raise a dust or starve in a gaol.'[80] Several years later, at the height of his political success in 1774, Wilkes publicly stated that 'if the King had sent me a pardon and a thousand pounds to Paris, I should have accepted them; but I am obliged to him for not having ruined me.'[81]

Wilkes wished to re-enter Parliament with éclat, at the general election due by March 1768. Election for a popular constituency was essential, with all the publicity and prestige that would ensue. He told Heaton on 12 July 1767 that he did not intend to purchase a seat: 'I will never give £2,000 nor £1,500 to come into Parliament.'[82] Despite an early rumour he never therefore contemplated a return to Aylesbury.[83] He was also to disdain all suggestions that he should sit 'quiet and undisturbed' for the pocket borough of some friend.[84] Wilkes had set his heart on being elected for his native City of London, a constituency with four MPs and an electorate of some 7,000. The obstacles were formidable, so Arthur Beardmore warned him in July. As an outlaw Wilkes would not be able to canvass or appear in person on the hustings. The 'eating and drinking' even at an uncontested City election cost each candidate £600 at least. One-quarter of the electorate was under ministerial control. Wilkes had no personal influence there, and had never been mentioned as a candidate. 'I fear you are only amusing yourself.'[85] This sound advice did not deter John, and two months later Heaton suggested an approach to Rockinghamite Sir William Baker, who was a prominent Alderman and merchant, and an MP for a Devonshire borough. He also proffered the shrewd suggestion that once Parliament was dissolved John could safely return to Britain. Private creditors would 'for their own interest be quiet', while any attempt at 'public prosecution . . . would make you returned for half the counties and boroughs in England'.[86] Rumours of his candidature began to appear in the press.[87] Although still ignorant of the opinions of such prospective allies as Baker, Wilkes proposed a draft election address for London in November.[88]

Impatient to ascertain news and expedite events, Wilkes now left France, and crossed the Channel on 3 December. A year later James Harris picked up the story that before finally leaving Paris Wilkes obtained £1,000 worth of jewels on approval, pawned them, and departed the next morning: 'that the matter was well known, and that the French ambassador had complained of it'.[89] He thought it unwise to stay in Britain for more than a few days, and leaving Polly in London, went to Holland for a couple of months to be safe, from his creditors rather than ministerial retribution.[90] When he visited his old University at Leiden on 24 December he received a warm welcome, and an invitation to take his degree. He frequently amused himself by skating on the frozen canals and rivers, and then went to Ostend to meet Cotes, who advised him both then and by letter to contest Westminster, since Charles Churchill's brother John had considerable influence there.[91] Wilkes, who was to ignore that advice, risked returning to London by 7 February, some weeks before the dissolution of Parliament. He took care to conceal his place of residence, directing his brother Heaton next day to send his luggage to John Churchill's house, whence it would be taken 'when it is dark' to his abode 'at Mr Thomsons . . . I have taken the name of Osborn'.[92] After the dissolution of Parliament on 11 March Wilkes openly rented a house in familiar territory, on the corner of Prince's Court, Great George Street. John Wilkes was back in British politics.

5

Election for Middlesex
1768

JOHN WILKES was in an anomalous position after his return to Britain early in 1768. Although he was an outlaw no attempt was made to apprehend him. When his presence, at first clandestine, became widely known he therefore sought to rectify or at least clarify the situation. His first move was to submit a respectful request to the King for a pardon, by a letter of 4 March delivered by his footman directly to the royal palace. Even a supporter like John Almon thought that this approach ought to have been made in a more formal manner, through the official channel of a Secretary of State. No reply was made.[1] When it became evident that no pardon would be forthcoming the only other recourse Wilkes had was to insist on surrendering himself to justice. On 22 March he therefore wrote to the Solicitor to the Treasury, now Thomas Nuttall, announcing his intention to do so at the Court of King's Bench when the next legal session began on 20 April.[2] That would be after the forthcoming general election, and Wilkes meanwhile busied himself in securing a Parliamentary seat, against a background of press speculation as to whether or not an outlaw could sit in Parliament.[3]

That the King's government studiously ignored the presence of John Wilkes has often been ascribed to a deliberate intention to avoid a repetition of what had happened under the Grenville ministry, the conversion of Wilkes into a political martyr by a prosecution that he would portray as persecution. That would have been a short-sighted attitude, for Wilkes was not a man to allow himself to fade into obscurity. The explanation was not policy but indecision, the result of the discordant composition of the ministry. During the months immediately before the return of Wilkes there had been significant changes in the cabinet. Chatham, Lord Privy Seal, was still nominal head of the ministry, but the effective Prime Minister since at least the spring of 1767 had been the Duke of Grafton, First Lord of the Treasury. Facing a formidable Parliamentary opposition of three parties, headed by Rockingham, Grenville, and Bedford, he had negotiated unsuccessfully with Rockingham in July, and had then done a deal with the Bedford group at the end of 1767. The resignations of two colleagues enabled Grafton to accommodate the Bedfordite demands. Lord Gower replaced Lord Northington as Lord President of the Council and Lord Weymouth became Northern Secretary instead of Henry Conway, who remained in the cabinet without office. Responsibility for America was transferred from Southern Secretary Shelburne to a new Secretaryship in the person of Lord Hillsborough. More important still as a step towards a stable administration was the accession to high office of Lord North: appointed Chancellor of the Exchequer on the death of Charles Townshend in September 1767, he now succeeded Conway as Leader of the House of Commons. Talented both as Parliamentarian and financier, North was the man around whom there soon developed a strong ministry.[4] All these changes betokened a hard-line attitude towards Wilkes, for the Bedford party, Hillsborough, and North had all served in the Grenville ministry. But the other half of the cabinet owed their appointment to Chatham and favoured leniency, Lord Chancellor Camden soon favouring even a pardon as a way out of the impasse. Shelburne, Lord Granby, and Conway seemingly followed the desire of Grafton to do nothing. The law officers of the Crown were not prepared to act against Wilkes without political guidance, and so he remained free to contest a seat in Parliament.[5]

Despite all the advice Wilkes had received to the contrary he was still determined to stand for the City of London. Already six strong candidates were in the field, and at the time of his return to Britain the prevailing opinion was that all four sitting MPs were safe. Top of the last poll in 1761 had been the popular Sir Robert Ladbroke, who had distilling and banking interests. His political record defied contemporary analysts, but he generally voted with the opposition in Parliament. Second then had come the current Lord Mayor, Thomas Harley. A man holding government contracts for clothing and financing the army and militia, he had the support of both the ministry and 'the monied interest'. Most famous of the City's MPs, and perhaps the most formidable politician within London, was William Beckford. His influence stemmed from vast wealth, derived from sugar plantations in Jamaica; from his close connection with Lord Chatham, albeit now a declining asset; and from radical views that enjoyed a wide appeal among the Livery. Looking somewhat more vulnerable, as an alleged supporter of Lord Bute, was the fourth MP, City banker Sir Richard Glyn. Long intent on election for London was Barlow Trecothick, a Rockinghamite who had played a key role in resolving the Stamp Act Crisis as Chairman of the American Merchants Committee. He had lived in Boston for over twenty years, and this American connection was held against him during the election campaign, because of colonial resistance to the taxation imposed by the late Charles Townshend. The sixth candidate was John Paterson. Already an MP at Bute's behest for a Cornish pocket borough, he now chose to contest the City, where he had long been a prominent supporter of government.[6]

All six candidates had issued election notices before the dissolution of Parliament on 11 March. Presumably acting on legal advice about his position as an outlaw, Wilkes delayed his own advertisement until then, and based his campaign on 'the two important questions of public liberty, respecting general warrants and seizure of papers'.[7] An unfounded rumour was soon afoot that Wilkes would ally with Rockinghamite Sir William Baker as 'friends of liberty, and oppressors of general warrants'.[8] The candidature of Wilkes at once dominated press coverage of the London election. It was soon reported that hundreds of voters intended to plump for him, and the reputed betting odds on his election success rapidly altered from ten to one against to five to two on. Heated debate on Wilkes filled the newspaper columns. He easily won the propaganda battle, although a correspondent in the *Gazetteer* derided him as 'an outlaw backed by an infatuated multitude'.[9]

Words bore no relation to votes, nor did the show of hands in his favour as the election began on 16 March, when Wilkes announced, 'I am happy to find myself once more among the friends and patrons of liberty'.[10] In the poll Wilkes began in bottom position and fell ever further behind. At the end of the second day he had only 172 votes, less than half the total for the candidate just above him in sixth place. He vainly sought to rally support by another circular, on 18 March: 'I am satisfied that in the great cause of Liberty I shall, by your generous assistance, rise superior to every act of oppression and malice.'[11] Wilkes was whistling in the wind, and the real battle was soon perceived to be between Trecothick and Glyn for the fourth seat. At the close of the poll on 23 March Harley came top with 3,729 votes. Ladbroke and Beckford were comfortably elected with 3,678 and 3,402 votes respectively, while Trecothick defeated Glyn by 2,957 to 2,823. Paterson trailed badly with 1,769 and Wilkes came last with a mere 1,247.

This humiliation was promptly forgotten in the excitement Wilkes caused by his announcement at the declaration of the London poll. He explained away his 'want of success' by the lateness of his candidature: 'My friends were of the opinion, that I should wait the dissolution of the last venal House of Commons, while the other candidates had been for many months soliciting your interest.' He then dropped a bombshell, by declaring his candidature for the county of Middlesex, which included London and where the election was due in only five days.[12] This news must have been a stunning blow to the two sitting members George Cooke and Sir William Beauchamp Proctor, who had not been expecting any opposition: for the *Gazetteer* of 26 March reported it as a well-kept secret: 'It is certain that Mr Wilkes's intentions for Middlesex were never so much as suspected till his public declarations at Guildhall, and it is equally as sure that it has given a very great alarm to his opponents as well as . . . the Ministry, who have already begun making interest against Mr Wilkes.'

Chathamite Cooke had been a Middlesex MP since 1750, and held the lucrative post of joint Paymaster-General of the Forces. Proctor, a county MP since 1747, was a local squire, from Tottenham, and in Parliament an independent who usually voted with the opposition. The two men sank their political differences to form a joint interest against this sudden threat, uniting in their election notices and in arranging the transport of voters to the poll.[13] Although most of the electorate lived in and around London and other points east, polling would take place in the county town of Brentford, ten miles to the west of the City. The morning after the London election the town was already festooned in blue, the Wilkite colour. Wilkes arrived there himself that day, with Charles Churchill's brother John, a Westminster apothecary.[14] Press comment implied that transport of his voters thither would be a particular problem for Wilkes:

The talk is that Mr Wilkes is sure of a very extensive interest in the eastern division of the county of Middlesex, and which alone contains, it is said, considerably more than one-third of the electors . . . The whole of freeholders in the county are estimated at between two and three thousand.[15]

All difficulties were solved by a clockwork campaign masterminded for Wilkes by an Election Committee that met regularly at those two centres of metropolitan politics, the King's Arms Tavern and the Mile End Assembly Rooms. In Brentford Wilkes promptly secured most of the public houses for his friends, helped by the local influence of John Horne, who was parson of New Brentford.[16] An efficient organization was created within the few days between candidature and poll. On the Saturday before the day of election, a Monday, 12,000 printed handbills were distributed, advertising where supporters of Wilkes could find the 247 carriages provided for their transport to the poll. On the Monday two men at each such venue took down names and sent off the coaches singly as soon as they were full. Not until then was distribution made of blue cockades and of cards printed 'Wilkes and Liberty'. The designated route was through Acton and not near the royal palace at St James's, to prevent any provocation of the King by 'those with more zeal than prudence'. Wilkes and his friends were anxious to preserve order, and this notice was sent to all the newspapers and printed in 40,000 handbills distributed over the weekend:

Mr Wilkes earnestly requests his friends and entreats that all possible measures may be used to preserve peace and good order through the whole of the approaching election for the county of Middlesex, to convince the world that Liberty is not joined to Licentiousness.[17]

Press reports of what happened on the day of election, 28 March, are confused and contradictory, even in a single issue of the same newspaper.[18] The returning officers for Middlesex were the two sheriffs elected for the City of London, Richard Peeres and William Nash. They prepared fifteen poll books, one for each division of the county, and set up booths at Brentford Butts. Crowds thronged the roads from London to Brentford, and while coaches with a blue cockade for Wilkes were unmolested, those conveying voters for his opponents often had their windows smashed and the slogan 'Wilkes and Liberty' scratched or painted on them, some being too damaged to continue their journey. Later it was to be claimed that hundreds of voters had been deterred by such violence from polling. 'At the last election, the cavalcade of Cooke and Proctor passed between a continual fire from London to Brentford and back again. The mischief to coaches, horses, and servants was incredible, and the many broken heads, and the blood spilt in the carriages on that occasion.'[19]

At Brentford Butts there was little disorder, for Wilkes was anxious to prevent success at the poll being nullified by a petition on the ground of violence, and he personally intervened to stop the only fight reported, when some Wilkites set upon a party of Cooke's supporters. Even the press account of this incident ended with the comment that 'the people were in general less tumultuous than at most of the contested elections', and no evidence has been found to contradict this claim in the *Gazetteer* for 30 March.

We can assure the public, from the best authority, that although the crowd was greater than ever known on the like occasion, yet was the whole poll conducted with the greatest regularity and order; and that there was not the least insult or violence offered to any of the electors that polled for either party; and it is very remarkable, that through the whole poll not one Freeholder that polled was in the least intoxicated with liquor.

The sheriffs had announced that the poll would commence at ten o'clock, and Wilkes was at the booth two hours before. But his opponents had advertised breakfast for their supporters in London for nine o'clock and did not appear until one o'clock, doubtless being delayed further by crowd trouble on the journey. During this interval Wilkes persuaded his restive supporters to remain orderly, and they even resisted the later provocation of banners being displayed with such slogans as 'No Blasphemer' and 'No

French Renegade' for some time after the arrival of Proctor and Cooke.[20] Voting took place for several hours during the afternoon.[21] It is about what happened in the evening that reports are most confused, perhaps because the sheriffs seem to have changed their minds, first announcing that the poll would continue the next day and then reversing that decision when they found no one ready to vote. They then closed the poll, but postponed the count until the next morning. Since the voting had been in public Wilkes could already see that he had won, and wrote jubilantly to his mother. 'I have the most brilliant success. I am first.'[22] Two newspapers the next day placed Proctor second. The *Gazetteer* put the totals at Wilkes 1,213, Proctor 740, and Cooke 645. The estimate in the *St. James's Chronicle* was Wilkes 1,300, Proctor 763, and Cooke 650. To the chagrin of Proctor, who anticipated re-election and unlike Cooke attended the count, the official poll result was Wilkes 1,292, Cooke 827, and Proctor 807. Wilkes was said to have polled over 1,000 'single voters', but to have favoured Cooke with enough second votes to defeat Proctor.[23]

The total poll was lower than was customary in Middlesex, a circumstance that gave credence to the opinion that violence had decided the result. Grafton wrote in his later memoirs of 'many of the freeholders of the other side being prevented, or intimidated from giving their votes'. That was an easy explanation for a ministry that does not seem to have anticipated a victory for Wilkes. Lord Chancellor Camden wrote from Bath on 3 April to Grafton: 'The event is disagreeable, and unforeseen, for I am persuaded that no person living, after Wilkes had been defeated in London would have thought it possible for him to have carried his election for the County of Middlesex.'[24]

That some voters might have been deterred or prevented from polling only affected the margin of victory for Wilkes, not the result: his success was achieved by a cocktail of superb organization and popular enthusiasm. But one myth that has been destroyed is that Wilkes received massive support from within the City itself. Examination of the Middlesex poll by George Rudé identified only 16 of the 260 Aldermen and Common Councilmen of the City as voting at all, most of them against Wilkes. His overall analysis shows that Wilkes obtained 681 votes from the urban sprawl outside rather than inside the City Walls, 152 from the City of Westminster, and 459 from the rural parishes to the north and west of these two Cities. By comparison with his opponents Wilkes secured a huge majority from the London area, whence Proctor obtained only 308 votes and Cooke 301, and more than held his own elsewhere.[25] Sociological analysis reveals a conflict very much on class lines. It was the shopkeepers, artisans, and the like who formed the bulk of the electorate in this highly urbanized county, and swept Wilkes to victory. The gentry, clergy, office-holders, and merchants voted overwhelmingly for his opponents.[26] This social contrast underlines the importance of the Wilkite organization: his supporters had had to be conveyed to the poll at Brentford.

Disorder occurred not so much at the election as in the victory celebrations afterwards, fully reported in the press. Brentford was illuminated that Monday evening. In London crowds had thronged the streets all day. American Secretary of State Lord Hillsborough had his coach windows broken that afternoon when going to his Whitehall office. The coach of the French ambassador was stopped, and he was politely asked to drink 'a glass of porter to "Wilkes and Liberty", which he did amiably'. By the early evening the occupants of all carriages were being made 'to huzza for Mr Wilkes', and 'about nine o'clock, . . . upon the return of the pollers from Brentford, the mobility grew extremely riotous and tumultuous in the Strand and Fleet Street, where the inhabitants, in obedience to their commands, very expeditiously and brilliantly illuminated their houses'. The crowds sought to enforce this edict throughout London and Westminster that night, houses not illuminated being liable to have their windows broken. Among those who suffered such damage were the King's own brother the Duke of Gloucester, Lord Bute, and Northern Secretary Lord Weymouth, but the unlit windows of opposition leader Lord Rockingham were spared. One mob ended up at the Mansion House and, since Lord Mayor Thomas Harley was a ministerial supporter, were happily smashing all windows within range of missiles when two companies of soldiers arrived. A confrontation was avoided when Wilkites persuaded the crowd not to damage the cause of liberty by improper conduct.[27] Blood might well have been shed if the crowd had veered towards St James's Palace, if this story about George III picked up by Grenvillite MP Thomas Whately was true:

He certainly sat up all the first night of the illuminations, the Monday night, full of indignation at the insult, and saying to those about him, who expressed apprehensions of the mob coming . . . that he wished they would push their insolence so far, he should then be justified in repelling it, and giving proper orders to the Guards.[28]

Wilkes himself had tried to avoid inciting disorder. On the Tuesday morning he made a short speech of thanks at the declaration of the poll, congratulating the electors on 'the true spirit of independency . . . I beg you to consider my past conduct as an earnest of the future'.[29] But he then refused to be chaired, and instead of a triumphant return to London set out quietly for Bath, with the intention of staying there until his appearance at the Court of King's Bench on 20 April to answer to his outlawry.[30] Events in London that day were less tumultuous because Wilkite patrols sought to maintain order. The highlight was an insult inflicted on the Austrian ambassador. When his carriage was stopped by a mob he was slower than his French counterpart in drinking the health of Wilkes, 'not directly understanding them', according to a newspaper report. He was taken out of his coach and had 'No. 45' chalked on his shoes. It was said that the cabinet ministers themselves found it difficult to conceal their mirth when this most dignified of men made a formal complaint.[31]

Such mob violence was a healthy symptom of British liberty. That was the claim of correspondent 'HS' in the *Gazetteer* of 7 April when arguing that Wilkes should not be blamed for the current disorders: 'There ever were and ever will be mobs in England, while we remain a free people.' Drawing a pointed contrast with France, he claimed that abuse of government power was more alarming as a threat to liberty than mere crowd trouble. Less sympathetic towards Wilkes, but on the same theme of believing him to be a symptom rather than a cause of mob violence, was a comment made on 3 April by lawyer Alexander Wedderburn to his political mentor George Grenville:

Wilkes, I dare to say, is vain enough to imagine that he has raised all this tumult, but in my opinion he is as innocent of it as the staff that carries the flag with his name upon it. The mob has been made sensible of its own importance, and the pleasure which the rich and powerful feel in governing those whom fate has made their inferiors, is not half so strong as that which the indigent and worthless feel in subverting property, defying law, and lording it over those whom they were used to respect. A Jack Straw, or a John Wilkes, are but the instruments of those whom they seem to lead.[32]

Such commentators might have deepened their analyses. That the first half of 1768 was a period of disorder in London was the result of a variety of causes. Bad weather—this was a winter when the river Thames froze over—and economic recession combined to produce social distress and unrest. The return of Wilkes added a political dimension to a situation already causing concern to the ministry. During the Middlesex Election Secretary at War Lord Barrington, in consultation with cabinet ministers Lords Gower and Weymouth, put on alert the soldiers stationed at the three London barracks of the Tower, the Savoy, and the War Office, and made contingency plans to call on all troops within sixty miles. Further instructions to both military and civil authorities were agreed by an emergency cabinet of those ministers in London on 30 March; but the meeting, so Grafton informed George III, decided not to issue a Proclamation against disorder because it might appear to be 'finding fault with the people for their joy too riotously testified at the late election'.[33] Wilkite mobs faded away after a few days during which many individuals were molested if their hats did not have 'Wilkes' or '45' on them;[34] and there seems to have been an April lull also in other disturbances. The ministry wanted to avoid if possible the provocation of an overt military presence in London, a sentiment the King fully approved, declaring himself 'averse to making any show of troops in the streets' even on 20 April, when it was anticipated that a crowd might assemble to watch Wilkes go to the Court of King's Bench.[35] That would be the next potential day of trouble: and it was perhaps in anticipation of what might happen then that on 17 April Secretary of State Weymouth wrote a fateful letter to the chairman of the Surrey Quarter Sessions at Lambeth, Daniel Ponton, one that Wilkes was later to utilize in his battle with the ministry. It was a reminder that troops were available 'at a time that so very riotous a disposition hath discovered itself among the common people', and warned that the magistrates would be blamed for allowing any riots to develop. There was nothing secret about this missive. Copies were sent to the two local MPs for Southwark, Henry Thrale and Sir Joseph Mawbey, and one reached the Duke of Newcastle within two days.[36]

Maintenance of order was an immediate problem: but during the interval between the Middlesex Election and the legal proceedings due against Wilkes on 20 April the cabinet also took the crucial policy decision that he should be expelled from Parliament, although exactly when it did so is unclear. Aware of the need to consider the implications of the election of Wilkes, the small cabinet meeting of 30 March decided to summon the ministers out of town, notably Lord Chancellor Camden and Lord North, to a full meeting on 8 April.[37] The reply from Camden to Grafton, written in Bath on 3 April, pointed out that, legal matters being the concern of the Court of King's Bench, the cabinet could consider only what steps to take in Parliament; but he did not shirk the issue: 'If the precedents and the constitution will warrant an expulsion that perhaps may be right.' The Lord Chancellor, although the same man as Judge Pratt of the *North Briton* case, evidently shared the shock and dismay of his colleagues: 'A criminal flying his country to escape justice—a convict and an outlaw—that such a person should in open daylight thrust himself on the country as a candidate, his crime unexpiated, is audacious beyond description.' But he added a warning note: 'It would be well to consider what may be the consequence if Wilkes should be re-elected. That is very serious.' And he ended the letter with the hint that it might still be the best tactic to ignore Wilkes: 'This gentleman will lose his popularity in a very short time after men have recovered their senses.'[38]

The cabinet eschewed such caution. After the meeting on 8 April, another was arranged for the next day. A letter of George III to Grafton shows that the King was pressing for a decision. 'I am of opinion that those conversant in the law must first declare what can legally be done. That once ascertained, I incline much to following that with vigour, that licentiousness may be curbed; and a general resolution to this effect is all I wish to be come to this evening.' It was decided then to instruct Jeremiah Dyson, the ministry's expert on Parliamentary procedure and precedent, to prepare an appropriate memorandum on expulsion, and the King returned this document to Grafton on 16 April. At a cabinet meeting on 19 April the decision was taken or confirmed to expel Wilkes as soon as Parliament met on 10 May, in the expectation that in the Court of King's Bench on the morrow he would be sentenced to prison.[39]

Such a hard-line decision was not anticipated by the opposition. 'The world will have it that the cabinet is almost equally divided with regard to strong and lenient measures', so MP James West reported to the elderly Duke of Newcastle, and the Duke himself had commented to Rockingham that he did not think that Grafton would be 'forward to come to a final resolution upon Wilkes's affair'.[40] During the general election the Duke had been observing events in the London area on behalf of the Rockingham party. He had not anticipated nor welcomed the success of Wilkes any more than had the ministry. Rockingham, absent in the north of England, did not even discuss the event in his correspondence with Newcastle.[41] But their ally the Duke of Richmond thought it good news. 'I confess that although I hate a mob, that rises against law and acts by force', he wrote to Newcastle on 3 April, 'I am not sorry the Ministry should see that there is in the people a spirit of liberty that will show itself on proper occasions as in the choice of their members.' The radical-minded Duke perceived that Wilkes was adding to the British political scene a dimension wider than that of Crown and Parliament.

For whatever men may think of Mr Wilkes's private character, he has carried his election by being supposed a friend to Liberty, and I think it will show the Administration that though they may buy Lords and Commons and carry on their measures smoothly in Parliament yet they are not so much approved of by the nation.[42]

Newcastle, unable to adapt to the new political concept, preferred to see the situation as reflecting the unpopularity of the ministry, but at the end of his reply he did concede Richmond's point: 'Wilkes's merit is being a Friend to Liberty, and he has suffered for it and therefore, it is not an idle symptom, that it should appear, that that is a merit with the Nation.'[43] Most Rockinghamites were more conservative than Richmond, and Newcastle became concerned about the divisive effect the Wilkes issue might have on the party: on 11 April he commented to the Duke of Portland that they should avoid 'entering into the affair of Wilkes, upon which there will certainly be differences of opinion, even among ourselves'.[44]

Wilkes made his much-advertised surrender to justice at the Court of King's Bench on 20 April, against the unanimous advice of his counsel.[45] There was much speculation beforehand as to what would happen, so James West told Newcastle the day before:

The opinions of mankind are very anxious as to the business of tomorrow. The populace, and not merely them, are by no means easy . . . Many think it will be only matter of form, and that he (Mr Wilkes) will be either admitted to bail or committed. Some say the Attorney-General will admit error in the proceeding and at law. Others that strong measures in support of government will be taken.[46]

Lord Chancellor Camden expected a simple outcome: the reversal of the outlawry, and a prison sentence for Wilkes for his 1764 libel convictions.[47] But Lord Chief Justice Mansfield, in his conduct of the case, was to confound expectations by his legal niceties. Wilkes entered the Court, not at the head of a London mob, as he had mischievously threatened,[48] but quietly with his brother Heaton, a few friends, and four counsel headed by Serjeant John Glynn. Proceedings began with a prepared speech by Wilkes. He claimed several irregularities in his outlawry, and then pointed out that his conviction for *North Briton, Number Forty-Five* was merely for republication of a paper written 'by he did not know whom', cheekily reminding his audience that no legal proof of his authorship had ever been established. That paper, he said, was 'full of duty and affection to the King . . . and not one word in it false'. As for the *Essay on Woman*, that was 'merely ludicrous, that it was never published, only twelve copies printed off, for the sake of merry laughing friends, and stole'. He hoped that God would forgive the jury who had found him guilty of publishing what had never been out of his possession. Wilkes formally requested bail, since there were errors in the outlawry. Attorney-General William De Grey asked for his commitment under the outlawry, so that he could be brought back for sentence on a future day. Lord Mansfield, instead of accepting either plea, ruled that as Wilkes had appeared in Court voluntarily, without legal process, he was free to leave.[49] 'There may be more law in that than there is reason', commented George Onslow next day when informing Newcastle that Mansfield had criticized the Attorney-General for not issuing a warrant of *capias utlegatum* to arrest Wilkes on his arrival in Britain. Such a warrant was promptly made out on 21 April![50]

Lord Mansfield's ruling of 20 April disrupted the ministry's timetable. The decision on expulsion was not to be implemented for nearly ten months, both because of second thoughts by several ministers, and because of difficulty in producing a credible reason for such a step, one that convinced a majority of the House of Commons. Camden wrote that same day to Grafton to point out the difficulty of expelling an MP 'either as an outlaw, or a convict' when he might 'turn out at last, to be neither'. Since the Court would not be pronouncing its judgment until after Parliament met the ministry would have to reconsider the matter.[51] The determination of the cabinet to expel Wilkes was nevertheless unchanged when it met on 22 April. Grafton informed the King afterwards that Lord North and Conway had been requested to summon a meeting of 'the Privy Councillors and men of business in the House of Commons' in order to communicate the cabinet decision 'that Mr Wilkes should not be allowed to sit in Parliament if it could be avoided by any means justifiable by law and the constitution, and conformable to the proceedings of Parliament'. But Grafton warned George III that it was probable that the outlawry, the most obvious ground for expulsion, would be reversed.[52]

The meeting of MPs was arranged for 25 April, sixteen being present. The King pressurized Lord North beforehand, writing that 'the expulsion of Mr Wilkes appears to be very essential, and must be effected'. George III was extremely angry about the behaviour of Wilkes on 20 April: 'If there is any man capable of forgetting his criminal writings, I think his speech in the Court of King's Bench on Wednesday last reason enough for to go as far as possible to expel him; for he declared Number 45 a paper that the author ought to *glory in*, and the blasphemous poem a mere *ludicrous production.'*[53] At that meeting Richard Hussey, a lawyer of high reputation, vehemently opposed a second expulsion of Wilkes for the same offence, and his argument influenced a number of those present; but North thought that most would support expulsion on the grounds of outlawry or conviction.[54] Until the legal position was clarified to provide some such pretext, the ministry would have to mark time in Parliament: but Lord Mansfield privately thought it incumbent on the Crown to inform the House of Commons if an MP was in prison, as Wilkes was likely to be before Parliament met.[55] Hardliners in the administration thought that this reason to delay any final decision was welcomed by the Chathamite group in the cabinet, a belief to be given some retrospective credence by later events: in a casual conversation on 7 May, three days before Parliament met, Bedfordite Richard Rigby told Grenvillite Alexander Wedderburn that 'he believed there would be no proposition made . . . at that minute he knew they had come to no resolution, that Camden, Grafton, Shelburne . . . and Conway, on account of their former conduct, were inclined to avoid it'.[56]

Wilkes had remained free even after the issue on 21 April of the writ for his arrest. When George III enquired why this was so, Grafton replied on 25 April that since Wilkes had gone to visit Sir Joseph Mawbey in Surrey a new warrant would have to be prepared, because the original one was valid only for Middlesex.[57] The ministry was obviously afraid of provoking a riot. What was rapidly becoming a ludicrous situation ended only when Wilkes, after prior notice to the Attorney-General, delivered himself into custody on 27 April.[58] At the Court of King's Bench that day he was given a writ of error to appeal against his outlawry, but Lord Mansfield rejected his application for bail, and he was committed to the King's Bench Prison in Southwark.[59] Pure farce ensued. The coach conveying Wilkes there was intercepted by a mob when crossing Westminster Bridge. The crowd turned it round, removed the horses, and pulled it through the Strand and Fleet Street into the City, the two custodial officers being ejected at Cornhill. Ignoring his request to go to prison, the crowd took Wilkes to the Three Tuns Tavern in Spitalfields. Not until late at night did he escape in disguise and make his own way to the prison. The episode gave rise to the witticism that many had used disguise to escape from prison, but only Wilkes had done the opposite.[60] The ministry was left with mud on its face. No precautions had been taken against such a contingency. No arrests had been made. That the whole matter had been 'a disgrace to civil government' was the irate opinion of Secretary of State Weymouth.[61]

Wilkes was to remain in prison for two years, a visible martyr to the cause of liberty, as he was prompt to point out to his Middlesex constituents, in an Address of 5 May: 'In support of the liberties of this country against the arbitrary rule of ministers, I was before committed to the Tower, and am now sentenced to this prison.'[62] It was a period when his political influence greatly increased: the time of the Middlesex Elections controversy, of the creation of the Bill of Rights Society in his support, and of the foundation of his political power in the City of London. Nor did prison stifle the flow of propaganda from his pen; printer John Almon claimed to have visited him every Sunday.[63]

The immediate consequence of his arrest was to increase the disorder in London. The King's Bench Prison, just south of the Thames, was close both to the City of London and to Westminster, and the assembling there of large crowds in the open space of St George's Fields by the prison was a disturbing phenomenon for the King's government. It proved to be a daily occurrence for the next fortnight. There was some property damage and a few arrests were made, but nothing happened to cause real alarm. A crowd threatening violence on 8 May quietened down at the request of Wilkes, and dispersed when a few soldiers arrived. Yet two days later there took place the so-called 'Massacre of St George's Fields', an event that was to prove a subsequent embarrassment to the administration, and became part of radical folklore about government tyranny.[64]

Parliament was to open on 10 May, and various rumours caused a crowd to assemble outside the King's Bench Prison that day: one was that Wilkes would be allowed out to attend, another that a mob would forcibly release him. The prompt dispatch to the scene of both a troop of horse and of soldiers from a Scottish infantry regiment was viewed as provocative by a crowd that swelled to upwards of 15,000: one estimate was 40,000. The mob was shouting 'Wilkes and Liberty! No Liberty, No King! Damn the King! Damn the Government! Damn the Justices!': and even, according to one magistrate, that 'this is the most glorious opportunity of a Revolution that ever offered'. It needed only a simple incident to spark off trouble, as when Daniel Ponton, one of six Surrey magistrates present, ordered the removal from the prison wall of a 'Wilkes and Liberty' poem stuck up there. The hostile crowd reaction to this move led another JP, Samual Gillam, to read the Riot Act, under which a crowd that did not disperse quietly could be broken up by force. Ponton told the soldiers not to fire because the place was a public thoroughfare; but an hour later Gillam, struck ten times already by missiles, announced that he would order them to do so unless the stone-throwing ceased. He was then felled by a piece of brick, gave the order to fire, and nervous soldiers became trigger-happy, killing and wounding bystanders as well as members of the hostile crowd. The list of seven dead included a woman orange-seller and a man on a passing haycart.[65] The incident that especially horrified contemporaries was the deliberate pursuit of a young man in a red waistcoat, marked out for his stone-throwing: because another man, similarly attired, one William Allen, was shot dead in his father's stable nearby, a case of mistaken identity. A coroner's inquest on him next day returned a verdict of murder against the ensign and two soldiers thought to have been involved. They were held in New Gaol prison from 11 to 16 May, when two were released on bail: none was found guilty at the subsequent trial in August.[66] Verdicts on all other deaths were 'chance medley'.

Anger at the 'Massacre' led to widespread riots in the metropolitan area later that day. In an early example of Luddism 500 sawyers in Limehouse demolished a windmill designed to saw timber, recently built for businessman Charles Dingley.[67] Other disturbances occurred outside both the Mansion House and the Palace of Westminster, where the peers and MPs could hear the shouts of 'Wilkes and Liberty!'[68]

The ministry was unrepentant at the bloodshed on 10 May. Secretary at War Lord Barrington wrote a public letter the next day to the officer in command of the soldiers, expressing royal approval of their conduct.[69] Also on 11 May a Royal Proclamation was issued for the suppression of 'Riots, Tumults and Unlawful Assemblies', directed specifically against seamen but of general application to the counties of Middlesex, Surrey, and Kent.[70] The House of Lords voted an Address of Thanks to the King on 12 May, and the Commons one on 13 May, after a debate in which the concern of the ruling propertied class about disorder overrode political alignments in Parliament. Opposition speakers joined with administration supporters to criticize not the deployment of soldiers but the ministry's failure to maintain order. Sir Joseph Mawbey, soon to be an ally of Wilkes, defended the conduct of the Surrey magistrates. Trecothick justified his own behaviour as a London magistrate. George Grenville declared, 'I saw the city of Westminster in a state, as if it was taken by an enemy', with not a magistrate in sight. He was one of several MPs who commended the example set to the ministry by Lord Mayor Harley, who had seized rioters with his own hands. Even Beckford testified to Harley's endeavours, and Commons Leader Lord North proposed that he be formally thanked by the House. But North sought to put the blame for the disorders on the magistracy, since the ministry had made soldiers available.[71]

The Commons duly thanked Harley on 16 May. When further complaints were then made of continuing disorder, Colonel Henry Luttrell said that every speaker had carefully avoided mentioning Wilkes, and asked whether he was 'Wilkes the outlaw, or Wilkes the member for Middlesex'. Why had this matter not been decided? That was a topic neither the ministry nor the opposition wished to discuss, and no answer was made.[72] But Parliamentary debate on the subject could be initiated by any MP, for or against Wilkes. The ministry had feared that on 16 May a new opposition MP Henry Cavendish was going to move that 'Mr Wilkes be brought' to the Bar of the House.[73] Luttrell's intervention was a Parliamentary intimation of discontent among the administration's hard-line supporters. At a meeting of the ministry's leading Commons spokesmen on 12 May Sir Gilbert Elliot had offered to move the expulsion of Wilkes, an idea strongly backed by Lord Barrington, Jeremiah Dyson, Bedfordites Rigby and Edward Thurlow, and those Newcastle described as 'Lord Bute's friends'. Moderates like Conway and George Onslow, the Duke's informant, opposed such a precipitate course of action, which Lord Granby hotly asserted might produce a rebellion.[74]

Whether or not Luttrell was the overt spokesman of much discontent in the ministerial ranks, he did make a motion on 18 May, 'that the proper officer of the Crown do inform the House why the laws were not immediately put in force against John Wilkes, an outlaw, when he returned to this Kingdom'. Rockingham had already picked up a rumour that Luttrell intended 'some motion about Wilkes. Whether he is set on or no, we dont know.'[75] Lord North now pronounced the motion to be irregular, since the King's servants did not answer to the House, and the Speaker, Sir John Cust, confirmed this opinion. The Attorney-General, amid some derision, denied that he was the proper officer. Henry Cavendish stated that he had also intended to raise the subject of Wilkes, but for a different reason, because the privilege of the House had been infringed: 'It is not the man, but the cause I mean to support.' The ministry disposed of the matter by an adjournment motion.[76] Rockinghamite MP Sir Matthew Fetherstonhaugh commented to Newcastle that 'the manner in which it was *received*, plainly indicated the *sense* of the House to let it remain *where* it is, until Westminster Hall has done something further in it'.[77]

No other Parliamentary debate on Wilkes took place during that short summer session. Luttrell and his friends were evidently persuaded not to embarrass the administration further, and the opposition leaders did not wish to raise the matter. Their dilemma over both the riots and Wilkes was reflected in the comment of Newcastle to Rockingham that 'we must be either governed by a mad, lawless Mob, or the peace be preserved only by a military force; both of which are unknown to our constitution'. Wilkes, the Duke still believed, would be 'half-forgot' by the winter meeting of Parliament if the ministry had the sense to ignore him.[78] That was a remarkably foolish prediction. Wilkes was not a man to subside into quiescence, and the 'Massacre' of 10 May had given him the fresh ammunition of martyrs to the cause of liberty with which to attack government.[79] Meanwhile several opposition politicians displayed public solidarity with his cause. Rockinghamite MPs Edmund and William Burke were among those who visited him in prison, and Lord Temple wrote on 28 April to arrange to do so.[80] Temple had not seen Wilkes since his return to Britain, but had made clear to both Rockinghamite and Grenvillite leaders that he would support his former protégé: 'His persecutions had been great, and though his faults were enormous, he had suffered abundantly, and his Lordship will continue to defend the laws and rights of this country against any attack whatever.'[81]

No decision was made in the Court of King's Bench when the outlawry of Wilkes was considered on 7 May. Arguments were heard respectively from Serjeant John Glynn and Bedfordite MP Edward Thurlow, deputizing for the Crown lawyers, but the matter was postponed until the next legal term began on 8 June.[82] Wilkes's lawyers had long been confident that his outlawry could be reversed on technical grounds, and that appears to have been the public expectation. Speaker Cust was anxious that Parliament should be prorogued before that happened, and not merely adjourned on 2 June, as was the ministry's known intention. 'His reason', so Treasury Secretary Thomas Bradshaw told Grafton on 31 May, 'is, an apprehension, that, if the House meets after Wilkes's outlawry is decided in the Courts, it will be impossible to avoid taking up that matter, whatever the decision may be'.[83] Lord Chancellor Camden also favoured 'a speedy prorogation', but Grafton and North wanted a three-week adjournment, so that Parliament could meet again if disorders continued. In the event they subsided, and the adjournment from 2 June to 21 June was then converted into a prorogation until November.[84]

On 8 June the outlawry of Wilkes was duly reversed, but not before Lord Mansfield had taken the opportunity to display his superior legal knowledge. He rejected all the points raised by the counsel for Wilkes.[85] Then he produced a trivial error, that the writ had omitted to state 'of the County of Middlesex' when describing the County Court; that invalidated the outlawry, so he ruled.[86] Thereby he achieved a temporary and unwonted popularity. 'I hear the *mob* had a mind to draw his coach home', wrote Rockingham to Newcastle. 'It would have been droll and would have half killed the proprietor of Hayes.'[87] The Attorney-General then demanded that sentence be pronounced for the two libel convictions of 1764, but that decision was postponed until 14 June.[88]

Wilkes lost no time in reactivating his prosecution of Lord Halifax as the Secretary of State who had authorized his imprisonment and the seizure of his papers under the 1763 general warrant, an action suspended in 1764 because of his outlawry. Misunderstanding the legal position, Wilkes had tried to do so on 29 April, when he wrote to his attorney John Reynolds, 'I hope to live to hear an English jury, by a formal verdict, condemn a Secretary of State, who violated the first right of this free nation, the personal liberty of our countrymen, in the most outrageous and illegal manner.' His counsel resumed the action on 9 June.[89] The declared illegality of general warrants now made the result of the case a foregone conclusion, and when it was eventually heard in the Court of Common Pleas on 11 November 1769 the issue was simply the size of the award for damages. Lord Chief Justice Wilmot advised the jury to give 'liberal and exemplary not excessive damages'. When the jury announced £4,000, instead of the £10,000 Wilkes had been expecting, 'there was an universal groaning', James Harris noted, 'and, as I heard it called, bellowing in Westminster Hall. The jury were abused by the names of rogues, rascals, etc, and even threatened'.[90] This popular disapproval missed the key point of the verdict itself, in the adulatory opinion of one Wilkite:

It is the decision which gives every well-wisher to the Constitution of England, cause to rejoice. It has put the grand, the indelible stamp of infamy, upon the arbitrary proceedings for which you sought redress, for all your countrymen, so grossly injured in your person. It has confirmed the rights of Englishmen, and stands a certain lesson to all Ministers, to teach them that neither Favour nor Station can prevent their being amenable to our happy laws. Laws which however require sometimes men of Mr Wilkes's steadiness and Patriotism, to revive and confirm them, by boldly standing forth, in their defiance, when corruption attempts their submission.[91]

Wilkes was then still in prison. After the judgment had been argued on 14 June 1768 between Glynn and the Attorney-General, sentence had been pronounced on 18 June by Judge Sir Joseph Yates. Wilkes was given ten months in prison for the *North Briton*, because he had been two months in gaol already, and twelve months for the *Essay on Woman*, the sentences to run consecutively. He was also fined £500 on each charge, to be paid before his release. George III was informed that 'Wilkes's behaviour was more indecent than upon former days. He affected ease and indifference by picking his teeth and talking to those near him while Mr Justice Yates was animadverting upon the nature of his crimes.'[92] Wilkes put the best possible face on his situation, publishing an Address to his Middlesex constituents pointing out that afterwards he would be a free man, and that he had secured a reversal of his outlawry and a declaration of the illegality of general warrants.[93]

The ministry did not have to take official cognizance of the circumstance that Wilkes was in prison until the next Parliamentary session, and its attention was meanwhile directed to more urgent and important problems, the French seizure of Corsica and renewed defiance in the American colonies. Nothing effective could be achieved to reverse the French coup, and political attention during the Parliamentary recess was mostly taken up by the American crisis. Colonial resistance to the taxation imposed in 1767 by Charles Townshend, and also to more rigorous enforcement of the trade laws, had in Boston developed into physical defiance of British authority. In June and July the Grafton cabinet ordered both army regiments and naval ships to that town, and during the autumn many in Britain anticipated an armed confrontation there when the soldiers arrived. Not until 4 November, shortly before Parliament met, did the news reach London that the military occupation of Boston had been bloodless.[94] Thereafter, for the next fifteen months, ministerial attention was engrossed by the Middlesex Elections case. That Wilkes so diverted official attention away from the colonial problem was, in a negative sense, as much a part of the causal connection between his career and the forthcoming American Revolution as the positive example he provided to the colonists of resistance to government 'tyranny'.

Even in the Parliamentary recess the ministry was not free from the repercussions of the Middlesex election. As if one had not been enough, the administration was faced with another, when the ailing George Cooke died on 5 June. The opportunity was too good for the Wilkites to miss and, although no writ for a by-election could be issued until Parliament met in November, John Glynn announced his candidature two days later.[95] But success would not be so easy for Glynn as it had been for Wilkes. There would be no element of surprise, and Sir William Proctor was early in the field.[96] He enjoyed the support not merely of the ministry but also of the main opposition party, the leading Rockinghamite in the county being George Byng. Newcastle, who was to die before the by-election, at once gave his support to Proctor, who, so Charles Yorke reported to the Duke on 12 June, 'dreads the going through a canvass for five or six months'. Proctor was afraid that like Wilkes Glynn would enjoy the mass support of 'the lesser freeholders . . . against the weight of the gentry and freeholders of another description'.[97] That fear was justified when a hard-fought campaign culminated in a controversial poll on 8 December. Accounts of the election scene at Brentford portray deliberate intimidation on Proctor's behalf. His thugs included a group of turbulent Irish chairmen headed by Edward McQuirk, an experienced election hooligan, hired by a man variously stated to have been an agent of Lord Halifax or the county's Lord Lieutenant the Duke of Northumberland, both men with ministerial connections. Open rioting began when Proctor ran out of voters while Glynn, already ahead by 147, had many left to poll. The sheriffs were forced to abandon the election as the violence became extreme, McQuirk and another Irish chairman Laurence Balfe being subsequently convicted of the murder of a Wilkite lawyer George Clarke.[98]

James Townsend, a Middlesex landowner who was soon to be a zealous partisan of Wilkes, raised the matter in the House of Commons that evening. George Byng disagreed with his contention that Proctor was to blame. The Speaker intervened to stop a heated argument, and MPs on both sides of the House, Sir Gilbert Elliot and George Grenville among them, urged that the matter be discussed calmly. The Commons then considered the problem of what should be done, after the sheriffs, Thomas Hallifax and John Shakespear, reported that eight of the thirty-three poll books were missing. Their evidence showed that the violence was a deliberate attempt to disrupt the poll, not a spontaneous riot: 'a large body of men' had arrived at the hustings 'with large sticks'. They had adjourned the poll to the morning, but would need protection to continue it. The House decided to postpone the poll, and ordered a search for the missing books.[99] They were found, and the poll resumed on 14 December, when Glynn won by 1,542 votes to 1,278.[100] The support of the local gentry had enabled Proctor to head Glynn by 574 to 508 in the more rural parts of the county, but Glynn led by 801 to 534 in the London area and by 233 to 170 in Westminster.[101] The duration and bitterness made it an expensive contest: informed opinion put the costs for Proctor at £10,000, and those for Glynn at £12,000.[102]

This by-election, rather than the snap victory of Wilkes in March, demonstrated the new-found strength of the Wilkite hold on Middlesex. A well-known local squire, backed by the combined interests of administration and the Rockingham party, had failed to defeat a man whose political fame was merely that of being Wilkes's lawyer. The memory of this event doubtless helped to deter any challenge for the next fifteen years; except, of course, for the unseating of Wilkes himself during the next few months.

6

Expulsion from Middlesex
1769

GRAFTON was Prime Minister before the problems of Wilkes and America came under further consideration. In October 1768 Chatham finally resigned as Lord Privy Seal, on the grounds of ill health, although his decision was initially made under a misapprehension that his leading supporter Lord Shelburne, long at odds with his cabinet colleagues, had been dismissed as Southern Secretary. This ostensible reason made it possible for the Chathamites to stay on in office without embarrassment, and only Shelburne resigned from the cabinet with him. Lord Chancellor Camden, Sir Edward Hawke at the Admiralty, Lord Granby as head of the army, all remained in post with Grafton: together with Conway, again without office, they formed a moderate bloc in the cabinet, reluctant to act harshly over Wilkes or America. The only newcomer to the cabinet was Lord Rochford, a diplomat who became Northern Secretary, Weymouth moving to replace Shelburne as Southern Secretary.[1]

Wilkes made the running before the cabinet considered what to do about him. He was under a misapprehension that Grafton had promised the King that he would be expelled, and thought that he had nothing to lose by boldness.[2] On 3 November he therefore published an Address to his Middlesex constituents, announcing his intention to petition the House of Commons for redress of his grievances.[3] Whether or not his aim was more subtle than merely to cause maximum embarrassment for the ministry, this public move produced a private offer of a bargain from the new Prime Minister. On 10 November Grafton sent William Fitzherbert to John Almon with this message for Wilkes: 'that if he would not present his petition, the Duke assured him, upon his honour, no attempt should be made in Parliament against him.' When Wilkes made no reply, Fitzherbert himself was sent to see him three days later, taking David Garrick as a witness, because, as Almon himself wrote, 'Mr Wilkes was not always correct in his reports of conversations'. The offer was repeated, with the warning that Wilkes would certainly be expelled if he presented his petition. Fitzherbert added 'in confidence' that Wilkes could then soon be released from prison if he made 'some small submission' to the King. Wilkes replied that 'as to the petition he thought it his duty to present it, and he would not alter his resolution'. Almon commented on this episode: 'It was a principal feature in Mr Wilkes's character that, when he had taken a resolution, he never changed it.'[4] But Wilkes knew that acceptance of such a compromise as Grafton proposed would have destroyed his reputation as an opponent of official tyranny.

Sir Joseph Mawbey presented the petition to the Commons the very next day, 14 November. It recounted the treatment Wilkes had received in the *North Briton* case, and made two specific charges: that Lord Mansfield had altered legal records the day before his trial on 21 February 1764, and that Treasury Solicitor Webb had bribed witness Michael Curry.[5] The petition was ordered to lie on the Table of the House, pending receipt of the relevant records of the Court of King's Bench. The debate witnessed a split between London Radicals. Alderman William Beckford, possibly anticipating that the Wilkite movement might threaten his own support in the City, declared, 'I have as little obligation to him as any man'. He himself had earlier been attacked in the *North Briton*, he stated; and, although saying that Wilkes ought to have been heard already, he ended with this ambiguous statement: 'I am tired of Wilkes and Liberty.' That gave an opening to Wilkite John Sawbridge: 'I shall not be tired with the name of Wilkes, till I see the constitution restored: as to liberty I shall never be tired of it.' Beckford rose to explain: 'as to being tired of Wilkes and Liberty I am as strenuous a supporter of liberty as any man.'[6] During the discussion ministerial speakers had warned that the consequences of the petition might not be what the friends of Wilkes desired, and Lord North's private opinion to his father was that Wilkes had now burnt his boats:

The administration were well inclined to do nothing upon the subject of Mr Wilkes, but he has resolved to force his cause upon them ... by presenting his petition.... We shall probably have much tumult, noise and clamour in the course of this business, but I do not see how it can end without his expulsion. He has brought it upon himself, and must answer for the consequences.[7]

Such a comment revealed the gap between the old political game and the new. For North Parliament was the playing-field, and expulsion the kiss of death. But to Wilkes Westminster was but part of a wider arena. He flourished on controversy, and obscurity was the fate to be dreaded. Wilkes had no intention of languishing quietly in prison, but before his next move he would await news of the reaction to his petition.

On 23 November copies of the Court of King's Bench records relating to Wilkes were laid before the House of Commons, which then debated how to proceed. Mawbey reminded MPs that 'it was not the refuse of the people, it was not the mob, who elected Mr Wilkes'. Lord North favoured a Committee for such a complicated matter, and so did procedural expert Dyson, who challenged any MP thinking there had been a breach of privilege to move for the discharge of Wilkes from custody. Conway wanted to drop the matter altogether. Lord Barrington called Wilkes 'criminal' and 'unfit to sit in the House'. That his denunciations reflected the mood of the Commons was demonstrated by the acceptance of his motion for the speedy procedure of a hearing of the petition at the Bar of the House on 2 December.[8]

Next day Mawbey moved for the attendance of several witnesses, and then, 'jocularly' he later said, for Wilkes to attend 'in his place' as an MP, afterwards altering that to the Bar of the House, since, so he remarked, Wilkes did not care how he attended.[9] Four days later, on 28 November, the ministry was tricked into agreeing to a motion to ask the House of Lords for the attendance of Lord Temple as a witness. With that precedent established, motions for Lords Sandwich and March could not decently be refused. But one for Webb's accounts as Treasury Solicitor was rejected, on the objection of Lord North that the charge of bribery ought to be proved first, despite opposition protests that such information was needed to provide the evidence. Grenville, defending his own corner as the then Prime Minister, blamed the ministry for allowing the business to proceed at all.[10] More witnesses were ordered that day and the next, when Dyson asked why so many were needed: forty-three had by then been summoned.[11] On 29 November, too, the House received a petition from Webb, denying the allegations of bribery, and ordered his attendance.[12] Wilkes, with his evidence prepared, and his witnesses ready, was anxious to proceed as soon as possible, to save legal and other costs; but the ministry on 10 December put off the hearing of his petition to 27 January 1769.[13]

This was evidently because the cabinet had not yet decided what to do about Wilkes. That same day, suspecting as much even before he knew of the postponement of his case, Wilkes gave the ministry a final prod. He handed to a John Swan two papers for Henry Baldwin, printer of the *St. James's Chronicle*, to publish at once in his newspaper, and Baldwin complied that day. One was a copy of the letter written on 17 April by Secretary of State Weymouth to Daniel Ponton, Chairman of the Lambeth magistrates, reminding him of the availability of soldiers. What outraged the ministry was the preface Wilkes wrote to the letter, claiming that it showed 'how long the horrid massacre in St. George's Fields had been planned . . . and how long a hellish project can be brooded over by some infernal spirits without one moment's remorse'.[14]

This outrageous accusation, and the language in which it was couched, finally goaded Grafton into deciding on the expulsion of Wilkes from Parliament. In the House of Lords on 15 December, after examination of Baldwin and Swan established Wilkes as the author, he moved a resolution that the preface was 'an insolent, scandalous and seditious libel, tending to inflame and stir up the minds of his Majesty's subjects to sedition'. The wording was significant and doubtless deliberate, for it was just such a condemnation of *North Briton, Number Forty-Five* that had been the ground for the expulsion of Wilkes from the Commons in 1764. The resolution was promptly passed and sent to the House of Commons the same day, when Lord North moved to concur with it, saying the question of authorship could be postponed. Several MPs, including Conway, criticized such haste, Mawbey pointing out that the Lords had not yet replied to their message for the three peers to attend. Edmund Burke feared for the liberty of the press if all attacks on ministers were to be deemed libels. Solicitor-General Dunning opposed voting the preface a libel so hastily and without knowing the author, and an angry North found he had to postpone the matter to 19 December.[15]

That day began with a message from the House of Lords stating that Lords Sandwich and March had been given leave to attend the hearing of the bribery charge against Webb. This news took the sting out of the opposition attempt to exploit jealousy of the Upper House. After a desultory debate, in which Conway urged MPs 'to wash our hands of the whole proceedings', because the House should not interfere in judicial matters, Baldwin and Swan were interrogated. Familiar with his distinctive handwriting, both confirmed that Wilkes had written the preface. This subject was then also postponed until 27 January.[16]

By the Christmas recess of Parliament no final decision to expel Wilkes had yet been taken by the cabinet.[17] Grafton's personal reaction to the libel of 10 December meant that he was now strongly in favour of that policy; and that Wilkes was deliberately courting such a fate was shown by a defiant Address to the Freeholders of Middlesex he published on 17 December. In this he stated that he had sent to the press Lord Barrington's letter of 11 May thanking the soldiers concerned for the 'foul murders' committed in St George's Fields on the previous day; and he confirmed his publication in the *St. James's Chronicle* of 10 December of Weymouth's letter, written in 'characters of blood'.[18] But Lord Chancellor Camden had now parted company with Grafton on the subject: whether through timidity, love of popularity, or some inkling of Chatham's opinion is unclear. On 9 January 1769, when promising attendance at a cabinet on the matter in four days' time, Camden told Grafton that he now favoured leniency on the ground of political expediency.

I do wish most heartily that the present time could be eased of the difficulties that Mr Wilkes's business has brought upon government: a fatality has attended it from the beginning, and it grows more serious every day. Your Grace and I have unfortunately differed. I wish it had been otherwise. It is a hydra multiplying by resistance and gathering strength by every attempt to subdue it. As the times are, I had rather pardon Wilkes than punish him. This is a political opinion independent of the merit of the case.[19]

The behaviour of Conway and Dunning in the Commons debates of December had suggested that other ministerial moderates would oppose expulsion. Three cabinet members, Conway, Lord Granby, and Sir Edward Hawke, now did so, presumably at the meeting of 13 January.[20] On 21 January Lord Temple, a man with a keen nose for political news, thought that expulsion, though much talked about, had not yet been decided upon.[21] Scruples about expelling Wilkes twice for the same offence could now be overcome by declaring the comment on Weymouth's letter to be a seditious libel, and on 22 January a meeting decided to proceed on that basis.[22]

The very next day in the House of Commons, either by coincidence or because he had got wind of the ministry's intention, a new opposition MP Joseph Martin proposed the motion that Wilkes, although convicted of seditious libel, was entitled to Parliamentary privilege. Such a resolution would cut the ground from under the ministry's strategy, and was an attempt to reverse the resolution of 24 November 1763 that Parliamentary privilege did not cover seditious libel. 'I never spoke to Mr Wilkes', Martin declared. 'It is the cause that animates me.' Lord North countered by an amendment designed to make the motion unacceptable by adding mention of obscene libel and stating that Wilkes was in prison on both counts. George Grenville, as Prime Minister during the *North Briton* case, spoke against the motion: 'I do not feel disposed to carry any question in favour of Mr Wilkes.' An opposition procedural tactic to avoid a decision on Martin's amended motion was defeated by 165 votes to 71, a thin attendance, perhaps because few MPs had known of Martin's intention. His motion was then formally rejected.[23]

Conway's opposition to expulsion had offended both his colleagues and George III, and he was not invited to a meeting, convened by Lord North on 26 January, to discuss how this policy could be implemented.[24] The next day in the Commons North proposed a tactic evidently agreed upon to dispose of Wilkes's petition: that proceedings on it should be restricted to two specific allegations, that Lord Mansfield had altered legal records, and that Philip Webb, then Solicitor to the Treasury, had bribed a witness. There followed a noisy debate in a crowded chamber, mostly conducted by lawyers. Diarist Henry Cavendish noted the treatment accorded to William Dowdeswell, the Commons spokesman of the Rockinghamite faction: 'Mr Dowdeswell spoke a long time, but the House was too noisy to give any attention to him, so much so, that the gentlemen who were next to him could not hear what he said.' North's motion was carried by 278 votes to 131, an attendance of 414 MPs.[25]

The next two Parliamentary days were taken up with settling those points. Proceedings on both 31 January and 1 February lasted until after midnight. The alterations Wilkes complained of proved to have been trivial. It was John Hatsell, Clerk to the House of Commons, who had for administrative convenience endorsed the *Essay on Woman* as 'blasphemy', and that word was not part of the legal record.[26] Lord Mansfield's own alteration had been purely verbal, the word 'purport' being changed to 'tenor'. Wilkes's agent had acquiesced at the time, 'though he said he could not consent'.[27] The alleged bribery of Curry by Webb was the payment of customary subsistence money for witnesses. After hearing witnesses, and debates in which opposition speakers argued that the charges were correct in form, the House resolved, without dividing for a vote, that the complaint against Mansfield was frivolous, and that Wilkes had not made good his charge against Webb.[28]

The way was now clear for the administration to initiate direct action against Wilkes, and 2 February was taken up with his introduction to Lord Weymouth's letter. Wilkes appeared before the House of Commons and, provocative to the end, proudly claimed authorship of the commentary on 'so bloody a scroll . . . I avow it. I think it a meritorious act.' Attorney-General William De Grey then moved that the preface was 'an insolent, scandalous and seditious libel', the same resolution as that voted by the Lords on 15 December. In the ensuing debate Dowdeswell pointed out that much of the justification offered for Weymouth's letter concerned subsequent events, and claimed that the real offence to the ministry was not what Wilkes had written himself but his publication of Weymouth's letter. That great lawyer of the age, William Blackstone, then announced that he could not this time vote for the administration, since the subject was a matter for the lawcourts, not Parliament. Grenville made the same point, though both condemned what Wilkes had written as libel. Later in the debate Mawbey declared as a Surrey magistrate that Weymouth's letter had led the county bench to fear censure if they did not send for soldiers. The central theme of the discussion was the ministerial contention that the army was an essential bulwark of the civil power, and the denial of this claim by opposition speakers. The debate lasted until after two o'clock the next morning, when the resolution was carried by 239 votes to 136.[29]

This declaration that Wilkes was guilty of another 'seditious libel' provided a reason for his expulsion, the main business when the House of Commons reassembled later that same day, 3 February. But the expulsion motion, proposed by Lord Barrington, was a composite one, listing five libels, two as seditious, those in the *North Briton* and the *St. James's Chronicle*, and three in the *Essay on Woman* as 'obscene and impious'. The first opposition speaker, Thomas Townshend, complained of the unfairness of this device. Wilkes had already been expelled for the *North Briton* libel, and only a dozen copies of the *Essay on Woman* had been printed, privately moreover. 'Leave libels to the law', he said, challenging the argument that conviction for a libel incurred expulsion. The significance of the ministerial tactic became apparent during the debate as several MPs, including lawyer Blackstone, declared that they would vote for expulsion because of the obscene and impious libels. Jeremiah Dyson produced the further argument for expulsion, that Wilkes could not represent his constituents while in prison. Rockinghamite Lord John Cavendish pointed out that when the voters of Middlesex had chosen Wilkes he was not legally incapacitated from election: 'Punishing a member, when that member is disagreeable to the majority of this House, will be a fatal precedent.'

George Grenville then rose for what his brother Lord Temple said was 'universally deemed the best speech he ever made'.[30] His attack on the expulsion motion centred on the 'complicated charge' against Wilkes. The tactic was novel and unfair, for already different speakers had given varying reasons for supporting the motion. 'Is it not evident, that by this unworthy artifice, Mr Wilkes may be expelled, although three parts in four of those who expel him should have declared against his expulsion upon every one of the articles contained in this charge?' He next discussed the various grounds for expulsion. The recent seditious libel on a minister should, 'as hitherto', be tried in a court of law. Nor should Wilkes be expelled again for the *North Briton* libel. As for the impious and obscene libels in the *Essay on Woman*, the House of Commons had ignored them five years ago, when Grenville himself had been Prime Minister, and should not now make them a reason for expulsion. When he later returned to this point near the end of his speech, Grenville declared bluntly that the provocation was the libel on Lord Weymouth and that the other charges were 'thrown into the scale, to make up the weight'. Dyson's additional argument that inability to sit in the House should incur expulsion Grenville countered by showing that all precedents were to the contrary, as in the instances of suspected Jacobite MPs arrested earlier in the century. It would have to be applied, moreover, to army and naval officers absent for years in time of war.

This brings me to the only part of the question which I have not yet touched upon. I mean the propriety and wisdom of the measure . . . I shall probably be told that it is to check and to restrain the spirit of faction and disorder, to re-establish the credit and authority of government and to vindicate the honour of this House by expressing our abhorrence of these offences . . . I have not changed my sentiments relative to Mr Wilkes, of whom I continue to think exactly in the same manner as I have long done; but whatever my sentiments are, it cannot be denied that he is now become an object of popular favour.

The ministry, Grenville argued, was playing into the hands of Wilkes, who 'thoroughly sensible that the continuance of his popularity will depend upon your conduct, uses every means in his power to provoke you to some instance of unusual severity'. Grenville then forecast what would lie ahead. Wilkes would be constantly re-elected and expelled. The two ways to avoid this impasse, both 'the subject of common conversation', were either to refuse to issue a new writ, which would deprive the Middlesex electors of representation, or to award the seat to a minority candidate.

Grenville's speech caused something of a sensation, not merely for the quality of argument, but because of astonishment that he should have spoken against the expulsion of Wilkes at all; for he had a low opinion of his character and had been the Prime Minister responsible for his expulsion in 1764. Wilkes was incensed at some disparaging comments Grenville made on his character, and when Grenville's speech was printed as a pamphlet later in the year he published a rejoinder, even though Lord Temple asked him not to do so: the two men never spoke again afterwards. The Wilkes pamphlet was presumably the one Grenvillite William Knox mentioned to Grenville on 10 November as 'a poor catchpenny pamphlet called *Observations on the Present Publication of the Speech*'.[31] That same day Wilkes told a French correspondent that 'it is a very large pamphlet, wrote for the nation, and against an odious fellow, although indeed he only furnished the pretence'.[32]

Grenville had avowedly voiced his own opinion without prior consultation with his friends, and not all were to follow his lead. In one sense an attack on the motion by Colonel Isaac Barré was more ominous for the ministry, for it betokened the hostility of Chatham, whose adherents still comprised a significant segment of the administration. On 30 January Lord Temple had received a letter from his sister Lady Chatham, 'assuring his Lordship that *Lord Chatham was strongly against the measure of expelling Mr Wilkes*'. Chatham's intention was to make known his opinion in order to 'check the foolish madness of your malicious enemies', John Almon told Wilkes the next day.[33] Barré, Shelburne's mouthpiece in the Commons, had accompanied his patron into opposition on Chatham's resignation. He declared that 'impiety and blasphemy' were a new political crime, but his main theme was that Parliament had better things to do with its time than punishing a libeller. The proceedings against Wilkes had given MPs 'the most fatiguing week' in memory. Foreign policy and colonial affairs had been neglected, while Wilkes would flourish by this folly. Attorney-General De Grey unfairly claimed that the logic of the opposition case was that an MP could be expelled for one crime but not for five. Edmund Burke provided a famous mockery of the whole proceedings:

The state of the night, the candles, put me in mind of the representation of the last act of a tragic-comedy, acted by his Majesty's servants, by desire of several persons of distinction, for the benefit of Mr Wilkes, at the expense of the constitution.

Lord North summed up for the ministry. In reply to Dowdeswell's claim that no court of law would accept an accumulation of offences as a ground for conviction, he pointed out that each taken separately was a libel, declared to be so either by the lawcourts or by Parliament. The libel on Lord Weymouth, moreover, was 'a crime . . . since he has been elected'. But the debate revealed that the ministry had not retained the support of all the customary adherents of administration. Some apparently absented themselves, while even after North had spoken the independent Herbert Mackworth told the House, 'I shall go against his Majesty's ministers, but my principle is to support them. There is no libel sufficient to ground a resolution of expulsion upon.' The administration carried the resolution by 219 votes to 137. Two of the three ministers who had opposed the expulsion in the cabinet, Hawke and Granby, voted for this, but Conway absented himself.[34] Twenty-five MPs had spoken in the debate, and the House rose at three o'clock, the fourth successive sitting after midnight.[35]

Events followed the course many had predicted. On 4 February Wilkes announced from his comfortable prison cell that he would stand again. Although no opponent was known, precautions were taken against the trick of a last-minute candidature. On 9 February Wilkes notified his constituents that the election would be at Brentford on 16 February, and on 15 February that carriages were to be stationed at eighteen venues. Two late rumours were that a friend would stand in place of Wilkes, and that Sir John Gibbons, a ministerial supporter unseated at the general election, would oppose Wilkes with Proctor's support. Neither was true. At both a nomination meeting at the Mile End Assembly Rooms on 14 February and at the election two days later Wilkes was proposed and seconded by two Radical MPs, James Townsend and John Sawbridge. Although it was a 'very wet day' some 2,000 freeholders and supporters attended to witness a unanimous election.

Townsend, saying that he had never spoken to Wilkes before his recent expulsion, declared that 'his cause was the cause of the people', and Sawbridge
quoted the part of Wilkes's Address that warned 'that if once the ministry
shall be permitted to say whom the freeholders shall not choose, the next
step will be to tell them whom they shall choose'.[36]

The next day in the House of Commons Lord Strange, on behalf of the
ministry, moved that since Wilkes had been expelled earlier, he was 'incapable of being elected a member to serve in this present Parliament'. William
Beckford challenged the argument of precedent. Lord Strange replied that it
was 'the certain law of Parliament that no man could sit after expulsion'.
James Townsend claimed that the return of Wilkes had been supported by
over 2,000 freeholders. They believed that Wilkes was legally qualified to sit
and that no resolution of 'any set of men' could deprive them of the right of
electing him. Edmund Burke questioned the claim that the proposed procedure was 'the law of Parliament'. Lord North replied that it was also 'the
law of reason and of common sense'. Other MPs thought that the reason for
expulsion should be included to avoid a general precedent, and an amendment to that effect was moved by Dowdeswell, supported by Grenville.
When this was rejected by 228 votes to 102, Dowdeswell announced that he
would oppose the main question, asking what would happen if Wilkes stood
again and an unsuccessful candidate petitioned. Barré also expressed concern about the precedent before the motion was carried by 228 to 89. There
was no further voting when Lord Strange moved that the election of Wilkes
was void and that a new writ be issued.[37]

An Address published by Wilkes next day assumed that the new election
would be on 28 February, but he corrected this date to 16 March on 22 February, when at a Mile End meeting of 400 freeholders Chairman James Townsend stated that the only precedents for incapacity were crimes, a claim
echoed by Sawbridge and John Horne.[38] The same precaution was taken of
stationing coaches at sixteen named venues, and this time there was a last-
minute opponent, Charles Dingley, possibly persuaded to stand by Grafton:
by now he had received £2,000 from the government as compensation for
the destruction of his sawmill in the riots of May 1768.[39] Dingley issued an
Address on the election day itself, 16 March, expressing the 'hope that every
freeholder will be permitted to come to the place of election without the
least molestation'. From his prison Wilkes denounced 'this plan of trick and
surprise', saying that Dingley's candidature was 'stolen upon us only this
morning'. Dingley appeared on the hustings before the arrival of the sheriffs, but withdrew in the face of physical assault. In a letter to the sheriffs he
announced his willingness to stand if put in nomination, but his messenger
was prevented from reaching them before, within half an hour, they

declared the return of Wilkes. Out of 500 voters Dingley claimed as supporters, and whom he later thanked for attending, not one was willing to
propose him.[40]

Next day in the Commons Richard Rigby moved to void the return. No
MP directly opposed this, although Dowdeswell did enquire whether it was
prudent to have a Middlesex election every month, and Grenville reminded
the House what he had forecast on 3 February. He accepted, however, that
the resolution of the House was binding and Wilkes in consequence in-
admissible. Lord North proved jocular about the financial support Wilkes
had received: 'I am not his enemy personally . . . I had as lief the money was
in his pocket as the pocket of the subscribers.' He then dropped a hint as to
what would be the ministerial solution to the problem: 'I shall deem that
man the true member for the county of Middlesex who shall have a majority of legal votes.' There was no division when the election of Wilkes was
again voided and a writ issued for a third by-election.[41]

The ministry, whether or not it had been involved in the Dingley fiasco,
took care this time to arrange for a candidate. On 24 March an election
Address was published by the Colonel Henry Luttrell who had sought
Parliamentary action against Wilkes in the previous May. Described in the
press as 'a young man of great courage and sense', he had distinguished himself in the Portugal campaign of the Seven Years War, winning promotion to
colonel at the age of 28. There were those who were puzzled why this young
war hero undertook such an 'unpopular and dishonourable task'. Certainly
the general presumption was that he had been promised the Middlesex seat
on petition. This time there was a press campaign against Wilkes, voters
being urged to choose 'a truly respectable man'. Wilkes himself had already,
on 23 March, put to the electorate what he saw as the constitutional point at
stake: 'My sole motive is the hope of establishing by perseverance your title
to a free election . . . The question is whether the people have an inherent
right to be represented in Parliament by the man of their free choice, not disqualified by the law of the land.'[42]

There was an obvious counter to the ministerial strategy: to arrange for a
Wilkite candidate to come second in the poll in order to deprive Luttrell of
the seat. This possibility may explain why Luttrell did not resign his Bossiney
seat until the last moment, on 11 April. One David Roche wrote to Wilkes, on
29 March, offering himself for this role: 'If you think it advisable I will declare
myself as a candidate forthwith that Mr Luttrell may not succeed agreeable
to the wishes of the ministry.'[43] This tactic was not adopted, perhaps because
the scheme would have been difficult to carry out, but more probably because
it would have concealed the full infamy, in Wilkite eyes, of the ministry's
behaviour. On 4 April Roche nevertheless issued a palpably spoof election

notice, satirizing Luttrell. A fourth, last-minute candidature, whimsical and inexplicable, came from a Serjeant Whitaker.

Both Wilkes and Luttrell advertised where their supporters could find coaches on election day, 13 April, when several Wilkes cavalcades set out for Brentford. One stopped at St James's Palace to annoy George III by playing music, but moved on when the guards came out. Luttrell had the protection of a party of horsemen, variously estimated to number between fifty and two hundred. As in March 1768 there was trouble at Hyde Park Corner, where Luttrell's party met a Wilkite mob. Luttrell's hat was knocked off by a missile, to 'a prodigious shout', and so his supporters put on 'a little gallop' to get through the crowd. Later press enquiries at nearby St George's Hospital established that there had been no serious injuries, even to a man who had seized the bridle of Luttrell's horse. At the poll itself an appeal for good order by Sawbridge and Townsend proved successful, even though Luttrell was proposed and seconded by two ministerial MPs, placeman John Dodd and the unpopular Stephen Fox. Sawbridge proposed Wilkes, announcing that the newly formed Bill of Rights Society had resolved to support 'the cause of liberty', and Townsend seconded. Whitaker did not appear. Roche did, but he had failed to produce any qualifications, and so his candidature lapsed. The poll was quick and quiet, beginning at eleven o'clock and closing four and a half hours later, when Wilkes had 1,143 votes, Luttrell 296, and Whitaker 5. Several thousand people subsequently marched to the King's Bench Prison to congratulate Wilkes, and the main streets of London were illuminated again that night.[44]

Next day George Onslow moved for the Middlesex return, and there followed a tedious wrangle about how to proceed. No speaker thought that Wilkes should keep his seat, the issue being, as Dowdeswell said, whether the election be voided or Luttrell returned. 'We go to establish the worst contest, between the house of representatives and their constituents', he asserted, professing to believe that Luttrell would not accept the seat as a minority candidate. No vote was taken on a motion by Onslow that the election of Wilkes was invalid, but his proposal to take the poll into consideration the next day was challenged, and carried by 207 votes to 115.[45]

That was 15 April, a Saturday, when the House did not usually sit. Disgruntlement may have contributed to the bad temper that day, when the House was noisy and speakers were often called to order, as when Stephen Fox abused the Middlesex voters as 'the lowest scum of the people. What could be lower than the inhabitants of Billingsgate and Wapping.' George Onslow began with the assertion 'that the House of Commons has assumed to itself, and put in practice, a legal power of expelling and incapacitating [its members]'. Moving that Luttrell ought to have been returned, Onslow said that the dispute was between the House and a few inhabitants of Middlesex, not 'the people at large'. For Edmund Burke it was 'a contest between the freeholders of England and the House of Commons'. Beckford warned that 'a corrupt majority of this House may expel whomsoever they please'.

The most notable contribution of the day, as on 3 February, came from George Grenville. Chatting to James Harris in the House on 6 April he had said that 'it was impossible to admit Wilkes this session, but that our resolution did not extend further, nor indeed could. For this reason . . .', Harris recorded, 'he seemed to think that though the election of Wilkes would be void, he being ineligible this session, another could not be voted into his place, for such election went to the whole Parliament'.[46] It was therefore 'in a tone exceedingly animated', diarist Cavendish noted, that Grenville now declared that 'the man who will contend that a resolution of the House of Commons is the law of the land is a most violent enemy of his country. . . . The law of the land, an Act of Parliament, cannot be altered, enforced, augmented, or changed, by a vote of either House of Parliament.' Later in the debate, to much applause, Grenville emphasized the distinction between a Parliamentary resolution and the law of the land. The House of Commons by itself had no right to impose a disqualification.

The ministerial case, as put by Lord North, was that the freeholders polling for Wilkes had thrown away their votes, since he was incapable of election. The only valid ones were those for Luttrell. In his peroration he urged, 'Let not Parliament fall into contempt. Let not liberty be established upon the ruin of law.' Precedents were cited on both sides, Rockinghamite Sir William Meredith producing the apposite one of 1712, when the candidate second on the poll to the disqualified Robert Walpole had been declared not duly elected. When the House divided, after one o'clock on Sunday morning, the ministerial majority had fallen to 54, 197 against 143.[47] 'Some of their friends quitted them', noted diarist Horace Walpole. 'Harley, the Lord Mayor, fearing for his personal safety in the City, was permitted by the Duke of Grafton to vote against the vote.'[48] Comparison of voting lists for 3 February and 15 April shows that six MPs who had voted to expel Wilkes now voted against the seating of Luttrell and that a further twenty-seven were absent.[49]

Presentation of the inevitable petition of Middlesex freeholders against this decision was deliberately delayed until the last possible day, 29 April, so that it could provide a basis for a renewed attack on the administration in the next Parliamentary session. This Rockinghamite tactic was defeated by the ministerial decision to fix the hearing for 8 May.[50] The debate then was long but unedifying, merely a rehearsal of arguments already deployed. Dowdeswell vainly sought to establish the question as 'not whether Mr Wilkes should take his seat in this House. The question is whether Mr Luttrell is duly elected.' Lawyer Blackstone announced that 'Mr Wilkes is disqualified by common law'. The highlight of the debate was the recantation of another lawyer, Alexander Wedderburn, who had silently voted for the expulsion of Wilkes and the seating of Luttrell. He now denied that a resolution of the House had 'the force of legality'. Wedderburn had been won over by Grenville, and was at once called upon to forfeit his Richmond seat by his indignant patron Sir Lawrence Dundas, a ministerial supporter angling for a peerage. This martyrdom, though it caused a contemporary sensation, was more apparent than real, for Wedderburn had already been promised another seat by Grenville's friend Lord Clive. Fears of the possible implications of the election decision were voiced by Chathamite Isaac Barré: 'A bold member may be expelled. It may be decided in the cabinet council, who are to sit in this House.' Grenville quoted Blackstone's own legal *Commentaries* against the opinion he had just given, and voiced a reflection that anticipated his Election Act of the next year: 'Is it wise, Sir, to vest in a majority of the House the law of elections?'[51] This time administration won by 221 votes to 152. Evidently alarmed by the fall in its majority on 15 April, the ministry had mustered a very large attendance. The number of MPs at the debate was estimated at well over 400, although only 378 voted at the division. Wedderburn was not the only MP with a troubled conscience, and numerous friends of government left the House rather than vote. Twenty-four MPs who had voted for the seating of Luttrell were now absent, among them Sir Edward Hawke.[52]

The Middlesex Elections dispute was not over. It had united the various opposition factions in a common cause and offered the prospect of toppling the Grafton ministry, for, as Lord Temple calculated, 'the minority is at least two hundred, or two hundred and twenty'.[53] They did not intend to let the opportunity slip. Morale was boosted by a dinner on 9 May at the Thatched House Tavern, attended by seventy-two MPs. All the leading figures of opposition were there, George Grenville, Rockinghamites William Dowdeswell and Edmund Burke, Chathamite Isaac Barré, and City Radical William Beckford. Such appropriate toasts were drunk as 'Freedom of Debate within doors and freedom of Election without'.[54]

During the Parliamentary summer recess these opposition politicians organized an extensive petitioning campaign throughout England, involving about twenty of the forty counties and a rather smaller number of boroughs. The common theme was the implicit threat of the Middlesex Elections case to the rights of electors, but Wilkites and some others also sought to include general statements of political and constitutional grievances. Members of the new Bill of Rights Society were foremost in instigating petitions from the metropolitan area and in some western shires, the Rockinghamite party in northern shires and in Dowdeswell's home county of Worcestershire, while Lord Temple was the key figure in Buckinghamshire.[55] They were confronted by widespread doubts over the constitutional propriety of petitioning the King for a dissolution of Parliament; and in some rural areas there was an unwillingness to lend support to Wilkes. Dowdeswell commented to Burke from Worcestershire on 5 September that 'Wilkes's character, of which men are inclined to think much worse than it really deserves, and the advantage which he necessarily must receive from the restitution made to the public of its rights at present lost, have checked this proceeding in most places'. In Yorkshire the next month Burke welcomed the support of many clergy because 'some people were willing to cast a stain of profaneness upon our conduct from our supposed patronage of Wilkes'.[56] Ministerial supporters were able to prevent projected petitions in some constituencies, but by 10 January 1770 at least fourteen counties and twelve boroughs had presented petitions to George III, signed altogether by some 60,000 Parliamentary voters, so it was to be repeatedly claimed in the ensuing Commons debates.[57]

The purpose of this campaign was to provide a foundation for a renewed attack on the Grafton ministry when Parliament reassembled in January 1770. But the decisive event that led to Grafton's resignation was not the petitioning campaign but the return in the summer of Lord Chatham to an active political role. His public denunciation of the proceedings over the Middlesex Elections threatened a ministry that still included men who might look to him for a political lead: Lord Chancellor Camden, Sir Edward Hawke, Lord Granby, and General Henry Conway within the cabinet itself.[58] The first omens occurred in the opening Commons debate of 9 January 1770 on the Address. The ministry triumphed by 254 votes to 138, and some observers therefore deemed the political crisis over. But Lord Granby publicly recanted his previous voting on the Middlesex Elections case, and others who now voted with the opposition included Solicitor-General Dunning, Sir Piercy Brett of the Admiralty Board, and three other Chathamite MPs. By contrast, Sir Edward Hawke and Conway spoke for the ministry.[59]

The next fortnight saw a Parliamentary hiatus, in part caused by fortuitous events like the resignation and death of Speaker Cust, but mainly due to the ministerial crisis. Camden and Granby resigned on 17 January, Dunning on 20 January. Sir George Yonge and Sir Piercy Brett left the Admiralty Board, but not Sir Edward Hawke. Parliamentary warfare resumed on 25 January, when Dowdeswell put forward a motion that no one could oppose in principle, but had obvious reference to the Middlesex Elections case: 'That the House of Commons, in judging of elections, ought to be regulated by the laws of the land, and the known and established law and custom of

Parliament, which make a part thereof.' This put the ministry in a procedural quandary. The usual evasive devices of an adjournment or a previous question could not be deployed, because the House was technically in a Committee, on the State of the Nation.[60] Yet Lord North and his colleagues were aware that they could not accept this motion and then defeat a subsequent one specifically on the Middlesex Elections case. Nor could they decently reject it. Diarist Henry Cavendish noted that confusion prevailed on the Treasury Bench until a message came from the absent procedural expert Jeremiah Dyson, and North then moved an amendment stating that the decision of 17 February last, declaring Wilkes ineligible to sit, was 'agreeable to the said law of the land'. The opposition, thus outmanœuvred, protested in vain at the alleged unfairness of this tactic. After a lengthy and acrimonious debate a division on the amendment took place, when the ministry won only by 224 votes to 180.[61] Examination of a minority voting list reveals what had happened. There were twenty-six more MPs now in opposition, sixteen of whom had previously voted for the administration on the Middlesex Elections case, with the other ten having been absent. The Chathamite connection explains the behaviour of seven of the former group, notably Lord Granby, and five of the latter, including John Dunning.[62]

This collapse of the ministerial position in the House of Commons was the event that precipitated Grafton's fall. Already demoralized by a whole series of events during the previous ten days, he decided to resign on 26 January when faced by this threat of impending Parliamentary defeat. A jubilant opposition then had victory snatched from their grasp by Lord North, who made good his acceptance of the Premiership by surviving the crucial Commons debate of 31 January. That was also on the Middlesex election, for Dowdeswell, again in Committee, put forward a motion even more difficult to counter than that of 25 January, the simple proposition 'that, by the law of the land and the known and established law and custom of Parliament, no person eligible of common right to serve in Parliament can be incapacitated by any vote or resolution of this House, but by Act of Parliament only'. The first speaker for the administration, Lord Clare, spelt out the dilemma:

There is certainly no Act of Parliament, upon which Mr Wilkes's incapacity is founded. You must infer then that injustice has been done to the county of Middlesex. Does the honourable gentleman mean to go further? You must give an answer. Because if you declare, that you have injured Mr Wilkes and the County of Middlesex, if you do not redress that injury, it is insult added to injury. Because you don't mean to vote Mr Luttrell out, and vote Mr Wilkes in.

Blackstone conceded that he would have to support the motion, but other lawyers on the ministerial side argued that incapacity was the natural consequence of the House's undoubted right of expulsion. Lord North nevertheless perceived that the wording of the motion might tip the balance in an evenly divided House, and countered by a procedural device, moving that the Chairman should leave the Chair. Anger at this tactic erupted on the opposition benches, Wedderburn denouncing it as a mean device and equivalent to a negative. Grenville said that he could see no problem in Dowdeswell's motion. Since it was a new session, the House could rescind any resolution of the previous one, such as that declaring Wilkes incapable of election. That had been his objection to the seating of Luttrell, he explained, for that must be for the whole Parliament, a procedural contradiction. The debate ended in noisy disorder. North's motion was carried by 226 votes to 186, and reporter John Almon believed that his tactic saved the day for the ministry: 'By this means the question was lost, as several of the majority had owned the truth of the proposition, and must have voted for it, but the question being on leaving the Chair, they saved themselves and only put off giving any determination on the motion at all.'[63]

Be that as it may, Lord North had won the day when many had anticipated his defeat and few such a majority. It was the political turning-point, for though Wilkes had felled a Prime Minister he had not brought down the King's government, and North during the next few weeks was to go from strength to strength.[64]

The Parliamentary and other political ramifications of the Middlesex Elections case did not, of course, end in January 1770. Later that session George Grenville successfully introduced his Election Act, transferring the decision of disputed cases from the House to a small Committee of MPs chosen by lot. In subsequent years the North ministry was to be occasionally harassed in Parliament over the case, notably by Sir George Savile, a Rockinghamite MP for Yorkshire. A man greatly respected in Parliament, Savile had been stirred to a rare anger by the decision to incapacitate Wilkes, and for the last four sessions of the Parliament proposed 'a Bill to secure the rights of electors with respect to the eligibility of persons to serve in Parliament'. As he explained on the first occasion, 7 February 1771, his aim was not to reverse that decision but to prevent a recurrence by condemning what he perceived to be the three principles behind it: that the House possessed a legislative power with respect to the rights of electors; that one decision of the House would make such law; and that incapacity to be re-elected was the consequence of expulsion. The ensuing debate was a rerun of those on the Middlesex election, young Charles Fox enhancing his reputation by a speech arguing that incapacity must follow expulsion and pointing out that Middlesex had not been deprived of a representative. Conway stated that he would oppose Savile's motion because the House was being asked to declare its own resolution illegal. John Glynn replied it was not undignified for the

House to reconsider a decision. Much interest centred on the behaviour of those Grenvillites who had recently joined the ministry on the death of their leader. Alexander Wedderburn, though now Solicitor-General, supported Savile's motion and the Grenvillites voted in the minority of 103 against the administration majority of 167. John Almon noted that the small attendance was explained by the pairing off of many MPs on such a stale subject.[65]

Subsequent debates on Savile's motions were shorter and badly reported. On 27 February 1772 Lord North deigned to speak, disputing Savile's contention that the law and common sense had been set aside, and carried the vote by 181 to 135.[66] That of the next session, on 26 April 1773, was preceded by a characteristic piece of Wilkes impudence. A Call of the House had been ordered for that day, all returning officers being instructed to summon their MPs. That was too good an opportunity for Wilkes to pass up, for the sheriffs of Middlesex were Radicals Richard Oliver and James Townsend. They summoned Wilkes, not Luttrell, to attend with John Glynn, and he duly presented himself at the Palace of Westminster, unsuccessfully demanding a certificate of his return from the Deputy Clerk of the Crown, Charles Trewen, so that he could take the appropriate oath. As soon as the Commons began public business Glynn proposed that Wilkes should be called in to make his complaint against Trewen, a motion seconded by Sawbridge but promptly rejected by 227 votes to 124.[67] This incident provoked a lively debate when Savile made his customary motion. Dowdeswell and Burke both reminded the House of the futile attempt in 1771 to stop Parliamentary reporting, and the failure then to punish Wilkes for his part in that episode.[68] Lord North commented that for Wilkes prison was a reward not a punishment, and said that the next general election would put an end to the whole question. He claimed popular backing over the Middlesex Elections case, whereupon Glynn derisively asked him where his supporters were hidden. The ministerial majority was half what it had been earlier in the day, 201 to 151.[69] That the Middlesex election remained a vulnerable point for administration was confirmed in the vote over Savile's motion in the next session on 15 February 1774: again the majority was only around the fifty mark, 206 to 147.[70] Thereafter, in the next Parliament and beyond, Wilkes himself raised the subject every session until success crowned his efforts in 1782.

In 1769 Wilkes had not expected the decision to deprive him of his seat for the entire Parliament, even after his first expulsion on 3 February. Diarist Sylas Neville, recording a conversation with him on 11 February, noted that 'Mr Wilkes thinks that since they did not disqualify him immediately after the expulsion . . . after continuing his time in prison he will be suffered to sit'.[71] The administration decision to declare him incapable of election and still more the bestowal of this seat on Luttrell, gave his political career a boost for which he was duly grateful. On 20 June 1769 he commented to his French correspondent Suard, 'I look upon the violence of the House of Commons in favour of Luttrell as one of the luckiest circumstances of my life.'[72] The Middlesex Elections case was the launching-pad for the Wilkite success story of the next few years.

7

The Bill of Rights Society
1769–1771

THE Parliamentary opposition had exploited the Middlesex Elections case as a weapon against administration. Wilkes, a passive observer of this Westminster battle from his prison cell, had no intention of being a mere cat's-paw for the factions intent on toppling North after their success against Grafton. That he intended to distance himself from that political game was shown by a letter of 2 March 1770 to French correspondent Suard:

At present the Rockingham, Grenville and Shelburne packs are united, and hunt well, but I doubt their success, nor indeed do I wish it on their terms, for I foresee a damned aristocracy, which Wilkes must at all events destroy, or he will be annihilated. But mark, my dear friend, the political events of this summer, and you will find what a firm support I have in the people, and how truly I follow *their* interests. I am determined never to have any connection with this *court*, nor with any minister, yet I mean to be the most active man in this country, without personal pique, passion or resentment, sacrificing every thing to the public good.[1]

It might be thought that Wilkes was simply adopting a realistic attitude to a different political situation. His exile, and his behaviour during that period, meant that he no longer had contacts with the leading Parliamentary politicians, and any prospect of government office, even as ambassador or colonial governor, had certainly vanished. Wilkes had alienated Grafton and Chatham by his pamphlet attacks, although some adherents of Chatham's chief lieutenant Shelburne were to be among his London supporters in the next few years. His association with Temple had cooled since the dispute of 1767, and was finally broken by the quarrel of 1769 over Wilkes's pamphlet reply to Grenville's speech on his expulsion. His financial demands had exasperated the Rockingham party, and in any case their former contacts with him, George Onslow and William Fitzherbert, were now both government men. But in striking out on his own Wilkes was not merely adapting to circumstances. In an earlier letter he had already spelt out his radical credentials: 'I am against all Lords. How many Lords had Cromwell?'[2] He had every intention of causing trouble for government as soon as he was out of prison, confident that he would be a major force in politics. 'I never knew the Court so greatly embarrassed', he wrote to Suard on 10 November 1769. 'America and Ireland are both ungovernable. Then Wilkes at home growing greater every day, and all eyes fixed on him.'[3] Modesty was never one of his virtues, and government had now learned the painful lesson that the best way to deal with Wilkes was to ignore him, whatever the provocation, as indeed he himself soon surmised. 'I rather suspect that Wilkes is too troublesome a fellow for any of them to chuse to meddle with again', he wrote four days before his release from prison.[4] Ministerial persecution would not again give him the immediate national attention he had secured over the *North Briton* and the Middlesex election.

Wilkes could be confident that, however outrageous his conduct in word or deed, his past record and present popularity would now render him virtually immune from government reprisal. It had soon become obvious to contemporaries that, deprived of a seat in Parliament until the next general election, which might not occur before 1775, Wilkes would seek to make London his power base. This strategy was initiated while he was still in prison, and as early as 1 May 1770 he described himself to Suard as 'a patriotic Englishman, in the high road to the Mayoralty of London'.[5] But before his political career could be thus relaunched there was a practical problem to be solved, that of his financial predicament. By early 1769 it had become evident to his friends that Wilkes would have to be freed from debt if his release from the King's Bench was not to be followed by his immediate transfer to the debtor's prison of the Fleet. His expulsion from the House of Commons had deprived him of Parliamentary immunity in that respect, a deliberate ministerial tactic in the opinion of John Horne, who later asserted that Wilkes's debts had swollen from £6,000 in March 1768, when a public subscription to pay them off raised only £1,116, to £14,000 in February 1769. In addition there were the two fines of £500 to be paid before his release, his various election expenses, and the cost of his lavish maintenance in prison.[6] Although this financial plight had been caused mainly by personal extravagance, or so most contemporaries thought, much had also arisen out of Wilkes's political career, and so a good argument in principle reinforced the practical motive why this burden of debt should be lifted from his shoulders.

On 20 February 1769, only three days after Wilkes had been declared incapable of election for the current Parliament, a meeting of his supporters at the London Tavern, presided over by John Glynn, promptly subscribed £3,340 and resolved to establish an organization that would 'contribute, as far as lies in their power, to the independence and support of Mr Wilkes'.[7] Five days later, on 25 February, this was created under the title of 'Society of Gentlemen Supporters of the Bill of Rights', a name deliberately chosen, John Horne recalled, in order to express 'the *public* intentions' of the society, which disclaimed the role of being merely a club for Mr Wilkes; and, still further to prevent any such misapprehension, Horne was invited to draw up the following public advertisement:

Many Gentlemen, Members of Parliament and others, divested of every personal consideration, and unconnected with any Party, have formed themselves into a Society at the London Tavern, under the title of SUPPORTERS OF THE BILL OF RIGHTS. Their sole aim is to maintain and defend the legal constitutional liberty of the Subject. They mean to support Mr WILKES and his cause, as far as it is a public cause. For this purpose only they solicit the countenance and encouragement of the public, whose emolument and advantage alone are intended.[8]

This advertisement, naming five bankers to whom subscriptions could be sent, appeared over the name of the Society's Secretary Robert Morris, a Welsh barrister who practised on the South Wales Circuit.[9] The Treasurer was a Surrey landowner William Tooke; later Tooke was to promise his fortune to Horne, who in anticipation added the name of Tooke in 1782.[10] Horne himself was the driving-force behind the Society during its first year. An early friend of Dunning when both were law students, Horne had been directed into the Church by his father, who purchased for him the living of New Brentford in 1760, the year he was ordained. This clerical status prevented Horne himself from seeking election to Parliament, but politics was his career preference. Horne did not take up his clerical duties until 1767 and virtually abandoned them the next year, when he played a key role in winning support for Wilkes in Middlesex. Horne made it his constant endeavour to prevent the Bill of Rights Society becoming 'a mere benefit fund for John Wilkes'.[11] That issue was to be the cause of the Society's split in 1771, but the two men were altogether incompatible. Horne thought the frivolous and selfish Wilkes an unworthy champion of liberty. Wilkes constantly ridiculed the serious demeanour of Horne, alleging that he 'cast a gloom' over every company where he appeared.[12]

The founding members of the Bill of Rights Society were drawn from a surprising variety of social and political backgrounds, but nearly all were men of substance, as befitted the Society's financial purpose, for the most part landowners, lawyers, and merchants. Six were current MPs, three prominent in the Middlesex Elections campaign. Lawyer John Glynn was to be a faithful and invaluable ally of Wilkes. James Townsend, by a nice irony, had been returned for the government-controlled borough of West Looe as a Shelburne nominee. John Sawbridge, a wealthy Kent landowner, had entered Parliament in 1768 for the borough of Hythe, near his family estate. His sister was the famous radical historian Catherine Macaulay, and his father-in-law Sir William Stephenson, City Alderman and also a Society member. The three other MPs were the wealthy Southwark distiller Sir Joseph Mawbey, knighted by Rockingham in 1765 but now a Parliamentary champion of Wilkes; Sir Cecil Wray, a Lincolnshire squire sitting for East Retford; and Sir John Molesworth, MP for Cornwall. Past MPs included Sir Robert Bernard; old Sir William Baker, a City Alderman since 1739 and an American merchant recently in the inner circle of the Rockinghamite party; and the Sir Francis Delaval whose family interest at Berwick Wilkes had challenged in 1754. With a Parliamentary record of support for each and every ministry Delaval was never fully trusted by other Wilkites. Other prominent members, some soon to become MPs as the Wilkite bandwagon rolled, were the brothers-in-law Thomas and Richard Oliver, whose wealth derived from sugar plantations in Antigua; London merchant Samuel Vaughan and Dover merchant John Trevanion; Portsmouth lawyer George Bellas, Chairman of the Middlesex county meeting on 14 February; and Glamorgan squire Robert Jones of Fonmon Castle. The personal following of Wilkes himself included his brother Heaton and brother-in-law George Hayley, second husband of Mary, whose dowry to him had been her first husband's mercantile business; attorney John Reynolds and apothecary John Churchill. By the summer of 1769 membership was about a hundred, the largest known meeting being sixty, on 6 June.[13] Conspicuous by his absence was William Beckford, not a man inclined to play second fiddle to John Wilkes. His attitude to the Society was to be one of alliance, but only his death two months after the release of Wilkes from prison averted a struggle for the leadership of London's Radicals.

The zeal and efficiency displayed by the Wilkites in the Middlesex Elections campaigns were to be equally manifest in the organization and achievements of the Bill of Rights Society. It was at once decided that meetings would be fortnightly, on the second and fourth Tuesdays of each month, members assembling for dinner at four o'clock at the London Tavern, with a different Chairman on each occasion. Money was raised at each meeting, and nationwide subscriptions were invited by newspaper advertisements to be sent to any of four London banking houses. Within a few weeks various Committees were established, to deal with accounts, correspondence, and subscriptions. Committees met on the alternate Tuesdays when the full Society did not assemble, and also sat during the summer when the Society, like Parliament, went into recess.[14] Conscious that it would be widely

regarded as a subversive organization, the Society publicized a re
passed unanimously at its meeting of 7 March: 'That no Member
mitted, but those who are of known loyalty to his Majesty, and affe
his illustrious family, the intent of this Association being to maint
defend the Liberty of the Subject, and to support the laws and constitution
of this country.'[15] This declaration did not free the Society from suspicion.
The *Gazetteer* stated on 15 March that 'some particular persons' saw the Society as similar to the Convention of delegates at Boston in September 1768
rumoured to have been plotting armed resistance to Britain. That had
broken up on the arrival in the town of British soldiers, and 'it is said that the
same measures will be taken to dissolve and disperse them'.

The Society promptly tackled the Herculean task of settling Wilkes's
debts. The meeting of 7 March, chaired by Sawbridge, appointed a Committee to examine 'the state of Mr Wilkes's affairs'. He was voted £300 'for his
immediate use' and another £600 on 11 April.[16] Serjeant Glynn meanwhile
negotiated with various creditors to compound for personal and political
debts of Wilkes at 25 per cent, apparently cancelling £10,800 by this method.[17]
A progress report to the Society on 23 May stated that £4,170 had been paid
out on behalf of Wilkes to discharge 'some of his debts and his election expenses'. The Society had spent no other money except on advertisements.[18]
By the last general meeting of the Society before the summer recess, on
6 June, so Horne later claimed, £4,553 had been spent on the composition of
debts and the treasurers were authorized to pay a further £2,500 during the
summer.[19]

But the flow of subscriptions was slowing down. On 9 May the Society
decided upon a national appeal to sympathizers, establishing for that purpose a 'Committee of Correspondence and Subscriptions', chaired by Serjeant Glynn. Other members included Bellas, Horne, Sawbridge, Townsend,
and Vaughan. The meeting of 23 May resolved that this Committee should
prepare a circular letter, the draft of which was amended and approved on
6 June. It invited 'the friends of liberty throughout the whole British Empire
to concur in promoting the constitutional purposes for which this Society
was established'. The Committee would meet fortnightly until the Society
assembled on 10 October.[20] The circular letter, dated 20 July and signed by
Robert Morris, stated that fear of the precedent of an individual being
crushed by government had led to the formation of the Society, and then explained why the circular was being sent: 'Many friends of liberty at a distance, have expressed the most earnest wishes to concur with them, and to
give their assistance.' Numbered accompanying letters, addressed to individuals, asked them to organize subscriptions on behalf of Wilkes in their
own localities, and to transmit a list of donors with the money. The circular

was sent to various members of the Parliamentary opposition and to certain boroughs.[21] This insensitive approach, the brash assumption that all critics of government would publicly support Wilkes, may well have been counter-productive. The reaction of William Dowdeswell, in a letter to Edmund Burke on 10 August, probably typified that of many opposition MPs: 'Myself and several others have received the inclosed circular letter. I think of writing no answer. For if I do, I must find fault with the forwardness of Mr Morris.'[22] Scattered subscriptions did come from all over England, but Horace Walpole's opinion that the circular 'produced nothing' was not wide of the mark.[23]

That summer of 1769 simultaneously witnessed the nationwide petitioning movement over the Middlesex election. Individual members of the Society were especially concerned in the metropolitan area. They were prominent in organizing the Middlesex and London petitions presented to George III on 24 May and 5 July respectively. Both contained lists of grievances other than those relating to the Middlesex election, but a Surrey meeting of 26 June refused to adopt a similar broad attack on government drafted by Horne. There followed a change of tactic. The Westminster petition, produced by Robert Jones at a meeting of 29 August, boldly asked the King for a dissolution of Parliament, and so did a Southwark one instigated by Mawbey on 17 October. Other Bill of Rights Society men were active in organizing petitions in their home counties, such as Sawbridge in Kent, John Glynn in Devon, and Sir John Molesworth in Cornwall.[24]

By the autumn the Society's collective concern was again the Wilkes debt problem, to ensure that Wilkes would be able to leave prison when his sentence expired on 18 April 1770. He was meanwhile voted another £300 on 24 October 1769 for his current expenses. But Wilkes, despite the entreaties of Horne, refused to hand over to the Society any of the £4,000 he was awarded in damages against Lord Halifax at the end of 1769. Horne accepted that £1,200 went to pay John Reynolds legal fees, and £800 to discharge old Buckinghamshire militia debts, long a notorious blot on the Wilkes record; but he disbelieved the claim by Wilkes that the other £2,000 had also been paid to Reynolds '*on account* for law-charges and debt'.[25] Horne was already critical of the extravagant lifestyle enjoyed by Wilkes even in prison, and this episode marked the beginning of the quarrel between the two men that peaked in 1771.

Wilkes could afford to disregard what anybody thought of this behaviour, for the Bill of Rights Society was publicly committed to securing his release by paying off his debts. On 23 January 1770 the Society reaffirmed its determination to ensure that there would be 'no impediment to his enlargement from prison at the expiration of his sentence'.[26] A fortnight later, on

6 February, the Society received the welcome news of a grant of £1,500 from the Assembly of South Carolina. On 13 March detailed accounts were presented to the Society. Personal debts of Wilkes to the amount of £19,792 had been identified, of which £7,149 had been incurred by Wilkes standing surety for other persons! £14,346 had been compromised at a cost of £4,199. The Society had also given Wilkes £1,000 for his personal expenditure while in prison; paid the fine of £500 due in the previous April at the expiry of his first sentence; and had contributed £1,705 to the cost of his three Middlesex by-elections. Altogether £7,404 had been spent on behalf of Wilkes, and nothing for 'any other purpose whatever'. There remained the second fine of £500, together with £5,446 of debt.[27] It became a race against time, Lord Hardwicke being told by his brother John Yorke on 3 April that 'John Wilkes is not yet sure of his liberty on the 18th of this month as so much of his debt is still unpaid'.[28] Wilkes himself remained confident of the outcome, writing on 10 April that 18 April would 'certainly see me a freed man. A free man you know I have ever been and will remain.'[29] But by a Society meeting that day only a further £946 had been subscribed, and it was decided to make a public appeal for funds and call a special meeting for 14 April. That merely authorized the payment of the second £500 fine, but at a final meeting on 17 April £2,201 was reported as cash in hand. Enough was done to satisfy the remaining creditors, and Wilkes was quietly released that evening to avoid disturbance the next day.[30] It was stated in the press that £3,195 was still owing on 24 April, when the Society's balance was only £250.[31]

John Wilkes was now free to embark on the take-over of the City of London as his power base. The democratic structure of the City government afforded the opportunity for such a popular hero to win control there. The 7,000 liverymen not only constituted the Parliamentary electorate: at Midsummer they elected the two sheriffs who served for Middlesex as well as London, and also chose various other City officials; at Michaelmas they elected two candidates for the Mayoralty, the final choice being with the Court of Aldermen; the latter were elected for life, one for each of the twenty-six wards, as occasion arose; and in December each year the Livery elected 236 of their number to serve with the Aldermen in the Court of Common Council, acknowledged as the City's representative body. In their manipulation of this corporate structure the Wilkites were to defy conventions. Notably they disregarded the custom of seniority in appointments. Political allegiance replaced affluence and respectability in the choice of Lord Mayors, Aldermen, and sheriffs, as propaganda, enthusiasm, and, so opponents said, intimidation enabled Wilkes and his supporters to dominate the Livery for several years. Special meetings of both the Common Council and the Common Hall of Livery were summoned for purposes of political propaganda, to vote instructions to MPs and petitions or remonstrances to the King.

Wilkes had already secured election as an Alderman while in prison. As early as April 1768 there was public speculation that he would stand for the first Aldermanic vacancy.[32] None occurred for nine months, and then Wilkes contested the Ward of Farringdon Without on 2 January 1769 with a Thomas Bromwich; described as 'a paper-hanger, by appointment to his Majesty', Bromwich may have been a ministerial candidate. He polled 69 votes as against 255 for Wilkes.[33] John Horne had organized the campaign for Wilkes, who had announced that he would seek to improve navigation of the Thames by demolition and reconstruction of London Bridge. Press comments on his success already forecast that he would be Lord Mayor within five years.[34] But on 24 January the hostile Court of Aldermen invalidated the election on a technicality, an announcement by Lord Mayor Samuel Turner before the poll that it would be continued a second day. Wilkes was re-elected without opposition three days later.[35] Next the Court of Aldermen, on 7 February, took official notice of Wilkes's imprisonment and sought legal advice as to his eligibility. Five of eight counsel ruled in favour of Wilkes, and the Court of Aldermen made no further challenge to his election.[36]

This success of Wilkes might be deemed a personal triumph, but events later in 1769 confirmed the growth of Wilkite power in the City. James Townsend and John Sawbridge both became Aldermen, on 23 June and 1 July respectively. On 24 June the two men were also elected sheriffs, at the Common Hall of the Livery that voted a petition on the Middlesex election after the Common Council on 5 May had ordered Lord Mayor Turner not to call a meeting for that purpose.[37] More success followed at Michaelmas with the election of William Beckford as Lord Mayor, in defiance of the custom of seniority by rota and in despite of the fact that Beckford had already served in that office, from 1762 to 1763. Although Beckford had kept aloof from the Bill of Rights Society, its members perceived that he was the only Radical likely to succeed. At the poll he won by 1,967 votes, as against 1,911 for Rockinghamite Barlow Trecothick and 676 for courtier Sir Henry Bankes, who should have been chosen on seniority. Beckford, reluctant to serve through age and infirmity, was disposed to urge the Court of Aldermen to choose Trecothick; but he was persuaded to accept at a Bill of Rights Society meeting he attended on 10 October.[38] Wilkite approval was publicly signified by the attendance at his Mayoral dinner on 9 November of Polly Wilkes, who, so her father was told, was 'prodigiously huzza'd by the whole people'.[39] But the Bill of Rights Society did not yet dominate the City political scene. Frederick Bull, a member associated with Wilkes, was defeated by 143 votes to 92 when standing for Alderman of Broad Street Ward in

December. The result led to premature speculation among Parliamentary politicians that the Wilkite cause was dead, especially when it was followed by apathy at the Common Council elections soon afterwards.[40]

The high-profile Mayoralty of Beckford was therefore a timely and invaluable boost to the radical cause in London. He used his wealth for lavish entertainments calculated to consolidate and maintain opposition to the new ministry of Lord North. These culminated in a great dinner at the Mansion House on 22 March 1770, attended not merely by City politicians but by virtually the whole Parliamentary opposition.[41] By then the City Radicals had launched a campaign of Remonstrances, upbraiding the King for his disregard of the petitioning campaign of 1769. After a Common Council vote on 1 March of 112 to 76 in favour of the proposal, Beckford duly summoned a Common Hall of the Livery on 6 March. The meeting approved a Remonstrance that condemned the continuance of the existing Parliament as illegal because of the Middlesex Elections decision, and ordered its formal presentation in the name of the City. It was duly presented to George III on 14 March by the Lord Mayor and only four Aldermen, Sawbridge, Stephenson, Townsend, and Trecothick, accompanied by 153 members of the Common Council and a deputation of the Livery. The King's reply described the Remonstrance as 'disrespectful to me, injurious to Parliament, and irreconcilable to the principles of the constitution'.[42] Indignation in the House of Commons was reflected in a motion condemning the Remonstrance, proposed on 19 March by an independent MP, Sir Thomas Clavering, who had voted against administration over the Middlesex election, and carried by the overwhelming majority of 284 votes to 127.[43]

Undeterred by this reception of the City Remonstrance, metropolitan Radicals organized others from Westminster and Middlesex before the end of March.[44] The City even voted a second Remonstrance, presented on 23 May, Wilkes having been on the drafting Committee. George III replied that his opinion was unaltered, adding that it would be an abuse of his prerogative to dissolve Parliament as requested. Beckford then had the audacity to reprimand the King to his face, deferentially requesting that 'you will not dismiss us from your presence without expressing a more favourable opinion of your faithful citizens, and without some comfort, without some prospect at least of redress'.[45]

Wilkes made no challenge to this ascendancy of Beckford at the time of his release from prison. Doubtless aware of the Mayor's poor health, he could bide his time, and the public relationship of the two men was one of mutual esteem. In his Address to his City Ward on 18 April Wilkes referred to 'so excellent a chief magistrate'.[46] Beckford, for his part, went in procession on 24 April from the Mansion House to the Guildhall to swear in Wilkes as

Alderman. He was attended by only six Aldermen, Ladbroke, Turner, Stephenson, and Trecothick, together with sheriffs Townsend and Sawbridge; but there was 'the greatest concourse of people ever known on any like occasion' to see Wilkes, who was 'dressed in a suit of black full trimmed'.[47] The respect Wilkes displayed for Beckford was genuine, for when informing daughter Polly of his death on 21 June Wilkes commented that 'he had of late behaved with spirit and honour in the cause of liberty, and was of singular service to what we all have the most at heart'.[48] He could afford to be generous, for the Lord Mayor's death had cleared the way for Wilkite dominance of the City.

Wilkes had adopted a low political profile even with respect to the ministry, apart from an Address to the electors of Middlesex in which he claimed that 'the measure of my expulsion and incapacity was previously settled in the cabinet, and only brought to Parliament by the minister in order to go through the common forms'. Even then he gave the assurance that 'I have no malicious revenge to gratify. I feel no passion, but that of gratitude to my friends, and my only enemies shall be those of my country.'[49] It was Wilkes who had requested the quiet release from prison in the evening before he was due to be freed, 'to avoid the people'. Nearby Southwark was illuminated at once, but London and Westminster not until the following night, many houses then displaying blue candles.[50] Next day Horace Walpole depicted the episode to Sir Horace Mann as an anticlimax:

The day so much apprehended of Wilkes's enlargement is passed without mischief. He was released late the night before last, and set out directly for the country. Last night several shops and private houses were illuminated, from affection, or fear of their windows, but few of any distinction, except the Duke of Portland's. Falling among the drunkenness of Easter week, riots were the more to be expected, yet none happened. Great pains had been taken to station constables, and the Light Horse were drawn nearer to town in case of emergency. The Lord Mayor had enjoined tranquillity—as Mayor. As Beckford, his own house in Soho Square was embroidered with 'Liberty', in white letters three feet high. Luckily the evening was very wet, and not a mouse stirred.[51]

Wilkes returned to London within a few days and set about obtaining a house. It so happened that Sir Edward Astley was just vacating the one Wilkes had previously occupied, but nothing came of discussions between the two men, and Wilkes took a fourteen-year lease on a smaller house nearby, off Prince's Court, Westminster, at fifty guineas a year. It is probable that Wilkes was now unable to afford his old house. His personal estate would seem to have survived the bankruptcy of Cotes, who had robbed him only of the income and other ready money: but although the gross income from his estate was £700, £200 was payable to his wife under their separation agreement, and an annuity of £150 to Reynolds, purchased for £1,000.[52] The Bill of Rights Society now planned to complete his financial rehabilitation by clearing his debts and buying for him an annuity of £600. This, Horne anticipated, could be accomplished by March 1771. That was an optimistic assessment, for Wilkes constantly demanded ready money and incurred new debts, faster, Horne later commented, than old debts could be discharged.[53] The financial problems of Wilkes were to divide the ranks of London's Radicals within a year: but meanwhile, despite personal antipathies and political quarrels, they contrived to fight together for 'liberty'.

Wilkes at first took little part in this activity, although he was formally elected to the Bill of Rights Society on 8 May and thanked the members for their support on 22 May.[54] He informed his French friend Suard that he did not even enjoy the social celebrations of his new freedom: for on 1 May he professed to be 'jaded with visitors and dinners. I abominate a great dinner, and all the good cheer of the Aldermen is lost upon me.' Wilkes took seriously his new duties as Ward Alderman and City magistrate. 'I held my first Wardmote yesterday. . . . The applause was prodigious. I have not yet been at any place of public diversion, nor visited a single lord. I have drudged through the vast arrear of City business.'[55] His quiet demeanour puzzled Horace Walpole. 'I don't know whether Wilkes is subdued by his imprisonment', he wrote to Mann on 6 May, '. . . or whether his dignity of Alderman has dulled him into prudence, and the love of feasting; but hitherto he has done nothing but go to City banquets and sermons, and sit at Guildhall as a sober magistrate.'[56]

Wilkes was not a man to stir himself unless he saw some personal advantage or perceived some public cause to champion, and during the summer of 1770 he lacked such incentives: instead he made a rural tour with his daughter Polly when she returned from a visit she had made to Paris to attend the Dauphin's wedding.[57] It was an irony that two metropolitan Parliamentary seats became vacant, for Wilkes had publicly stated in 1769 that he could not stand for Parliament, being already the legal member for Middlesex.[58] On 21 April one of Westminster's MPs, Edwin Sandys, succeeded to his father's peerage. 'Wilkes will not stand himself, adhering to his pretensions for Middlesex,' wrote Walpole, 'but may name whom he pleases.'[59] It was immediately understood that Sir Robert Bernard would be this candidate. Edmund Burke commented to the Duke of Portland that 'perhaps the thing most to be wished is, that Wilkes should stand; that is what would thoroughly distress administration'. Failing that, Burke thought that the best tactic would be to give public support to Bernard, for that would show that he was not the candidate of 'the mere clubs of tradesmen': and William Dowdeswell was one of Bernard's sponsors at a nomination meeting on

24 April.[60] George III had already advised his Prime Minister not to 'occasion a tumult in this City by encouraging a contest'.[61] Bernard was returned unopposed on 30 April, when he demonstrated his radical credentials in his acceptance speech by promising to work for 'equal and true representation of the people' as well as for the older country programme of Place Bills and Shorter Parliaments.[62]

The other by-election was for Beckford's London seat. His death had created vacancies also for the Lord Mayoralty and an Aldermanship. It so happened that the Midsummer meeting of the Common Hall of Livery took place on the following day, 22 June. A show of hands for the Mayoralty favoured Rockinghamite Trecothick and Wilkite Brass Crosby, but a poll was demanded for Sir Henry Bankes. This closed on 29 June with Trecothick on 1,601 votes, Crosby 1,434 and Bankes 437. Trecothick was chosen by the Court of Aldermen the same day.[63] Two other Rockinghamite MPs had been elected sheriffs at the Common Hall without a contest, Joseph Martin, who had spoken up for Wilkes in the Commons, and William Baker, son and heir of Sir William, who had died in January.[64] The Parliamentary seat was reserved for a Bill of Rights Society man. After George Bellas declined nomination as either MP or Alderman, Thomas Oliver became the Society's candidate; but illness caused his later withdrawal in favour of Richard Oliver, who was elected both MP and Alderman without opposition. In his Parliamentary acceptance speech on 10 July he made the same political pledges as Bernard.[65] This Wilkite alliance with the Rockinghamite party was uneasy and temporary. In a letter of 6 August, published in the *London Evening Post* on 6 September, Robert Morris denounced 'the great leaders of Parliamentary opposition' for having failed to support Wilkes: 'I shall look upon them as interested men, more studious to do themselves good, than their country.'[66] That Trecothick would at the Michaelmas election lose the prized Lord Mayoralty to a Wilkite seems to have been taken for granted. Newspapers during September do not discuss his retention of that office, the only challenge anticipated being one again from Sir Henry Bankes. He did not, however, force a poll when Brass Crosby and James Townsend were acclaimed as candidates by the Livery on 29 September, and the Court of Aldermen the same day selected Crosby. He was formally sworn in as Lord Mayor on 8 November.[67]

Those last weeks of Trecothick's Mayoralty saw him clash with the Wilkites over an issue that occasioned the return of Wilkes himself to an active political role. Spain's seizure of the British base of Port Egmont in the Falkland Islands opened up the prospect of war in late 1770, and the Admiralty issued warrants to press men in the streets of London, which within the City needed the backing of a magistrate. These warrants authorized the seizure for service in the navy of men not named. There was an obvious analogy to make, Robert Morris writing to Wilkes on 27 October that 'it rests upon no better footing than general warrants. All the usage in the world would not have made *them* legal, as the Judges declared, and I don't see why the same might not be said of press warrants.'[68] In the event Wilkes and his allies resorted to practical obstruction rather than a legal challenge. Trecothick had co-operated with the Admiralty by providing lists of City constables, whose assistance was necessary to authorize any such action in London. He informed a Court of Common Council of his decision when questioned by Wilkes on 12 October, adding the palliative that City freemen, and their servants, were to be exempt. Wilkes commented that 'there was now a suspension of Magna Carta in the City by their chief Magistrate', quoting the Latin text of that document. The Common Council signified its displeasure by transferring the City's legal business from the official Recorder, James Eyre, to John Glynn, who was to be elected formally to that post in 1772.[69]

Trecothick himself, anxious to redress his blunder, then virtually established the immunity from seizure of 'mechanics, and other working people' by correspondence with the Admiralty that elicited the assurance on 26 October that only seamen should be impressed. He implemented this by insisting that the City constables should not hand over any men to the navy before they had been examined by a magistrate. On 29 October Trecothick released men brought before him, six out of nine, and Wilkes, Oliver, and Sawbridge were among other magistrates that did the same.[70] But the liberty of the subject had to be balanced, in the scales of popularity, against the needs of the navy, and Wilkes had already on 12 October suggested bounties to aid recruitment. As soon as Crosby became Mayor he went to see Chatham, on 10 November. Chatham forthrightly condemned the obstruction of the press warrants, and next day Serjeant Glynn went to visit him, making a most favourable impression. 'I find him a most ingenious, solid, pleasing man, and the spirit of the constitution itself', Chatham wrote. 'I never was more taken by a first conversation in my life.'[71] The evident outcome of these consultations with the political oracle was the decision of the Common Council on 15 November to offer for the next month additional bounties of £2 or £1 for seamen who voluntarily signed on at the Guildhall for naval service.[72] The controversy died down when the Falkland Islands Crisis was resolved without a war in January 1771.[73]

This episode, in its deployment of City privileges, anticipated the spectacular quarrel of 1771 with the House of Commons over Parliamentary reporting. Ironically that great triumph of London radicalism took place at the very time when the Bill of Rights Society finally split asunder. Hardly had the Society been formed before animosity between Wilkes and Horne was being reported in the press.[74] It was a clash of principles as well as person-alities. Wilkes conceived of the Society in personal terms. Its sole functions were the payment of his debts and the redress of specific grievances relating to his career. But the Society had attracted men of zeal, ambition, and sub-stance, notably Sir Robert Bernard, John Sawbridge, James Townsend, and Richard Oliver. They intended to make the Society a radical organization, concerned not only with traditional opposition demands for Place Bills and Shorter Parliaments, but also with such forward-looking measures as elect-oral reform, and current issues like American grievances over taxation. These men, among whom John Horne was the driving force, included the majority of those Society members who were MPs and City Aldermen. Horne and his allies saw themselves as genuine and altruistic reformers, de-voting time, effort, and finance to radical causes, and they regarded Wilkes as egocentric, a man who relished the attention and money bestowed on him, and who judged political matters solely by the criteria of his reputation and his purse. That was an unfair judgement, as later events would demon-strate: but the behaviour of Wilkes during 1769 and 1770 did provide much evidence to support it.

While Wilkes remained in the King's Bench Prison this tension did not develop into open confrontation. Horne within the Society and Beckford in the City directed radical activities, which in any case were chiefly concerned with payment of Wilkes's debts and redress of his grievances. But from April 1770 Wilkes was free, with the bulk of his debts paid, and with no prospect of reviving the issue of the Middlesex Elections. His assumptions as to the pur-pose of the Bill of Rights Society seemed increasingly implausible and came under challenge from Horne and his supporters. An early sign that all was not well came with the resignation of Society Secretary Robert Morris on 6 August: ostensibly this was because he had expected the post to rotate among members and was finding it burdensome, but he also stated that 'the cause of Mr Wilkes, as an injured and persecuted individual, has been the first and hitherto the only motive of my appearing in publick'.[75] His replace-ment, on 27 November, was an adherent of Horne, Thomas Boddington.[76]

Matters initially came to a head at a stormy interview between Wilkes and Horne on 28 October. Wilkes pressed for ready money rather than payment of his remaining debts, voicing what Horne claimed was his invariably cavalier attitude to personal debts: 'He urged to me his old argument, which he has often repeated to many people, that "those who do pay make amends for those who do not, and that tradesmen always charge accordingly." ' When Horne remained adamant in his refusal to comply with the demand, Wilkes angrily said 'that if he was to be treated so, it was plain the Society had only made a *decoy-duck* of his name, and that he was used only as an *instrument*'.[77]

Part of this quarrel concerned what tactic to adopt at a meeting of Westminster freeholders called for 31 October. Wilkes persuaded a Bill of Rights Society meeting on 30 October that a motion should then be put to instruct the Westminster MPs to impeach Prime Minister Lord North. Wilkes chaired the Westminster meeting, only to find the proposal opposed by John Sawbridge, who argued that impeachment was an archaic procedure and impractical when North controlled both Houses of Parliament. Sawbridge successfully moved instead for a Remonstrance calling for the dissolution of Parliament, much to the chagrin of Wilkes, whose private opinion was that such a document would be 'only another paper kite' for the young Prince of Wales. Bernard, reputably refusing to kneel, presented this on 7 November to George III, who received a similar City one from Lord Mayor Crosby on 21 November.[78]

This public rebuff to Wilkes was followed by a newspaper war, as Horne tried to rub salt into his wounds and Wilkites returned the abuse, as in this charge that Horne owed all his importance to Wilkes: 'The life of Mr Horne began, as I understand, about four years ago, when he was produced to the world as the friend of Mr Wilkes, and, as such, received a degree of public countenance and favour, which his merit or abilities would never have entitled him to.'[79] Simultaneously there commenced the final power struggle within the Society.[80] On 11 December Horne carried against Wilkite opposition a motion that the £744 remaining of the debts owing at the release of Wilkes on 17 April should be compounded at 50 per cent by Richard Oliver, now Society Treasurer. Horne was evidently anxious to settle that matter so that the Society could pursue a more constructive policy. But later that month the Society was faced with a demand for £600 from Lauchlin Macleane, who had lent Wilkes £1,000 in Paris but was now himself in financial difficulties: the sum requested was the balance outstanding after Macleane had cancelled £400 on the formation of the Society.[81] Wilkes responded by packing the next Society meeting, on 22 January 1771, with members who had seldom attended before. Resolutions were passed, by 24 votes to 18, that the Macleane debts should be given a priority claim on the Society's funds; that a new subscription be opened to discharge all debts of Wilkes outstanding in February 1769; and, by a majority of 23 to 12, as a final snub to Horne's party, that the conduct of Wilkes since his release from prison had been 'such as merits the approbation of the Society'.[82] Horne subtly counter-attacked at the next meeting, on 12 February, by a motion assuming that the Society's objectives extended beyond support of Wilkes: for he successfully proposed an immediate subscription to raise £500 for William Bingley, a printer imprisoned since November 1768 for contempt of court arising out of a political libel case.[83] Wilkes, absent on that occasion, took care to attend the next meeting on 26 February, when his supporters passed these two motions:

That the first object of this Society, in order to promote the public purposes of its institution, was to support JOHN WILKES Esq. against ministerial oppression, by discharging his debts, and rendering him independent.

That this Society having resolved, that the public conduct of John Wilkes, Esq. has continued such as merited their approbation, and not having as yet fully accomplished their declared purpose of discharging his debts, no new subscriptions shall, for the future be opened in this Society for any other purpose whatever, until all the debts of John Wilkes Esq.; which shall appear to have been bona fide due at the time of the formulation of this Society, and have already been given in to any Committee or general meeting thereof, shall be fully discharged or compromised.[84]

This endorsement of the Wilkite view of the Society appeared to signify Horne's final defeat. But the battle was not yet over. Horne, in order to assert the wider purposes he thought the Society should pursue, switched his point of attack by seeking to exploit the dispute over the reporting of Parliamentary debates which was then being waged between the House of Commons and the City of London. On 12 March the Society postponed consideration of this matter until its next meeting on 9 April; but the Horne faction persuaded Secretary Thomas Boddington to convene a special meeting on 19 March. Horne was among twenty-four members present, as were some Wilkites, one of whom, Robert Jones, handed in a written protest about the invalidity of the meeting, signed by Wilkes and fifteen other members. The meeting nevertheless proceeded to conduct business, voting £100 each to the three printers most directly concerned in the defiance of Parliament.[85] That decision was confirmed by the meeting of 9 April, but acrimony over the extraordinary meeting soon developed into an altercation between Wilkes and Horne, who then moved for the dissolution of the Society. With James Townsend in the Chair this was defeated only by 26 votes to 24, the Wilkite majority including Robert Jones, Frederick Bull, James Adair, Robert Morris, and American Arthur Lee.[86] The Horne faction promptly seceded to form the new Constitutional Society. But members of both factions co-operated in the ongoing contest with the House of Commons over Parliamentary reporting.

8

The Reporting of Parliamentary Debates: The Wilkes Coup of 1771

THE *causes célèbres* of the *North Briton* and the Middlesex Elections have over-shadowed the triumph of John Wilkes in establishing the freedom of the press to report Parliamentary debates. Yet, in contrast to those hard-fought battles over freedom from arrest and the rights of electors, Wilkes in 1771 achieved an immediate success in what has often been known as 'the Printers' Case'.[1] The episode highlighted an implicit contradiction in contemporary interpretations of the constitution. Although Parliament's moral authority derived from its representative nature, the great majority of MPs were un-willing to acknowledge direct personal responsibility to the electorate, whether their own constituents or the wider political nation. This attitude was encapsulated in the declaration of young Charles James Fox that 'he knew nothing of the people, but through the medium of their representat-ives there assembled'.[2]

The reporting of Parliamentary debates had therefore hitherto been re-peatedly and successfully suppressed by direct action of both Houses of Parliament.[3] Despite the political excitement caused in the earlier 1760s by such events as the Peace of Paris, the *North Briton* case, and the Stamp Act Crisis, no periodical ventured then to report the proceedings in Parlia-ment. The successful challenge to this censorship owed much to Wilkes, in a double sense. He masterminded the tactical coup: and the episode itself resulted from the greater public interest in politics generated by the Middle-sex Elections case. The years from 1768 witnessed a significant expansion of the metropolitan press, until by the middle of 1770 there were being published in London at least five daily, eight thrice-weekly, and four weekly papers. Notable among the newcomers was the *Middlesex Journal or*

Chronicle of Liberty, a thrice-weekly founded on 4 April 1769 by William Beckford.[4]

To contemporaries, however, the outstanding feature of the political press during these years was not the cautious and slow development of Parliamentary reporting but the polemical writing, in the daily *Public Advertiser*, of the anonymous Junius. His polished, sardonic attacks on government and individual ministers began on 21 November 1768 with this brief stab at Grafton and Camden, even before the ministerial decision to expel Wilkes: 'Other men have been abandoned by their friends. Mr Wilkes alone is oppressed by them.'[5] During 1769 there was a widespread belief that Junius was Wilkes himself, writing from the King's Bench Prison. This assumption tickled his vanity. 'Would to Heaven I could have written them' was his reputed reply when accused of being the author.[6] That idea was killed by the publication on 19 December 1769 of *Letter XXXV* addressed by Junius to the King. 'The opinion that Wilkes was Junius has been very general', Thomas Whately wrote then to George Grenville, 'but the Junius of today will, I think, destroy the supposition.'[7] That letter is replete with scorn for the popular hero: 'Mr Wilkes brought with him into politics the same liberal sentiments, by which his private conduct has been directed, and seemed to think, that, as there are few excesses, in which an English gentleman may not be permitted to indulge, the same latitude was allowed him in the choice of his political principles, and in the spirit of maintaining them.' Junius advised the King that the best way to deal with Wilkes would be a contemptuous pardon: 'He will soon fall back into his natural station—a silent senator, and hardly supporting the weekly eloquence of a newspaper.'[8]

The contemporary attention given to Junius owed as much to the mystery of his identity as to the power of his prose. If the author had been known to be War Office clerk Philip Francis the writings would have attracted far less attention: and, in truth, their political significance was no more than a propaganda contribution to the fall of the Grafton ministry.[9] In retrospect the significant press development of that time can be seen as the beginning of Parliamentary reporting in the newspapers. John Almon, in the role of journalist rather than printer, later claimed the credit for this initiative:

When the spirit of the nation was raised high by the massacre in St. George's Fields, the unjust decision upon the Middlesex election, etc., Mr Almon resolved to make the nation acquainted with the proceedings of Parliament: for this purpose he employed himself sedulously in obtaining from different gentlemen, by conversation at his own house and sometimes at their houses, sufficient information to write a sketch of every day's debate, on the most important and interesting questions; which he printed three times a week regularly in the *London Evening Post*.

... During two sessions, this practice of printing sketches of the debates continued, without any notice being taken; and Mr Almon furnished them constantly, from the best information he could obtain. Though they were short they were in general pretty accurate, and their accuracy was perhaps the cause of the printer's security.[10]

The immunity from Parliamentary prosecution led other newspapers and the monthly magazines to follow Almon's example. Gradually the press cast caution aside and abandoned early brief sketches and disguised reports in favour of ostensibly full and increasingly inaccurate accounts of debates. By early 1771 over a dozen papers, daily, thrice-weekly, or weekly, were publishing Parliamentary reports.[11] The initiative to stop this practice was thought by London's Radicals to have come from George III himself. In a public letter to Wilkes on 10 July 1771 John Horne gave this account of what he had told the Bill of Rights Society meeting of 26 February:

Mr Horne observed, that he had some small time since received information from an authority which he could not doubt, that a certain great personage had conversed with the elder Onslow at St James's near half an hour; that in that conversation it was mentioned to Mr Onslow as matter of surprise, that the House of Commons permitted their debates to be published; and it was asked, if it was ever suffered before, and why something was not done to prevent it? This question from such a person was well understood to be an order.

George Onslow of the Treasury Board, that erstwhile friend of Wilkes, was 'the elder Onslow' to whom the King had allegedly spoken: but it was his cousin, Colonel George Onslow, who 'soon after' moved in the House of Commons on 5 February that a 1729 order of the House prohibiting the publication of debates should be read. Horne claimed responsibility for then inserting in the *Middlesex Journal* for 7 February this provocatively insulting comment: 'It was reported, that a scheme was at last hit upon by the ministry, to prevent the public from being informed of their iniquity; accordingly, on Tuesday last, little *cocking* George Onslow made a motion, that an order against printing debates should be read.'[12] There followed a report of the ensuing debate. This item was reprinted next day by the *Gazetteer*, but without the offensive reference to Onslow. This precaution did not prevent a motion by Colonel Onslow that afternoon for its printer Roger Thompson to attend the House of Commons on 11 February together with John Wheble of the *Middlesex Journal*. The two Onslows had beforehand approached Speaker Norton for assistance; but, so Colonel Onslow told James Harris a year later, 'he contemptuously clapt his hand on his backside and said "No, Damme if I do." '[13]

Colonel Onslow, who told the House that he had not given prior notice of his previous action to Prime Minister Lord North, complained not of

Parliamentary reporting as such but of the two newspapers as 'misrepresenting the speeches and reflecting on several of the Members of this House'. In the ensuing debate Alderman Trecothick spoke in favour of Parliamentary reporting, arguing that the public had the right to be informed of debates. William Dowdeswell also urged that the votes and speeches of MPs should be made public: otherwise, he asked, what was the purpose of having elections? His Rockinghamite colleague Edmund Burke was more cautious. He did not oppose the standing orders of the House, but questioned the prudence of enforcing them and opined that speeches could be published after the session. Other opposition speakers also doubted the wisdom of any attempt to prevent reporting, but the arguments of misrepresentation and of the threat to freedom of debate prevailed, Onslow's motion being carried by 90 votes to 55 in a thin House.[14]

Months later, in the *Middlesex Journal* of 24 October, Wheble stated that after this summons he was introduced to John Horne, who instructed him to disobey it; and, if he afterwards lost his nerve, authorized him to declare Horne to be both the author of the offending paragraph and the instigator of his defiance.[15] Wheble accordingly did not attend the Commons on 11 February, when pressure of business caused the House to postpone the orders for the printers until 14 February, and again on that day until 19 February. Wheble never attended at all. Thompson was present on 11 February, but afterwards joined Wheble in his defiance. When on 19 February both printers were found to be absent, the Commons' messenger was called in, and he gave evidence that orders had been served for their attendance only on 11 February. Fresh orders were then issued for the printers to attend on 21 February. On that day they were again given the benefit of the little doubt that remained; but the order for their attendance on 26 February was accompanied by another order that leaving a copy of a summons at the party's last place of abode would be deemed equal to personal service. Sterner action at last came on 26 February, when Lord of the Treasury George Onslow moved that Wheble should be taken into the custody of the Serjeant at Arms for his contempt. The feeling of members that the authority of the House had to be vindicated was shown by the majority for the motion of 160 votes to 17. A similar order was then made for Thompson.[16] The very small minority, however, had included nearly all the leaders in the Commons of the two main opposition parties headed by Rockingham and Chatham: this salutary experience was to make them cautious in future criticisms of the measures against reporting.[17]

John Wilkes chanced to be away from London early in February, but on his return snatched the initiative from Horne. Wheble later recalled how he had succumbed to incessant pressure from Wilkes, after Horne had refused to disclose what, if any, plan he had in mind.[18] There was, by contrast, soon very little secret about the bold scheme Wilkes concerted with John Almon and Robert Morris. It was a deliberate attempt to pit against the power of the House of Commons the privileges of the City of London, which claimed an exclusive right under its charters to all jurisdiction within its boundaries. Wilkes and his confederates realized that proceedings were not likely to be confined to two newspapers. Rather than rely on Wheble, with his Horne links, they chose to make use of their own man, John Miller, printer of the *London Evening Post*. A plan was therefore devised, to await the time when Miller should become the subject of complaint.[19] Wilkes, in his capacity as Alderman, would be able to act as a City magistrate, and the support was obtained of other City officials, among them Lord Mayor Brass Crosby. Secrecy was perhaps not intended, and certainly proved impossible. By the middle of February it was widely known that some scheme involving the privileges of the City was afoot. Lord Chatham was informed on 18 February by Isaac Barré, and they persuaded Sawbridge and Townsend to take no part.[20] Lord North, too, heard that resistance was being planned in the City, and on 20 February warned George III that some Aldermen might prevent the arrest of the printers. The King replied next day that he had 'very much considered the affair of the printers that is now coming before the House. I do in the strongest manner recommend that every caution may be used to prevent its becoming a serious affair.' George III then suggested that a confrontation might be avoided if the Commons officials deliberately failed to find the printers. It was not that the King meant to back down, for he declared that 'it is highly necessary that this strange and lawless method of publishing debates in the papers should be put a stop to'. What George III suggested was recourse to the greater powers of the House of Lords, 'as a Court of Record the best Court to bring such miscreants before, as it can fine as well as imprison; and as the Lords have broader shoulders to support any schism that this salutary measure may occasion in the minds of the vulgar.'[21]

This royal idea was impractical, for the Commons could not now abandon the course of action on which the King himself, if Horne had been correctly informed, had launched it. The North ministry was powerless to avoid the trap set by Wilkes. On 4 March the House's Deputy Serjeant at Arms John Clementson reported that he had failed to find either Wheble or Thompson, and his account made it clear there had been deliberate evasion. Colonel Onslow therefore moved for an Address to the King 'that he will be graciously pleased to issue his royal proclamation for apprehending the said John Wheble and R. Thompson, with a promise of reward for the same'. The motion passed without a word being said.[22] A proclamation, offering a reward of £50 for the arrest of each of the delinquents, duly appeared in the *London Gazette* of 9 March.

Despite this impasse over Wheble and Thompson the ministry responded to royal pressure and Parliamentary indignation by supporting Colonel Onslow when on 12 March he announced to the Commons his intention of extending his campaign:

If it is right to have the speeches printed, it would be right to employ two clerks to take them down, that they may not be misrepresented. . . . [It is] nonsense to have these rules and orders, and not put them in execution. I have three brace—Woodfall of the *Morning Chronicle*, Baldwin of the *St. James's Chronicle*, Evans of the *London Packet*, Wright of the *Whitehall Evening Post*, Bladon of the *General Evening Post*, and Miller of the *London Evening Post*.[23]

Onslow's first motion was carried after a heated debate by 140 votes to 43. Thereafter the opponents of his measures resorted to deliberate obstruction. Although the minority seldom numbered more than a dozen, the House was forced to divide on twenty-three occasions, and it was five o'clock on the next morning before the six printers had been ordered to attend on 14 March.[24]

Events now moved rapidly towards a crisis. The House of Commons had played into the hands of John Wilkes and his allies. A brief glimpse of their activity is provided in a letter of 13 March from Robert Morris to Wilkes himself:

I have been all this day upon the wing about the business of the printers and hitherto unable to call upon you, agreeable to my inclinations. I would not have the affair sleep for the universe. The ministry take care it shall not on their side; we must therefore be staunch on ours. You know what they proceeded to yesterday. Some of the six newly ordered to attend, I believe make their appearance tomorrow at the House—those are Bladon (Gen. Evg.), Wright (Whitehall) and possible Evans (L. Pack). There will be business new for all of us; and each must have his share. Different games must be played. But if we can, we must take into our assistance some more of the Aldermen; and I hope also we shall have the Sheriffs.[25] Messengers may yet be sent to Newgate, and printers lodged there be let out. I saw Wheble and Thompson Tuesday. The direct opposite of each other in patience; and the hasty one is the former. I gave your message to the latter. He thanks you, as he has much reason, for your alacrity to serve him; though I know it is also to serve the public. You have too great a regard for that consideration, ever to alter in your conduct from paltry jealousies. . . .[26]

But, apart from Miller, the other printers proved unwilling to defy Parliament. When the Commons met on 14 March, four out of the six newly summoned were in attendance. Baldwin, Wright, and Bladon apologized for their offence, and were discharged after promising not to publish further reports. Thomas Evans went home before his case was heard, because his wife had broken her leg; this circumstance was solemnly entered in the Journals of the House, and an order made for him to attend again on 19 March.[27] The absent William Woodfall was found to be already in the custody of Black Rod. John Miller was the only printer who had defied the House, and he was ordered to be taken into the custody of the Serjeant at Arms for contempt.[28]

The time was at last ripe for Wilkes's plan, but it was preceded by two deliberate insults to the dignity of the House. While the Commons had been sitting on 14 March, John Wheble wrote a public letter to the Speaker, declaring that he had returned from business in the country on 11 March, and had been astonished to hear of the proceedings against him. He had accordingly taken the advice of learned counsel, in the person of Robert Morris, and enclosed a copy of the lawyer's opinion. The document, written in a vein of insolent humour, affected to show that the summons, warrant of apprehension, and proclamation were all illegal because the House of Commons was not an appointed Court of Justice. Morris concluded, 'I do give it as my opinion, that Mr Wheble may well institute an action upon the case, against the counsellors, promoters, aiders, abettors and publishers thereof'.[29] On the next day, 15 March, this piece of impudence was followed by a more audacious step. A collusive arrest of John Wheble was made by one of his servants, Edward Carpenter, by reason of the proclamation in the *Gazette* of 9 March.[30] Wheble was taken before Alderman John Wilkes, who was the sitting magistrate that day at the Guildhall. Wilkes established that Wheble was a freeman of London, that Carpenter was neither a constable nor a peace officer of the City, and that the cause of the arrest was merely the proclamation and not any felony or breach of the peace. Wilkes therefore rebuked Carpenter: 'As you are not a peace officer, nor constable, and you accuse not the party of any crime, I know not what right you have to take his person; it is contrary to the chartered rights of this City, and of Englishmen.' He released Wheble, who made a formal complaint of assault, and was bound over to prosecute Carpenter at the next Quarter Sessions. Carpenter, however, was given a certificate of his having apprehended Wheble in order to obtain the £50 reward from the Treasury. As a final touch, Wilkes hastened to report the incident to his old enemy the Earl of Halifax, who was again Secretary of State as he had been during the general warrants case:

As I found that there was no legal cause of complaint against Wheble, I thought it clearly my duty to adjudge that he had been apprehended in the City illegally, in direct violation of the rights of an Englishman, and of the chartered privileges of a citizen of this Metropolis, and to discharge him.[31]

These were token acts of defiance. The real challenge to the authority of the House, from which later events were to stem, also took place on 15 March.[32] Early in the afternoon William Whittam, a messenger of the House of Commons, attempted, in pursuance of a warrant from the Speaker, to arrest John Miller at his house. The plot long concerted with Wilkes then came into operation. Miller resisted arrest, a City constable was conveniently at hand, and the messenger found himself charged with assault and false arrest.[33] Together with some witnesses, the three men went to the Guildhall, but by this time Wilkes had finished the business of the day and departed for the Mansion House. They followed, and there applied to Lord Mayor Crosby, who was confined to his bedchamber with gout. At Whittam's request, the hearing was adjourned until six o'clock. The affair was reported to the Speaker, Sir Fletcher Norton, who sent Deputy Serjeant at Arms Clementson to demand both the release of the messenger and the restoration of Miller to his custody. When the case was resumed at six o'clock, the Lord Mayor, assisted by Aldermen Richard Oliver and John Wilkes, conducted the proceedings in his bedchamber. Robert Morris acted as counsel for John Miller, and made repeated interventions on legal points to add to the discomfiture of the Commons' officials.[34] Clementson at once demanded possession of Whittam and Miller, but the Lord Mayor refused. Crosby ascertained from Whittam that he was not a constable of the City, and that the Speaker's warrant had not been backed by any City magistrate. The Mayor and Aldermen thereupon ruled that Miller's arrest was illegal. They then heard Miller's complaint. Evidence was given by Miller himself and three other printers to prove the offence. Whittam was ordered to appear at the next Quarter Sessions to answer the charge, and released only after he had given bail.

About an hour later the last pinprick was delivered, in what was evidently a carefully prepared scenario. The third defiant printer Roger Thompson was arrested outside his own house and taken before Alderman Oliver, now in solitary state at the Mansion House. Oliver released Thompson, for the same reasons Wilkes had freed Wheble, but gave a certificate to his captor to obtain the Treasury reward.[35]

The administration now faced a political crisis. Three meetings of leading ministerial MPs were promptly held, two at 10 Downing Street and the third at the Speaker's House on Sunday, 17 March. George III did not scruple to inform the Prime Minister of his own opinion before this last meeting:

The authority of the House of Commons is totally annihilated if it is not in an exemplary manner supported tomorrow, by instantly committing the Lord Mayor and Alderman Oliver to the Tower; as to Wilkes, he is below the notice of the

House; then a Secret Committee or any other mode of examining further into the affair is open for the wisdom of the House.[36]

Sir Gilbert Elliot and others thought to be close to the King therefore urged strong measures, but Richard Rigby argued for moderation. So did Lord North, who favoured a plan of Speaker Norton for a Committee of Inquiry. Treasury Lord George Onslow offered to persuade his cousin to drop the matter, but the ministry evidently decided to take further action against the printers.[37] The Parliamentary management of the case was entrusted to a junior office-holder and experienced debater, Welbore Ellis.

When the Commons next met, on Monday, 18 March, a crowded House heard a full account of events from the Speaker and the Deputy Serjeant at Arms. Since both Crosby and Oliver were MPs, Ellis, according to precedent, moved for the attendance of Crosby on the following day. The House approved this step by 267 votes to 80, after objections from many opposition speakers. The stance of the opposition factions in Parliament nevertheless incurred radical criticism for its implicit or explicit acceptance of the right of the House of Commons to take action against reporting. The Rockingham group based their stand simply on the inexpediency of such measures, while Barré for the Chathamites merely challenged the idea of punishing the printers.[38] In the City those associated with Chatham stood aloof from the Wilkes plot, as Barré had informed him the previous day: 'Mr Townsend and Mr Sawbridge have taken no sort of part in these proceedings, and differ in opinion from those who have.' Chatham had replied approving this conduct:

I am not a little happy that Mr Townsend and Mr Sawbridge are upon clear ground, and would fain hope that they may venture to continue in the right, without losing all their weight with the livery. . . . That the proceeding of [the] Lord Mayor is censurable, I have no doubt . . . but I am of opinion that to go further than . . . noise without effect, would be neither wise nor becoming.[39]

But anything less than full support of the printers would forfeit all popularity in the City, and in the debate of 18 March Sawbridge backed the conduct of the Lord Mayor: 'I think he has defended in a very proper manner the liberty of his fellow-citizens.' James Townsend, absent through illness, asked Sawbridge to say the same on his behalf.[40] This change of attitude was an ominous indication of the growing intransigence within the City. On the next day the administration was threatened with a further embarrassment. Anxious to avoid a direct encounter with John Wilkes, the ministers had been disposed to concur with George III's view that his part in the affair was best ignored, but that matter was forced on their attention as soon as the House met on 19 March, when Sir Joseph Mawbey moved that Wilkes be summoned to attend the next day.[41] The King expressed regret to Lord North at this step:

I own I could have wished that Wilkes had not been ordered before the House, for he must be in a jail the next term if not given new life by some punishment inflicted on him, which will bring him new supplies; and I do not doubt he will hold such a language that will oblige some notice to be taken of him.[42]

George III knew his man. Wilkes, who had just taken the precaution of leaving his Westminster house and lodging within the City boundaries, made a reference to the Middlesex election in his answer the next day to the Speaker:

I observe that no notice is taken of me in your order as a Member of the House, and that I am not required to attend in my place. Both these circumstances, according to the settled form, ought to have been mentioned in my case, and I hold them absolutely indispensable.[43]

Sir Joseph Mawbey produced a copy of this letter as soon as the order for Wilkes was read in the Commons on 20 March. The Speaker refused to allow him to read it out to the House, and another order was made for Wilkes to attend on 25 March.[44] In view of his defiance this was a moderate step, and George III approved 'the apparent intention of not examining Wilkes'.[45] This reluctance to endure another direct confrontation with Wilkes was soon public knowledge, Chatham being informed on 24 March by his supporter John Calcraft: 'The ministers avow Wilkes too dangerous to meddle with. He is to do what he pleases; we are to submit. So his Majesty orders: he will have "nothing more to do with that devil Wilkes".'[46] When the House met on 25 March the administration's first step was a motion to postpone the order for Wilkes. Mawbey tried to press the matter, declaring that Wilkes was involved equally with the other two magistrates. North retorted that Wilkes was obviously courting punishment, and the motion passed without a division. The House escaped the procedural difficulty by a new order at the end of the day for Wilkes to attend on 8 April. That date fell within the Easter recess, and the order therefore lapsed.[47]

The ministers had avoided a sensational clash with Wilkes himself, but they still had to weather the storm he had raised. The dilemma of an angry Commons and a defiant City remained. In the House on 19 March Lord Mayor Crosby rested his whole argument on the oath he had taken as an Alderman to protect the rights of the City, and he made no attempt to conciliate the feelings of MPs. 'I must glory in my own breast in having executed what I was sworn to do.' His request for permission to use counsel sparked off two days of debate over motions on the subject made by Alderman Trecothick.[48] The House decided that Crosby could be heard by counsel only as far as did not affect the privileges of Parliament. Further delay was caused by the ill health of the Lord Mayor, and the whole case was postponed until 25 March.[49]

A week of discussion had shown that most MPs shared the indignation of the King. Few even among opposition speakers directly challenged the official view that the privileges of the House had to be vindicated. Many administration supporters, led by Sir Gilbert Elliot and Charles Fox, demanded punitive measures. Lord North himself, at first an advocate of moderation, was provoked by the intransigence of the City. On 20 March he compelled the Lord Mayor's clerk to expunge from his minute-book the entry concerning Whittam's arrest. This action was followed by a resolution of the House that no suit should be commenced on the ground of 'the said pretended assault'.[50] Two days later North made a warm speech in the Commons on 'the necessity of doing ourselves right, and the disgrace and extinction of the Members, and the authority of the House, if this violent act was submitted to'.[51] On 24 March the ministry openly revealed its role by this Treasury whip to supportive MPs: 'You are most earnestly requested to attend early tomorrow, on an affair of the last importance to the constitution, and the rights and privileges of the people of England.'[52]

The City was also united by *esprit de corps*, and even ministerial supporters there aligned themselves behind the Lord Mayor.[53] A Court of Common Council met on 21 March, with Trecothick presiding instead of the gout-ridden Crosby. A unanimous vote of thanks was passed to the Mayor and Aldermen Wilkes and Oliver 'for having on a late important occasion supported the privileges and franchises of this City and defended our excellent constitution'. A Committee was appointed, of four Aldermen and eight Commoners, to assist them in their defence. The Committee was empowered to employ counsel, and to spend up to £500.[54] Alderman John Kirkman, usually a supporter of the administration, made an able speech on the popular side, and Sawbridge spoke 'extremely well in defence of the franchises of the City, and the common rights of mankind'.[55]

The case now reached its climax. On 25 March the House of Commons was surrounded by a vast crowd, many with labels in their hats inscribed 'Crosby, Wilkes, Oliver, and the Liberty of the Press'. They included, according to the radical newspapers, 'a great number of gentlemen, merchants and respectable tradesmen, many of whom went in their carriages'.[56] The noise could be heard inside the building, and MPs had difficulty in passing through the mob. It was under the threat of physical force that the Commons began to consider the conduct of the City magistrates. After Crosby had announced his refusal to employ counsel under the restrictions imposed by the House, Welbore Ellis moved a resolution that the discharge of Miller was a breach of privilege. City spokesmen remained belligerent. Aldermen Sawbridge and

Townsend both declared that they would have taken the same action as the accused; and Townsend warned members not to embark on a fruitless contest: 'The worthy magistrates may, for a time, be committed to the custody of the Serjeant at Arms, but should they be shut up, there are other magistrates ready and willing to do the same duty for them.' The Rockingham group took their ground on a previous question moved by Sir George Savile, who declared that he could not conscientiously give a vote when counsel had been refused. Administration speakers urged the need of some decision, and when the House divided shortly before midnight the previous question was negatived by 270 votes to 90. Immediately Savile, Lord John Cavendish, and other prominent Rockinghamites walked out, but Barré and the Chathamites preferred to wait for the punishment.

Since the Lord Mayor had retired during the debate through ill health, an order was made for his attendance on 27 March, and attention turned to Alderman Oliver. The Speaker asked him to make his defence, but the reply was uncompromising: 'I know the punishment I am to receive is determined upon. I have nothing to say . . . I defy you.' An angry North then prompted Ellis to move Oliver's commitment to the Tower, 'a length he meant not to go', so thought MP John Calcraft, who the previous day had told Chatham that 'reprimand only is now the language'.[57] But there had been a widespread belief that expulsion was the punishment the ministry intended for Crosby and Oliver.[58] Prudence prevented a course of action that would have revived the issues of the Middlesex Election case in a popular constituency: for while Crosby sat for the Devonshire borough of Honiton, Oliver was an MP for the City of London. Barré at once rose, made a short fiery speech, and left the House, followed by Sawbridge, Townsend, and others. After an amendment to substitute a reprimand had been defeated by 170 votes to 38, the motion was carried, and the House adjourned.[59] Next day 160 coaches were said to have visited the Tower.[60]

The Commons was due to consider the case of Lord Mayor Crosby on 27 March. On the morning of that day he presented Robert Morris to the freedom of the City, in recognition of his part in the scheme. At one o'clock Crosby left the Mansion House in procession for the House of Commons, which was again surrounded by a large and excited mob, estimated by one newspaper at 50,000. Several MPs had their carriages stopped. The windows of Lord North's coach were smashed, and the vehicle wrecked. North himself was hurt, and had to be rescued by an opposition member, Sir William Meredith.[61] Speaker Norton refused to begin the proceedings of the House until order had been restored outside. When the Westminster magistrates found themselves unable to read the Riot Act, sheriffs Baker and Martin went out and dispersed the crowd.

After a long argument over an allegation by Solicitor-General Alexander Wedderburn that the mob had been organized, the business appointed for the day commenced. A motion by Ellis that Crosby had been guilty of a breach of privilege was carried without a division. Ellis next proposed the commitment of Crosby only to the custody of the Serjeant at Arms, out of consideration for the Mayor's health. Crosby at once rose to say that he was much better, and desired the same punishment as Oliver. Ellis therefore altered his motion accordingly. At this point Barré and the Chathamites left the House rather than vote on the matter. Most of the Rockingham party had deliberately absented themselves, and the motion to commit Crosby to the Tower was carried by 202 votes to only 39. The ministry did not intend to stop with the imprisonment of Crosby and Oliver. After the Mayor had left, Ellis declared that other persons were also concerned, and moved for a Committee to inquire into the circumstances of 'the late obstructions to the execution of the Orders of the House'. The motion was carried after a brief debate, and an order made for a Select Committee of twenty-one members to be chosen by ballot on the next day.[62] Rigby and the advocates of moderation refused to have anything to do with it, and the three opposition MPs included by the ministry declined to attend.[63] The Committee sat on every weekday from 28 March to 30 April, when Ellis presented the report to the House. This set out the evidence, but made only the lame recommendation that John Miller ought to be taken into custody.[64] Lord North tried to put a good face on the matter by declaring that the Commons had already vindicated its authority by imprisoning two magistrates. The report, he said, now confirmed the powers claimed by the House.[65]

The martyrdom of the prisoners in the Tower had meanwhile been solaced by gifts and expressions of support from many parts of the country, while Crosby and Oliver received votes of thanks from all the wards of the City. The Court of Common Council voted them the cost of their tables, but both refused the offer to save the City such additional expense.[66] Opposition politicians publicly signified their disapproval of the punishment. Lord Temple was one of those who visited Oliver on 26 March, while on 30 March the leaders of the Rockingham party made a formal journey to the Tower.[67] More practical efforts to assist the prisoners were made by the Committee appointed by the Court of Common Council. On 3 April it resolved that application should be made to three lawyers of opposition sympathies, Glynn, Dunning, and John Lee, to move for a writ of habeas corpus for the two prisoners. Dunning refused to act, but Glynn and Lee made four unsuccessful attempts to obtain their release, pleading before the two Lord Chief Justices De Grey and Mansfield in their respective chambers on 5 April, before the Court of Common Pleas on 22 April, and before the Court of Exchequer on 30 April.[68]

Crosby and Oliver had to wait for their release until the close of the Parliamentary session, when the powers of the House automatically lapsed. The prorogation was expected on 9 May; but in order to avoid the disturbance of a large mob outside the Tower, the King suddenly put an end to the session on the previous day. As soon as the news was known, the attendance of the Aldermen and Common Council was requested at the Guildhall. Amid a cheering crowd fifty-three carriages escorted the Lord Mayor and Alderman Oliver to the Mansion House.[69] The City, however, did not yet regard the affair as closed. No heed was paid to the resolutions of the House of Commons on 20 March, prohibiting progress in the suits brought by the printers. At the Quarter Sessions on 8 April at the Guildhall the grand jury found bills of indictment for assault and wrongful imprisonment against both William Whittam, the messenger who had arrested Miller, and Edward Carpenter, who had apprehended Wheble on the strength of the royal proclamation.[70] The case against Whittam was removed into the Court of King's Bench, where it was stopped on 13 May by the entering of a *nolle prosequi* on behalf of the Crown by Attorney-General Thurlow. It was not fit, he said, that the King should be the prosecutor of a servant of the House of Commons who had merely been carrying into execution an old privilege.[71] Carpenter, however, was tried at the Guildhall on 1 July, found guilty, fined 1s., and imprisoned for two months. That 'he lived like a prince' until his release on 26 August confirmed the collusive nature of the incident; the purpose of his punishment was simply the assertion of the City's authority within its boundaries.[72] As a final gesture the Court of Common Council on 24 January 1772 voted to give silver cups to Crosby, Wilkes, and Oliver 'for the noble stand they made in the business of the printer'. That for Crosby was to cost £200, the others £100 each. Oliver asked for his to be kept with the City plate, but Wilkes said he would treasure the one given to him, as each tried to score political points off the other.[73]

The whole episode had been a public humiliation for the King's government. Although Lord North had known a month beforehand that some resort would be made to the City's privileges, the administration had been outmanœuvred by Wilkes. He had astutely calculated the outcome of events. It had not mattered that both the main opposition groups led by Chatham and Rockingham had shunned the project, or even that many City officials had at first been reluctant to give assistance. Once the fatal step had been taken, the uncompromising attitude of the City spokesmen both inside and outside Parliament deprived the ministers of any chance of extricating themselves from the situation. As Wilkes had foreseen, the corporate feeling of the City, aroused by the attack on the privileges, made his success inevitable. For the victory lay with Wilkes, and the ministry could derive little satisfaction from the final result. Certainly a policy of undignified evasion had cut short the development of another Wilkes case. The authority of the House of Commons, too, had been formally vindicated by the punishment of Crosby and Oliver. But this triumph was a hollow one. The campaign had completely failed to stamp out Parliamentary reporting. The elusive Miller, Wheble, and Thompson had continued to publish debates throughout the crisis in their three newspapers, the *London Evening Post*, the *Middlesex Journal*, and the *Gazetteer*. The printers of the *St. James's Chronicle*, the *Whitehall Evening Post*, and the *General Evening Post* all promised to discontinue reports when they appeared before the House of Commons on 14 March; but the *General Evening Post* was printing debates again within a week, and the *St. James's Chronicle* soon followed this example.[74] Early in April reporting was resumed even by the cautious *London Chronicle* and *Lloyd's Evening Post*, which had both stopped the printing of debates immediately after Colonel Onslow's warning on 5 February. No action whatever had been taken by the House against the weekly and monthly periodicals. Long before the release of Crosby and Oliver reporting was in progress as if there had never been any interruption.[75]

The House of Commons faced the entire task again, after having suffered both loss of dignity and the dislocation of business for several weeks. At the beginning of the next session, in January 1772, Wilkes did contemplate the possibility that 'the old battle' would be 'renewed with the Commons';[76] but the North ministry sensibly avoided another fiasco. The Printers' Case, however, did have a sequel, with respect to the House of Lords. The basic premiss for the reporting of the debates of the House of Commons, that constituents had the right to know the behaviour of their representatives,[77] did not apply to that unelected chamber; and there was the practical difficulty that from December 1770 the House of Lords shut out the public from its debates. Wilkes nevertheless, in late 1771, planned a similar trap concerning the right of imprisonment recently exercised by the House of Lords against several printers. A provocative libel against a court peer would be followed by the release, by City magistrates, of any printers seized in consequence of it.[78] Wilkes did not pursue this idea, but the wider issue of the reporting of Lords debates arose when in December 1774 that House again opened its doors to strangers. The reporting of debates there began, and on 31 January 1775 complaints of such publications led the House to order the arrest of the printer of the *Public Ledger*. Wilkes, then Lord Mayor, threw down the gauntlet by instructing the printer to inform the Lords of his whereabouts, in the City of London, of course. He made it publicly known that Black Rod himself, the official emissary of the House of Lords, would be imprisoned if he sought to execute the order, and the ministry backed down.[79] The consequences of a committal of Wilkes himself to the Tower were too disagreeable and dangerous to contemplate. From 1771 and 1775 the debates of the House of Commons and House of Lords respectively have been regularly published in the press. That victory over authority was perhaps the most significant gain for 'liberty' achieved by Wilkes.

9

City Politician
1771–1775

WILKES would not return to the national political stage of Parliament until the next general election, and that need not take place until 1775. In the meantime the City of London engrossed his political attention, as he deployed his popularity there to good effect in combating and embarrassing the King's government as embodied in the North ministry. If the Printers' Case was his greatest triumph, there were more successes to celebrate than failures to contemplate. Exactly what role the Bill of Rights Society played in this activity is impossible to determine. It faded from prominence to obscurity during these years, vanishing altogether in 1775. How far it was the Wilkite organization power base, and how far merely a propaganda machine, must remain unknown; but it was certainly the focus of attention in 1771, despite the Hornite secession on 9 April. After the narrow failure then of Horne's motion to dissolve the Society the defeated minority formed a new Constitutional Society that same day. Horne took with him most of the wealthy and influential members, particularly those linked with Lord Shelburne: John Sawbridge and his father-in-law Sir William Stephenson, James Townsend, Richard and Thomas Oliver, Sir Robert Bernard, Sir Cecil Wray, Sir Francis Delaval, Lauchlin Macleane, George Bellas, Secretary Thomas Boddington, and Horne's patron, William Tooke.

This split also cost London radicalism the services of former Society Secretary Robert Morris. He became estranged from Wilkes, whom he had at first supported, over the latter's attempt to involve him in the quarrel with Horne, writing a public letter to Wilkes on 27 May:

I am unwilling to interfere in the dispute between you and Mr Horne, who have both deserved well of the public, and are so fully qualified to fight your own battles.

. . . As to the parties who are now contesting, I have no reason to wish success on one side more than on the other. . . . It is the cause of liberty I wish to promote, and I care not by whose hand it triumphs. Of that cause alone I desire to be esteemed a partisan, and not of any individual.[1]

That was not a realistic attitude to adopt, and Morris dropped out of the political scene. But he was soon to call upon Wilkes for personal assistance, after he eloped to Europe the next year, aged 29, with a 12-year-old heiress. The escapade ended in fiasco; by the end of 1773 the girl rejected Morris as her husband despite two dubious marriage ceremonies. But Wilkes was caused embarrassment by numerous appeals from Morris for help to extricate him from such legal consequences of his behaviour as foreign prisons.[2]

The Hornites claimed that the Bill of Rights Society had been dealt a fatal blow, the *Middlesex Journal* stating that only thirty-two members remained, such relatives and friends of Wilkes as his brother Heaton, brother-in-law George Hayley, attorney John Reynolds, John Churchill, and John Glynn.[3] Sixty-three members had in fact remained in the Society, including such leading figures as Sir Joseph Mawbey, Robert Jones, and John Trevanion, together with other men soon to rise to prominence, lawyers James Adair and Watkin Lewes, and London merchant Frederick Bull, and three lively Americans, Stephen Sayre and Virginians Arthur and William Lee.[4] Wilkes, moreover, acted promptly to repair the damage done to the Society. At the next meeting, on 16 April, chaired by Robert Jones and attended by twenty-eight members, Boddington and Richard Oliver were replaced respectively as Secretary and Treasurer by Arthur Lee and Frederick Bull. The Society resolved that all who had resigned would have to seek formal readmission, and no problem was encountered in restoring the Society to its former numerical strength. Fourteen new members were proposed that day, including the imprisoned Lord Mayor Crosby.[5] At the next meeting, on 30 April, sixteen more members were proposed, and by September the membership was claimed to be over 130.[6]

A lull in the Wilkes–Horne propaganda battle during the Printers' Case ended in May, when Horne launched a press campaign, a dozen letters in the *Public Advertiser* intended to expose Wilkes as selfish and treacherous, often citing trivial incidents from a few years back. This tactical error allowed Wilkes to adopt a disdainful attitude, well aware that his popularity rendered him invulnerable to the accusations and comments of Horne. His effective retort was to remind Horne and his allies that they owed their political importance solely to him, and they were reproached for their association with the notoriously untrustworthy Lord Shelburne. Wilkes brought what is generally known as the 'Controversial Letters' episode to an end in his reply of 20 June to Horne's twelfth letter, and Horne conceded defeat in a final bitter rejoinder of 10 July. His attacks on the character of the popular hero had rebounded to his own disadvantage, rendering him, according to his first biographer, 'one of the most odious men in the kingdom'.[7]

In the wider field of political propaganda, the Bill of Rights Society at first seemed to be in danger of being outpaced by the Constitutional Society. That began with about forty members, appointing the former Bill of Rights Society Secretary and Treasurer, Thomas Boddington and Richard Oliver, to act in the same capacity. The new Society also met fortnightly, but remained very much a private club. It did not invite public subscriptions, did not advertise its activities, and was restrictive about its membership. On 15 May it demonstrated political purity by imposing on each member a promise to campaign for Shorter Parliaments and redress of the Middlesex Elections decision. Already two of the Society's members, John Sawbridge and James Townsend, had manifested their political zeal on 26 April by proposing and seconding in the House of Commons a Shorter Parliaments Bill, which the ministry defeated by 105 votes to 54 without debate.[8]

Wilkes, well aware that his enemies would seek to portray the Bill of Rights Society as his personal clique, had responded to earlier criticism as soon as the Hornites left. On 16 April Wilkes himself moved to rescind the order of 26 February prohibiting any new subscriptions until his debts were settled, thereby mollifying waverers like James Adair, who seconded him. Another move to answer past and anticipate future attacks from Horne was one to improve financial accountability. It was resolved that the Society's 'cash-book' should be open to inspection at every meeting, and that a full statement of income and expenditure should be prepared for the next meeting on 30 April.[9] On news of the Constitutional Society's political announcements the Bill of Rights Society decided on 11 June to draft an extensive political programme, appointing a Committee of twelve for this purpose, and adding six more on 25 June.[10] That was too unwieldy a body, and the document presented to the Society on 23 July was essentially drafted by one man, Secretary Arthur Lee. Wilkes later told Junius that even he did not see it until the morning of that day, and that he disliked the 'extreme verbiage', although 'the substance I indeed greatly approve'. Both he and Mawbey wished to postpone the adoption of the programme in order to redraft it, but they found the majority of members impatient to publish it. Wilkes ruefully commented to Junius: 'The Society of the Bill of Rights have been called my Committee, and it has been said that they were governed entirely by me. This has spread a jealousy even among my friends. I was therefore necessitated to act the most cautious and prudent part.'[11]

The heart of the document, after a long declamation about grievances, was a list of eleven pledges that electors were urged to obtain from Parliamentary candidates. It was a mixed bag. Some were long-standing 'country programme' matters, such as a bribery oath for all Parliamentary candidates, annual Parliamentary elections, and a comprehensive Pension and Place Bill to exclude from Parliament any recipients of pecuniary rewards, direct or indirect, from government. But to these traditional demands there was added a new one of Parliamentary Reform, 'a full and equal representation of the people in Parliament'. Another group of resolutions referred to such recent events as the St George's Fields Massacre, the Middlesex Elections, and the Printers' Case, seeking such redress or retribution as was appropriate. The last two drew attention respectively to the unspecified grievances of Ireland and to those of the American colonies with special reference to the right of taxation.[12] On 7 September Junius privately sent Wilkes a scathing denunciation of the document: the preamble was pompous and pretentious, the pledges for the most part impractical and unwise. Junius himself favoured only moderate change, a Triennial Act and an increase of the county representation. Wilkes briefly replied five days later, saying that he wanted annual elections and the disfranchisement of decayed boroughs like Old Sarum and Gatton.[13]

The propaganda battle between Wilkites and Hornites formed the backdrop to a City contest over the midsummer election of sheriffs. Before the radical split the Bill of Rights Society had planned to run Wilkes and Richard Oliver on a joint ticket. Within two days, on 11 April, Oliver wrote from his Tower prison cell to inform Wilkes that he would refuse to do this because he thought their political views were different. Wilkes disagreed in his reply next day: 'Our sentiments have always coincided, although our expressions have varied.' And he outscored Oliver by stating that he would serve as sheriff with any man, since the choice belonged to the Livery.[14] On 13 April the Hornite *Middlesex Journal* gave a different and unconvincing reason for Oliver's refusal: that if Wilkes was sheriff he could not, as returning officer, stand for Parliament if Luttrell resigned his Middlesex seat.[15] The newspaper also claimed that finance was the real motive behind Wilkes's response to Oliver, since Richard and Thomas Oliver had between them contributed one-tenth of all the money subscribed for Wilkes, who now wanted Richard Oliver to pay all the costs of being sheriffs, at least £1,400.[16] A reply appeared on 15 April in the *Public Advertiser*, which also recalled how 'tardy' James Townsend had been in the cause of liberty with respect to both press warrants and the Printers' Case. The entire Shelburne connection, including Horne, was lambasted for attacking Wilkes more than the ministry.

Wilkes chose wealthy Frederick Bull to stand with him for sheriff in place of Oliver, who persisted in his candidature. This was a situation that the ministry sought to exploit, and Treasury Secretary John Robinson even issued a canvassing letter on behalf of the two government candidates, Aldermen John Kirkman and Samuel Plumbe.[17] George III was at first hopeful of success, believing that 'Wilkes has been in his various struggles supported by a small though desperate part of the Livery, while the sober and major part of that body have from fear kept aloof'.[18] His optimism was unfounded. Oliver failed to split the radical vote, polling a mere 119. Wilkes with 2,315 and Bull with 2,194 finished well ahead of the 1949 and 1875 votes for Kirkman and Plumbe respectively. The Wilkites thereupon sought to emphasize their hold over the Livery by another Remonstrance calling for the dissolution of Parliament. Lord Mayor Crosby and the two new sheriffs headed the delegation that presented it to George III on 10 July.[19] Secretary of State Lord Rockford had advised the King that because of 'the designs of the faction' the best tactic would be a gracious reception: 'Wilkes hopes the City will be ill received, and from that he has expectations of getting a pension from them of £600 a year.'[20]

This Wilkite triumph was a false dawn. Horace Walpole might write that 'Wilkes is another Phoenix revived from the ashes. He was sunk. It was over with him; but the ministers too precipitately hurrying to bury him alive, blew up the embers, and he is again as formidable as ever.'[21] But other political observers had noted the strong government influence in the Livery, and the Wilkite cause was not assisted by a foolish attack made by Junius on John Horne during July and August, one that proved as counter-productive as Horne's own earlier onslaught on Wilkes had been.[22] Junius accused Horne of sacrificing everything to his hatred of Wilkes, the case for whose support he stated on 24 July:

Indeed Mr Horne, the public should and *will* forgive him his claret and his footmen, . . . as long as he stands forth against a ministry and Parliament, who are doing every thing they can to enslave the country, and as long as he is a thorn in the King's side. You will not suspect me of setting up *Wilkes* for a perfect character. The question to the public is, where shall we find a man, who, with purer principles, will go the lengths, and run the hazards that he has done? The season calls for such a man, and he ought to be supported.[23]

Junius meanwhile privately urged Wilkes, since Horne was 'completely defeated', to reunite the two radical factions before the election of the next Lord Mayor at Michaelmas. This should be done, he suggested on 21 August, by sponsoring the candidature of John Sawbridge, a man respected for his probity and independence of mind, who might in any case be won back from the Horne faction. By then it was widely known that for this 1771 Mayoral election Wilkes was again going to put forward Mayor Crosby, who wished to retain the office, in tandem with William Bridgen, a man deemed to be so unpopular because of his tight-fisted behaviour when Mayor in 1763–4 that it was anticipated the Court of Aldermen, faced with a choice between the two, would opt again for Crosby.[24] Wilkes replied on 12 September that Sawbridge, whom he described as 'honest', the dupe of the Shelburne faction of Horne and Townsend, and 'not the best-bred man in the island', would not accept such an offer, and that in any case he had earlier promised Crosby his support. On 18 September Junius warned Wilkes that while he seemed to fear success for the Shelburne party 'the real danger is from the interest of government', and this proved a shrewd assessment.[25] The strategy devised by Wilkes collapsed when Bridgen refused to play the role of stalking-horse. James Townsend, a Hornite candidate along with Sawbridge, then rejected a Wilkite suggestion that he should stand down, in order to allow the joint return of Sawbridge and Crosby, unless he himself was promised support in 1772, a condition rejected by the Crosby campaign committee.[26] The consequence of the radical split was that the ministerial candidate William Nash headed the poll with 2,199 votes. Sawbridge polled 1,879 and Crosby 1,795, with three other candidates well behind, Townsend obtaining a derisory 151. George III was well pleased with the result, and regretted only that another courtier Thomas Hallifax, who polled 846 votes, had not joined Nash 'from the first', since if they had headed the poll together such a result 'would have been the fullest disavowal of the strange conduct held of late by the Livery'.[27] The Court of Aldermen then chose Nash to be Lord Mayor. This outcome, confided new Bill of Rights Society member Edmund Dayrell to Lord Temple, 'we do not secretly dislike, as he is more likely to be with us, than any of the Shelburnes can be'.[28] Certainly the acrimony between the radical groups had been intensified. During the election Sawbridge had attacked Wilkes for conducting an underhand press campaign against him, while Wilkes had again reminded the Livery how backward Townsend had been in the Printers' Case.[29]

The election of Nash as Lord Mayor was a salutary warning to the City Radicals, Wilkite and Hornite alike, of the continuing weight of government influence there. Alderman Sawbridge now took upon himself the role of mediator between the two factions for which his moderation and integrity so fitted him, and by the summer of 1772 the *London Evening Post* was commending his 'zeal to unite the leaders of the popular party'. Such prominent members of the Hornite faction as Sawbridge and Richard Oliver contributed to the success of Wilkite Frederick Bull in a contested Aldermanic election, while for the midsummer election of sheriffs Wilkite Watkin Lewes stood with Oliver on a joint candidature. Both were chosen, the poll closing on 1 July with 1,586 votes for Oliver and 1,327 for Lewes, as against 762 for ministerialist Samuel Plumbe.[30]

This result seemed to herald a new unity among London's Radicals, despite the ongoing enmity between Wilkes and Horne.[31] For at the time of the shrievalty elections Wilkes agreed to stand on a joint ticket for the Mayoralty with James Townsend, whose candidature Shelburne had pushed.[32] This news was generally welcomed by City Radicals. Sawbridge wrote to Bull on 4 July: 'I am convinced that whenever the friends to the liberties of their country act in concert, neither the power nor corrupt influence of the ministerial faction can prevail against them.' And on 22 September the Bill of Rights Society resolved to support the plan.[33] For the Wilkites this was a strategy to prevent the name of a government candidate being forwarded to the Court of Aldermen along with that of John Wilkes. Townsend's role was merely to facilitate his election as Mayor, and he tacitly accepted this arrangement, taking little part in the election campaign.[34]

Never one to miss a propaganda trick, Wilkes on 28 September, the day before the Mayoral election began, published with Bull a report to the Livery on their shrievalty. Cultivation of his public image and a genuine concern for 'liberty' had led Wilkes to adopt a high profile as sheriff. One much publicized move was an attempt to stop what many Radicals believed to be ministerial 'packing' of special juries in libel and other cases of political portent. Wilkes and Bull therefore decided to draw up official lists of all men eligible to serve on such juries in Middlesex, London, and Westminster, so that jurymen would be selected in rotation. From 1 January 1772 a 'Freeholders Book' for Middlesex and a 'Jurors Book' for Westminster were in use, but it is unclear whether a London list was ever completed.[35] More of a gesture, to keep alive the memory of the St George's Fields Massacre, was a promise by the sheriffs on taking office in September 1771 not to allow the deployment of soldiers at public gatherings.[36] Motives of humanity as well as publicity may be ascribed to two instructions sent by Wilkes and Bull on 16 October to the Keeper of Newgate Prison, one ordering that prisoners should not be brought into court in chains, the other forbidding the customary public admission charges for the Old Bailey.[37] Both gestures misfired. Wilkes discovered that prisoners expecting conviction preferred not to have their chains painfully removed and put on again. Unrestricted admission converted the Old Bailey into a scene of disorder as criminals crowded in to see the fun. Wilkes had to withdraw this concession on the pretence that Horne had deliberately sabotaged his reform by hiring a riotous mob.[38] Despite such setbacks, the genuine concern of Wilkes about practical aspects of the judicial system had been made manifest, and the report of the sheriffs criticized the severity of the penal laws that inflicted capital punishment equally for petty crimes and those of 'the most shocking depravity and turpitude': the allusions here were to the pardons given to the St George's Fields 'murderers' and to a man recently convicted of sodomy.[39]

During the Mayoral poll the two ministerial candidates, Thomas Hallifax and John Shakespear, took an early lead, much to the delight of George III, who insisted on a daily report, and when the Radicals went ahead commented to Lord North on 5 October that 'Wilkes is not bound by any ties, therefore would poll non-freemen rather than lose the election'. The seven-day poll closed next day with Wilkes gaining 2,301 votes, Townsend 2,278, Hallifax 2,126, and Shakespear 1,912. The Prime Minister's account of the poll reinforced his sovereign's suspicions:

As Mr Wilkes has polled at this election, above 500 more than Crosby, and above 400 more than Sawbridge did at the last, there is the greatest reason to believe that many of his votes are illegal. The strange ragged figures whom he brought up today were such as were never seen at any poll before, except at his own when he stood for sheriff. A scrutiny has been demanded, and, if it succeeds for Mr Hallifax and Shakespear, will more effectually ruin Wilkes than any thing which has yet happened.[40]

Alderman Thomas Harley accused sheriffs Lewes and Oliver of having altered the poll figures. Wilkes countered that the scrutiny was demanded only to cause him extra expense, and it was abandoned by the defeated candidates after five days. On 29 October the election of Wilkes and Townsend was confirmed, and the Court of Aldermen proceeded to the choice of Mayor.[41] Townsend now played Wilkes false. He had long nurtured both an animosity towards Wilkes and an ambition to play a leading part in London politics. At the end of 1771 he won some cheap popularity by refusing to pay land tax on his Tottenham estate because Middlesex was not represented in Parliament, thereby suffering distraint upon his goods to the value of £200.[42] It must remain a matter of doubt as to whether Townsend had always intended to betray Wilkes. A few days before 29 October suspicions on that point appeared in the press; now his friend Oliver, acting as sheriff, suddenly convened a Court of Aldermen early on that day, and Townsend was voted Lord Mayor by 8 votes to 7.[43]

'Wilkes was thunderstruck, and for once, angry in earnest', noted Horace Walpole in his account. 'His rage, and that of his partisans, broke out in every kind of outrage against Townsend.' A Wilkite mob attacked the Guildhall during the ball on Lord Mayor's Day, when the hot-tempered Townsend had some of the rioters committed to Newgate, thereby increasing his unpopularity.[44] This spectacular betrayal of 1772 rendered permanent the radical split of the previous year. At a meeting on 3 November the Bill of Rights Society resolved to support Wilkes as a future Lord Mayor, 'he having been deprived of the Chair, in direct opposition to the sense of the Livery, by the malice of ministerial Aldermen' and the treachery of Sawbridge and Oliver.[45] Yet a fortnight later, in a temporary alliance of convenience, the radical factions did combine to secure the election of Serjeant Glynn as City Recorder. On 17 November the Court of Aldermen divided 13-all in the choice between Glynn and a ministerial candidate proposed by Thomas Harley. Lord Mayor Townsend then gave a second and casting vote in favour of Glynn, to the plaudits of that day's *London Evening Post*:

It is happy that the citizens of London have at last by their noble struggles, obtained a majority in the Court of Aldermen in favour of constitutional liberty. Notwithstanding the private quarrels subsisting among the Patriots, yet we see they heartily join against the common enemy.

But Wilkes had not forgiven Townsend. He maintained an incessant personal attack on the Lord Mayor in the press and at the Guildhall;[46] and in the spring of 1773 engineered a subtle and appropriate stroke of revenge. Townsend called a Common Hall of the Livery on 10 March 1773, to vote a resolution for Shorter Parliaments, the aim being to reinforce his radical credentials as established by the now annual Commons motion on the subject which had been as usual unsuccessfully proposed and seconded by Sawbridge and Townsend on 26 January.[47] At the Common Hall Wilkes persuaded the Livery to adopt also a Remonstrance to the King complaining of his 'neglect and disregard' of earlier petitions. This deliberately put Townsend in a dilemma, with Wilkes boasting that he would be 'undone at St. James's if he presented it, and stoned by the people if he did not'.[48] Townsend, after taking legal advice, found himself obliged to present this on 26 March, but sent an advance personal disclaimer. George III dismissed the petition as 'disrespectful' and 'void of foundation'. Wilkes meanwhile had shrewdly excused himself from attendance:

As I have long been personally obnoxious to the King, I have not for many years been at St. James's. It would now be rude and indecent to force myself into the Royal presence on an occasion not the most pleasing, I believe, to his Majesty. I am not used to go into any gentleman's house who does not wish to see me.[49]

One consequence of the radical split was frequent non-coöperation and occasional acrimony between sheriffs Oliver and Lewes.[50] On 7 April 1773, however, they were at one when an order came from the House of Commons Speaker for all sheriffs to summon MPs for a Call of the House on 26 April. That was too good an opportunity to miss. Their precept was sent on 13 April to Wilkes, who on the due date attended to claim his seat. The Deputy Clerk of the Crown refused to swear him in. In the House John Glynn proposed and Sawbridge seconded an unsuccessful motion that Wilkes should be heard on his complaint against that official.[51]

An uneasy truce between Wilkites and Hornites still prevailed at the Midsummer Court of Livery. The Court first voted instructions to the City

MPs to support Sawbridge's motion for Shorter Parliaments next session, and then elected as sheriffs, without a contest, Hornite William Plomer and Wilkite Stephen Sayre, an American; when Plomer was persuaded by the Constitutional Society to refuse to serve with Sayre, his place was taken by another American Wilkite, William Lee.[52] But the two factions clashed three months later at the Mayoral election, with the ministry content to stand aside, as Wilkes and Bull fought Sawbridge and Oliver. Already at the previous Mayoral election Wilkes had spelt out from the hustings on 29 October 1772, after the Townsend coup in the Court of Aldermen, what would be the consequence of repeated Aldermanic refusals to select him as Mayor. The Livery would choose the Mayor directly, by returning 'a friend to Liberty along with Mr Wilkes'.[53] Wilkes was now to drive that lesson home.

At the hustings on 29 September 1773 Sawbridge complained that he had been accused of dividing 'the friends of freedom' and thereby giving an opportunity of success to a ministerial candidate. He counter-attacked by denouncing a man who devoted all his time to traducing others, an obvious hit at Wilkes. Sawbridge was another to learn the folly of embarking on a war of words with him. Wilkes retorted, 'I glory in being a public writer, unpaid'. He accused Sawbridge of betraying the London Livery by allowing the election of Nash and assisting that of Townsend, ridiculed his pomposity, and questioned his integrity.[54]

The absence of an overt government interest led to a lower than usual poll. Wilkes obtained 1,690 votes and Bull 1,655, as against 1,178 for Sawbridge and 1,094 for Oliver. At the close of the poll a coach containing Wilkes, Bull, and Lewes was hand-pulled by supporters amid a cheering crowd of many thousands. In the Court of Aldermen on 8 October, after a tie of nine votes each, Lord Mayor Townsend gave a second and casting vote in favour of Bull, who in his acceptance speech expressed the wish that Wilkes had been chosen in view of 'the transcendent abilities of that gentleman'.[55] Such treatment of Wilkes was counter-productive, as Horace Walpole noted:

This proscription of Wilkes, though for two years together he was first in the poll, did but serve to revive his popularity from the injustice done him, and in this instance did not hurt his power, Bull being entirely his creature, and the odium on Townsend, Horne, Oliver and Sawbridge increasing. The first two were knaves and the latter weak men. Wilkes was the only man, except Ministers, who preserved credit in spite of character.[56]

A few weeks later a London Parliamentary by-election took place, caused by the death of Sir Robert Ladbroke on 31 October. That same day Lord North told the King that he expected Bull to be chosen: 'Every attempt to overturn Wilkes in Guildhall will, at present, be fruitless, as the Liverymen, who are not his friends, though they are a majority, have not zeal enough to hustle through a tumultuous election in order to disappoint him.' Alderman Thomas Harley confirmed this pessimistic judgement in a report to Treasury Secretary John Robinson, so North informed George III on 3 November: 'The great aversion which all men of fortune and character have to any of the City honours gives a terrible advantage to Mr Wilkes and his adherents.' This time suitable candidates did come forward. On 5 November 'a reputable merchant' Robert Peckham took Ladbroke's place as Alderman, and the King was even more pleased a week later when 'an eminent merchant', East India Company Director John Roberts, agreed to fight the Parliamentary seat. His chances seemed good when a meeting of 500 supporters on 17 November was attended by Aldermen Sawbridge, Townsend, and Oliver![57]

The Wilkites faced what they must have deemed an unholy alliance of the ministry and the Hornite party, and perhaps only the advantage Bull enjoyed of an early start to his canvass enabled them, as North feared it might, to defeat this challenge. On the day of the by-election Wilkes proposed and Crosby seconded Bull, but Roberts demanded a poll after the Wilkite sheriffs declared Bull elected on a show of hands. When the poll ended on 4 December, Bull had won by 2,695 votes to 2,481.[58] He was the first MP to be returned on the radical programme of the Bill of Rights Society, for before the election he had given a pledge to the Livery to work for Shorter Parliaments, Place Bills, 'more free and equal representation in Parliament', and the rights of the American colonists. He also promised not to accept any reward whatsoever from the government.[59] Bull's victory and his political pledge foreshadowed events in the metropolitan area during the general election of 1774.

Two by-election defeats earlier in 1773 made this London triumph all the sweeter for the Wilkites. At Dover on 2 April John Trevanion, who had lost a by-election there in 1770 by 483 votes to 456, was more heavily defeated by 524 votes to 385, the government interest outweighing his local connections.[60] At Worcester Watkin Lewes, who had been knighted in February, was a last-minute candidate on the independent interest: arriving only an hour before the poll began on 25 November, he obtained 635 votes as against 900 for the corporation candidate Thomas Rous. This election was declared void on 8 February 1774, on the ground of corruption, but Lewes lost once more on 1 March to another candidate by 796 votes to 713. Both Trevanion and Lewes were to fight those seats again at the general election, but the London area was the focus of Wilkite attention.

Although the general election did take place in the autumn of 1774, it was not due until 1775, and for most of the year the candidature of Wilkes for Lord Mayor was the centre of London interest. Here the midsummer election of sheriffs proved a setback for the Wilkite cause. Hornite William Plomer declined an invitation to stand with Wilkite John Williams, and came forward on a joint candidature with ministerial man John Hart. Wilkes hastily produced a second Bill of Rights Society candidate, an obscure solicitor George Grieve. But his candidates, professedly standing on 'independent principles', were heavily defeated. Plomer and Hart had received 908 and 900 votes respectively, as against 312 for Williams and 300 for Grieve, when the two last declined the poll on 28 June. The *London Evening Post* pointed out that Wilkes would now face hostile returning officers at the general election.[61]

That was not to matter in the end. But after this defeat Wilkes made careful preparations for the Mayoral election. On 15 September a well-attended meeting of the Livery agreed upon the joint candidature of Wilkes and Lord Mayor Bull, and five days later the Bill of Rights Society endorsed this plan.[62] When the official Court of Livery met on 29 September John Sawbridge made a hustings speech urging that there should be no division among the friends of liberty. He said that he did not intend to stand and so give ministerial candidates a chance of success. Sawbridge was speaking only for himself, not for the Hornite Constitutional Society; and he was generally understood to have made a private arrangement to secure Wilkite support for a London seat at the general election now perceived to be imminent and officially called the very next day. Lord Mayor Bull announced that he was standing merely to facilitate the election of Wilkes. A poll was then demanded by ministerialists Sir James Esdaile and Brackley Kennett. It ended on 6 October, when Wilkes had 1,957 votes, Bull 1,923, Esdaile 1,474, and Kennett 1,410. As in his two previous contests Wilkes polled a few plumpers near the end to ensure that he came first. Two days later the Court of Aldermen chose him as Mayor by 11 votes to 2, Townsend and Oliver displaying their personal enmity by perversely supporting Bull.[63] The ministerial Aldermen absented themselves after an analysis by Treasury Secretary John Robinson forecast a 13–9 majority for Wilkes.[64] This event gave Horace Walpole occasion to marvel at the political durability of Wilkes:

Thus, after so much persecution of the Court, after so many attempts on his life, after a long imprisonment in a gaol, after all his own crimes and indiscretions, did this extraordinary man, of more extraordinary fortune, attain the highest office in so grave and important a city as the capital of England, always reviving the more opposed and oppressed, and unable to shock Fortune, or make her laugh at *him*, who laughed at everybody and everything. The duration of his influence was the most wonderful part of his history. . . . Wilkes was seen through, detected, yet gained ground: and all the power of the Crown, all the malice of the Scots, all the abilities of Lord Mansfield, all the violence of Alderman Townsend, all the want of policy and parts of the Opposition, all the treachery of his friends, could not demolish him. He equally baffled the King and Parson Horne, though both neglected no latitude to compass his ruin. It is in the tenth year of his war on the Court that he gained so signal a victory![65]

By the time Wilkes became Lord Mayor the general election campaign was in full swing. A Middlesex county meeting on 26 September had already nominated Wilkes and Glynn as Parliamentary candidates, and they signed a pledge to work for the Bill of Rights Society programme, including Shorter Parliaments and 'a more fair and equal representation of the people', and also for the repeal of the recent legislation on America, including the Quebec Act.[66] Lord North told the King that despite intensive advertising only 300 had been present, 'all of them of the lowest of the people, and many of them certainly not freeholders'. Wilkes was so conscious of the poor attendance that he blamed the bad weather, but North could draw little comfort from the circumstance:

One might hope, that this appearance might give to some gentlemen of the county an inclination to oppose Mr Wilkes; but the spirits of the gentlemen of this part of the world are either so intimidated, or so indolent, or so fond of Mr Wilkes, or so averse to the present administration, that I do not think anything is to be expected from them.[67]

The ministry spared no effort to find two candidates for Middlesex: one alone would at best only keep out Glynn, not Wilkes, as George III realized. For a brief moment early in October there were two, William Blackstone's brother-in-law James Clitherow, and Sir Charles Raymond, thought by many ministerial men to have a good chance of success; but by 10 October both had withdrawn.[68] 'The Court . . . had used every endeavour to get candidates, but no one would venture', noted Horace Walpole, who thought that James Townsend, about to lose the government borough he had been representing, had also threatened to stand.[69] Wilkes and Glynn were unopposed at the election on 20 October, and the day was marked by a triumphant procession from the Mansion House to Brentford.[70]

There was more excitement elsewhere in the metropolitan area. In the City of London the Mayoral contest had provided an opportunity of 'trying the strength of the two parties', so George III commented to North on 30 September.[71] On 3 October there took place a Common Hall of the Livery, for the purpose of nominating Parliamentary candidates. The four Wilkes named were Frederick Bull, John Sawbridge, Brass Crosby, and George Hayley, and all took the same political pledge as Wilkes and Glynn. Two other candidates nominated, Rockinghamite William Baker and Richard Oliver, refused to do so, and were as much hissed by the 2,000 crowd as the others had been applauded, while James Townsend met with such abuse that he declined to stand. North hoped that Baker and Oliver would be joined by 'two other tolerable candidates', and next day two ministerial men, John Roberts and Alderman Benjamin Hopkins, announced a joint candidature. But on 6 October Hopkins withdrew at a meeting of 350 'friends of government', which then unanimously nominated Roberts, and, with only five dissentients, agreed that he should join with Oliver and Baker. Ministerial hopes of an anti-Wilkite alliance were unfounded, and it was soon apparent that Roberts had little chance.[72] He came last with 1,398 votes, when the successful candidates were Sawbridge, Hayley, Oliver, and Bull, with 3,456, 3,390, 3,354, and 3,096 votes respectively. But Crosby came a poor sixth, with 1,913 as against 2,802 for Baker. If the Wilkite success was thus incomplete, it was still better than it might have been. Wilkes himself admitted that Thomas Harley would have topped the poll if he had stood: but he 'took fright', according to Walpole, and sought to defend a family interest in Herefordshire, losing both the contest and court favour.[73]

Wilkite candidates also contested Surrey, Southwark, and Westminster. Sir Joseph Mawbey quitted his Southwark seat to fight Surrey, but was defeated by nearly 300 votes, being unpopular both as a distiller and as a Radical, even though he omitted Parliamentary Reform from his version of the Wilkite political programme. His old constituency of Southwark was contested by two candidates who took the Wilkite political test, local tobacco merchant Nathaniel Polhill and American William Lee. Polhill headed the poll, but Lee came a bad third. The large and prestigious constituency of Westminster presented a complicated scene. Sitting member Sir Robert Bernard, elected when a Bill of Rights Society man, had since joined the Constitutional Society, and did not stand again. Bill of Rights member Lord Mountmorres was soon in the field, and it was at first conjectured that the other Wilkite candidate would be Humphrey Cotes, who in 1772 had returned to financial prosperity by marrying a wealthy widow, and remained on good terms with Wilkes.[74] But early in September Chathamite Lord Mahon twice visited Wilkes to seek his endorsement. Wilkes, knowing little about him, 'had been rather cautious in what he said', so Chatham was informed on 16 September. Lord Mahon, despite having been advised by Wilkes 'not to be precipitate in declaring himself', published an election address on 15 September. Nor had he made a good impression on John Churchill, still a leading Wilkite in Westminster.[75] Wilkes did in the end favour the candidature of Mahon as well as Mountmorres after both subscribed to his political creed, although he voted for Cotes when his old friend also decided to stand. But the government interest in Westminster proved to be impregnable against this radical challenge, the ministerial candidates, Lord Percy and Lord Thomas Clinton, winning by over 2,000 votes. 'Wilkes went one day to support the losing candidates, and could amass but 15 votes', Walpole dryly noted. He was soon distancing himself from the débâcle, denying that he had proposed Mountmorres or sanctioned Mahon's advertisement.[76] Altogether the Wilkes candidates had won six seats in the London area. Elsewhere there was Wilkite success only for John Trevanion, now returned unopposed for Dover. Sir Watkin Lewes was again narrowly defeated at Worcester, while Stephen Sayre failed at Seaford. The Wilkite cause had little appeal to the electorate outside London.[77]

The Mayoralty of Wilkes was one of the most splendid in the City's history. His generosity, popularity, and flair for publicity contributed to this memorable circumstance; but the role of his elegant daughter Polly as Lady Mayoress was an important part of the scene, and affection for her much of the reason why Wilkes put on such a show. His first task was to wait upon Lord Chancellor Apsley to receive the King's formal approval of the City's choice. Newspapers reported that a refusal had been debated in cabinet, until one minister was said to have commented that 'it was much better to permit him to be Lord Mayor for one year than King of the City for life'. Wilkes was reputed to have been ready for a rebuff, prepared to tell the undistinguished Apsley that he was 'at least as fit to be Lord Mayor as he is to be Lord Chancellor'.[78] The occasion passed off without incident on 3 November.[79] Lord Mayor's Day on 8 November was even more resplendent than usual with the customary highlights of a procession of barges up and down the Thames to Westminster, and the Lord Mayor's Dinner in the Guildhall, although this function was boycotted by many grandees who customarily attended.[80] Throughout the year Wilkes gave frequent and lavish entertainments, highlighted in a magnificent Easter Ball on 17 April 1775. His daughter's special occasion as Lady Mayoress was a 'most brilliant rout' in the Mansion House on 7 April, attended by nearly a thousand people, including many peers.[81] The Mayoral expenses Wilkes incurred of £8,226 exceeded by £3,337 his official allowances, and he ended the year of office heavily in debt.[82]

Notwithstanding these public displays Wilkes took his duties seriously. He displayed administrative zeal and enterprise as Lord Mayor, just as he had done when sheriff. He was actively concerned with the regulation of Smithfield cattle market, and of food prices generally, in the interests of the consumer. Among his other initiatives were the organization of a charity for prisoners, and a campaign to clear prostitutes from City streets. Thereby he gained respect, and respectability: the Archbishop of Canterbury was one of his guests on 17 February 1775.[83]

Heavily involved in his Mayoral duties as genial host and busy administrator, Wilkes failed to exploit the political potential of his status as much perhaps as many had expected him to do. His political activity in the City was mainly concerned with the American crisis and the organization of protests against ministerial policy. Here his characteristic contribution was to resort to that popular body, the Livery, rather than the more conservative institutions of the Courts of Aldermen and Common Council; until George III declined to play this Wilkes game.[84]

The ascendancy of Wilkes in City politics remained virtually unchallenged at the end of his Mayoralty in November 1775. His own brother-in-law George Hayley had been one of the sheriffs chosen in midsummer, and at the Michaelmas election of Mayor there was no poll after Wilkes had made clear his intention that Sawbridge should succeed him. The Court of Aldermen chose Sawbridge after Wilkes himself had been the other candidate put forward. But soon the American War proved a solvent of Wilkite control of the City. Radical power there declined, and the heat went out of London politics as elections to City offices reverted to the earlier practices of custom and seniority.

*

The role of Wilkes in City politics had a postscript, a longer one than he anticipated in 1775. Then he hoped to take advantage of the popularity he had acquired as Lord Mayor by securing his election to the profitable if demanding post of City Chamberlain, which involved management of the City's finances. During the summer he had already sounded the incumbent, Sir Stephen Janssen, as to whether he was going to resign, and pushed the matter more pointedly in a letter of 18 November 1775:

I am told by my friends that the City are almost unanimous in their approbation of the late Mayor. . . . Your great kindness emboldens me to hint that if it corresponds with your ideas of resignation, *in a short time*, I might probably have the honour of succeeding a gentleman whom I highly venerate, and wish to imitate. After being harassed for so many years, I cannot but earnestly desire to arrive in a safe post, and acquire an honourable independence by a continuance of services in the best way I am able.[85]

Janssen yielded to this pressure, and was willing to assist Wilkes in his candidature.[86] 'It is generally believed that Alderman Wilkes will be elected, being the most capable of filling that important post', declared the partisan *London Evening Post* when Janssen formally signified his resignation on 6 February 1776. But even then the newspaper mentioned that there were other candidates, and two days later it reported that 'every step is being taken by the ministerial party in the City to keep Alderman Wilkes out of the Chamberlainship'. The rival candidate was Alderman Benjamin Hopkins, eight years a Director of the Bank of England, who had voted with the administration when an MP from 1771 to 1774, notably over the Printers' Case. These points were voiced at a Livery meeting of 12 February. Partisans of Hopkins retaliated with the argument that a man with such a cavalier attitude to money as Wilkes was unfit to take charge of the City's finances, and the advertisement for Hopkins reminded voters that he was 'a gentleman of unimpeachable integrity, well affected to his Majesty King George, and the present happy constitution in church and state'.[87] As the campaign hotted up aspersions on the financial integrity of Wilkes were countered by charges of ministerial bribery and by imputations that Hopkins was a recipient of such government rewards as business contracts and lottery tickets.[88] But for Wilkes there was the unfortunate circumstance, as his opponents often reminded him, that, at the height of his 1771 controversy with Horne, he had publicly declared, in answer to a taunt, that he would 'never' accept the post of Chamberlain. 'I know it indeed to be the most lucrative office in the gift of the City, but . . . I am not avaricious. My wishes are now few, and easily gratified.'[89]

To Wilkite partisans like Dr Thomas Wilson in Bath it was unthinkable that the City Livery would not now elect a man who had 'so bravely stood up, in the worst of times, for . . . the Liberties of the City of London'.[90] To his role in the famous controversies of 1763–4, 1768–9, and 1771 there was added the record of Wilkes as sheriff, Mayor, and MP. All these had been 'an honourable expense. He is now a candidate for the first time, for an office which unites profit with honour.'[91] Wilkes sought to clinch this case for his election by pledging himself, when the poll began on 20 February, to use at least one-third of his income, if chosen Chamberlain, to repay the debts incurred as Lord Mayor. Hisses greeted a declaration by Hopkins that 'honesty is the best policy',[92] and after the first day Wilkes led by 330 votes to 168. Thereafter he steadily lost ground, and the *London Evening Post* made a desperate appeal on 24 February:

Will the independent Livery let their old firm friend, John Wilkes, be overpowered by ministerial influence. The ministry and the ministerial Aldermen . . . are running our champion down. Come on then, my brave boys, and let us support our hero, John Wilkes, against his opponents and our oppressors.

A late rally failed to avert defeat for Wilkes by 2,887 votes to 2,710 on 27 February after a seven-day poll.[93] Wilkites attributed this, to them, shock result to such factors as the continued support by Wilkes of the American cause even after the outbreak of war in the previous April, and, more obviously, to ministerial interference. That 'dint of money' had carried Hopkins to victory was the popular belief, voiced at an unofficial Livery meeting of 14 March chaired by Alderman Lee, which resolved to raise a subscription to defray the expenses of Wilkes in his next challenge for the post.[94] That took place at the annual election of City officials on Midsummer Day, 24 June. A circular by Wilkes on 17 June claimed that Hopkins had been elected through perjury and bribery, and alleged that being a Bank of England Director was incompatible with the City Chamberlainship. A carefully timed publication on 20 June of the accounts of Wilkes as Lord Mayor showed the deficit of £3,358, together with the claim that the debt would not be cleared by four years' income as Chamberlain. The *London Evening Post* of that date also asserted that the contest was 'a struggle, whether the Liverymen of London, or the Ministry, shall, for the future, have the disposal of the important offices of this City'.

All this effort was to no avail. When the poll closed on 1 July Hopkins had triumphed by the much greater majority of 2,869 votes to 1,673. Wilkes had lost over 1,000 voters, many clearly resentful of his defiance of precedent in contesting again an office that although nominally annual was by convention deemed to be held for life.[95] Nor had Wilkes helped his cause by announcing that if elected Chamberlain he would not resign as Alderman.[96] That was another breach of conventional practice, one based on the sound reason that simultaneous tenure of both offices led to an incompatible conflict of interests between employer and employee.[97] Wilkes, unabashed by such criticism and desperate for money, nevertheless stood in 1777, being defeated by 2,132 votes to 1,228. This setback Wilkes attributed to treachery and indifference, announcing that he would stand again in 1778.[98] That was a foolish piece of bravado. Wilkes was trounced by 1,216 votes to 287, and did not contest the post in 1779.[99] But the unexpected death of Hopkins a few months later gave Wilkes the opportunity to take a prize that seemed to have passed beyond his reach.[100]

10

Wilkes and America

THAT the career of John Wilkes exacerbated the problem for Britain of the American Revolution has never been in doubt: that Wilkes himself welcomed that event has often been an unproven assumption. The treatment accorded to him by the ministries of Grenville and Grafton seemed to colonists confirmatory evidence that the government of George III threatened the liberty of his subjects in both Britain and America, thereby stiffening colonial resistance to administration policies.[1] More recently perceived is a second and fortuitous circumstance, that the Middlesex Elections case had the consequence of diverting ministerial attention away from the American problem arising out of the imposition of the Townshend taxes of 1767, and so worsening it by causing postponement of decisions on colonial policy.[2]

The coincidence of the Wilkite heyday with the coming of the American Revolution led London Radicals to cite colonial grievances in their campaign against government. That was a dangerous game to play, and ultimately contributed to the collapse of the Wilkite movement. The colonial cause was by no means as popular in Britain as contemporary Americans believed. Championship of American rights was never in the forefront even of any radical political programme, and the sincerity of Wilkes himself in the colonial cause has been the subject of continual controversy. To compare Wilkes in this respect with such wholehearted champions of America as the so-called Real Whigs is manifestly unfair. That precious group of thinkers and talkers could afford to indulge in open support of the colonists because they were not active in politics, their role being the Richard Price one of providing propaganda support in pamphlets and other modes of publicity.[3] But in the world of practical politics championship of the colonies could be a liability. During the general election of 1768 the American connections of Barlow Trecothick proved to be a disadvantage even with the voters of London, and politicians seeking influence and power there had to temper any enthusiasm they might possess for the colonial cause with a dose of caution.

'Mr Wilkes had always hated the Americans, was always the declared foe of their liberties, and condemned their glorious struggles for the rights of humanity.'[4] John Horne's sweeping condemnation of his rival in their public controversy of 1771 formed part of his attempt to discredit Wilkes as 'a friend to liberty'. But it has sometimes been accepted as a benchmark for assessments of the degree of sincerity with which Wilkes championed the colonial cause. Certainly Horne's biographer sought to convert this contention into historical fact: 'Mr Wilkes always hated, or rather despised the Americans; and even during his confinement in the King's Bench, laughed at and ridiculed their pretensions to an independent legislative right of internal taxation.'[5] Such private behaviour would have been at variance with the public stance of Wilkes, but it was certainly true that by 1771 he had done little to justify any claim to be a friend of America. He had been in France when the first storm of the Stamp Act Crisis erupted, and his reaction to the colonial resistance of 1765 can only be deemed hostile. 'You are much mistaken as to my ideas of America', he wrote to his brother Heaton on 17 November. 'I am too well informed of what passes there by some gentlemen I have seen, and there is a spirit little short of rebellion in several of the colonies. If I am to be an exile from my native London, it shall not be in the new world: so far I can command.'[6] The Rockingham ministry then in office solved the Stamp Act Crisis by combining repeal of that measure with the Declaratory Act of 1766, asserting the right of Parliament to legislate for the colonies 'in all cases whatsoever'. An ideological hostage to fortune, that measure was to make it impossible for the Parliamentary opposition to resist the North ministry's American policy on principle during the next decade.

This initial reaction by Wilkes anticipated his reluctance a decade later to support the idea of American independence. For Wilkes was a true patriot in the modern as well as the contemporary sense, and the outbreak of the American War revealed that his zeal for liberty was matched by his love of country. But during the intervening period he did adopt the idea of a common cause of 'liberty' on both sides of the Atlantic. At first his relationship with American resistance groups was one sided. Wilkes was willing to accept colonial acclaim and support, but in return he offered only private words of encouragement. The few public declarations of support for America from his partisans during the Middlesex Elections case seemingly owed nothing to Wilkes himself. It was American Arthur Lee who contrived, with professed difficulty, to insert in the Middlesex and London petitions what were no more than postscript references to colonial grievances.[7]

It was nevertheless that episode that sparked off regular contact between

Wilkes and America.[8] The Boston Sons of Liberty opened a correspondence with him by a letter of 6 June 1768. 'You are one of those incorruptibly honest men', it began, commending his 'perseverance in the good old cause'. Wilkes would have deemed unexceptionable the sentiments expressed next: 'We wait for constitutional redress, being determined that the King of Great Britain shall have subjects but not slaves in these remote parts of his dominions.' Enclosed with this epistle was a copy of the *Farmer's Letters*.[9] That was a recent series of anonymous tracts written by Philadelphia lawyer John Dickinson, who in response to the Townshend revenue duties of 1767 completely denied Parliament's right to tax the colonies. Wilkes, in his reply of 19 July, declared that in the *Farmer's Letters* 'the cause of freedom is perfectly understood, and ably defended', and then continued: 'I will ever, gentlemen, avow myself a friend to universal liberty. . . . Liberty I consider as the birthright of every subject of the British empire, and I hold Magna Carta to be in as full force in America as in Europe.'[10] Wilkes had displayed his customary talent for voicing appropriate sentiments, and the answer of the Boston Sons of Liberty on 5 October requested permission to publish his letter.[11]

The chief refrain of the subsequent correspondence from Boston was 'the military occupation' of that town from September 1768, a ministerial response to riots over the trade laws.[12] In a letter of 30 March 1769 Wilkes replied that it was 'with grief and indignation' he had heard about the dispatch of troops to Boston, 'as if it were the capital of a province belonging to our enemies or in the possession of rebels', and he congratulated the Bostonians on avoiding an incident similar to that in St George's Fields by displaying prudence and moderation when the soldiers arrived. With respect to the broader colonial dispute over taxation his opinion was unequivocal, condemning the Townshend duties not only as 'highly impolitic and inexpedient, but on my idea likewise absolutely unjust and unconstitutional, a direct violation of the great fundamental principles of British liberty'.[13] Before Wilkes emerged from prison the Bostonians were able to claim that they too had suffered an event similar to the St George's Fields Massacre, the 'Boston Massacre' of 5 March 1770 when five members of an aggressive crowd were killed by soldiers.[14] The obvious comparison was promptly made by the Boston press, but curiously not in the report sent to Wilkes on 23 March, the day after a Boston town meeting had decided that he should be personally informed of 'the late horrid Massacre'.[15]

During his sojourn in the King's Bench Prison Wilkes received practical testimony of support from various colonists; gifts for him included two turtles from Boston, and forty-five hogsheads of tobacco from both Maryland and Virginia.[16] The most famous donation was the £2,500 of local currency, equivalent to £1,500 sterling, voted on 8 December 1769 by the South Carolina Assembly 'for the support of the just and constitutional rights and liberties of the people of Great Britain and America'. Next day the Committee empowered to carry out this resolution instructed the colony's London bankers to pay the money to the Bill of Rights Society, and to obtain a receipt from its Secretary Robert Morris.[17] On 6 February 1770 Morris received the appropriate letter and informed Wilkes the same day of the stipulation that the money was to be used 'particularly for supporting such of our fellow-subjects who by assisting the just rights of the people have or shall become obnoxious to Administration and suffer from the hand of power'.[18] Despite this clear hint that the money was to be used on behalf of Wilkes he was annoyed that the gift had not been made to him by name and wrote a peevish reply.[19] The release of Wilkes from prison in April 1770 was widely celebrated in America as well as in Britain; but by that date the North ministry had defused the colonial crisis by the repeal of all the Townshend duties except that on tea, and thereafter America faded in British political consciousness until the Boston Tea Party of December 1773 precipitated a new and final crisis.

During this period Wilkes maintained his American contacts. A letter of 28 December 1770 to him from Boston Radical Sam Adams contains what can be seen in retrospect as a significant hint that Britain might lose America if the colonies were not permitted 'the fullest exercise of their rights'.[20] But within the ranks of the Bill of Rights Society it was the Horne clique that took the lead on America. At the London Parliamentary by-election of July 1770 John Horne declared that 'when the people of America are enslaved, we cannot be free'; and the successful Society candidate Richard Oliver, whose own Caribbean background may have afforded him some insight into colonial grievances, made a hustings pledge that he would endeavour 'to remove the just complaints of America which operate to your [London's] present disadvantage, in a commercial connexion, as well as in a political view'.[21] There is some evidence that later in the year Wilkes himself favoured the idea of organizing a City Remonstrance to the Crown over America, but nothing came of it.[22] Yet he was capable of berating American attitudes to score a political point. In an anonymous pamphlet *Annals of the Mayoralty of the Right Hon. Barlow Trecothick Esq.*, designed to prevent Trecothick's re-election as Lord Mayor, Wilkes made a scathing reference to 'the true *levelling* principle of his countrymen, the *Bostonians*'.[23] That was published in the autumn of 1770. Horne, whether or not he knew Wilkes to be the author of this tract, deemed the colonial question to be an issue over which he was vulnerable in their public controversy of 1771. Wilkes took care to defend himself, writing on 24 May of the repeal of the Stamp Act as one of the glorious achievements of the Rockingham ministry by which 'the subjects, both at home and in the colonies, have been restored to their personal liberty'.[24]

At the time of the Hornite secession the three American members of the Bill of Rights Society, Arthur and William Lee and Stephen Sayre, remained loyal to Wilkes, and Arthur Lee became the new Secretary. During the Stamp Act Crisis of 1765–6 he had been active in the press campaign for repeal and more recently had written newspaper articles as 'Junius Americanus';[25] and it was he who inserted in the Society's political programme of July 1771, albeit as the last of eleven items, this comprehensive statement on America:

You shall endeavour to restore to America the essential rights of taxation, by representatives of their own free election; repealing the acts passed in violation of that right, since the year 1763; and the universal excise, so notoriously incompatible with every principle of British liberty, which has been lately substituted in the Colonies for the laws of customs.[26]

The Bill of Rights Society might adopt a policy stance on America, but the colonial issue remained dormant until the Boston Tea Party of 16 December 1773. That act of defiance, when £9,000 worth of taxed tea was thrown into Boston harbour, alienated virtually all British politicians except the radical factions in London. During the first half of 1774 the latter tacitly acknowledged this public indignation by adopting a low profile on America in the City, although in Parliament there was some radical resistance to the ministerial legislation. John Sawbridge at once made his position clear by declaring on 14 March that 'there can be no such thing as liberty when you can be taxed without your consent'.[27] The occasion was the introduction of the Boston Port Bill, designed to shut Boston harbour until the town paid compensation for the tea. The measure passed without a vote, but among the few MPs who opposed it were Richard Oliver at the Committee stage on 23 March and Bull and Sawbridge two days later on its passage.[28]

The American cause afforded Radicals welcome new ground on which to attack government, for the Middlesex Elections case had lost its appeal to a wider audience, and such other radical ideas as Parliamentary Reform attracted little popular support. 'No taxation without representation' was by contrast a battle-cry that evoked folk memories of the earlier contests in Britain between Crown and Parliament. The Parliamentary opposition groups headed by Rockingham and Chatham, sharing with the North ministry a belief in Parliament's right to tax America, did not adopt it; but they did offer resistance to later policy measures of the ministry. What most aroused Radicals and Chathamites alike was the Massachusetts Justice Bill, because of its contingency provision for transferring to Britain trials of soldiers and officials accused of capital offences. Sawbridge opposed the measure at its introduction on 21 April as unfair, since only ministerial witnesses would cross the Atlantic, and subsequently opposed the Bill at every stage.[29] He and Sir Cecil Wray were the tellers for the small minority of twenty-four against its passage on 6 May, a group that included Bull, Oliver, and James Townsend.[30]

Sawbridge frequently made the point that his support of the colonies did not derive 'from a desire of gaining popularity. For certainly the cause of America is not a popular cause in this country. It doth proceed from the love of liberty.'[31] The City Radicals, however, struck a more popular chord, at least in London, by resistance to the Quebec Bill, albeit for reasons of prejudice rather than principle. The retention of French civil law, and the protected status of the Catholic Church, were two provisions that, while commended by posterity, were susceptible to contemporary political exploitation, though more so in the City than in the House of Commons. Serjeant Glynn criticized both features at the second reading on 26 May.[32] On 3 June Lord Mayor Bull held a Court of Common Council that voted a petition against the Quebec Bill.[33] Presented to the Commons that same day, it objected to the measure on three grounds: that the introduction of French law would threaten the freedom of both persons and property; that the preference for the Catholic Church as 'the only legal established religion' would be oppressive to Protestants; and that the legislative power would be vested in a Council nominated by the Crown, 'totally inconsistent with the liberty and principles of the *English constitution*'.[34] A further objection was added by Glynn on 10 June when he attacked the absence of jury trials in French law. They were a notable safeguard of liberty, he said, citing the *North Briton* case of 1763 as an example.[35] Sawbridge, Oliver, and Townsend also spoke against the Bill during its passage.[36] On 22 June, the day when the King was due to give his royal assent, a Common Council petition vainly asking him to refuse to do so was presented to George III by Lord Mayor Bull, attended by Aldermen Crosby, Lewes, Sawbridge, and Plomer, together with 156 Common Councillors.[37] The King then went to Westminster to signify his consent to the Bill. Crowds thronged the streets, groaning, hissing, and shouting 'No Popery. No French laws.' On the return journey there was an unexpected cheer, because Wilkes was standing at the window of a nearby house. Misunderstanding the situation, 'the King bowed, but the people, too honest to deceive his Majesty, instantly shouted "Wilkes for ever!" '[38] Thwarted in all their endeavours to stop or modify the Quebec Act, the City Radicals subsequently gave way to frustrated spite, taking advantage of the circumstance that public Roman Catholic worship was still illegal in Britain. On Sunday, 18 September, Lord Mayor Bull closed two Catholic churches in London, 'to stop the progress of Popery, at least within the City, so long as the law is on his side'.[39]

John Wilkes had not hitherto taken a prominent part on the American question. In London it had been Arthur Lee who organized petitions against the Boston Port Bill, presented respectively on 25, 28, and 31 March to the Commons, Lords, and King.[40] On the Quebec Act there hangs a question-mark over his attitude. On 3 June Wilkes 'retired very early' from the Common Council meeting that voted a petition against the measure, and he was conspicuously absent from the delegation to George III on 22 June.[41] This behaviour reflected his strong personal belief in religious toleration, and anticipated his role in the anti-Catholic Gordon Riots six years later. On the main American question he was more active from the autumn of 1774, when election both as MP and Lord Mayor provided him with a dual chance of political participation. Wilkes did not speak in Parliament on America until 6 February 1775. A brief summary of the debate next day in the *London Chronicle* reported only that he had 'denied the right of taxation independent of representation'; but the fullest public exposition of his views on America before the outbreak of war was provided by John Almon's paper, the *London Evening Post*, on 11 February.[42] Wilkes, indeed, began with a forecast that ministerial policy would lead to 'the horrors of a civil war' and asked the House before it was too late to 'reflect whether justice is on our side. The assumed right of *taxation without* the *consent* of the subject is plainly the primary cause of the present quarrel. Have we, Sir, any right to tax the Americans?' Wilkes then produced a plan that, as reported, was confused on that very point of principle. This was that there should take place that spring a joint meeting of MPs and colonial delegates, in order to establish quotas for each colony, analogous to the fixed land tax assessments on each county in England. The annual burden would then vary in accordance with the rate of land tax levied by Parliament.

American resistance had been exaggerated, Wilkes insisted, pointing out that the recent petition from the Congress at Philadelphia did not mention the Navigation Act or the Declaratory Act, and specifically acknowledged the authority of George III. He deplored the reference in the Address at the beginning of the session to Massachusetts being in a state of rebellion, making this prescient comment: 'This I know, a successful resistance is a *revolution* not a *rebellion*. Who can tell, Sir, . . . whether in a few years the Americans, may not celebrate the glorious aera of the revolution of 1775, as we do that of 1688.' Wilkes ended by warning that Britain would not be able to subdue America in a war: 'A few fortresses on the coast, and some sea-ports only, you will keep.' Boston would be like Gibraltar in Spain, while 'the Americans will rise to independence'.

This speech by Wilkes forecast much of what was soon to happen: but it also exemplified the misunderstanding by the London Radicals of the colonial crisis. The Bill of Rights Society programme at the general election of

1774 portrayed the American grievance as 'taxation without representation'. The Wilkites, more so even than most British politicians, failed to perceive that the challenge of the Continental Congress to the so-called 'Intolerable Acts' of 1774 was one to the legislative rights of Parliament, and no longer merely a dispute over taxation. On the contrary, some Radicals had come to believe their own paranoid propaganda: on 5 April 1775 Frederick Bull voiced in the Commons the unfounded suspicion that the 1773 export of taxed tea to the colonies had been a sinister plot against American liberty.[43]

Wilkes made no other Parliamentary speech on America that session. Indeed, in order 'to show he was not connected with the Rockingham party', he did not even stay to vote for Edmund Burke's Conciliatory Plan of 23 March 1775.[44] But if Wilkes neglected the American cause at Westminster, it was in order to promote it at the Guildhall. Aware that only in the City did he possess an opportunity to make any political impact, he exploited his position as Lord Mayor to launch a propaganda campaign, and the overall effort was impressive. His brother-in-law George Hayley organized a petition of London merchants trading to America, which was presented to the House of Commons on 23 January.[45] On 10 February William Saxby, a Bill of Rights Society member, successfully proposed in Common Council a motion of thanks to Chatham for the conciliation plan for America he had put forward in the Lords on 1 February. The Common Council also thanked all peers and MPs who had opposed ministerial policy towards the colonies.[46] On 21 February the same body passed further resolutions on America, including the declaration that 'we are therefore of opinion that our fellow-subjects the Americans are justified in every constitutional opposition' they made to the Parliamentary legislation of 1774.[47] Three weeks later, on 14 March, it voted a petition to the House of Lords against the New England Trade Bill.[48]

Common Council was acknowledged to be the authentic political voice of the City. What was innovative about the mayoralty of Wilkes was his deployment for propaganda purposes of the Common Hall of Livery, whose size and political zeal made possible the voting of more popular and extreme resolutions. On 5 April Lord Mayor Wilkes opened a Livery meeting with a speech in which he expressed feelings of 'justice and humanity to our persecuted brothers in America' and apprehensions about the threat to London's prosperity. The City Remonstrance then voted declared that the consequences of ministerial policy were 'a deep and perhaps fatal wound to commerce, the ruin of manufactures, the diminution of the revenue, and consequent increase of taxes, the alienation of the colonies, and the blood of your Majesty's subjects'. It alleged that 'the real purpose' was 'to establish arbitrary power over all America', and proclaimed that it was 'a principle of liberty' that 'no part of the dominion can be taxed without being represented'.

Such statements were predictable. But the remarkable feature of the Remonstrance was this implicit adoption of the American denial of Parliament's right to legislate for the colonies at all, except with regard to trade: 'Subordination in commerce, under which the colonies have always cheerfully acquiesced, is, they conceive, all that this country ought in justice to require.'[49]

Perhaps because the City Radicals now understood and were eager to endorse the colonial viewpoint, this assertion went far beyond what Wilkes had said in Parliament only two months earlier. George III, indignant at what he deemed the insolence of the Livery, had to be persuaded by his Prime Minister to receive this formally on the throne, in accordance with precedent. Lord North had given him this advice:

We know, by experience, that these Addresses when received, and rejected in the usual manner fall into contempt, and are attended with no other evil consequences than the trouble and disagreeable circumstances of receiving them on the throne. . . . It seems likewise inadvisable to alter the method of proceeding in the Mayoralty of Mr. Wilkes. His importance, which was greatly over-rated in the most violent times, is now certainly much fallen, but it would revive in the opinion of some part of the world, if his presence should seem to be too studiously avoided.

The King, as North reminded him, had earlier accepted from the City Livery other Remonstrances even more objectionable, as on 6 March 1770 and 11 March 1773.[50]

George III reluctantly took this advice, receiving the Remonstrance on 10 April, when his reply expressed astonishment that rebellion was being thus encouraged.[51] This was the occasion, so Horace Walpole noted, when 'Wilkes behaved with so much respect, that the King himself owned he had never seen so well-bred a Lord Mayor'.[52] But the next day George III sent a message, through his Lord Chamberlain, Lord Hertford, to Lord Mayor Wilkes, announcing that he would not receive future Livery petitions on the throne.[53] As Lord North had anticipated, Wilkes sought to exploit this royal breach with precedent, pointing out the theoretical danger that the sovereign might not know the grievances of his subjects unless he received their complaints in person. At the midsummer meeting of the Livery on 24 June a strong petition on the subject was voted. Drafted by Arthur Lee, it condemned those who had advised the King to take this stand. It was never presented, after George III told the London sheriffs four days later that he would not receive it on the throne, a procedure that had been insisted upon by the Livery. On 4 July Lord Mayor Wilkes reported these events to another Livery meeting, which voted a series of resolutions denouncing the King's behaviour as a breach both of the 1689 Revolution Settlement and of the rights of the City. Yet even now the King's decision, which was palpably his own, was ostensibly attributed to bad advice.[54] This City indignation reflected radical impotence in the face of the King's attitude. George III had effectively countered the new propaganda tactic of utilizing the City Livery devised by John Wilkes.

Simultaneously with this challenge to the King's government in Parliament and City the radical clubs engaged in competitive support of the colonial cause. The Constitutional Society voted £100 for Boston on 7 February 1775, and another £100 on 21 March after being outbid by the Bill of Rights Society with £500 on 14 March.[55] John Horne then went too far when on 7 June, after news of actual hostilities had arrived, he persuaded the Constitutional Society to vote £100 for 'the relief of the widows, orphans and aged parents' of Americans 'inhumanely murdered' by the King's troops at Lexington and Concord on 19 April.[56] This advertisement was deemed seditious libel by the ministry, and eventually led to Horne's conviction on that charge in 1777, when Lord Mansfield sentenced him to a year in prison.[57]

The outbreak of the American War eroded the popular support hitherto enjoyed by Wilkes, a trend symbolized by the demise of the Bill of Rights Society, which held its last known meeting on 24 October.[58] Only a month earlier, on 26 September, the Society had resolved to recommend to those of its members who were MPs that they should endeavour to stop the American War and seek 'to establish a connection between the two countries, upon the generous principle of equal liberty'.[59] But already by that date the Wilkite hold on London was under threat. On 5 July the Common Council postponed for two days resolutions on America after a heated debate during which Alderman Harley had the 1766 Declaratory Act read out to make the point that Parliamentary sovereignty over America was supported by the great majority of British politicians.[60] The King was encouraged by this to hope that the next meeting might be 'prevented from taking any step with regard to the rebellion in America', but deemed the outcome as unimportant. 'The comfort is by the many absurd steps taken by that body if they act otherwise it will not be of much effect', he commented to North. 'I have no doubt but the Nation at large sees the conduct of America in its true light.'[61] On 7 July the adjourned Common Council meeting debated whether or not the Americans were in a state of rebellion and then carried by 74 votes to 59 a motion asking the King to suspend hostilities.[62] Opponents had objected to the implication that George III had begun the war, and to the denial of Parliament's right of taxation, a doctrine the King deemed 'subversive to all authority'. But he thought the Address couched in 'the most decent and moderate' wording 'that has been for some time fabricated on that side [of] Temple Bar', and approved the answer North drafted for him to make when Lord Mayor Wilkes presented the Address on 14 July.[63]

Wilkes never relaxed his opposition to the American War. When on

23 August the King issued a Proclamation of Rebellion, as Lord Mayor he 'let nobody but the common crier attend the Proclamation, and would not lend any horses to the heralds'.[64] A month later, when the City Livery met to choose Sawbridge as his Mayoral successor, Wilkes produced a letter he had received from John Hancock, President of the American Congress, asking the City of London as 'the patron of liberty' to moderate for peace. Wilkes thereupon persuaded the Livery to vote an Address to the electors of Great Britain criticizing the war as 'bloody, expensive, and a threat to liberty'.[65] Wilkes also took the opportunity of his retirement Mayoral speech to attack ministerial 'plans to establish despotism in New England, and popery in Canada', the latter claim, so contrary to his usual stance of toleration, perhaps a desperate ploy to retain popular support.[66] And it was doubtless at his instigation that the Court of Common Council on 25 October 1775 and 14 March 1776 voted Addresses to Parliament and King respectively against the war.[67] Wilkes was fighting a losing battle. Even within the metropolitan area radical opposition to the war came under increasing challenge. At a Middlesex county meeting of 25 September, summoned to vote instructions to its MPs, objection was made to the presence of Wilkes, who declared himself 'the servant of the electors'. Several speakers had the temerity to oppose the radical resolutions, declaring that America had been taxed earlier and that colonial charters reserved Parliamentary rights. Sayre replied that only the Pennsylvania charter did so, and instructions to oppose the war were voted by 'an immense majority'.[68] But the autumn campaign of loyal Addresses stimulated by the Proclamation of Rebellion revealed how fast opinion was changing in London. Loyal Addresses were presented by the magistrates both of Middlesex and the Liberty of the Tower of London. An Address from 941 London merchants on 14 October countered a conciliatory petition of 1,100 merchants three days earlier. Most remarkable of all was a loyal Address submitted on 20 October by 1,029 members of the Livery.[69] That London was no longer a Wilkite stronghold was demonstrated by the failure of Wilkes himself to secure election by the Livery in February 1776 to the coveted and lucrative post of City Chamberlain, a setback widely attributed to his support of the colonial cause.[70] The American Revolution proved a kiss of death to Wilkite radicalism.

Wilkes, effectively deprived of his City power base, became more of a Parliamentary politician. But on America he spoke only twice in the session of 1775–6, the period between the outbreak of war and the Declaration of Independence. In the opening debate of 26 October 1775 on the Address, Wilkes denounced the American War as 'unjust', since it originated from attempts to tax the colonists without their consent. Claiming to be a friend to 'universal liberty', he accused the North ministry of provocative measures, and denied that independence was the American aim, although it might well prove to be the result of the war. Wilkes virtually endorsed the American denial of Parliament's legislative powers over the colonies, just as the City petition of 5 April had done. The colonists, he declared, simply wanted parity with Britain. That could be either commercial restrictions and no taxation, or taxes and freedom of trade.[71]

The other occasion when Wilkes championed the cause of America was on 27 November, when Richard Oliver moved for an Address to George III to ascertain responsibility for a wide range of government measures. It had been previously agreed among City Radicals that Lord Mayor Sawbridge should propose such a motion, but Oliver usurped the role by advertising his intention, to the disgust of the Wilkites, Frederick Bull commenting to Wilkes on the 'pride, insolence, vanity, conceit, self-sufficiency, obstinacy, malice, envy . . . [of] this dirty fellow'.[72] Despite this annoyance with its proposer Sawbridge, Wilkes, and Hayley spoke for it, with Wilkes declaring that it was the duty of the House 'as the grand inquest of the nation, to find out and punish the delinquents . . . We owe it to the people at large, and several of us have it in express charge from our constituents'. The motion he claimed to be an 'olive branch', presumably because punishment of the culprits was intended to follow their disclosure. America could not be conquered, he warned the House, and must be conciliated. Samuel Adams and John Hancock, Wilkes said provocatively, were 'two worthy gentlemen, and, I dare to add, true patriots'. Lord North jocularly derided the attempts of other Radicals to emulate their mentor, saying that one Wilkes was sufficient. 'Though, he said, to do him justice, it was not easy to find many such.' Oliver's motion implied criticism of all ministries since 1763, thereby offending the opposition parties of Rockingham and Chatham as well as the North administration. On two divisions it obtained the derisory support of 16 and 10 votes.[73] MP Anthony Storer told Lord Carlisle that 'Wilkes counted twelve who divided with him; . . . he dignified them by calling them his twelve Apostles'.[74]

News of the American Declaration of Independence on 4 July 1776 changed the whole political argument. That was a watershed even for such a champion of colonial rights as John Wilkes. 'I will never give up the supremacy of Great Britain' was his reputed comment.[75] Indirect confirmation that Wilkes held this opinion appears in a letter written to him on 24 September 1776 by former Bill of Rights Society member Samuel Petrie: 'If nothing is either done or attempted this campaign, American independence is for ever established.'[76] Wilkes, like many other opposition politicians, was in the dilemma of wishing military success to neither the King's government nor the rebels. But, in contrast to the main opposition parties of Rockingham and Chatham, whose support of the Declaratory Act confined their criticism to the conduct of the war, Wilkes blamed the ministry for 'the wicked war' itself. In a half-hour speech during the debate of 31 October 1776 on the Address he attributed the conflict to 'a spirit of violence, injustice, and obstinacy in our ministers'. For Wilkes the fatal step had been the refusal to respond in the autumn of 1775 to the Olive Branch Petition from the American Congress. The ministers should not now pride themselves on having forecast the colonial demand for independence, because it had been caused by their own 'unjust and sanguinary measures'. Britain's European enemies would take advantage of this situation, but in any case America could never be conquered by 'this island'. The only way 'to save the empire', Wilkes urged, was 'to recall our fleets and armies, repeal all the acts injurious to the Americans passed since 1763, and restore their charters'.[77]

Privately Wilkes thought little of both the Parliamentary opposition and the American rebels. In the House of Commons on 15 May 1777 he commented to MP James Harris that 'the Americans thought their friends in England so profligate, they would not trust them': but then went on to say that 'a good cause (meaning the Americans) had been defended there by cowards'.[78] That was at a time when the British armies seemed to be on the brink of victory. Yet even before news came in December of the surrender of General Burgoyne at Saratoga, Wilkes publicly repeated his opinion that Britain could not win the war. Speaking on an opposition amendment to the Address on the first day of the next Parliamentary session, 20 November 1777, Wilkes deplored the evident intention of the ministry to continue 'this unnatural, unjust and barbarous war', which was expensive and futile. Especially did he denounce the use by the British army of Red Indians, whose favourite repast was 'human flesh'. Britain, he reiterated once again, lacked the resources to subdue such a vast country; but his clinching argument was that 'men are not converted, Sir, by the force of the bayonet at the breast'.[79]

It was Wilkes who seized the Parliamentary initiative when the Saratoga disaster became known. On 10 December 1777 he boldly moved for the repeal of the Declaratory Act of 1766. In an oration that expounded his personal view of the contest, Wilkes began by deploring the ministry's reluctance to seek reconciliation:

Scarcely a hint of a wish for peace has been made by any member of administration. I will not, however, Sir, be dispirited. Some late events unknown to the House at that time, may induce the most violent to listen to those healing measures, which in the insolence of our imagined triumphs, we rejected with disdain. The preliminary of peace, which I shall take the liberty of submitting to the House, strikes at the root of the evil, the confessed cause and origin of the American war. I mean, Sir, the right of taxation, which is enacted in the Declaratory Act.

Taxation without consent was contrary to 'the law of England', Wilkes declared. 'While that act remains in the statute book, you never can think of any negotiation with the Congress. . . . This one statute, the Declaratory Act, is the foundation from whence not only waters of bitterness, but rivers of blood, have flowed.' Parliament had no right to pass it, for Parliament was not omnipotent: 'We cannot fill up our own vacancies, as the late House of Commons indeed did in the case of the Middlesex election, but all good men abhorred the usurpation.' Wilkes praised the Rockingham ministry for its achievements in the cause of liberty: the resolutions condemning general warrants; the repeal of the cider tax, obnoxious because of the alleged right of excise men to enter private houses; and the repeal of the Stamp Act, perhaps made possible, Wilkes conceded, only by the simultaneous passage of the Declaratory Act. He regretted that such expediency had been necessary, and was 'satisfied that it was not meant to be acted upon'. But the next ministry, under Chatham, 'built on this solid foundation of a right to taxation' by the Townshend duties of 1767. Having devoted most of his speech to the Declaratory Act, Wilkes announced that afterwards he meant to move the repeal of all American measures since 1763, thereby acceding to the request of Congress. His list included the Quebec Act, which had 'established French tyranny and the Romish religion in their most abhorred extent'.

The motion caused embarrassment for opposition and administration. The Rockingham and Chatham parties, with both of which Wilkes had disclaimed any connection, found it unacceptable. Shelburne told Chatham next day that Barré's initial reaction had been to support it, but after consultations with their friends he and Dunning headed a group of abstainers.[80] The Rockinghamites, however, voted against the motion after Charles Fox defended the Declaratory Act. The vote took place over a previous question moved by the ministry, a procedural device to avoid a direct negative. Lord North had claimed that the concessions proposed by Wilkes would not satisfy the 'unreasonable demands' of the colonists. At the same time he did not rule out the possibility of concessions 'on similar ground to that now before the House' at a more appropriate time, and explained that under Parliamentary rules rejection of a motion precluded its proposal again in the same session. Hence his use of the previous question, which was carried by a majority of 116 to 10.[81]

The Prime Minister was generally understood to have informed the House that he would introduce a conciliatory plan after the Christmas recess.[82] When this was revealed to Parliament early in 1778 it bore a remarkable similarity to the proposals of Wilkes. Lord North adopted the principle of renouncing Parliamentary taxation of the colonies, albeit by a different method, a Bill specifically for that purpose rather than repeal of the Declaratory Act.

A second Bill appointing a Peace Commission to negotiate with the colonists authorized it to suspend laws 'so far as the same doth relate to them', a formula that excluded the Quebec Act.[83]

Wilkes did not speak on these measures until the third reading of the Bill relating to taxation on 2 March 1778. He could not forbear from pointing out their parentage. 'There is scarcely an idea in either of the two acts . . . which has not been suggested' by the opposition, Wilkes declared, mentioning his own proposal 'not three months since'. But the recent American negotiations with France had now changed the situation, while the legislation proposed was 'more calculated for this country than America. . . . The Bills hold out what ministers know to be a fallacious hope, a reconciliation with the colonists on terms short of independence.' The Americans would not accept them. The taxation measure before the House Wilkes described as 'a kind of second Declaratory Act', for it referred to the abandonment of only 'the exercise of the right of taxation' of the colonies by Parliament. 'Was this meant as a healing measure?' The second Bill mentioned the American 'misrepresentations of danger to their liberties and legal rights', a phrase Congress would construe as an insult. After contending that the colonists could not be expected to trust British promises, and a scathing denunciation of the employment of Indians in the war, Wilkes nevertheless concluded by saying, 'I heartily wish success to these two conciliatory bills and that we may regain by treaty, what we have lost by tyranny and arms. . . . I entirely approve the effort, although I have my fears that it is made too late.'[84]

In his American speeches Wilkes had been a repeated critic of General Burgoyne, especially over his use of savage Indians against the colonists; and this conduct resulted in a personal confrontation between the two men in the House of Commons on 26 May 1778, when Burgoyne was back in Britain on parole after his surrender at Saratoga. Independent MP Robert Vyner put forward a motion for an inquiry into the wretched plight of Burgoyne's army in captivity, and the freedom of its general. Wilkes rose to second and to express the wish that the inquiry would include an examination of the Saratoga campaign. Since procedural rules precluded a seconder from amending a motion, Charles Fox did so on his behalf. Wilkes declared that he was not bringing any charge against Burgoyne, but rather giving him an opportunity to answer criticism. Burgoyne dryly retorted that he would treat this conduct of Wilkes as 'some reparation for the very free, and not very generous comments he made upon my conduct in my absence'. He had made every effort to prevent Indian atrocities, but one incident had been generalized into a policy of deliberate savagery. Wilkes denied any personal animus: 'I am on this occasion merely the echo of the public voice.' But he did raise as a matter of public concern 'the charge I have repeatedly read of the burning villages and houses, and the wanton destruction and devastation of property, during the progress of the northern army under his command'. Burgoyne thereupon denied all knowledge of such behaviour and of any orders to that end, asking Wilkes to consider an apology. This was not made, but the debate ended with the rejection of Vyner's motion.[85]

The failure of the Peace Commission was known before Parliament met for the next session on 26 November 1778. During the debate that day on the Address Wilkes, the voice of realistic common sense, had no doubt as to what policy the ministry should now adopt: 'I believe the acknowledgement of the independency of the revolted colonies is the only measure, which can re-establish the public tranquillity. I sincerely think it would both with America and France, and probably prevent a future Spanish war.' The colonists, driven to declare their independence by British policy, had since been further alienated by the deployment against them of Germans and Red Indians, and it was 'beyond credibility that, now assured of French support, they would renounce independence'. There was no practical alternative. 'A series of four years disgraces and defeats are surely sufficient to convince us of the absolute impossibility of conquering America by force, and I fear the gentle means of persuasion have equally failed.' Acceptance of independence would detach America from France, and perhaps lead to a commercial treaty. In any case, the gesture would be nominal: 'The fact cannot be dissembled, nor disguised. America is, in my opinion, irrecoverably lost. It is indifferent to her, whether you think proper to acknowledge her independency.'[86] This candid and shrewd appraisal was to be justified by subsequent events, but in 1778 neither the ministry nor the majority of MPs deemed America to be lost.

That Wilkes believed American independence to be inevitable was misinterpreted by his former Bill of Rights associate, American William Lee, then in Paris, into a desire to expedite that development. For in 1779 Lee wrote to him a letter secreted under two covers, the outer addressed to George Hayley, the inner to 'Miss Wilkes'. The letter, dated 17 June, reached Wilkes on 20 July. Asserting that 'every true Englishman' should wish 'success to the enemy, until our liberties are secured', Lee asked Wilkes to act as a paid spy. If he sent information on all operations planned against America and her allies, from details of all expeditions to news of cabinet meetings and dockyard activities, Wilkes would be paid £200 a quarter![87] That was a total misjudgement of the man. Wilkes did not favour American independence, and in any case he would never have acted as a traitor to his own country: fierce patriotism in the modern sense was always part of his political creed.

Only one more Parliamentary speech by Wilkes on America is known, made on 27 November 1780 against a proposal to thank generals Clinton and Cornwallis for their successful campaign during the summer in the Carolinas. That was the first Wilkes speech heard by diarist Nathaniel Wraxall, who noted this impression:

Wilkes, rising in his place, pronounced a speech of great length, and of still greater severity which (as he was accustomed to do) he had prepared, not without evident labour, for the occasion. It was, like every composition of his, spirited, classic, and stamped with the characteristic energy of his fearless mind.[88]

The motion implied approval of the American War, which Wilkes denounced as 'unfounded in principle, and fatal in its consequences to this country. I condemned it at the beginning and have regularly opposed its progress in every stage, both in and out of Parliament.' Wilkes did not want Britain to lose her colonies. He would 'subscribe to almost any conditions' to obtain peace with America. But he repeated what he had said in 1778, that American independence was inevitable, whether or not Britain formally agreed. America would possess it *de facto* if not *de jure*.[89] Wilkes did not share the optimism induced by temporary success in the war. Within a couple of years events demonstrated the truth of what Wilkes had perceived much earlier than most British politicians. By that time the wheel of political fortune had put him in the ranks of government supporters.

11

Parliamentary Politician
1774–1790

THE return of Wilkes to Parliament in 1774 aroused varying expectations among contemporaries. From time to time ministers had been advised to allow him to take his seat there, in the confident expectation that he would subside into silent back-bench obscurity. This prognosis was evidently based on the dismal performance of Wilkes as a speaker when in the House of Commons from 1757 to 1763; but events from 1774 were to show it to have been a significant underestimate of his talent and pertinacity.[1] Equally mistaken was the anticipation that he would now create a Radical Party in the Commons, centred on a nucleus of those MPs associated with the Bill of Rights Society. That was never his intention, nor ever a possibility. Wilkes lacked the requisite personal stature, character, and financial resources to sustain any such role. Nor did Wilkes sacrifice his independence or risk his popularity by attaching himself to either of the two opposition parties. 'Wilkes could not properly be considered as a Member of the Minority; because, though he always sate on that side of the House, and usually voted with them, yet he neither depended on Lord Rockingham, nor on Lord Shelburne.'[2] So recalled memoir-writer Nathaniel Wraxall, who entered Parliament in 1780. Wilkes, indeed, thought better of Lord North than of his Parliamentary critics, as he told James Harris privately in the Commons on 15 May 1777: 'He commended Lord North, and his candid behaviour in the House. . . . Speaking of Burke and other orators, *apparently* vehement, mentioned a story he had heard from D'Alembert concerning a missionary, who laughed to think he could make twenty thousand men believe, what he did [not] believe a syllable of himself.'[3] Wilkes for the most part treated the House of Commons simply as a platform from which to propound those views on 'liberty' that maintained his popularity. For, as Wraxall noted, he ensured press publicity for speeches that were usually drafted with care:

Representing, as he did, the County of Middlesex, he spoke from a great Parliamentary eminence. He was an incomparable comedian in all he said or did; and he seemed to consider human life itself as a mere comedy. In the House of Commons he was not less an actor, than at the Mansion House, or at Guildhall. His speeches were full of wit, pleasantry, and point; yet nervous, spirited, and not at all defective in argument. They were all prepared, before they were delivered; and Wilkes made no secret of declaring, that in order to secure their accurate transmission to the public, he always sent a copy of them to William Woodfall, *before* he pronounced them.[4]

On his return to Westminster Wilkes produced a level of Parliamentary performance surpassed only by the leading debaters for government and opposition. During the poorly reported Parliament of 1774 to 1780 he is known to have made forty-two speeches, most of them set orations.[5] He attracted especial attention because of his character and reputation, and he merited it, because of the impressive knowledge he usually displayed of each subject he discussed. Much detailed research, as well as literary polish, sustained his clear and forceful presentations.

The main thrust of Wilkes's oratory was to confirm his radical credentials. He did not speak as MP for Middlesex until 26 January 1775.[6] Then he mocked the ritual observance of the execution of Charles I on 30 January 1649 by an annual sermon preached to the House of Commons. While several MPs were complaining that this ritual reflected adversely on the Glorious Revolution, Wilkes intervened to declare forthrightly that the anniversary should be 'celebrated as a festival, not kept as a fast: that the death of that enemy of our liberties . . . ought to be celebrated as the most glorious deed ever done in this or any other country'.[7] A few days later, on 1 February, Wilkes spoke in support of the annual motion by his new ally Alderman Sawbridge for a Shorter Parliaments Bill. After commending Sawbridge for 'his truly patriotic endeavours and noble perseverance', Wilkes put forward the argument that Parliament merely exercised powers delegated by 'the people'. Seven years was too long a period for such a trust. An additional argument Wilkes adduced from the spate of election petitions currently before the House, that there would be less motivation for ministerial and other bribery if elections were more frequent.[8]

Wilkes is not recorded as speaking again on this subject, in subsequent sessions, but he had his own annual motion to make: to rescind the resolution of 17 February 1769, declaring him incapable of election after his expulsion. Horace Walpole scarcely exaggerated when he described the first occasion, 22 February 1775, as 'a day which had long given the Court a greater panic' than the American question. 'This was the motion Wilkes had threatened of rescinding every step of the last Parliament in the Middlesex election. Lord North had even declared he would resign if he could not throw out the motion.' The Parliamentary danger to the ministry was two-fold, 'the obligation members for counties and popular boroughs were under of humouring their constituents by voting for Wilkes, the idol of the people', and the probability that those MPs who were former oppositionists but now ministerial men would demonstrate the political virtue of consist-ency by doing likewise.[9]

Wilkes took his stand on the claim that 'the freedom of election is the common right of the people'. He had prepared his argument thoroughly, citing precedents, of 1704 and 1712, and legal authorities alike to show that incapacity had not been a consequence of expulsion: 'This House, Sir, is created by the people, as the other is by the King. What right can the majority have to say to any county, city or borough, you shall not have a particular person your representative, only because he is obnoxious to us, when he is qualified by law?' Even Charles I had not dared to go so far, Wilkes declared. Edward Gibbon, who sat next to him, reported to a friend that he 'spoke well and with temper, but before the end of the debate fell fast asleep'.[10]

After Serjeant John Glynn had seconded Wilkes, Colonel George Onslow replied with a counter list of precedents, and challenged those of Wilkes: in 1712 Robert Walpole had been declared incapable of election and had put up a friend at the ensuing by-election. The electors of Middlesex ought to have similarly found another person, British or American, 'of equal abilities, patriotism and virtue, with Mr Wilkes' to represent them. When General Charles Fitzroy rather foolishly reminded MPs that it was his brother the Duke of Grafton who had decided on the expulsion of Wilkes, this gave Wilkes the opportunity to attack such interference by a peer. John Luttrell, brother to the Henry who had replaced Wilkes for Middlesex, then made this remarkable claim: 'When the colonel undertook this ministerial job, it was upon the fullest confidence and assurance of being returned by a major-ity of legal votes. Sir, he never meditated the violation of the sacred right of election, but he was unfortunately doomed to be the vehicle through which the machinations of a certain faction were to be carried into execution.' As for Wilkes, John Luttrell made this declaration:

I have no knowledge of him in his private capacity, but in his public one I have ever held him respectable; he has exercised the great offices of magistracy, in this metropolis, with an assiduity and firmness that is scarce to be paralleled; he has ever displayed that consistency and uprightness in all his public actions, that in these times of supiness and ductility, claim peculiar admiration.

Charles Van, a fiery ministerial backbencher, declared that Wilkes should be content with regaining his seat, and charged him with blasphemy. Wilkes called him to order, as no such word appeared in the Parliamentary resolutions. 'This occasioned much laughter', a reporter noted, but Van refused to retract, saying that impious and profane were 'pretty much the same thing'. Lord North briefly recapitulated some precedents and won the day only by 68 votes, 239 to 171, being pushed harder on this issue than on any other subject. For if the need of consistency caused Charles Fox, now in opposition, to side with the ministry, the same motive caused a number of MPs, including Solicitor-General Wedderburn, to vote with Wilkes.[11] George III, annoyed that Wedderburn had not even given a silent vote, was pleased at a majority deemed 'very creditable' by his Prime Minister: 'I flatter myself we shall in future not hear that old bone of contention brought into agitation.'[12]

The King was to be disappointed in that respect. Wilkes made the same motion during every subsequent session of North's ministry; but it was an annual ritual, not a political event. On 30 April 1776 Wilkes cited the Abingdon case of 6 March 1775, when a petitioner against an ineligible candidate secured only a void election, not the seat. Wilkes was seconded by Glynn and supported by two other speakers, but the ministry made no reply before rejecting the motion by 186 votes to 92.[13] Disdainful silence was thereafter the invariable administration response, nor was there public interest. Only the speech of Wilkes was reported for 29 April 1777, and no debate at all was recorded for 12 March 1778 and 18 February 1779.[14] In 1780 Wilkes put forward his motion on 15 March, at the height of a great Parliamentary battle over government corruption, and lost only by twelve votes, albeit in a thin House, 113 to 101.[15]

On 5 April 1781 Wilkes, in a new Parliament, jocularly remarked that he did not doubt that the new Speaker Charles Cornwall would be able to declare the expunging of the resolution of 17 February 1769. 'The House could not refrain from a loud laugh.' Rockinghamite George Byng, Wilkes's new colleague for Middlesex, seconded the motion, claiming that 'out of that House, he did not meet with a person who pretended to disapprove of it'. Another opposition MP Charles Turner reproved the display of levity, claiming that the treatment of Wilkes had led the Americans to distrust Parliament, and that nothing would more effectively restore colonial confidence than the passage of his motion. It failed by 116 votes to 61.[16] A year later the jest of Wilkes became fact, after the fall of North's ministry. He made what the press now called his 'annual motion', on 3 May 1782. After Byng had seconded, Charles Fox, although now a Secretary of State in Rockingham's new ministry, maintained consistency on this point to the end. The House of Commons should retain the power of expulsion, he said, but not use it 'against the people'. The danger that Wilkes had always emphasized, that a ministry would expel political opponents, did not exist: for in 1771 Crosby and Oliver had kept their seats. Fox ended by claiming that legislation on the matter was necessary, since the mere expunging of a resolution would settle nothing. At the end of a short debate the resolution was carried by 115 votes to 47.[17] Despite the forebodings of Fox, this Parliamentary vote was henceforth deemed sufficient to safeguard the rights of electors.

If the Middlesex Elections issue was for long Wilkes's political stock in trade, it is, above all else, the distinction of having made the first motion for Parliamentary Reform that secures him a place in the Pantheon of British Radicalism. This aim of altering the constitution, as distinct from merely removing abuses by more frequent elections or the elimination of corruption, was what distinguished the Wilkite movement from early 'country party' ideas. The Bill of Rights Society had adopted the principle of Parliamentary Reform in its 1771 programme, and on 23 March 1775, when there was a large Commons attendance on Edmund Burke's American plan, Wilkes gave notice that in the next session he would put forward a motion for 'the more equal representation of the people'.[18] He did so on 21 March 1776, in a characteristically well-prepared speech that drew upon knowledge of Roman as well as British history, and also cited John Locke and Richard Price. After commenting on 'the present unfair and inadequate state of the representation of the people of England in Parliament', Wilkes expounded the theory of representation. 'Every Englishman is supposed to be present in Parliament, either in person, or by deputy chosen by himself.' In a historical recapitulation of how that original principle had deteriorated into current practice, during which he could not resist pointing out that the Prime Minister was returned by only seventeen electors, he produced a calculation that a working majority of 254 MPs could be elected by only 5,723 voters. Amputation was the remedy he prescribed for such decayed boroughs as Old Sarum and Gatton, 'which ought not to retain a privilege, which they acquired only by their extent and populousness'. The defects of the electoral system had led the Americans to believe that ministerial policy had not enjoyed popular support, an interpretation that Wilkes claimed to be correct 'as to the actual hostilities now carrying on against our brethren and fellow-subjects'. He announced that he did not intend to make any detailed proposals: 'I will not intrude on the indulgence of the House, which I have always found so favourable to me.' For the moment he would merely put forward some general ideas:

That every free agent in this kingdom should, in my wish, be represented in Parliament. That the metropolis, which contains in itself a ninth part of the people, and the counties of Middlesex, York, and others, which so greatly abound with inhabitants, should receive an increase in their representation. That the mean and insignificant boroughs, so emphatically stiled the rotten part of our constitution, should be lopped off, and the electors in them thrown into the counties; and the rich, populous trading towns, Birmingham, Manchester, Sheffield, Leeds and others, be permitted to send deputies to the great council of the nation.

Such reform of the constituency structure should be matched by reform of the franchise. Votes attached to property, such as burgage tenures, were 'monstrous absurdities in a free state'. Every man, even a poor mechanic or a peasant, was affected by Parliamentary legislation, and should have 'some share' in 'the power of making those laws'. In his peroration Wilkes declared that without a true system of representation Parliament was 'a delusive name', and such other remedies as Shorter Parliaments or Place Bills, both equally necessary, would be ineffectual. After Alderman Bull seconded his motion, 'that leave be given to bring in a bill for just and equal representation of the people of England in Parliament', Lord North rose to reply. Employing his characteristic weapon of humour, the Prime Minister jocularly remarked that Wilkes must have been pleased with his own electoral success in London and Middlesex. 'He supposed the honourable gentleman was not serious', for those who had an interest in boroughs would not sacrifice their property. North then made a comparison of the dangers of physical and political amputations, to show by analogy that such experiments were dangerous, and might destroy the whole constitution: 'The proposition could do no good, and might do much harm.' After Wilkes had made a short reply, his motion was rejected without a vote.[19]

It could never be said of Wilkes that he lacked political pertinacity; but even he saw no purpose then in further advocacy of electoral reform, and he took little part in the reform campaigns of the next decade. He was nevertheless still recognized as a champion of the cause. Early in 1780 Granville Sharp offered to send Wilkes copies of his recent pamphlet in favour of 'more equal representation' and annual Parliaments, for distribution at the country meetings then being widely held.[20] A few years later the role of the Younger Pitt as the leading advocate of Parliamentary Reform was a significant reason why Wilkes gave support to his ministry.

The same broad principle of the responsibility of MPs to their constituents had been behind the establishment of Parliamentary reporting in 1771; and it led Wilkes to second a motion by maverick opposition MP Temple Luttrell on 30 April 1777 for the official admission of strangers to the House, on the ground that the people had the right to know what their delegates were saying on their behalf. For strangers, even reporters, were still admitted only on sufferance, liable to eviction at the whim of a single MP. Wilkes warmly endorsed Luttrell's argument, declaring that the voters were 'the very erectors of their authority'. Lord North opposed the motion, and said that the constituents admitted would in practice only be those of Wilkes, from Middlesex. It was defeated in a thin House, by 85 votes to 18.[21]

If few MPs adopted the Wilkes view of responsibility to constituents, more would respond to his championship of 'liberty', both individual and constitutional: as on 17 February 1777, when in 'a long speech' described by Horace Walpole as made 'with great rudeness but great wit' Wilkes took part in vigorous opposition criticisms of a Bill to suspend Habeas Corpus 'out of the realm'.[22] The outbreak of the American War reopened the issue of naval impressment that had briefly been a matter of contention in the Falkland Island dispute of 1770, with City obstruction of press-gangs. City officials of Wilkite persuasion now again sought to prevent this practice within London, sometimes claiming that press warrants were as illegal as general warrants.[23] But there was the crucial difference that obstruction of the war effort itself was now an additional motive, and the City did not offer bounties as an alternative method of recruitment. In 1776 Lord Mayor Sawbridge ordered City officials to arrest naval officers leading press-gangs; and in the debate of 31 October on the Address Wilkes criticized the ministry for hastily issuing press warrants before offering bounties for naval recruitment, and boasted that no press-gangs dared to roam the streets of the City of London.[24] That was not true, and the next two years saw both street violence and legal contests as City officials and navy officers clashed repeatedly over the issue. On 16 January 1778 the current Lord Mayor, Sir James Esdaile, a ministerialist and army contractor, sought to resolve the problem by convening a Court of Common Council and proposing there a subscription to offer bounties to encourage navy and army enlistment. But not only was this motion defeated. Another was passed stating that any support of the war would 'reflect dishonour upon their humanity and in no wise advantage the commercial interests of this great city'.[25] This rebuff to ministerial policy, evidence of continuing Wilkite influence in the City, was seen by George III as 'a mortifying circumstance'.[26] Controversy over this matter soon faded thereafter as the outbreak of war with France and Spain transformed the conflict, in radical eyes, from a civil war to one with Britain's natural enemies.

Close scrutiny of royal or government finance is a perennial feature of political radicalism, with a view to detecting abuse as well as extravagance; and Wilkes spoke at length when George III's request for payment of his Civil List debt was debated on 16 April 1777, making what Walpole described as 'a very offensive speech'.[27] He began with this bland assurance: 'There is not a gentleman in this House, or the kingdom, more anxious than I am, to see the splendour and dignity of the Crown of England maintained in its

1. 'John Wilkes Esq. Drawn in the Life and Etch'd in Aquafortis by Will.m Hogarth. Price 1 shilling. Published according to Act of Parliament May 4e 16.1763.'

2. 'John Wilkes and his Daughter' by J. Zoffany, 1779.

THE NEW COALITION.

Sure! the worthiest of Subjects & most Virtuous of men.

I now find that you are the best of Princes.

Geo. 3.   I. Wilkes.

O rare Forty five!
O dear Prerogative!

The Wolf shall dwell with the Lamb, & the Leopard
shall lie down with the Kid; & the Calf & the young Lion
& the Fatling together; & a little Child shall lead them.

Pub.ᵈ May 1.ˢᵗ 1784 by I. Cooke, Fetter Lane.   Isaiah. Chap. xi. V. xvi.

West. Elect. P. 317. 329. 138.

3. 'The New Coalition.' Caricature showing the reconciliation of George III
and Wilkes, 1 May 1784.

4. 'A (Quondam) Friend to Liberty, "So Politic as if one Eye | Upon the other were a spy"'. A contemporary caricature of John Wilkes, 1797.

utmost lustre, although for above a course of fifteen years I have received from the Crown only a succession of injuries, and never at any moment of my life, the slightest favour.' But Wilkes then recalled how the King at the beginning of the reign had gladly accepted an annuity of £800,000 in exchange for the hereditary revenues of the Crown, with the assurance that he would not apply to Parliament to make up any deficiencies on this Civil List. Yet £513,511 had been paid in 1769 to meet arrears, and now Parliament was being asked for another £618,340, a singularly ill-timed request during what Wilkes described as an expensive civil war. After a detailed survey of royal revenues that did credit to his assiduity, Wilkes voiced the widespread contemporary belief that the debt had been incurred through corruption of that House; the accounts showed £438,000 as paid in pensions and £285,000 paid to the two Secretaries of the Treasury during the last eight years. This imputation provoked North into a presumption that Wilkes did not mean that every ministerial supporter was bribed, a feeble rejoinder that North himself at once corrected: 'He, and those who thought with him, might act upon principle, and not, as the honourable gentleman termed it, be influenced by a temporary pension.' Wilkes had had the better of that exchange.[28]

That too little of the King's Civil List was allocated to other members of the royal family was another criticism of George III that Wilkes was foremost in voicing. On 9 May 1777 he spoke in support of an unsuccessful motion by Sir James Lowther that the King be asked to increase the incomes of the Dukes of Gloucester and Cumberland, two brothers of the King who had both made marriages to unsuitable commoners.[29] In the next session a Bill was introduced to settle annuities on various members of the royal family, but only after George III's death. On 10 April 1778 Wilkes professed to welcome the circumstance that the Hanoverian tenure of the throne, and thereby the 'perpetual preservation of our liberties', was guaranteed by so extensive a royal family:

The kingdom at large contemplates with rapture his Majesty's numerous, and still I hope, increasing progeny, as insuring even beyond our children's children . . . the blessings and glories of his reign. It is the duty of his faithful Commons here to do more, to provide for them in a manner adequate to their exalted birth and royal dignity.

This touch of irony was a preliminary to another attempt to embarrass the King. Wilkes said that the other members of the royal family should not be left in 'a state of the most absolute dependence on the Crown'. The proposal before the House should therefore take effect immediately. He then sought to rub salt into royal wounds by an amendment asking the King to supply the House with evidence as to the marriages of Gloucester and

Cumberland, but withdrew this motion on requests from friends of the two Dukes.[30]

Already Wilkes had himself introduced a debate on what he claimed to be a threat to the basic constitutional principle that the Crown should derive its income solely from Parliament. On 2 April 1778 the Speaker called on Wilkes to make a motion of which he had given notice. Control over government finance, Wilkes declared, was the safeguard for regular meetings of Parliament, and the Crown had to apply there even in emergencies. Now, with ministerial encouragement, army regiments were being raised by private subscriptions, and he named ten, while other efforts were being made to secure voluntary donations. All this activity, Wilkes asserted, was 'contrary to what has been demonstrated to be the established doctrine of the constitution, that the Crown cannot receive the money of the subject, for public purposes, but through the medium of Parliament'. After a long digression on the American War Wilkes returned to his theme of the perennial need for Parliament to keep a watch on government: 'Sir, the spirit of liberty is a spirit of jealousy.' Wilkes reminded MPs how in 1772 Sweden had lost its liberty in one day to a treacherous King, and ended by stating that he was calling for the assistance of 'the real Whigs, and friends of this excellent constitution'. He then moved for a Bill 'to prevent the dangerous and unconstitutional practice of giving . . . money to the Crown . . . for public purposes, without the consent of Parliament'.

Few MPs shared his perception of a constitutional danger in these voluntary enlistments, although Edmund Burke did take up the point of the King raising soldiers without Parliamentary consent. After a brief debate the motion was defeated by 71 votes to 40.[31] That Wilkes had more sensitive political antennae than most contemporaries was also shown on 29 and 30 November 1779, when he alone objected to a proposal to move the next Hampshire county election from Winchester, then a garrison town. The reason was that electoral law forbade the presence of soldiers near a polling station; but Wilkes feared that a threat to the freedom of elections might arise if ministers could so alter the venues.[32]

*

'Liberty' for Wilkes embraced wider objectives than such purely political aims as personal freedom and the constitutional power of the House of Commons, purified and made more representative. It also included religious toleration in the broadest possible sense, and on that issue, with respect to Roman Catholics, Wilkes was to part company with many of his radical allies. But on the question of concessions to Protestant Dissenters the Wilkites were as one. Many were themselves Dissenters, and his mother had ensured that John was brought up a Dissenter, at both school and university. By the 1750s Wilkes had become an Anglican, and in 1759 was chosen churchwarden for St Margaret's parish, Westminster; but he was not reappointed a year later although he had been a regular worshipper. Thereafter he never wavered in his religious allegiance, assuring his daughter a few years later, 'I remain sound in the faith, and I will keep to my good orthodox mother, the Church of England, to the last moment of its legal establishment.'[33] When occasion arose in the House of Commons Wilkes always described himself as an Anglican, and his speeches displayed considerable knowledge of the Bible and religious matters in general. But for a man with a lifestyle like Wilkes's, the depth of his personal religious faith must remain a matter of doubt.

Only in 1779 did Wilkes speak on behalf of Protestant Dissenters. In that year their chief Parliamentary champion Sir Henry Hoghton introduced legislation to exempt dissenting ministers and teachers from the current requirements that they should subscribe to thirty-six of the thirty-nine Articles of the Church of England.[34] In the first debate, on 10 March, Wilkes argued that the Dissenters had 'a stronger claim on government' than the Roman Catholics to whom concessions had been made in 1778: 'They have steadily supported the cause of freedom.' He lamented the uncharitable spirit of many of his fellow Anglicans: 'I think it would do honour to our church, to treat with tenderness all those who are unhappy enough not to be in her bosom.'[35]

When it became apparent that the Bill was going to pass, Lord North, to mollify angry Anglicans, moved in the Committee stage on 20 April an amendment requiring Dissenting ministers to make this declaration: 'I A.B. do solemnly declare, that I am a Christian, and a Protestant Dissenter; and that I take the holy scriptures, both of the Old and New Testaments, as they are generally received in Protestant countries, for the rule of my faith and practice.' This was carried by 88 votes to 58, after Wilkes had made the only speech reported against it.[36] 'I am against the old test; and when we have got rid of that, my voice will never be for fresh shackles on tender consciences.' Speaking 'as a steady friend to religious liberty and the right of private judgement', Wilkes pointed out that various governments in other parts of the world enforced different religions, before launching out into a plea for universal toleration. The sincerity of his opinions is attested by the circumstance that a month earlier he had expressed the same views privately to James Harris: 'John Wilkes, in describing to me his ideas of Toleration, said they were so general and unlimited, that he wished to see a Mosque on one side of [St] Pauls, and a synagogue on the other.'[37] Now he expounded them to the House of Commons:

I wish to see rising in the neighbourhood of a Christian cathedral, near its Gothic towers, the minaret of the Turkish mosque, the Chinese pagoda, and the Jewish synagogue, with a temple of the Sun, if any Persians could be found to inhabit this island, and worship in this gloomy climate, the God of their idolatry. The sole business of the magistrates is to take care that they did not persecute one another.

Even the famous Toleration Act of 1689 implied a possible persecution of Protestant Dissenting ministers: and, to ram this point home, he instanced the men who were currently at risk.

I will venture, Sir, to affirm, that there are not in Europe men of more liberal ideas, more general knowledge, more cultivated understandings, and in all respects, men better calculated to form the rising generation, to give the state wise and virtuous citizens, than the Doctors Price, Priestley, and Kippis. Yet the rod of persecution hangs over them by a single thread, if they do not subscribe thirty-five articles and a half of our church.

To prevent such a possibility was the sole object of the current Bill, which in his opinion did not go far enough: 'I contend for the most general and universal toleration, and I wish the bill more extended, to take in all sects and all religions.' Wilkes ended by extolling the practical benefits of toleration, citing the prosperity of Holland and Prussia. He was subsequently given a formal vote of thanks by the Protestant Dissenters for his efforts on their behalf. On 2 June 'the general body' of Dissenting ministers unanimously voted their gratitude for 'his generous and active zeal in support of the cause of religious liberty', and this was conveyed to Wilkes by four of their number on 11 June.[38]

Many of his fellow Radicals did not share these admirable sentiments of Wilkes with respect to Roman Catholics. Frederick Bull, his predecessor as Lord Mayor, had been active in organizing protests against the Quebec Act of 1774, proceedings from which Wilkes had been a conspicuous absentee. The furore over that measure paled into insignificance by comparison with the consequences of the Catholic Relief Act of 1778. The idea of making concessions to Roman Catholics originated in an administration plan to recruit Catholics openly into the army: but the legislation was to be initiated by opposition politicians, with ministerial acquiescence. The Bill was drafted by John Dunning, now the leading Shelburnite lawyer, and introduced by Rockinghamite Sir George Savile. It was very limited in scope. Catholics were now to be allowed full rights of inheriting and purchasing land; and Catholic clergy were no longer to be punished for conducting private services.[39] When it was introduced into the Commons on 14 May Attorney-General Thurlow publicly assured the sponsors that there was no government objection, and the measure passed both Houses with little debate and no resistance. But the Bishop of Peterborough had expressed concern about popular reactions, and his forebodings were soon to prove well founded.[40]

At a time when Britain was soon fighting Catholic France and Spain, popular anti-Papist prejudice fed on alarmist rumours and on encouragement by Methodist and Dissenting preachers. Protestant Associations were formed in England, and also in Scotland; for although the Act did not apply to that country the Lord Advocate of Scotland, Henry Dundas, had told the Commons that he would introduce a similar measure next session. Dundas did not appear in the House again until 15 March 1779, when Wilkes at once called on him to fulfil his promise. Dundas replied that there was such hostility to the idea in Scotland that the leading Catholics there had advised him to postpone it. Wilkes thereupon claimed that 'the honour and independence of this House' had been sacrificed to 'the seditious populace in Scotland'. The mobs of Edinburgh and Glasgow had given an example to the mob of London, he presciently declared over a year before the Gordon Riots. The Edinburgh mob had been quietened only by a promise that there would be no legislation in favour of Scottish Catholics: 'Is it possible, Sir, to imagine a more ignominious surrender of the dignity of Parliament? . . . We are forbidden even beginning an act of justice or humanity by an ignorant and insolent mob.' No other MP echoed his indignation, and the matter was dropped.[41]

Wilkes therefore had scant sympathy with the aims of the Protestant Association, whose monster petition, purporting to have 120,000 signatures, was presented to the House of Commons on 2 June 1780 by the London President, 28-year-old MP Lord George Gordon.[42] A man already notorious for his eccentric behaviour, Gordon was seconded by Alderman Bull. Although the mob around the Parliament building dispersed soon afterwards, rioting broke out elsewhere in London that night, and continued for several days, as mobs of fanatics and criminals looted and burned the houses and private chapels of Catholics. Other targets were prisons, taverns, and the homes of men unpopular for upholding authority. Individual Aldermen-magistrates were unwilling to order the deployment of soldiers, some like Bull being openly sympathetic towards the rioters.[43] Lord Mayor Brackley Kennett proved a broken reed in this time of crisis. The Court of Aldermen met three times on 5 and 6 June, to no avail. On 7 June, after news that Newgate Prison had been sacked during the night, Wilkes visited Kennett to urge immediate action.[44] The same day George III issued a Royal Proclamation authorizing the army to act without instructions from magistrates, and the tide began to turn. Wilkes personally assisted that evening in defence of the Bank of England, when several rioters were killed.[45] Thereafter his diary of the riots shows him to be active in both a military and civil capacity. Horace Walpole recalled that he 'showed great spirit and zeal during the riots';[46] and he won applause for his endeavours in unexpected circles. 'Wilkes was *the* heroic Justice', wrote Lord Clarendon to James Harris on 13 June.[47] Wilkes served on night watch with soldiers and militia on at least three occasions. He was daily attending Courts of Aldermen, making arrests, and questioning prisoners; and several passages from his diary appear ironic in the context of his own earlier career. Wilkes, who had made his name by opposing general warrants, noted that he issued on 10 June a 'warrant for searching for and securing all idle and disorderly persons, and all concealed arms, in the Ward of Farringdon Without', and on 16 June 'a special warrant to search for rogues and vagabonds' in the same ward: while on 13 June he committed to prison one William Moore 'for being the printer and publisher of two seditious and treasonable papers, entitled *England in blood* and *The Thunderer*'.[48]

There is much contemporary evidence to confirm the verdict of diarist Wraxall that Wilkes, who had made 'so glorious a resistance to general warrants, displayed as manly a resistance to popular violence, . . . and had he filled the chair of Chief Magistrate, instead of Kennett, would unquestionably by his vigour, have prevented many or all the disgraceful scenes which took place in the capital'.[49] The transformation of Wilkes almost into a respectable pillar of the establishment was signified a few days later by the acceptance of his request to Secretary at War Charles Jenkinson that the cavalry posted outside the Guildhall should be withdrawn. Wilkes had mentioned the reason in confidence, the midsummer election of City officials due within a few days. Jenkinson recommended this move to the army Commander-in-Chief Lord Amherst, 'as I am persuaded that Mr Wilkes is sincere in what he says', and was able to inform Wilkes that his request would be granted.[50]

When the House of Commons debated the Gordon Riots on 19 June Wilkes was quick to blame the Lord Mayor, and he returned to this point on 27 June by successfully moving that copies of papers relating to the Mayor's role in the riots should be laid before the House for perusal next session: that order was to be invalidated by the autumn dissolution of Parliament.[51] Already the split between London's Radicals had been revealed on 19 June, when Sawbridge presented to the Commons a City Petition asking for repeal of the Catholic Relief Act. Wilkes opposed the petition, as having been procured clandestinely in the Court of Common Council after most members had gone home. He then launched a personal attack on Alderman Bull for taking no action against the rioters, for having indeed permitted the constables of his ward to wear the blue cockades of the petitioners, 'the ensign of riot', a charge Bull virtually admitted. Lord North, however, had already on 6 June promised that the House would consider such petitions, and next day it resolved into a Committee to do so. Repeal was urged by Bull and Sawbridge, and also by Mawbey, who took Wilkes to task for his ingratitude towards Bull: 'because the worthy magistrate, in times of distress and difficulty, had supported that Alderman, and he thought personal and friendly obligations should restrain him from undeserved abuse.' The sense of the Committee, voiced by North, Charles Fox, and Edmund Burke among others, was overwhelmingly in favour of retaining the Act.[52]

The Gordon Riots had divided London Radicals even before the constitutional crisis of 1782–3 created a permanent split. Some commended the behaviour of Wilkes. One hailed him as 'a true Patriot', and Thomas Wilson wrote from Bath on 17 June to congratulate Wilkes on 'his late noble behaviour. . . . Go on and try all in your power to establish civil government'.[53] But it was soon to be evident that the role of Wilkes as an apparent defender of Popery had cost him much popularity in London.

*

The transformation of Wilkes into respectability was buttressed by new-found financial stability. When Benjamin Hopkins died on 9 November 1779, at the age of 45, Wilkes had an unexpected opportunity to secure the City Chamberlainship. Two days later the *London Evening Post* put the case for him of political gratitude:

There is no man that has added more uniformity to principle than Mr Wilkes. He has been an active friend of the public for these sixteen years past, during which he has never, in any one action of his life, deserted for a moment the popular cause. He has, by his persevering endeavours, enlarged the circle of British freedom, and established peace and security in an Englishman's habitation.

Wilkes did not issue his election notice until nominated at a Livery meeting on 17 November.[54] By then there were other candidates in the field. Two soon disappeared from view, a William Montague and a Henry Cranke, who described himself as 'well known in the silk trade' for over forty years.[55] A more serious threat was posed by banker William James.[56] He claimed in his election notice of 10 November to rely 'entirely on your uninfluenced suffrages', but was clearly identified by the press as a ministerial candidate.[57] He adopted an obvious propaganda line, as in a sarcastic newspaper paragraph that since Wilkes had squandered his own property he was therefore entitled to be trusted with that of the City.[58]

The supporters of Wilkes reacted promptly to this challenge. By 12 November £1,500 had already been raised to finance his campaign, a sum swelled to £2,400 by 16 November. One newspaper calculated that the volume of support given to Wilkes forced any opponent to spend £10 for every £4 by the popular hero. A Committee to secure his election had immediately been formed, and Hayley promised to provide whatever financial guarantee the Court of Aldermen would require for Wilkes; this was to be £40,000, and the four sureties included Hayley and Sawbridge, as London's Radicals united behind Wilkes. Alderman Townsend busily canvassed for him, together with many members of the London Association. Richard Oliver was now back in Antigua, but Thomas Oliver subscribed generously to the cause. Fourteen Aldermen named as active on behalf of Wilkes included Bull, Crosby, Kirkman, Lewes, and, of course, Sawbridge.[59]

What was described as the most numerous Common Hall of Livery since the second election of Beckford as Mayor, in 1769, assembled on 22 November. At the hustings Wilkes promised to devote half the profits of the office to extinguishing his Mayoral debts, and announced his intention to serve for life. Despite a show of hands supposedly being 5,000 to 100 for Wilkes, James demanded a poll, but gave up two days later when Wilkes was ahead by 2,332 votes to 370. With the poll open one hour a day until 30 November, by statutory requirements, the final result was 2,343 to 371. Wilkes was formally named as City Chamberlain on 1 December, when he congratulated the Livery on 'your attachment to the cause of liberty'.[60] This triumph was the last success of the united City Radicals before they fell out over the Gordon Riots; but Wilkes owed his victory also to the unpopularity of the American War, which had caused such economic distress among London's merchants that, so the jubilant London Evening Post claimed on 27 November, 'those who had no personal attachment to the man and the cause, now support him out of abhorrence to the Minister'.

This success followed one in Middlesex, where a by-election had been caused by the death on 16 September of John Glynn, whose health had been deteriorating for some years, so much so that on 18 February he had been unable to second Wilkes's annual motion on the Middlesex Elections. The North ministry, aware that no administration candidate could win the seat, sought to counter the Wilkite interest by assisting George Tufnell, an opposition MP who had aspirations to represent his native county. Lord North promised him the conventional sinecure of the Chiltern Hundreds so that he could vacate his seat at Beverley, and George III agreed that Tufnell's ministerial sponsor in Middlesex, the Duke of Northumberland, could be given financial support, 'some gold pills for the election'.[61] The Wilkites, looking to a future alliance, did not put up their own candidate and supported George Byng, an important landowner in north Middlesex and a leading Rockingham MP; but North refused to grant Byng the Chiltern Hundreds to vacate his Wigan seat. This public avowal of ministerial partiality destroyed any chance in Middlesex for Tufnell, who withdrew his candidature in embarrassment. At the by-election on 28 October there was no challenge to Thomas Wood, the 71-year-old Chairman of Byng's election committee, who was put up to hold the seat until Byng could take it at the next general election. With a view to a joint candidature then with Byng, Wilkes wrote to congratulate Wood on 'his very honourable election'. Wood's reply expressed the hope that it would keep the county 'free and independent'. By the end of October the Wilkite understanding was that Byng and Wilkes would be standing together at the general election.[62]

This behaviour of North provided obvious ground for attack in Parliament. On 12 November a meeting of Middlesex freeholders unanimously voted a petition to the House of Commons about his refusal to allow Byng to vacate his seat, for the Prime Minister had decided who could and who could not stand at the recent by-election. The meeting also passed a resolution thanking Wilkes for 'his able and disinterested conduct in Parliament', after one of his supporters, evidently with the imminent election for City Chamberlain in mind, had declared that 'fidelity and rectitude, such as Mr Wilkes had invariably pursued, as it obtained no pecuniary reward, called loudly on his constituents for approbation and applause'.[63] Wood presented the petition on 10 December, and moved for a Bill to allow existing MPs to fight vacant seats. Wilkes seconded, and North said he had no objection, since he found his power in this respect disagreeable. Byng stated that the petition was the work of 'temperate freeholders, many having wished to come to the House with other instruments than parchment'. The motion passed, but the ensuing Bill was defeated on 29 February 1780.[64]

The Middlesex episode led Temple Luttrell, also on 10 December, to complain about ministerial influence in Hampshire, proposing a motion that such interference was criminal and unconstitutional. Wilkes seconded this, and cited an election letter of the Duke of Chandos, which was referred to the Committee of Privileges.[65] Wilkes explained both then and later that his complaint was about such misbehaviour by a peer who was also a Lord Lieutenant, and therefore doubly atrocious as an abuse of royal power as well as a breach of privilege; but the matter was killed by an indefinite postponement on 2 February 1780.[66]

Wilkes at this time was anticipating a lifetime tenure of both his City office and his Parliamentary seat; for he wrote this comment on 5 May 1780 to his friend Sam Petrie: 'I believe there will be no opposition to the Chamberlain of London either at Midsummer Day or at the general election. His prospect into futurity for the eve of life is pleasing.'[67] But the subsequent behaviour of Wilkes during the Gordon Riots led to a hostile reception at the

Midsummer meeting of Livery on 24 June; here is the report by the sympathetic *London Evening Post* on the same day:

Mr Wilkes met with marks of displeasure from some of the Livery. The Livery, many of them, called out 'No Popish Chamberlain' and it was near half an hour before they would allow Mr Wilkes to vindicate his conduct. His speech, after all, could not be heard, but by a few, so great an uproar was there in the Guildhall. This was very cruel in the Livery to condemn the man who has often so nobly stood forth as the advocate of liberty—to condemn him unheard. However, when he was again nominated, in order to make some reparation for their heat and zeal for public freedom, they received his name with great acclamation, and he was again re-elected.

Further evidence of a decline in Wilkes's popularity was manifest before the general election, which was called unexpectedly in September 1780. Criticism of him appeared in the press, accusing Wilkes of devoting his time to his office of Chamberlain and of 'having neglected the common cause of public freedom'. Wilkes replied that the assiduous pursuit of his duties as Chamberlain had not caused him to neglect his political role. Throughout the recent Parliamentary session he had sat out long debates to vote 'among the supporters of the constitution', while he had attended public meetings in Buckinghamshire, Cambridgeshire, and Westminster in the cause of reform.[68] At the Westminster meeting, a gathering of 3,000 in Westminster Hall, Wilkes had seconded Sawbridge's motion for a petition, and had been appointed to the Westminster Committee; but he attended only two of twenty meetings before the summer of 1780.[69]

Public opinion was nevertheless reflected in the comment of Sir William Jones to Wilkes on 7 September: 'No man, I trust, will be hardy enough to oppose your election for the county of Middlesex.'[70] Wilkes and Byng issued a joint Address, promising 'zeal for the security of the invaluable rights of Englishmen, and a watchful care for the preservation of the constitution of our country, as settled on the broad basis of public liberty'. They were elected without opposition.[71]

In the first two sessions of the new Parliament Wilkes was a mostly silent member of the opposition to the North ministry. When Rockingham succeeded North as Prime Minister Wilkes wrote on 2 April 1782 to congratulate the Marquess on his appointment to 'the most important department of the state', and also to ask for the post of Receiver-General of Land Tax for Middlesex, since that had been attached to the office of City Chamberlain until Janssen's time. Ten days later he withdrew this request, having found out that the post was incompatible with a seat in Parliament.[72] On 3 May 1782, when successfully moving the erasure of the Middlesex Elections resolutions, Wilkes welcomed the sight of 'the Treasury Bench filled with the friends of the constitution, the guardians and lovers of liberty'.[73] But there soon occurred a seismic change in his political career. After Rockingham's death on 1 July, when Charles Fox led the bulk of his party back into opposition to George III's choice of Shelburne as his successor, Wilkes chose to side with the King's ministry. As diarist Wraxall perceived, the professions of loyalty to the Crown Wilkes had always made were not mere formality:

Notwithstanding the personal collision which may be said to have taken place between the King and him, during the early portion of His Majesty's reign; Wilkes . . . nourished in his bosom, a strong sentiment of constitutional loyalty. He gave indelible proofs of it, during the riots of June 1780. . . . And although Wilkes lent his aid to overturn Lord North's administration, yet he never yoked himself to Fox's Car.

Wraxall misled sundry historians and biographers by ascribing the change in Wilkes's political attitude to the East India Bill Fox introduced in 1783.[74] For it was Fox's attempt to dictate to George III who should be Prime Minister that caused Wilkes to gravitate to the Court even before the India Bill was conceived. On 9 August 1782 Wilkes had a two-hour interview with Shelburne, and then attended the King's levee.[75] Soon afterwards it was being rumoured that Wilkes had then made a deal with government. 'Johnny Wilkes did not pay an *idle* visit of late to Berkeley Square and St. James's', claimed the *Morning Herald* of 28 August: 'this patriotic *Cerberus* being said to have got a sop at last that will keep him from snarling during the course of the present Premiership.' Whether or not Wilkes did receive any inducement, before the next Parliamentary session he was avowedly 'the zealous partisan' of Shelburne's ministry.[76] Yet his only known intervention in debate led to its discomfiture. On 27 January 1783, when the ministry was resisting in the Commons a proposal to print the peace terms recently agreed with America, France, and Spain, Wilkes rose to say that 'he could cut the matter short by informing them . . . that their Lordships had already ordered them to be printed. This raised a great laugh', as Wilkes no doubt intended.[77] Next month Wilkes voted for the Shelburne ministry when it was defeated and forced to resign over the peace terms by the newly formed coalition of Fox and Lord North. On 26 February he was among the supporters of the fallen minister who attended the King's levee, and he did so again on 14 March, when he had a private audience with George III.[78]

Wilkes had meanwhile suffered the unique, for him, experience of being called upon to explain his behaviour to his constituents, at a county meeting on 5 March. Wilkes claimed that his instructions from them were 'positively for peace', and sought to justify himself by arguments used by the Shelburne ministry in Parliament. The Bourbon navies were superior to the British by 130 ships to 105, besides 30 Dutch ones. The peace had been necessary to save

India and Canada. Wilkes then went on the attack, portraying Lord Shelburne as a political reformer: 'Therefore he held it to be his absolute duty to support him.' A press report noted that this speech was 'very animated, and expressive of the self-conviction of the rectitude with which he had acted'. Wilkes nevertheless failed to carry the meeting after Byng had defended the Fox–North Coalition, and at a subsequent political dinner at Covent Garden on 7 April the customary toast of 'the members for Middlesex' was replaced by that of 'Mr Byng and the independent freeholders of Middlesex'.[79]

Unabashed by this loss of popular support, Wilkes opposed the Fox–North coalition ministry that took office in April 1783 against the King's wishes, and made a long speech on 8 December on the third reading of Fox's India Bill. It breached the charter of the East India Company, 'a charter purchased of the public, and secured by the sanction of Parliament'. He recalled how the violation of American charters had cost Britain an empire in the west, an example that would have deterred any minister 'less rash, less impetuous'. Wilkes said that he did not believe the Company should be a territorial power, and he would approve a Bill to curb it in that respect. His main theme was the alleged ministerial motive of corruption. 'It is a swindling Bill', Wilkes declared, a measure of confiscation by which the ministry would acquire the means to bribe Parliament. At stake was patronage of £2,000,000 a year. 'If we do not strangle the monster in its birth, it will destroy the freedom of Parliament and people.'[80] Wraxall rated this speech highly, quoting it at length, notably to show how a polished compliment to North's personal character was neatly turned into a political attack: 'Would to heaven I could commend his reverence for the constitution, his love of freedom, and his zeal for the preservation of those privileges and franchises, which constitute the birthright of Englishmen.' Wilkes then attacked Fox, first recalling how 'by his side I fought in all the struggles to repress the power of the Crown'. Now he was allied to the man he had threatened to impeach as 'the corrupter of Parliament, the author and contriver of our national destruction'.[81]

Opponents of Wilkes thought that he defended the East India Company in order to strengthen his support among London's commercial community.[82] Certainly he was to need all the help he could obtain when, early in 1784, a general election was called by the minority administration of the Younger Pitt, appointed in December, 1783 on the King's dismissal of the Coalition. Wilkes was now fighting Middlesex as a ministerial candidate; according to Wraxall, he had been 'among the foremost supporters of Pitt in Parliament . . . re-appeared at St. James's where he met with the most gracious reception'.[83] Wilkes stood on a joint interest with a William Mainwaring against George Byng, now a Foxite. Mainwaring was very much an establishment figure, Chairman of the county magistrates, and in receipt of £1,000 Treasury money towards his expenses. A contemporary cartoon, entitled *The New Coalition*, mocked 'the two Kings of Brentford', with Wilkes describing his monarch as 'the best of princes' and George III greeting him as 'the worthiest of subjects and most virtuous of men'.[84]

It was Wilkes who was in danger from Byng. His recent behaviour had cost him much popular sympathy for two reasons, support of the Court and simple lack of effort. Less than a fortnight before the poll was due on 22 April, Wilkes was warned that many freeholders would be voting for the other two candidates, because his alliance with Mainwaring had not been sufficiently publicized. Since Mainwaring was certain to head the poll, Byng's agents were canvassing for him also, in evident hopes of reciprocity, and alleging that Wilkes was 'seldom in the House and a man of no business (but upon very extraordinary occasions)'.[85] Although Wilkes tried to rekindle radical enthusiasm by emphasis on the commitment of Pitt and himself to Parliamentary Reform, he probably owed his narrow victory to the national surge of popular support for the ministry. His nomination at the hustings met a mixed reception, the hostile *Morning Herald* commenting that the enthusiasm for Pitt's administration would not embrace 'countenances for vice', Wilkes being 'an example of notorious depravity'.[86] Byng polled well in his home area of north Middlesex, but residual support for Wilkes in the East End of London enabled him to defeat Byng narrowly for second place in the two-day election. Mainwaring secured 2,118 votes, Wilkes 1,858, and Byng 1,792.[87] Byng attributed his defeat to 'the combined attempts of power, ambition and treachery'.[88] He demanded a scrutiny of the poll, but soon abandoned both that and the alternative threat of a petition. Wilkite partisans responded by attributing the narrowness of his victory to 'the well known fact that his canvass did not begin till about ten days since'.[89]

The old radical persona of Wilkes survived with regard to Parliamentary Reform. During the general election campaign Pitt, who had vainly proposed reform in 1782 and 1783, had secured the support of reformers by a promise to introduce another reform bill. Wilkes was evidently anticipating this measure, when, late in 1784, he commented to a Scottish correspondent that 'the great business of a Parliamentary reform will, I suppose be agitated early in the ensuing session', urging that there should be 'the same anxiety, as well as necessity, for this important object in the more northern parts of the island as among the patriots of the south'.[90] A few months later, when the reform campaign was in progress, organizer Christopher Wyvill sent Wilkes a report of the Yorkshire county meeting of 10 February 1785 that had unanimously decided to support 'a reformation of Parliament'.[91] When Pitt introduced his Reform Bill on 18 April 1785, again unsuccessfully, Wilkes voted for it, though he did not speak.[92] That at least to the end of his career as an MP Wilkes remained a champion of Parliamentary Reform, as well as of repeal of the Test Act for Protestant Dissenters, is attested by his correspondence in 1790.[93]

Wilkes did not mend his Parliamentary ways after 1784, failing to respond to the charge of neglecting his duties that had so nearly cost him his seat then. He sat as an occasional and silent supporter of Pitt's ministry, though apparently still on the opposition side of the House, as a demonstration of his independence.[94] This behaviour may have been more than affectation; for before the 1784 election the government's political expert John Robinson, advising Pitt as he had previously done North, had made this note: 'Mr Wilkes's support of any government is very uncertain, because the safety of his situation depends on his watching as he calls it all administrations and having no apparent connection with any, but taking the side of all popular questions.'[95] But there is insufficient evidence to determine whether Wilkes maintained at all this vestigial role of 'patriot' after 1784.[96] Only one speech by him is recorded for the six years of the ensuing Parliament.

That was on behalf of his friend Warren Hastings. The two men exchanged correspondence and hospitality from at least 1782, and in his 1783 speech on Fox's India Bill Wilkes had spoken favourably about his friend.[97] From 1786 there loomed before Hastings the prospect of impeachment for his behaviour when Governor-General of India, and on 19 May 1787 there was before the House of Commons a motion to read the report of the Select Committee appointed to draw up such articles of impeachment. Wilkes, recalling that Hastings had saved India for Britain during the American War, professed astonishment that 'a faction in that House' should have been able to carry the prosecution thus far, and expressed the hope, one that proved vain, that 'it would be put an end to that night'. Hastings, so Wilkes claimed, had 'laid the foundation for the present prosperous state of India'. Not a single complaint against him had come from there. During the exigencies of the American and other wars Hastings had proved 'a profound politician, who had acted in times of singular peril and difficulty with equal vigour and wisdom'. The House of Commons had now given to the current Governor-General Lord Cornwallis greater powers than those assumed by Hastings, thereby implicitly acknowledging that Hastings had acted by necessity. This is how diarist Wraxall noted the last major speech of Wilkes:

Wilkes, though during the two or three last sessions he had rarely taken any active part, and though he already began to feel the infirmities of approaching age, came forward on this occasion. The same unconquered spirit, wit and classic fire, which he displayed on the 30th April 1763, when brought before the Earls of Egremont and Halifax, by virtue of a *general warrant*, pervaded every sentence that he uttered. But his articulation, which never had been perfectly distinct even in youth, grew annually more embarrassed from the inroads of time on his organs of speech.

His spirited defence of Hastings made Wilkes one of the targets of the witty and uninhibited Foxite John Courtenay in a speech that Wraxall deemed the most outrageous he had ever heard in the House of Commons; here is his diary account of the attack on Wilkes:

Then turning towards Wilkes, who sate next to him, 'The worthy Alderman', continued he, 'possesses more sense than to feel anger, when I mean him a compliment; as I do, when I assert that his country owes him great obligations, for having, at one period of his life, diffused a spirit of liberty throughout the general mass of the people, unexampled—except, indeed, in the times of Jack Cade, and Wat Tyler.' The cry of Order! that had been so violent only a minute before, was lost in the universal burst of laughter which followed this observation. 'The honourable magistrate', said Courtenay, 'has defended Mr Hasting's treatment of the *Begums*, by asserting that those princesses were engaged in rebellion. Surely he must have looked upon the transaction *obliquely*, or he never could have formed so erroneous an idea. Two old women in rebellion against the Governor-General! Impossible. Nor would the worthy Alderman have made an *Essay on Woman* in the manner that Mr Hastings did. The House well knows, he would not.'

Wraxall noted that 'the humour of this last observation was lost in its superior indecency', and that neither the Speaker nor any other MP had curbed 'the studied indecorum of the allusions . . . reflecting on the personal infirmities, or on the licentious productions, of the member for Middlesex'. On the contrary, the riposte to Wilkes produced 'an almost universal roar of laughter', according to one reporter.[98] Wilkes, the master of sarcastic invective, had finally been hoist with his own petard.

Despite the clear warning of the 1784 contest Wilkes seems to have believed that he had a Middlesex seat for life, whatever or how little he did as an MP. In an advertisement of 19 December 1789 he announced that he would not campaign for the next general election, but await 'the sanction of a nomination from a county meeting'.[99] Already this strict constitutional propriety had nearly cost him his seat in 1784. Such nonchalance did not help his cause, nor did his failure to attend the debate on a Middlesex petition against Pitt's Tobacco Act that he had presented himself on 19 March 1790.[100] And unpopular with many was his public plumper vote at the Westminster election on 16 June for his old enemy John Horne, now surnamed Tooke, who thanked Wilkes for 'your conduct to me in the hustings. It was judicious and handsome.'[101] This gesture, like Tooke's candidature itself, annoyed both Pittite ministry and Foxite opposition. After an expensive by-election contest in 1788, administration and opposition had agreed to share the two Westminster seats at the general election, with Admiral Hood and Charles Fox as their respective candidates. This cosy arrangement angered London's Radicals, and Tooke unexpectedly came forward on polling day, forcing a contest: he obtained 1,697 votes, as against 3,516 for Fox and 3,217 for Hood.

In Middlesex Wilkes was challenged by the younger George Byng, namesake son and successor, in 1789, of his former colleague and rival, and like his father a Foxite. *The World* sought to help Wilkes by reminding voters of his past record: he had been 'chosen by the freeholders of Middlesex twenty years ago, because he was known to be an enemy . . . to everything of which his constituents disapproved'. The newspaper also castigated young Byng for promising to emulate the conduct of his late father, since he had disobeyed the instructions of his constituents in 1783 by supporting 'Mr Fox's most pernicious India Confiscation Bill'.[102] The opposition *Gazetteer* forecast on 19 June that 'Byng will certainly throw out Wilkes for Middlesex', yet he professed to perceive no threat. The county meeting was fixed for 25 June when, Wilkes said, he had 'not the least doubt of being nominated'.[103] His notice requesting the attendance there of his friends seems to have been published only the day before.[104] Whether all this was self-delusion or merely whistling in the wind, Wilkes suffered a rude awakening at the county meeting, where, so the *Gazetteer* jibed, only forty-five of his voters appeared.[105] Faced with the collapse of his support Wilkes announced his withdrawal. He did not appear at the election on 28 June, when the sheriffs announced that 'it was not the intention of that gentleman to give the county any further trouble'.[106] The *Gazetteer* next day published a scathing valediction on the end to Wilkes's political career. As an MP he had been inattentive and indolent, except when summoned by Pitt; whereas a better attendance record and a greater independence of attitude might have secured for him the seat for life he had clearly thought his due.

To Mr Wilkes. You are now compelled to retire into that obscurity, to which your subserviency to a Court which you rose into notice by insulting, your dereliction of those principles by which you became popular, ought long since to have consigned you . . . For you, Mr Wilkes, the language of patriotism and unmeaning promise, will no longer pass. . . . We have found your promises to have been, as you once was in our esteem, great; and your performance, as you now are, nothing.

The World noted that 'Mr. Wilkes stole out of Middlesex without even a parting Address', and suggested that he had been more concerned with his office of City Chamberlain than with the House of Commons.[107] By the end of the year the same paper was reporting that Wilkes was so sad a figure at Court that he had been dubbed 'the Knight of the woeful countenance'; for there was a rumour that he would soon be Sir John Wilkes. Certainly, 'from the variety of his vision, they consider him as a gentleman upon the look out for every thing'.[108]

Wilkes received no reward from government, neither honour nor office, for his support during the last fifteen years of his life: but his innate loyalty to the monarchical system of government established at the Glorious Revolution of 1688, so lauded in the introduction to his otherwise unwritten *History of England*,[109] was demonstrated in 1792 in what may well have been his last public political pronouncement. The occasion was a ward meeting of Farringdon Without, called on 14 December to express loyalty to the Crown at a time when Revolutionary France had just declared itself a republic. In his speech Wilkes extolled the virtues of 'a limited monarchy, as a government founded on laws', for the eighty years of Hanoverian rule had been the happiest and most prosperous in our history. 'We are governed by wise and equal laws, the same laws for the poor as for the rich, for every subject of the state. Our persons are safe, our property secure, and our commerce most extensively flourishing; especially during the reign of his present Majesty.' Wilkes pointed the contrast with both autocratic rule and republican government:

I have spent no small part of my life abroad; in countries where the government depended on the caprice of an individual . . . where no one was secure. . . . In a republican government there is a continued struggle who shall be the greatest . . . But here the line is clearly chalked out by law; no subject can with us be so ambitious, or so mad, as to contend for the sovereign power. We are preserved from all those evils which necessarily attend a republican government.[110]

The public political career of John Wilkes ended with an exquisite piece of irony. On 17 April 1794 he spoke in the Court of Common Council in favour of a proposal to raise a force of Loyal London Volunteers, to help to defend the country against France.[111] But on 11 June, a Loyalist mob, with cries of 'Down with the English Jacobins' and 'God save the King', included, by mistake, or perhaps from folk-memory, his home among those whose windows were smashed.[112] The characteristic magnanimity of Wilkes on this occasion was reported in the *Morning Post*:

Mr Wilkes bears the loss of his fine windows with that pleasant humour so peculiar to him, and absolutely refuses to prosecute any of the mob. 'They are only', said he, 'some of my pupils, now set up for themselves'.[113]

12

Work and Leisure
1776–1797

THE gradual fade-out of John Wilkes as a politician during the last two decades of his life was caused only in part by the deterioration of his faculties sometimes noted by contemporaries. Rather was his attention engaged by other interests of work and leisure as he continued to lead a full and varied life. His duties as City Chamberlain took up much of his time. He had extensive family and social commitments. His sexual drive remained unimpaired. And he took up again his first love, study of the classics. The backdrop to all this activity was one of financial difficulty, a situation eased but evidently not solved when he became City Chamberlain. Wilkes could never be deemed a provident man, and lived an easygoing existence, seemingly oblivious to anything except immediate needs, and certainly so ignorant of his true financial situation that the bequests genuinely intended in his will could not be honoured.

The failure of Wilkes to obtain the City Chamberlainship in 1776 left him encumbered by a new load of debt accumulated as Lord Mayor. Very soon there was a campaign by his partisans to secure payment by the City of London for those financial burdens incurred in its service. The Court of Common Council appointed a committee to investigate the City's accounts, and specifically asked recent Mayors about their income and expenditure. Wilkes replied in detail on 15 June 1776, recounting how onerous a burden in time and money that office had been, and suggesting that the episode of being sheriff should also be taken into account, his own cost in that respect having been over £1,800 in 1772. The Mayoral accounts presented by Wilkes showed receipts of £4,889 and expenditure of £8,227. His two immediate predecessors reported similar deficits, Townsend an income of £3,896 as

against £7,592 expenses, and Bull one of £5,647 and costs of £9,293. The crucial difference was that both of them had sufficient personal wealth to afford
such losses.[1]

When nothing came of this initiative, various creditors of Wilkes, perhaps at his instigation, petitioned the Court of Common Council in 1777,
asking that the City should pay the debts he had incurred as Mayor. The petition was rejected, after a long debate, by 80 votes to 73, when the matter was
finally resolved on 20 November. A motion that Wilkes should be paid £500
a year 'for his past services' was defeated by 108 votes to 73. Common
Council then carried by 105 votes to 74 a resolution stating that granting an
annuity to Wilkes or paying his debts whether or not contracted as Lord
Mayor would be improper and 'a most dangerous precedent'.[2]

With that avenue to financial salvation closed Wilkes had to fall back on
his customary recourse, the charity of his friends and supporters. Here the
evidence is scanty. In the earlier 1770s Wilkes was still receiving payments
from the Rockinghamite leadership, with MP Chase Price acting as conduit;
for on 6 November 1773 Wilkes wrote to Price what was less a begging letter
than an assumption of support:

I don't know who is your banker, but I know you are the best I ever had; and as I am
poorer now than for a monstrous long time, I shall be much obliged to you, if you
could contrive for me a note of £150 in two months or thereabouts, which would
bring it to about the time you mentioned, a little after Christmas . . . If you had a
very small bank-note useless in any idle corner of your bureau, I should thank you
for it in part.

Price passed this letter on to Rockingham, saying that he had complied with
the request, by giving Wilkes £10 and a note payable after Christmas for £140,
'supposing that as the Dukes of Devonshire and Portland continued *another
year* their gratuity, your Lordship would have no particular objection'. He
also reminded the Marquess that £100 was still due to himself out of 'the
original payment to J.W. when he was sheriff'.[3] There is no information as to
how much longer these payments continued, but within a few years Wilkes
certainly had an alternative source of income. By 1776 there was in existence
a trust fund, intended to produce £600 a year, financed by private contributions and administered by Bull. There is no evidence to support the tempt-
ing assumption that the origin of this fund was the 1770 Bill of Rights Society
plan to provide Wilkes with a £600 annuity; nor to make any connection
with those earlier Rockinghamite donations. On 2 September 1776 Bull,
when sending Wilkes £40 he could spare, told him that he had already been
advanced more than he was due. The next month Wilkes was in such distress
that he thought of pawning the £100 silver cup given him by the City in 1772

for his part in 'the Printers' Case'. Bull thereupon offered to advance him £50, with the cup as security.[4]

The financial situation of Wilkes remained precarious. Subscribers to any voluntary scheme were likely to default, and any money Wilkes received was liable to be swallowed up by his debts. By early 1778 Thomas Wilson had floated a plan to pay Wilkes an annuity that would be immune from his creditors, hoping that Bull could devise the method.[5] Some such arrangement was evidently formulated, for the young Chathamite MP Lord Granby wrote to Wilkes on 9 March 1778 to say that he was 'extremely happy that the Friends of Liberty had proposed to extricate Mr Wilkes from difficulties in which his zeal for and attachment to the constitution of his country have contributed to involve him'. Lord Granby enclosed notes for £300 of debts Wilkes owed him, and later that month Sir James Lowther cancelled another £202.[6] There were suspicions, however, so John Almon later recalled, that Bull in his role as administrator of such funds deceived Wilkes as to the financial situation.[7] Such a circumstance would explain this otherwise puzzling comment about Bull made by Wilkes to his friend Sam Petrie on 2 January 1780, before their difference over the Gordon Riots: 'I have been very unworthily treated by him.'[8]

All such palliatives were no substitute for the regular substantial income Wilkes had by then secured as Chamberlain. In the 1779 contest for that post the opponents of Wilkes cited even his poverty as an argument against his appointment to an office of financial responsibility: 'He has but three suits, the Blue, the Green, and the Scarlet, and not one of them has been new these ten years.' This press jibe was answered in the *London Evening Post* of 20 November by the claim that such poverty was the hallmark of political integrity:

A man of Mr Wilkes's parts, activity, and interest, might have shone in the political hemisphere, with all the trappings of magnificence. . . . But Mr Wilkes persisted in obstinate indigence, and with his threadbare Blue, Green and Scarlet, maintained the privileges of his fellow-subjects, against the mean resentments of his Sovereign, and the lawless encroachments of Administration.

Financial salvation was at hand with his election as Chamberlain. Wilkes was delighted at his success, and not merely over the money. 'It is a post adequate, after the payment of my debts, to every wish I can form at fifty-three; profit, patronage, and extensive usefulness, with rank and dignity', he wrote to Petrie on 2 January 1780.[9] The City Chamberlain had two main sources of income, various fees appertaining to the office, and the income to be gained from the substantial cash balances in his keeping: for it was a widespread contemporary practice that office-holders in both national and local government could use to their own advantage public funds in their care. The fees

each year included an 'ancient fee' of £110; an 'annual fee' of £100; the right
to nominate to six City freedoms, worth £150; a £100 allowance for duties at
Smithfield Market; £100 as stationery allowance; and small fees for the
admission of individual freemen. To them was added on 19 November 1779,
obviously at the behest of Wilkes and just before his formal appointment,
£100 in lieu of use of the Chamberlain's official residence. The income from
these sources has been estimated by a biographer knowledgeable in such
matters as about £1,200 a year.[10] But an 1801 calculation was that a gross income of £930 was reduced by expenses to £553.[11] More lucrative, but extremely liable to fluctuation, due to variations in both the capital and the
interest rates, was the income to be earned on the City's cash balances.
While Wilkes was Chamberlain this income seemingly fluctuated between
£1,200 and £2,000. The income Wilkes received as Chamberlain might then
have varied from over £3,000 to barely more than half that total; and he
seemingly faced a mini-crisis in 1791, for on 3 March a City Lands Committee
report recommended the payment of £600 to Chamberlain Wilkes to com-
pensate for the current low cash balance. The resolution stated that this was
'his right', since Wilkes had advanced money to the City during the previous
three years. What the Chamberlain had presumably been doing was to move
money from accounts in credit to those in deficit: for critics of the motion
claimed that Wilkes had under his control twenty-eight separate funds, and
'*at all times* a large balance of public money in his hands', sometimes as much
as £80,000 or more. That was a gross misrepresentation, for a modern estimate puts the average total balance at £22,000. The motion was carried in
Common Council by 62 votes to 29, but the episode revived the old complaint that it was improper for Wilkes to be simultaneously Alderman and
Chamberlain.[12]

Already in 1790 the loss of popularity that cost Wilkes his Parliamentary
seat had spilt over into the annual City elections on 24 June. The nomination
of Wilkes as Chamberlain was 'received with considerable marks of applause, but not without some signs of disapprobation', according to the next
day's *Public Advertiser*. He was re-elected without opposition, but only after
Alderman Richard Clark, whose name had been put forward, had 'declared
that while the Chamberlainship was so ably filled as at present, he could not
think of giving them the trouble of a poll; but should he outlive the worthy
Alderman, he would then call upon them for their kind assistance'. That
implicit assumption that Wilkes would be Chamberlain for life was challenged in 1791, when on 10 June a Livery meeting voted that the two offices
of Alderman and Chamberlain were incompatible. It decided to support the
candidature of John Cowley if two other persons known to be interested,
Alderman Clark and Sir Watkin Lewes, declined to stand.[13] Cowley was a

Common Councilman who for some years had been criticizing the failure of Wilkes to produce detailed financial accounts.[14] Now a public campaign was launched against Wilkes, as in this *Morning Post* paragraph on 14 June:

Since Mr Wilkes held these offices the City accounts have been kept back for eight years together: in consequence the City became so poor, as to be obliged to borrow large sums, and at the same time the Chamberlain became rich, and therefore the citizens have wisely determined that the two offices are incompatible. Mr Wilkes opposed Mr Hopkins through successive years, giving no other reason than that the office was annual.

Two days later Cowley announced that despite obstacles placed in his way by Wilkes he had made a close study of the City accounts for several years. Another meeting of Livery on 21 June decided to support his candidature because of his exertions in 'favour of a reform in the said revenues and expenditure'. Next day Wilkes issued a notice asking his friends to attend the Midsummer meeting of the Livery on 24 June.[15] Clarke and Lewes also mustered their supporters, but on behalf of Wilkes. This alliance deterred Cowley from insisting on a poll, even though hundreds of hands were raised for him. He was howled down when he tried to speak, the *Morning Post* claiming that 'a vulgar rabble was hired to shout for Wilkes'.[16] The same paper on 1 July made this sour comment on the re-election of Wilkes:

The Livery of London can have no respect for Wilkes. He owes his election more to their pity than their love, as they suppose that he will not long enjoy their favours, and therefore they do not wish to send his 'grey hairs with sorrow to the grave'.

Wilkes was thenceforth unchallenged in his tenure of the post until he died in 1797. Cowley, when withdrawing his candidature, claimed success in the real object of his campaign, condemnation of the failure of Wilkes hitherto to present annual accounts.[17] But Wilkes did not mend his ways. An otherwise laudatory obituary notice in the *Annual Register* more or less said so: 'The same candour that dictates these observations, obliges the author at the same time to confess that he was dilatory in the production of the City accounts, and rather too attentive to the emoluments of office.'[18] These issues of breach of trust and dereliction of duty were raised again at his death, as a ground for the projected candidature of Cowley. 'It is a fact', wrote a correspondent in the *Morning Herald* of 30 December 1797, 'that your Chamber has been in such disorder that the salaries even of your Lord Mayor, your Recorder . . . as well as those of other officers, have been in arrears.' Especially reprehensible had been a cosy arrangement whereby Wilkes lent the City Corporation money from the 'other funds under his care', and pocketed the interest. Such practices had been commonplace in mid-century, but now invited public censure. Wilkes had outlived the *mores* of his time. In the event, however, Cowley was sidelined, as Richard Clarke easily defeated Sir Watkin Lewes.[19]

The post of City Chamberlain was no sinecure, as Sir Stephen Janssen's 1776 resignation letter had made clear, claiming that during his eleven years in office over 60,000 persons had attended on him.[20] The chief function was that of City Treasurer, with responsibility for administration of various official and charitable funds. A heavy workload was necessitated by the number and complexity of the accounts held in the City Chamber. The most important were the City's own cash fund; the Finsbury Estate; the Gresham Account; the Thames Navigation Fund; the Orphan Fund, used during this period for repairing bridges and rebuilding Newgate Prison; and the funds for paving, cleaning, and lighting the City streets, for which annual rates were levied. All these funds had to be managed separately. This financial business necessitated the employment of a staff of seven in the Chamberlain's office.[21] Other functions attached to the post of Chamberlain included control over the City apprentices, and responsibility for the admission of freemen; and the Chamberlain also enjoyed the ceremonial task of the bestowal of the honorary freedom of the City voted to distinguished individuals.[22] That was a duty at which the facility of Wilkes for making prepared orations enabled him to excel, and he prided himself on the quality of these addresses. He had the opportunity of congratulating several eminent men, including Lord Cornwallis and Admirals Howe and Nelson, the last on 28 November 1797.[23] The most famous of such occasions was the presentation of the City's freedom to William Pitt on 27 February 1784, at the height of the political struggle that was to confirm the young Prime Minister in office. It was a Pittite triumph as a London mob pulled the carriages of Pitt, Wilkes, and Sir Watkin Lewes to the Guildhall. Wilkes began with a compliment to, and comparison with, Pitt's father, past animosities so far forgotten that the recollection brought tears into the orator's eyes.[24] After this emotional opening the speech became a propaganda piece directed against Pitt's opponents in the Fox–North Coalition:

We look up, Sir, to that superior ability and purity of public virtue, which distinguishes you, for the reformation of many and great abuses; as well as for the steady protection of our chartered rights, our property, and our freedom. A late administration undertook an unjust and wicked war; which dismembered the empire, by depriving us of our most valuable colonies, and has brought us almost to the verge of bankruptcy.[25]

Almon's memoirs of Wilkes are full of praise for the performance of his duties as City Chamberlain. At one point he claimed that 'the Livery could not have selected in the City of London a more proper person for this situation';

and he later added that 'perhaps a more punctual, patient and penetrating Chamberlain has not filled the office during the last century'.[26] Other, less partial, comments endorse this broad verdict, and certainly within a year of taking the post Wilkes himself had to deny the charge that his zealous conduct of his duties as Chamberlain had caused him to cut down on his Parliamentary activities. But he nevertheless did take the opportunity to claim that he had 'never neglected a single day the duties of the Chamberlain's office'.[27] Wilkes took his work as Chamberlain seriously, and even towards the end of his life attended at the Guildhall three or four days a week.[28] His obituary notice in the highly respectable *Gentleman's Magazine* was but one of several testimonies to his conscientious and able performance of his duties there: 'As Chamberlain his regularity of attendance and superior merit were generally acknowledged. Patience and candour distinguished his decisions in the many causes which came daily under his cognizance in that office.'[29] This skill as an administrator, already displayed as Buckinghamshire magistrate and London Alderman, City sheriff, and Lord Mayor, is an aspect of the character and career of Wilkes neglected by those whose gaze is fixed on his political virtues and moral vices.

*

Long before the financial security afforded him by the post of Chamberlain, John Wilkes had settled into a regular lifestyle centred on his family and a select circle of friends. Resident since 1770 with his daughter Polly at Prince's Court, Great George Street, Westminster, he was in a sense paterfamilias of an extended family. His widowed mother soon afterwards moved to live nearby, until her death in 1781, at Old Palace Yard, to be close to her famous son and favourite grandchild. His elder brother Israel sought fame and fortune in foreign parts, Europe, Africa, and America, evidently without success: for when John became a ministerial supporter, Israel tried to take advantage of his brother's new contacts. In 1783 he asked John to obtain a general letter of recommendation from Admiral Rodney, and in 1790 vainly requested the New York Packet Agency.[30] Their younger brother Heaton took over the family business on the death of their father in 1761, but contrived to bankrupt it within a dozen or so years, writing to John on 9 March 1774: 'I have been for months past very unhappy, it being out of my power to go on with the distillery.' He was then sounding his brother about becoming London's Town Clerk.[31] Such a hope was as fruitless as his idea in 1770 of standing for City Chamberlain, when John Horne had deterred him by saying that he would certainly fail and damage his brother's political image in the process.[32] Amiable but rather feckless, Heaton became a coal merchant, remaining an emotional and financial dependant of John to the end of his brother's life.[33] Of all John's siblings his only source of strength was his formidable sister Mary, wife of George Hayley.

Exactly what role in the Wilkes family circle was played by his son John Smith is unclear, the more so as the young man was seldom in London. Wilkes acknowledged him only as his nephew, and he in turn addressed his father as his uncle. He was born on 10 December 1760 to Wilkes's house-keeper Catherine Smith; but, according to Almon, she 'being a very low illiterate woman, the boy was removed from her as soon as possible, that he might not attain any of her vulgar idiom or coarse phraseology'.[34] She bore no resentment at this decision, for her enduring affection for Wilkes shines through a letter of 30 September 1793. 'I have no friend in the world but you', she wrote, fondly recalling 'that day I had the honour of meeting you. I often dream of you and wish myself young again.'[35]

John Smith was educated privately in London and at Harrow, and then spent four years in Paris, whence he returned in about 1774 so Frenchified that he could hardly speak English. By 1776 he was in Hamburg, and the next year in Berlin, where he met Arthur Lee.[36] His paternity was an open secret, with Wilkes dropping humorous hints to his friends about papal nephews.[37] In 1782 Wilkes was able to set up a career for him, a cadetship in the Bengal Cavalry of the East India Company, possibly arranged through his friendship with Warren Hastings. John Smith did not prosper in India. In a desultory correspondence with his father during the next decade he complained of poverty and asked for letters of recommendation. Wilkes supplied these, but not until 1800 did Smith become a captain.[38]

Wilkes was evidently disappointed in his son, and his existence must have been an awkward reminder of his promiscuous behaviour. A recital of the numerous amours of John Wilkes would itself fill a volume, for he never re-mained faithful to the women selected as successive mistresses.[39] Even Wilkes, never a man to feel embarrassment, felt obliged to pen this letter of justification to his daughter in 1778:

In my non-age, to please my indulgent father, I married a woman half as old again as myself, of a very large fortune, my own that of a gentleman. It was a sacrifice to Plutus, not to Venus. I never lived with her, in the strict sense of the word, nor have I seen her for near 20 years. I stumbled at the very threshold of the temple of Hymen.

> The God of love was not a bidden guest
> Nor present at his own mysterious feast.

Are such ties at such a time of life binding? And are school-boys to be dragged to the altar? I have since often sacrificed to beauty, but I never gave my heart except to you.[40]

In the middle 1770s the lady most favoured by Wilkes was a Mademoiselle Charpillon. He had succeeded with her where even Casanova had failed, but this courtesan of Parisian extraction was an expensive luxury he was glad to shed after four years, in 1777. Within a year he formed a liaison that lasted for the rest of his life, bringing back to London from a winter sojourn at Bath one Amelia Arnold. Born on 29 May 1753, and so three years younger than Polly, she was, Almon recalled, 'a woman of some education and not of very humble origin'.[41] The affair caused some scandal, and was deemed detrimental to Wilkes's political career, so an anonymous professed well-wisher wrote to inform John's old mother:

He has *now* a young woman in keeping, who was induced by him to leave her place in the country. . . . Now be pleased to consider the criminality and infamy of such conduct. . . . He has lost many generous friends by his licentious practice, for what wise and virtuous man will be accessory to such vices by any contribution.[42]

Wilkes at once organized a residence for Amelia, about the time their daughter Harriet was born, on 20 October 1778: he obtained the lease of a house, number two at Kensington Gore, where mother and daughter resided for the rest of Wilkes's life.[43] It was a second home for Wilkes, who carefully supervised the education of his younger daughter, his paternity openly acknowledged by her surname of Wilkes.

He was a regular visitor to, and frequent guest at, the Kensington Gore house, but this long-standing relationship did not inhibit him from pursuing other women, a circumstance publicly highlighted by his affair with one Sally Barry. His diary records frequent dining engagements with 'Mrs Barry and Sally' between late 1793 and early 1796.[44] The relationship led to this mocking press comment in September 1795: 'Alderman Wilkes is *finishing* his Essay on Woman in the neighbourhood of Soho; but it is a *weak* and *miserable* performance.'[45] It may well have been with respect to Sally Barry that the later story was told of Wilkes running one day along St James's Street when a friend interrupted him, to meet this answer, 'Don't stop me. I have got an *erection* now. Did it go down I don't know when I shall have another.'[46] It was characteristic of Wilkes to jest about such a matter as his failing sexual powers: he is reputed to have commented to his apothecary, shortly before his death, 'my sins of *omission* are daily increasing, my sins of *emission* daily diminishing'.[47]

The social life of John Wilkes, quite apart from the delights of family and the pleasuring of women, was more extensive than is implied by the obituary notice in the *Gentleman's Magazine*: 'Full of wit, easy in his conversation, elegant in his manners, and blessed with a retentive memory, his company was a perpetual treat to the chosen few whom he selected as his intimate friends.'[48] His engagement diary from 1770 records a great many occasions when Wilkes was either attending public dinners or at private houses.[49] And the recollection of diarist Wraxall shows that if ever a man was the life and soul of a party, it was John Wilkes:

In private society, particularly at table, he was pre-eminently agreeable; abounding in anecdote; ever gay and convivial; converting his very defects of person, manner, or enunciation, to purposes of merriment or of entertainment. If any man ever was pleasing, who squinted, who had lost his teeth, and lisped, Wilkes might be so esteemed. His powers of conversation survived his other bodily faculties. I have dined in company with him not long before his decease, when he was extenuated and enfeebled to a great degree; but, his tongue retained all its former activity, and seemed to have outlived his other organs. Even in corporeal ruin, and obviously approaching the termination of his career, he formed the charm of the assembly.[50]

Wraxall knew Wilkes only in his declining years. The most famous instance of his deliberate use of his charm was on 15 May 1776, the occasion of his first meeting with Dr Samuel Johnson. The two men were poles apart in politics and character, and each had made press attacks on the other. In 1762 Wilkes, in the twelfth number of the *North Briton*, had cited Johnson's dictionary definition of a pensioner and branded the author as one himself. Johnson, in his 1770 pamphlet *The False Alarm*, described Wilkes as 'a retailer of sedition and obscenity' and derided the Middlesex Elections controversy as whether or not that county should be represented by a criminal in gaol. James Boswell, a friend of both men, amused himself by contriving that they should meet at a dinner party on that day, and noted how Wilkes pampered the older man: 'Mr Wilkes placed himself next to Dr Johnson, and behaved to him with so much attention and politeness, that he gained upon him insensibly.' They soon got on famously, indulging in abuse of the Scots, but also sharing a love of the classics.[51]

For Wilkes was a man renowned among his contemporaries for his learning. It was his old adversary Lord Mansfield who pronounced at a private dinner in 1783 that 'Mr Wilkes was the pleasantest companion, the politest gentleman, and the best scholar he knew'.[52] His youthful classical education was an enduring influence throughout his life, and a circumstance that, according to one obituarist, had unfitted him for business.[53] A strong cultural thread was woven in the rich tapestry of his life, albeit concerned with literature and scholarship rather than the visual and performing arts. Already, by the time of his French exile in 1764, his personal library reflected the catholic tastes of a cultivated mind, and its enforced sale upset him deeply. The catalogue of 949 items listed classical and modern literature, political tracts, Parliamentary treatises and debates, and no less than 188 books and pamphlets in French.[54] Wilkes was fluent in that language, and in

1769 described his years in France as the happiest period of his life.[55] Much of his later correspondence was written in French, to men like Diderot who had become firm friends.

In 1764 he beguiled away the early part of his French exile by reviewing an astonishing variety of literature: a book of lectures on Hebrew poetry, an edition of John Locke's political writings, and a volume of translated Welsh bardic poetry.[56] That was before he decided to fill his enforced leisure with writing his projected 'History of England'. After his release from prison in 1770 Wilkes set about rebuilding his personal library. At his death this comprised nearly 1,700 items, that fetched a total of £825 in the sales of 1799 and 1802.[57]

That Wilkes did read these books is apparent from both his private correspondence and his Parliamentary speeches. The latter were thoroughly prepared in their political and historical context, and almost invariably adorned by Latin quotations and allusions to both classical and modern literature. A reflection of a well-stocked mind rather than an affectation to impress contemporaries, this hallmark of his speeches evoked admiration even from political opponents, as when Governor George Johnstone began a reply to Wilkes on 26 November 1778 with this handsome acknowledgement: 'Sir, I shall not dispute with the honourable gentleman about matters of verbal criticism, concerning the purport and tenor of which I know he is a perfect master, and much my superior.'[58]

The abiding love Wilkes cherished for literature in particular and culture in general was strikingly demonstrated in a Commons debate of 28 April 1777. The occasion was a customary biennial petition of the Trustees of the British Museum for a Treasury payment to meet the yearly deficit of about £1,000. Wilkes supported the petition, urging a more generous allowance to permit the Museum to extend its opening hours: 'It is a general complaint that the Museum is not sufficiently accessible to the public. This must necessarily happen from the deficiency of their revenues; the Trustees cannot pay a proper number of officers and attendants.' Wilkes then took the opportunity to make a visionary and far-sighted plea for the expansion of the Museum by the establishment of both a National Library and a National Art Gallery. 'I wish their plan much enlarged, especially on two important objects, books and paintings. This capital after so many years remains without any considerable public library', he said, pointing the contrast with Rome and Paris, where the Vatican Library and the King's Library respectively were open to the public. 'The British Museum, Sir, is rich in manuscripts, the Harleian collection, the Cottonian library . . . but it is wretchedly poor in printed books. I wish, Sir, a sum was allowed by Parliament, for the purchase of the most valuable editions of the best authors, and an act passed, to oblige, under a certain penalty, every printer to send a copy bound of every publication made to the British Museum.' After expressing the hope that private benefactors might be encouraged by such a move, Wilkes pursued another theme: 'The British Museum, Sir, possesses few valuable paintings.' An opportunity to rectify this defect would soon present itself, he said, for 'one of the first collections in Europe, that at Houghton, made by Sir Robert Walpole', was to be sold. 'I hope it will not be dispersed, but purchased by Parliament, and added to the British Museum. I wish, Sir, the eye of painting as fully gratified as the ear of music is in this island, which at last bids fair to become a favourite abode of the polite arts. A noble gallery ought to be built in the garden of the British Museum, for the reception of that invaluable treasure.' That would be compensation for the withdrawal from public view of 'the cartoons of the divine Raphael', displayed at Hampton Court in rooms built for that purpose by William III, but in the present reign removed to the Queen's House, the modern Buckingham Palace, and 'entirely secreted from the public eye; yet, Sir, they were purchased with public money'. They were a national treasure, not private property, Wilkes declared, adding pointedly that 'the Kings of France and Spain permit their subjects the view of all the pictures in their collection'.[59]

No other MP took up or even commented on these ideas, and in 1779 the Houghton paintings were to be purchased by Catherine II of Russia for just over £40,000.[60] On 28 April 1777 the House of Commons duly resolved into a Committee of Supply on the British Museum petition. When Treasury Secretary Grey Cooper moved that £3,000 should be granted, Edmund Burke proposed an amendment for £5,000, perhaps following up the earlier suggestion of Wilkes, who seconded this; but the Treasury resolution was carried by 74 votes to 60.[61] The very next day, 29 April, Wilkes spoke in support of a Bill to license a Birmingham Playhouse, denying that drama had the pernicious social influence that opponents of the measure claimed. The play 'Macbeth', Wilkes declared, was 'a greater deterrent to murder than any sermon'; but the Bill was defeated by 69 votes to 18.[62]

During the last decade of his life, after his virtual retirement from politics, Wilkes gave fuller vent to that 'literary turn of mind' recalled by one obituarist.[63] In 1788 he published, at the press of John Nichols, one of his Aldermanic deputies, an edition of the minor Latin poet Catullus, whose role as an indigent and witty defender of liberty in his own time evidently struck a chord with Wilkes. It was a private edition, not for sale, of three vellum copies and a hundred on fine paper, of small quarto volumes, distributed to friends. Among the letters of thanks was one from Prime Minister Pitt, dated 15 July 1788.[64] Another came from Lord Mansfield on 1 August, congratulating Wilkes 'upon those enjoyments which an early taste for the

Classics has put in his power'.[65] Two years later he published in Greek an edition of *The Characters of Theophrastus*. William Holwell, a Greek scholar resident in Bristol, made many corrections to a proof sent to him by a mutual friend.[66] The work was published in a private edition identical to *Catullus*. Among the grateful recipients were Horace Walpole, Warren Hastings, Sir Joshua Reynolds, and, again, Lord Mansfield.[67] It was the first complete edition, but lacked accents, notes, or introduction. A reviewer commended Wilkes for his 'natural force of genius and affection for polite literature', describing how Wilkes had been diverted from his early love of learning: 'He was driven, by a fortuitous coincidence of events, into the most tremendous storm of politicks. . . . In maturer years we see him continuing to cultivate the Muses . . . Long may he continue to enjoy this rational delight.'[68] That wish was fulfilled, for as late as 1796 Wilkes was busy on Greek translation.[69] But that scholarship rather than politics was his true *métier* is not an interpretation of John Wilkes that carries conviction.

That Wilkes should have given away to friends these expensive classical editions was characteristic of the man. 'We may add', wrote one obituarist, 'that, though his income was handsome, his liberality kept equal pace with it. Hence the vague reports of his having amassed an ample fortune cannot possibly be deserving of credit.'[70] His intended beneficiaries under his will found that to be all too true after his death. For Wilkes never did put his finances in order, despite the advantage of a substantial income as City Chamberlain, or even after the death of his wife on 3 April 1784 substantially improved the financial position of his household. If Wilkes himself only gained thereby from the termination of the £200 annual payment he had made since their separation, his wife's fortune was bequeathed to Polly. It was a substantial inheritance, for in addition to landed estates in several counties she listed over £15,000 worth of Bank of England and South Sea Company stock in the will she made in 1800. Her income was said to exceed £2,000.[71] John Wilkes, perhaps aware of her impending demise, made a last-minute visit to his wife. 'We are happy to hear that after a long separation Mr Wilkes had a conciliatory interview with his lady a short time before her death', reported the *Gentleman's Magazine*.[72] And he observed formal mourning for the customary six months.[73]

To the very end Wilkes lived a hand-to-mouth existence. It was evidently bad news that only twelve freemen were admitted during one week in July 1793, for that meant a diminution of fee income; and later that year Wilkes had to borrow £300 from a friend.[74] Where did his money go? He did not enjoy an extravagant lifestyle. He was not a gambler, a glutton, or a heavy drinker.[75] He walked from his own home to Kensington and to the City, several times a week, instead of taking hackney coaches. Nor did he spend much on clothes, as one obituarist commented: 'Towards the latter part of his life he became regardless of his dress, and his wardrobe for the last fifteen years seems to have consisted of a faded scarlet coat, white cloth waistcoat and breeches, and a pair of military boots.'[76]

Where Wilkes seemingly spared no expense was in the maintenance and embellishment of his properties. Extravagant sums were spent on his own house at Prince's Court and that of Amelia Arnold; and, later, on a cottage he acquired on the Isle of Wight and on a new home in London.[77] Long on the look-out for a summer residence, he obtained in 1788 a fourteen-year lease of one at Sandown, which he called his 'villakin', and thereafter spent several months each summer there, usually July to September, visited by the Arnolds and Polly, separately not together, and by other friends.[78] In a letter of 1 September 1790, written from 'Sandham Cottage', one invitation for a weekend included the suggestion, mock or otherwise, of a visit to church on the Sunday![79] In 1790, after twenty years at Prince's Court, Wilkes moved to a larger residence, at number thirty, Grosvenor Square, with brother Heaton taking over his old home. Wilkes took out a £1,500 mortgage to purchase the lease of the new property.[80] Although his new home was considerably further from the City, nearly three miles from the Guildhall, he still walked there 'every day when his duty required his attendance', so Almon recalled.[81] 'In his person Mr Wilkes was tall, agile', stated his *Annual Register* obituarist; but it would be unwise to assume that his predilection for walking was responsible for this physique, that he was an early and successful fitness fanatic: for the report continued, 'and so very thin towards the latter part of his life, that his limbs seemed cadaverous'. Marasmus, a disease of malnutrition, was suspected to be a cause of his death, aged 72, on 29 December 1797.[82]

He had made his will on 21 May 1795. Amelia Arnold was bequeathed the lease of the Kensington Gore house, with contents, and £1,000. Harriet was left that of Sandham Cottage, together with £2,000. There were small bequests to some officials in the Chamberlain's office and to his household servants. His daughter Polly, formally named Mary in the will, received the Grosvenor Square house and the rest of his estate.[83] But Wilkes, who thought himself affluent, died virtually insolvent. The residue of his estate, after payment of his debts and funeral expenses, did not amount to a fifth of the modest legacies. That was a great shock to all concerned. Shortly before his death he assured his chief beneficiaries that he had a 'considerable balance' at the bank: and his close friend Joseph Paice, a merchant much respected for his altruistic beneficence, had 'thought it moderate' to estimate this at between £8,000 and £10,000, so he wrote afterwards. Paice undertook the task of breaking the news to Polly, Amelia Arnold, and Harriet, who all received it, he recalled in 1804, with 'humility and disinterested resignation'.[84] Polly, who became a close friend of Harriet during the few years before her sudden death in 1802, sought to carry out her father's wishes in her own will, dated 18 July 1800. Harriet was given £3,400 worth of stock, the interest thereupon until she married, when she would receive the capital; and Amelia Arnold was bequeathed £2,500 of South Sea Stock for her lifetime only, with £1,000 of this to go to Harriet on her death.[85] So did money from the estate of the wife of John Wilkes pass to his mistress and their child. He would have enjoyed that ironic postscript to his life.

13

Radical or Rascal

'To the various merits of Mr Wilkes impartial Posterity will do ample justice', the *Gentleman's Magazine* predicted in 1798.[1] That was not to be so, and yet the immediate verdict of contemporaries was favourable. The brief first obituary notice of Wilkes in the same periodical had opened with this compliment: 'A Patriot in the truest sense of the word, his exertions and intrepidity added legal security to the liberties of Englishmen.'[2] Almost as favourable was the lengthy notice in the *Annual Register*. His skill of popular journalism was commended: 'As an author, he possessed the singular merit of always writing to and for the people. . . . His merits can only be appreciated by the benefits he has conferred on his country.' After recounting the political achievements of Wilkes, in securing the freedom of the press, especially with respect to Parliamentary reporting, and such other gains for liberty as the abolition of general warrants and the freedom of elections, the obituarist came to this conclusion:

In short, with all his faults, Mr Wilkes possessed something more than the vapour of patriotism; he could face poverty and banishment, despise a jail, resist corruption, attack and overcome tyranny. . . . He outlived his reputation and . . . when he died . . . he was nearly forgotten. Distance blends and softens the shades of large objects. Time throws her mantle over petty defects. The present age already confirms that he was persecuted, the next will probably consider him as a great man. At all events, his name will be connected with our history.[3]

Immediate posterity gave Wilkes a bad press. Tory historians from John Adolphus onwards portrayed him as lacking ability and integrity. Nor did Wilkes fit easily into a Whig historiography intent on lauding Charles James Fox and other Parliamentarians. Lord Brougham denounced him as a hypocrite. Lord John Russell, perhaps mindful of the antipathy between Wilkes and his ancestor the fourth Duke of Bedford, described the demagogue as 'a profligate spendthrift, without opinions or principles, religious or political; whose impudence far exceeded his talents, and who always meant license when he cried liberty'. Lord Macaulay, that doyen of Whig historians, simply dismissed Wilkes as a nobody.[4]

Later generations of historians and politicians were more disposed to acknowledge his achievements, but often with a reluctance to accept that such a man, notorious as a womanizer and blasphemer, and with a cynical sense of humour, could possibly have possessed political principles. Victorian Liberals were embarrassed by such a political ancestor, an attitude encapsulated in the famous comment of William Gladstone that 'the name of Wilkes, whether we choose it or not, must be enrolled among the greatest champions of English freedom'. Few politicians have been as virtuous as Gladstone, and Wilkes has too often been judged by standards not applied to such of his contemporaries as Charles James Fox, whose range of deplorable habits was far wider. Appraisal of Wilkes should take note of his double-edged boast that he had 'no *small* vices'. He did not indulge in many fashionable pursuits of the age. Wilkes was never a noted gambler, whether at dice, cards, or on horses. After his youth he was abstemious in his consumption of food and drink. Although he enjoyed riding, he did not hunt or shoot, professing a metropolitan disdain for such rural activities, as in this letter of 20 June 1769 to French correspondent Suard: 'A proper vacation must be allowed the English for partridge shooting and all field sports; then they return to the smoke, dirt and politics of London with fresh gout.'[5]

But vices are weighed, not counted, and for contemporaries the wickedness of Wilkes lay in his overt sexual promiscuity, emphasized by bawdy language and lack of shame, an attitude epitomized in his comment that he 'loved all women except his wife'.[6] Two lines of defence have been offered to palliate if not excuse his behaviour. One is that he was not a seducer of innocents, preferring experienced and willing partners. 'A man cannot be wicked if a woman says nay', claimed one biographer.[7] This line of argument is not borne out by the evidence of his life, and it is apparent that his notorious behaviour and ribaldry caused him to be deemed a danger to all women. The other, obvious, explanation of his conduct is that Wilkes, estranged from his wife since 1756 and unable to obtain a divorce, could not have been expected to adopt a celibate way of life. That argument will not stand. Wilkes began his notorious lifestyle when a young man and never changed his ways even when, as with Amelia Arnold, he had a permanent lady friend. Contemporaries judged correctly when they regarded Wilkes as a profligate.

His alleged lack of political principle, supposedly implied by this personal immorality, was seemingly confirmed by both his tongue-in-cheek humour and his instantaneous 1782 conversion from an opponent into a supporter of government. His witty comments, so often directed at himself or his supporters, were common knowledge, as Horace Walpole stated when recounting what Wilkes said during his speech of 22 February 1775 on the Middlesex Elections: 'Though he called the resolutions of the last Parliament a violation of Magna Carta, he said, in a whisper to Lord North, he was forced to say so to please the fellows who followed him. This was his constant style; and though certainly conveyed to the mob, they still followed him.'[8] More damaging to his popularity, and to his contemporary reputation, was his 1782 decision to support the King's government, for the last fifteen years of his life as it proved to be. It is evidently to that period that the variously attributed story belongs of his rebuke to an elderly woman who had called out 'Wilkes and Liberty' on seeing him in the street: 'Be quiet, you old fool. That's all over long ago.' Political opponents made much of his supposed apostasy from the cause of liberty, the most famous jibe being one attributed to R. B. Sheridan, opposition politician as well as playwright:

> Johnny Wilkes, Johnny Wilkes,
> Thou greatest of bilks,
> How changed are the notes you now sing!
> Your famed Forty-Five,
> is Prerogative,
> And your blasphemy, 'God save the King'.[9]

That final twist in the Wilkes story helps to explain why Whig historians have been reluctant to commend his achievements. But it is irrelevant to an assessment of his political role during the preceding two decades. Wilkes was a political journalist first and foremost, and two of his three major confrontations with government arose from official attempts to curb political activities of the press, criticism of ministers, and Parliamentary reporting. The furore over the *North Briton* case had the incidental effect of deterring future ministerial prosecutions of what were deemed to be political libels, but Wilkes took little interest in the subsequent legal and political battles on that issue, when he was not personally involved. The issue that he seized upon, and that launched his political career, was the theoretical threat to 'liberty' implicit in general warrants, for they exposed unnamed individuals, everyone in theory, to invasion of their homes and seizure of their persons and property. Two centuries later it is apparent that there was no danger that any British ministry would make deliberate and extensive use of general warrants to arrest political opponents, or stifle press criticism. Nor that any ministry would embark on systematic disqualification of political opponents from sitting in the House of Commons, the theoretical implication of the Middlesex Elections case. But contemporaries were very sensitive to any abuse of executive power, an attitude Wilkes exploited to the full. His successes over general warrants and the Middlesex Elections episode helped to define practical limits to government control over individuals and Parliament respectively. He was defending the boundaries of a liberty that already existed. To posterity the extension of that boundary to include the freedom to report Parliamentary debates would seem to be an achievement of greater potential significance than the two more famous episodes that engrossed contemporary opinion. And the political significance of Wilkes was greater than the sum of his successes in the cause of liberty.

After Wilkes the Georgian political world was never to be the same again. His career widened the political dimension beyond the closed world of Westminster, Whitehall, and Windsor. George Rudé demonstrated a generation ago that the men who gave Wilkes his political importance were not the impoverished working class, but their small-scale employers: merchants, shopkeepers, artisans, craftsmen, and the like. Men of wealth like Beckford, Bull, Crosby, and the Olivers might take the lead, and pauper crowds helped to throng the streets and sometimes rioted; but the Wilkite movement reflected the evolution of new social groupings of men whose economic self-sufficiency generated an independence of attitude. The simultaneous growth of the press was the torch that illuminated political matters for them, and Wilkes the spark that lit the torch. In the Wilkite era the politicization of the press was the key to its expansion, symbolized by the rapid spread of Parliamentary reporting, soon deemed essential to secure viable circulations for most newspapers.

Wilkes was swimming with the political tide, and 'the fourth estate' was henceforth a factor in politics; but these circumstances do not explain how one man had so successfully confronted the power of government. Sheer audacity was part of the answer. The legality of general warrants had been a matter of some doubt before 1763; but it took a John Wilkes, backed by the purse of Lord Temple, to challenge their validity. In 1768–9 his persistent and unprecedented refusal to accept the traditional power of the House of Commons to decide disputed elections, one originally established to safeguard Parliament against the Crown, outraged the political establishment of the day. And, for many contemporaries, the most blatant example of his cheek was his 1771 success in pitting the City of London against the House of Commons.

To political courage Wilkes added tactical skill. What a close study of Wilkes reveals is the clever way in which he outwitted government time and again. In both of the crises commenced on his own initiative, those of 1768–9 and 1771, he contrived to manoeuvre administration into untenable positions. In 1763–4 and 1769 the Grenville and Grafton ministries were compelled to alter the rules of the political game to defeat him; and in each case Wilkes later nevertheless won the constitutional point. The Grenville administration adopted dubious and unfair tactics, beginning with the smear campaign based on the irrelevant *Essay on Woman*. The decision of 23 November 1763 to withdraw the protection of Parliamentary privilege from seditious libel was contrary to previous usage, however logical the argument of criminal offence Grenville and others put forward to justify it. The expulsion of Wilkes from Parliament on 20 January 1764 anticipated the legal conviction that provided the pretext for that decision. What happened in 1769 over the Middlesex election can likewise be analysed into a triple injustice to Wilkes. The decision of the Grafton ministry to expel him was taken first, and then a reason for it sought. The libel on Lord Weymouth was dubious ground in itself, and the composite motion of expulsion on 3 February 1769 manifestly unfair. Worse was to follow. The House of Commons, faced on 17 February with the new problem of an MP who refused to accept expulsion, created a disqualification on the basis of its own authority, and thereby prevented a constituency electing as MP a man not otherwise debarred from sitting in the Commons. When Wilkes forced the issue, the ministry awarded the seat to a minority candidate. Ministers were constantly and consistently wrong-footed by 'that devil Wilkes'.

If for many contemporaries Wilkes did too much, for some historians he did not do enough. The judgement that Wilkite radicalism was limited and conservative, however, is one based on abstract criteria taken out of context. In the early decades of George III's reign advocacy of any change in the much-revered constitution was a daring innovation. John Wilkes should not be judged by the levelling principles of the French Revolution, a development he publicly condemned as soon as it ceased to resemble Britain's Glorious Revolution. Wilkes was no role model for later generations of Radicals. His disdainful attitude to the lower social orders was illustrated by the frequent disparaging remarks about his followers, and exemplified by his treatment of the workers at his private printing press in 1763. Even in his heyday his political opinions were less radical than those of some of his followers, as he himself well knew. Lord Eldon recorded this account by George III of a reply by Wilkes after the King had enquired about his friend Serjeant John Glynn:

'Sir', rejoined Wilkes, 'he *was* my *counsel*—one *must* have a counsel; but he was no *friend*; he loves sedition and licentiousness, which I never delighted in. In fact, Sir, he was a Wilkite, *which I never was.*' The King said the confidence and the humour of the man made him forget at the moment his impudence.[10]

The concept Wilkes had of the British constitution embraced the importance of the monarchy, as his comments on the French Revolution demonstrated. He had respect for the institutions of the state, never challenging the
powers of the Crown to govern, Parliament to legislate, and the Courts of
Law to enforce their decisions. But the defects of the system were his targets,
and especially could his attempts to establish the responsibility of the House
of Commons to the electorate be construed as a restoration of a basic principle of Parliamentary government. Even electoral reform was in that sense
a removal of abuses that had crept into the system. Most contemporaries
regarded Wilkes, however, merely as a foolish and self-seeking trouble-maker,
this opinion of the serious-minded and honourable Edmund Burke in 1768
being typical: 'He is a lively, agreeable man, but of no prudence and no principles.'[11] Yet by then Wilkes had already suffered exile and financial ruin because of his political conduct, and was soon to be imprisoned, disdaining a
deal with Prime Minister Grafton for his release later that year. In all the evidence of his political views, whether in correspondence, papers for the press,
and public speeches, there is a consistency of argument, attitude, and conviction that only a cynic would disregard. Biographers of Wilkes, familiar
with this evidence, have taken a more favourable view of him as a principled
politician than historians with more impressionistic opinions. 'Few historical characters have been the victims of more hasty generalisations', wrote
Horace Bleackley in 1917.[12] Detailed assessments establish that John Wilkes
was a genuine Radical as well as an undoubted rascal.

Select Bibliography

PRIMARY SOURCES

A. Manuscripts

British Library (cited as BL)

Eg[erton] MSS 215–63, 3711. The Parliamentary Diary of Henry Cavendish, 1768–74.
Eg. MSS 2136–7. Original Letters of English Statesmen, 1734–1847.
Add[itional] MSS 6804–71. Sir Andrew Mitchell Papers.
Add. MSS 20733. John Almon Papers, 1766–1805.
Add. MSS 22131–2. Papers relating to the trial of John Wilkes, 1762–9.
Add. MSS 30865–96. John Wilkes Papers.
Add. MSS 32559–75. John Mitford Papers.
Add. MSS 32686–3072. Newcastle Papers.
Add. MSS 35349–6278. Hardwicke Papers.
Add. MSS 38190–468. Liverpool Papers.
Add. MSS 38593–4. Minutes of Westminster Committee, 1780–3.
Add. MSS 42083–8. Grenville Papers.
Add. MSS 59679–80. The Life of John Wilkes by John Jaques (1836).
MS Facs 340 (1–5). John Robinson Papers in the possession of Lord Abergavenny at
    Eridge Castle.

Public Record Office

Treasury Papers (cited as T).
State Papers Domestic (cited as SP).
Chatham Papers (cited as PRO 30/8).

Guildhall Library

MS 214. The King versus Wilkes. Crown Solicitors papers.
MS 2892. Papers relating to John Wilkes.
MS 3332. English Liberty. MS notes and supplement by Isaac Hitchcock, 1762–80.
MSS 14173–6. Correspondence of John Wilkes.

Other Repositories

Malmesbury MSS. Hampshire County Record Office (photocopies and tran-
    scripts). By permission of the Earl of Malmesbury.
Sandwich MSS. National Maritime Museum. By permission of the Trustees.

Wilkes MSS (1–6). William L. Clements Library, Ann Arbor. Cited as Wilkes MSS (Clements).

B. Printed Sources

Legal and Parliamentary Proceedings

A Complete Collection of State Trials, ed. T. J. Howell and T. B. Howell, 34 vols. (London, 1809–28). Cited as Howell, *State Trials*.

Journals of the House of Commons

Journals of the House of Lords

ALMON, J., *The Debates and Proceedings of the British House of Commons from 1743 to 1774*, 11 vols. (1766–75). Cited as Almon, *Debates*.

—— *The Parliamentary Register . . . 1774 to . . . 1780*, 17 vols. (1775–80). Cited as Almon, *Parl. Reg.*

WRIGHT, J. (ed.), *Sir Henry Cavendish's Debates of the House of Commons during the Thirteenth Parliament of Great Britain*, 2 vols. (1841–3). Cited as *Cavendish Debates*.

COBBETT, W., *Parliamentary History of England from . . . 1066 to . . . 1803*, 36 vols. (1806–20). Cited as Cobbett, *Parl. Hist.*

DEBRETT, J., *The Parliamentary Register . . . 1780 to . . . 1796*, 45 vols. (1781–96). Cited as Debrett, *Parl. Reg.*

THOMAS, P. D. G. (ed.), 'The Parliamentary Diaries of Nathaniel Ryder 1764–1767', *Camden Miscellany XXIII* (Royal Historical Society, 1969), 229–351. Cited as *Ryder Diary*.

SIMMONS, R. C., and THOMAS, P. D. G. (eds.), *Proceedings and Debates of the British Parliaments Respecting North America 1754–1783*, 6 vols. (New York, 1982–6).

STOCKDALE, J., *Debates and Proceedings of the House of Commons and Lords*, 19 vols. (1785–90). Cited as Stockdale, *Debates*.

Contemporary Correspondence and Memoirs

Memoirs of John Almon, bookseller, of Piccadilly (London, 1790). Cited as Almon, *Memoirs*.

Correspondence of John, Fourth Duke of Bedford, Selected from the Originals at Woburn Abbey, with an Introduction by Lord John Russell, 3 vols. (London, 1842–6). Cited as *Bedford Papers*.

Boswell on the Grand Tour: Italy, Corsica and France 1765–1766, ed. F. Brady and F. A. Pottle (London, 1955).

The Correspondence of Edmund Burke, i, ed. T. W. Copeland (Cambridge, 1958); ii, ed. L. S. Sutherland (Cambridge, 1960); iii, ed. T. W. Copeland (Cambridge, 1961); iv, ed. J. A. Woods (Cambridge, 1963). Cited as *Burke Corr.*

Letters from George III to Lord Bute 1756–1766, ed. R. Sedgwick (London, 1939). Cited as *Bute Letters*.

Carlisle MSS. Reports of Historical Manuscripts Commission. 15 Report. App., Part VI (1897). Cited as *HMC Carlisle*.

Alexander Carlyle: Anecdotes and Characters, ed. J. Kinsley (London, 1973). Cited as *Alexander Carlyle Anecdotes*.

Correspondence of William Pitt, Earl of Chatham, ed. W. S. Taylor and J. H. Pringle, 4 vols. (London, 1838–40). Cited as *Chatham Papers*.

Anecdotes of the Life of . . . the Right Honourable William Pitt, Earl of Chatham . . . 1736 to 1778, ed. J. Almon, 3 vols. (London, 1810). Cited as *Chatham Anecdotes*.

The Public and Private Life of Lord Chancellor Eldon with selections from his correspondence, ed. H. Twiss, 3 vols. (London, 1844).

The Papers of Benjamin Franklin, x–xxii, ed. L. W. Labaree, W. B. Willcox (New Haven, 1966–82). Cited as *Franklin Papers*.

The Correspondence of King George the Third from 1760 to December 1783, ed. Sir John Fortescue, 6 vols. (London, 1927–8). Cited as *Corr. of George III*.

The Letters of Edward Gibbon, ed. J. E. Norton, 3 vols. (London, 1956).

Gibbon's Journal to January 25th 1763, ed. D. M. Low (London, 1929).

Autobiography and Political Correspondence of Augustus Henry, Third Duke of Grafton, ed. Sir William R. Anson (London, 1896). Cited as *Grafton Autobiography*.

The Grenville Papers; being the correspondence of Richard Grenville, Earl Temple, K.G., and the Right Hon. George Grenville, their friends and contemporaries, ed. W. J. Smith, 4 vols. (London, 1852–3). Cited as *Grenville Papers*.

Memoirs of John Horne Tooke, ed. A. Stephens, 2 vols. (London, 1813). Cited as *Horne Tooke Memoirs*.

The Diary and Letters of his Excellency Thomas Hutchinson, Esq., ed. P. O. Hutchinson, 2 vols. (London, 1883–6). Cited as *Hutchinson Diary*.

The Jenkinson Papers 1760–1766, ed. N. S. Jucker (London, 1949).

Boswell's Life of Johnson, ed. G. B. Hill, rev. L. F. Powell, 6 vols. (Oxford, 1934–50).

The Letters of Junius, ed. J. Cannon (Oxford, 1978).

Radical Adventurer: The Diaries of Robert Morris 1772–1774, ed. J. E. Ross (Bath, 1971).

The Diary of Sylas Neville 1767–1788, ed. B. Cozens-Hardy (London, 1950).

Peter Oliver's Origin and Progress of the American Revolution: A Tory View, ed. D. Adair and J. A. Schutz (San Marino, Calif., 1963).

Parliamentary Papers of John Robinson 1774–1784, ed. W. T. Laprade (Royal Historical Society, London, 1922).

Memoirs of the Marquis of Rockingham and his Contemporaries, ed. George Thomas, Earl of Albemarle, 2 vols. (London, 1852).

Horace Walpole. Memoirs of King George II, ed. J. Brooke, 3 vols. (London, 1985). Cited as Walpole, *Memoirs of George II*.

Horace Walpole. Memoirs of the Reign of King George the Third, ed. G. F. Russell Barker, 4 vols. (London, 1894). Cited as Walpole, *Memoirs of George III*.

The Last Journals of Horace Walpole, during the Reign of George III from 1771–1783, ed. A. F. Stewart, 2 vols. (London, 1910). Cited as Walpole, *Last Journals*.

The Letters of Horace Walpole, Fourth Earl of Orford, ed. Mrs Paget Toynbee, 16 vols. (Oxford, 1905). Cited as Walpole, *Letters* (Toynbee).

The Correspondence of the late John Wilkes with his Friends, printed from the original manuscripts, in which are introduced Memoirs of his Life, ed. John Almon, 5 vols. (London, 1805). Cited as Almon, *Wilkes*.

The Correspondence of John Wilkes and Charles Churchill, ed. E. H. Weatherly (New York, 1954).

John Wilkes, Patriot. An Unfinished Autobiography, ed. W. F. Taylor (Harrow, 1888).

Historical Memoirs of His Own Time by Sir N. W. Wraxall, Bart, 4 vols. (London, 1836).

Posthumous Memoirs of His Own Time by Sir N. W. Wraxall, Bart, 3 vols. (London, 1836).

Contemporary Periodicals

Annual Register   *Middlesex Journal*
Daily Advertiser   *Morning Chronicle*
The Gazetteer   *Morning Herald*
General Evening Post   *Morning Post*
Gentleman's Magazine   *North Briton*
Lloyd's Evening Post   *Public Advertiser*
London Calendar   *Public Ledger*
London Chronicle   *St. James's Chronicle*
London Evening Post   *Whitehall Evening Post*
London Magazine   *The World*

SECONDARY WORKS

A. Books

BEAVEN, A. B., *The Aldermen of the City of London*, 2 vols. (London, 1913).

BLACK, E. C., *The Association: British Extra-Parliamentary Political Organisation 1769–1793* (Cambridge, Mass., 1963).

BLEACKLEY, H., *Life of John Wilkes* (London, 1917).

BONWICK, C., *English Radicals and the American Revolution* (Chapel Hill, NC, 1977).

BOWEN, H. V., *Revenue and Reform: The Indian Problem in British Politics 1757–1773* (Cambridge, 1991).

BRADLEY, J. E., *Popular Politics and the American Revolution in England: Petitions, The Crown, and Public Opinion* (Macon, Ga., 1986).

BREWER, J., *Party Ideology and Popular Politics at the Accession of George III* (Cambridge, 1976).

BROOKE, J., *The Chatham Administration 1766–1768* (London, 1956).

—— *King George III* (London, 1972).

CANNON, J., *The Fox-North Coalition: Crisis of the Constitution 1782–4* (Cambridge, 1969).

—— *Parliamentary Reform 1640–1832* (Cambridge, 1973).

CHRISTIE, I. R., *The End of North's Ministry 1780–1782* (London, 1958).

—— *Wilkes, Wyvill and Reform: The Parliamentary Reform Movement in British Politics 1760–1785* (London, 1962).

—— *Myth and Reality in Late Eighteenth Century British Politics and other Papers* (London, 1970).

DEANE, S., *Sales Catalogues of Libraries of Eminent Persons*, viii. *Politicians* (London, 1973).

EHRMAN, J., *The Younger Pitt: The Years of Acclaim* (London, 1969).

ELLIOTT, G. F. S., *The Border Elliots and the Family of Minto* (Edinburgh, 1897).

FITZGERALD, P., *The Life and Times of John Wilkes, MP, Lord Mayor of London and Chamberlain*. 2 vols. (London, 1888).

FITZMAURICE, LORD, *Life of William Earl of Shelburne, afterwards First Marquess of Lonsdowne*, 2 vols. (London, 1912).

HAIG, R. L., *The Gazetteer 1735–1797: A Study in the Eighteenth Century English Newspaper* (Carbondale, Ill., 1960).

HAMILTON, A., *The Infamous Essay on Woman, or John Wilkes Seated Between Vice and Virtue* (London, 1972).

HIBBERT, C., *King Mob: The Story of Lord George Gordon and the Riots of 1780* (London, 1958).

HILL, B., *The Republican Virago: The Life and Times of Catherine Macaulay, Historian* (Oxford, 1992).

HINKHOUSE, F. J., *The Preliminaries of the American Revolution as Seen in the English Press, 1763–1775* (New York, 1926).

KEMP, B., *Sir Francis Dashwood: An Eighteenth-Century Independent* (London, 1967).

LANGFORD, P., *The First Rockingham Administration 1765–1766* (London, 1973).

LAWSON, P., *George Grenville: A Political Life* (Oxford, 1984).

MACCOBY, S., *English Radicalism 1762–1785: The Origins* (London, 1955).

McCORMICK, D., *The Hell-Fire Club. The Story of the Amorous Knights of Wycombe* (London, 1958).

MACLEAN, J. N. M., *Reward is Secondary: The Life of a Political Adventurer and an Inquiry into the Mystery of Junius* (London, 1963).

MARTELLI, G., *Jemmy Twitcher: A Life of the Fourth Earl of Sandwich 1718–1792* (London, 1962).

MASTERS, B., *The Chamberlain of the City of London 1237–1987* (London, 1988).

NAMIER, SIR LEWIS, and BROOKE, J. (eds.), *The House of Commons 1754–1790: The History of Parliament*, 3 vols. (London, 1964).

NOBBE, G., *The North Briton: A Study in Political Propaganda* (New York, 1939).

NORRIS, J., *Shelburne and Reform* (London, 1963).

O'GORMAN, F., *The Rise of Party in England: The Rockingham Whigs 1760–1782* (London, 1975).

OLSON, A. G., *The Radical Duke: The Career and Correspondence of Charles Lennox third Duke of Richmond* (London, 1961).

PETERS, M., *Pitt and Popularity: The Patriot Minister and London Opinion during the Seven Years' War* (Oxford, 1980).

POSTGATE, R., *That Devil Wilkes* (London, 1930).

REA, R. R., *The English Press in Politics 1760–1774* (Lincoln, Neb., 1963).

RODGER, N. A. M., *The Insatiable Earl: A Life of John Montagu 4th Earl of Sandwich* (London, 1993).

RUDÉ, G., *Wilkes and Liberty: A Social Study of 1763 to 1774* (Oxford, 1962).

—— *Paris and London in the Eighteenth Century: Studies in Popular Protest* (London, 1970).

SAINSBURY, J., *Disaffected Patriots: London Supporters of Revolutionary America 1769–1782* (Gloucester, 1987).

SHARPE, R. R., *London and the Kingdom: A History Derived Mainly from the Archives at Guildhall*, 3 vols. (London, 1894–5).

SHERRARD, O. A., *A Life of John Wilkes* (London, 1930).

SUTHERLAND, L. S., *The East India Company in Eighteenth-Century Politics* (Oxford, 1952).

—— *The City of London and the Opposition to Government 1768–1774* (London, 1959).

THOMAS, P. D. G., *The House of Commons in the Eighteenth Century* (Oxford, 1971).

—— *British Politics and the Stamp Act Crisis: The First Phase of the American Revolution 1763–1767* (Oxford, 1975).

—— *Lord North* (London, 1976).

—— *The Townshend Duties Crisis: The Second Phase of the American Revolution 1767–1773* (Oxford, 1987).

—— *Tea Party to Independence: The Third Phase of the American Revolution 1773–1776* (Oxford, 1991).

TRELOAR, W. P., *Wilkes and the City* (London, 1917).

TRENCH, C. C., *Portrait of a Patriot: A Biography of John Wilkes* (London, 1962).

WILLIAMS, B., *The Life of William Pitt Earl of Chatham*, 2 vols. (London, 1913–14).

WILLIAMSON, A., *Wilkes: 'A Friend to Liberty'* (London, 1974).

YARBOROUGH, M. C., *John Horne Tooke* (New York, 1926).

B. Articles

CHRISTIE, I. R., 'The Wilkites and the General Election of 1774', *The Guildhall Miscellany*, 2/4 (1962), 155–64.

COLLEY, L., 'Eighteenth-Century English Radicalism before Wilkes', *Transactions of the Royal Historical Society (TRHS)*, 5th ser., 31 (1981), 1–20.

DICKINSON, H. T., 'Radicals and Reformers in the Age of Wilkes and Wyvill', in J. Black (ed.), *British Politics and Society from Walpole to Pitt 1742–1789* (London, 1990), 123–46.

DILKE, C. W., 'Wilkes and the "Essay on Woman" ', *Notes and Queries*, 2/4 (1857), 1–2, 41–3, 74–5.

DITCHFIELD, G. M., 'The Subscription Issue in British Parliamentary Politics, 1772–79', *Parliamentary History*, 7 (1988), 45–80.

FORD, W. C., 'John Wilkes and Boston', *Proceedings Massachusetts Historical Society*, 47 (1914), 190–215.

GREENE, J. P., 'Bridge to Revolution: The Wilkes Fund Controversy in South Carolina 1769–1775', *Journal of Southern History (JSH)*, 29 (1963), 19–52.

HUGHES, E., 'Lord North's Correspondence 1766–1783', *English Historical Review* (*EHR*), 62 (1947), 218–38.

LOWE, W. C., 'Peers and Printers: The Beginnings of Sustained Press Coverage of the House of Lords in the 1770s', *Parliamentary History*, 7 (1988), 241–56.

MAIER, P., 'John Wilkes and American Disillusionment with Britain', *William and Mary Quarterly* (*WMQ*), 3rd ser., 20 (1963), 373–95.

MONEY, J., 'The Masonic Movement: Or Ritual, Replica and Credit: John Wilkes, the Macaroni Parson, and the Making of the Middle-Class Mind', *Journal of British Studies* (*JBS*), 32 (1993), 358–95.

PETERS, M., 'The "Monitor" on the Constitution, 1755–65: New Light on the Ideological Origins of English Radicalism', *EHR* 86 (1971), 706–27.

RUDÉ, G., 'The Middlesex Electors of 1768–1769', *EHR* 75 (1960), 601–17.

THOMAS, P. D. G., 'The Beginning of Parliamentary Reporting in Newspapers, 1768–1774', *EHR* 74 (1959), 623–36.

—— *Sources for Debates of the House of Commons 1768–1774*, *Bulletin of the Institute of Historical Research* (*BIHR*), Special Supplement, No. 4 (1959).

—— 'John Wilkes and the Freedom of the Press (1771)', *BIHR* 33 (1960), 86–98.

—— 'The St. George's Fields "Massacre" of 10 May 1768: An Eyewitness Report', *London Journal*, 4 (1978), 221–6.

—— 'The House of Commons and the Middlesex Elections of 1768–1769', *Parliamentary History*, 12 (1993), 233–48.

WATSON, E. R., 'John Wilkes and the "Essay on Woman" ', *Notes and Queries*, 11/9 (1914), 121–3, 143–5, 162–4, 183–5, 203–5, 222–3, 241–2.

C. Unpublished University Theses

DAVIES, N. C., 'The Bill of Rights Society and the Origins of Radicalism in Britain', MA Thesis (University of Wales, 1986).

DURRANT, P., 'A Political Life of Augustus Henry Fitzroy, Third Duke of Grafton, 1735–1811', Ph.D. Thesis (University of Manchester, 1978).

HAMER, M. T., 'From the Grafton Administration to the Ministry of North 1768–1772', Ph.D. Thesis (University of Cambridge, 1970).

NICHOLAS, J. D., 'Lord Bute's Ministry 1762–1763', Ph.D. Thesis (University of Wales, 1987).

TOMLINSON, J. R. G., 'The Grenville Papers 1763–1765', MA Thesis (University of Manchester, 1956).

Notes

Chapter 1

1. *Gentleman's Magazine*, 68 (1798), 81.
2. Those with the wrong date of birth include the *Dictionary of National Biography*; Treloar, *Wilkes and the City*, 1; Fitzgerald, *Wilkes*, i. 8; and Sherrard, *Wilkes*, 1. Postgate, *That Devil Wilkes*, 1, and Williamson, *Wilkes*, 15, evade the issue. Bleackley, *Wilkes*, 6, and Trench, *Portrait of a Patriot*, 2, give 1725.
3. Evidence that John Wilkes was born in 1725 is reviewed in Bleackley, *Wilkes*, 445–6.
4. In his manuscript autobiography the last number of his year of birth was altered to seven (BL Add. MSS 30865A, fos. 6–7).
5. *Public Advertiser*, 30 Oct. 1769 and 23 May 1771.
6. Wilkes MSS (Clements), i, no. 2.
7. For a Wilkes family pedigree see Bleackley, *Wilkes*, at p. 448.
8. BL Add. MSS 30865A, fo. 7.
9. Ibid. 30867, fo. 4.
10. Wilkes MSS (Clements), i, no. 13.
11. Ibid. 10.
12. *Alexander Carlyle Anecdotes*, 86–7. I owe this reference to David Wilkinson.
13. Brady and Pottle (eds.), *Boswell on the Grand Tour*, 58.
14. BL Add. MSS 30867, fo. 11.
15. Bleackley, *Wilkes*, 6–14; Nobbe, *North Briton*, 3–6.
16. BL Add. MSS 30880B, fo. 71; Almon, *Wilkes*, i. 22.
17. Ibid., v. 107, 145.
18. Her given name was Mary, but that was used only for formal purposes, perhaps because she had a grandmother, mother, and aunt also called Mary.
19. Almon, *Wilkes*, i. 20–2.
20. BL Add. MSS 30867, fo. 65.
21. See McCormick, *Hell-Fire Club*, and Bleackley, *Wilkes*, 48–51. There are retrospective references, naming Wilkes as a member, in the *St. James's Chronicle* for 26 May and 4 June 1763. In the face of abundant evidence Kemp, *Sir Francis Dashwood*, 130–6, seeks to query its existence.
22. Bleackley, *Wilkes*, 69.
23. Potter added that he and William Pitt had read it together (BL Add. MSS 30867, fo. 103). That information explains the disgust felt by Wilkes at Pitt's hypocritical denunciation of the *Essay* in the House of Commons on 24 Nov. 1763 (*Letter to the Duke of Grafton* (1766), printed in Almon, *Wilkes*, iii. 184–93). The detail in

this pamphlet by Wilkes, read in conjunction with Potter's letter of 27 Oct. 1754, makes it clear that the 1754 'parody' was indeed the *Essay on Woman*. Wilkes in 1766 acknowledged his authorship, moreover, whereas in 1763, when prosecution threatened, he had been content to allow his by then deceased friend Potter to take the blame. The view that Potter was the main or sole author has been held by some historians, misled by the arguments of C. W. Dilke in *Notes and Queries*, 2/4 (1857), 1–2, 41–3, 74–5. On this subject see also E. R. Watson, *Notes and Queries*, 11/9 (1914), 121–3, 143–5, 162–4, 183–5, 203–5, 222–3, 241–2; and Bleackley, *Wilkes*, 437–44.

24. BL Add. MSS 30867, fo. 103.
25. Ibid., fos. 75–6.
26. Wilkes MSS (Clements), vi, no. 18.
27. BL Add. MSS 30867, fo. 95; *Grenville Papers*, i. 102.
28. BL Add. MSS 30867, fo. 99; 30877, fo. 1; Almon, *Wilkes*, i. 23–4; *Public Advertiser*, 9 Nov. 1763.
29. Almon, *Wilkes*, i. 25–7; *Gentleman's Magazine*, 38 (1768), 123.
30. BL Add. MSS 30877, fo. 1.
31. Ibid. 32735, fos. 50, 176. A story soon circulated that the Delavals bribed the ship's captain to go to Norway instead of Northumberland. This version was in time reversed, to make Wilkes the perpetrator of such a trick so in keeping with his reputation (Bleackley, *Wilkes*, 33).
32. BL Add. MSS 30867, fo. 99. There was some basis to Potter's claim, for in Bristol Robert Nugent, standing sole on the local Whig interest, had headed the poll against two Tories.
33. Wilkes MSS (Clements), vi, no. 207.
34. *Grenville Papers*, i. 125–6; *Commons Journals*, xxvii. 30–1.
35. Walpole, *Memoirs of George II*, ii. 24–5; Bleackley, *Wilkes*, 34–5.
36. BL Add. MSS 32857, fo. 594; 32861, fo. 314; *Commons Journals*, xxvii. 430.
37. In 1763 diarist James Harris noted this conversation with Wilkes. 'I met him in Palmal [*sic*] . . . He talked with his usual vivacity. Among other things said he had put off his wife, who had brought a large fortune, but was a most disagreeable woman, twenty years older than himself, and had the most odious relatives' (Malmesbury MSS, photocopies, B. 57).
38. Wilkes MSS (Clements), vi, no. 37.
39. Almon, *Wilkes*, i. 28–32, 35–7; Bleackley, *Wilkes*, 40–2, 46–7.
40. Wilkes MSS (Clements), vi, nos. 27–8.
41. Ibid., no. 29.
42. BL Add. MSS 30867, fos. 125–6.
43. Wilkes MSS (Clements), iv, Wilkes to Suard, 27 Oct. 1766.
44. Ibid., vi, no. 11.
45. Ibid., no. 14.
46. BL Add. MSS 30867, fos. 130–4. This correspondence does not support the later claim of Almon that the arrangement cost Wilkes £7,000 as the bill for all these by-elections. 'He was the person who paid all' (Almon, *Wilkes*, i. 34).

47. BL Add. MSS 30867, fo. 137.
48. Ibid., fo. 138; printed, *Chatham Papers*, i. 240.
49. BL Add. MSS 30877, fo. 5.
50. Ibid., fo. 4.
51. *Chatham Papers*, ii. 93–5; in 1759 he had asked Pitt a favour for his brother, presumably Israel, a contract for Chelsea College, only to be told it depended on the Paymaster-General, Henry Fox (BL Add. MSS 30877, fo. 14).
52. Almon, *Wilkes*, i. 57–8.
53. Wilkes MSS (Clements), vi, no. 28.
54. Ibid. 57.
55. Ibid., i, no. 37; vi, no. 58.
56. Ibid. 65.
57. Ibid. 67.
58. Ibid. 68.
59. *Grenville Papers*, i. 479. Wilkes himself did later say that when Bute was Secretary of State he once attended his levée, but Bute failed to appear. It is unclear whether this was before or after the resignation of Pitt and Temple (Almon, *Wilkes*, i. 59 n.).
60. Ibid. 59–60.
61. Malmesbury MSS, Memo of 9 Jan. 1765.
62. Walpole, *Memoirs of George III*, i. 280–1.
63. Hamilton, *Essay on Woman*, 69.
64. The note is printed in Nobbe, *North Briton*, 66.

Chapter 2

1. *Burke Corr.*, i. 349.
2. Malmesbury MSS, Memo of 9 Feb. 1772.
3. As by a recent advocate of this thesis, Colley, *TRHS*, 5th ser. 31 (1981), 1–20.
4. For the campaign see Christie, *Wilkes, Wyvill and Reform*, 68–153.
5. Cannon, *Parliamentary Reform*, 1–46.
6. *Grenville Papers*, ii. 239.
7. Brewer, *Party Ideology and Popular Politics*, 139–60.
8. The dailies were the *Daily Advertiser*, *Gazetteer*, *Public Advertiser*, and *Public Ledger*. The thrice-weeklies were the *General Evening Post*, *Lloyd's Evening Post*, *London Chronicle*, *London Evening Post*, *St. James's Chronicle*, and *Whitehall Evening Post* (Thomas, *EHR* 74 (1959), 624).
9. *Grenville Papers*, i. 404–5. The references are respectively to Bute, Newcastle, and Pitt.
10. Ibid. 406. Temple was referring not merely to Pitt's loss of office, but also to widespread opprobrium heaped on him for the acceptance of a pension, and a peerage for his wife.
11. Malmesbury MSS, Harris Diary, 13 Nov. 1761; Walpole, *Memoirs of George III*, i. 71–7.
12. Ibid. 90.

13. Ibid. 127; Malmesbury MSS, Harris Diary, 12 May 1762.

14. Ibid. 26 Mar. 1762.

15. Walpole, *Memoirs of George III*, i. 142.

16. The full title was *Observations on the Papers relative to the Rupture with Spain, laid before both Houses of Parliament on Friday, Jan. 29th, 1762*.

17. Almon, *Wilkes*, i. 66; Bleackley, *Wilkes*, 60–2.

18. Almon, *Wilkes*, i. 75.

19. BL Add. MSS 30867, fo. 176.

20. Ibid., fos. 178–9.

21. Low (ed.), *Gibbon's Journal*, 145.

22. Wilkes MSS (Clements), iii, no. 26, Wilkes to Suard, 4 Dec. 1769.

23. Peters, *EHR* 86 (1971), 706–27.

24. Peters, *Pitt and Popularity*, 240–1.

25. Guildhall MSS 2892; quoted Nobbe, *North Briton*, 73. According to Leiden fellow student Alexander Carlyle Wilkes had not hitherto displayed animosity towards the Scots. 'The people of that nation were always Wilkes's favourites, till 1763, . . . when Wilkes became a violent party writer and wished to raise his fame and fortune on the ruin of Lord Bute' (*Alexander Carlyle Anecdotes*, 87).

26. Hamilton, *Essay on Woman*, 45.

27. BL Add. MSS 22131, fos. 175–6; 35400, fo. 160; Nobbe, *North Briton*, 62–5.

28. BL Add. MSS 30878, fo. 1.

29. Quoted in Nobbe, *North Briton*, 47.

30. *Grenville Papers*, i. 459–60.

31. Nobbe, *North Briton*, 45, 48–9, 66–7.

32. Walpole, *Memoirs of George III*, i. 140–1.

33. Nobbe, *North Briton*, 73, 86, 266.

34. Weatherly, *Churchill–Wilkes Letters*, pp. xii–xiv; Nobbe, *North Briton*, 64.

35. Guildhall MSS, no. 14174; Almon, *Wilkes*, iii. 41–9, 52–5; *Grenville Papers*, i. 477; *Burke Corr.*, i. 149–51; Nobbe, *North Briton*, 76–81.

36. Almon, *Wilkes*, iii. 24–5.

37. *Grenville Papers*, i. 469–73. Yet on 10 Oct. Temple disclaimed to his sister Lady Chatham, Pitt's wife, any connection with the *North Briton*: 'I hope . . . it is universally known how much Mr Pitt and I disapprove of this paper war, and the daily abominations which are published, though, because Wilkes professes himself a friend of mine, I am for ever represented infamously as a patron of what I disapprove' (*Chatham Papers*, ii. 193).

38. This issue is reprinted in Hamilton, *Essay on Woman*, 57–62.

39. *Grenville Papers*, ii. 5.

40. It was drawn from a sketch made when Wilkes appeared at the Court of Common Pleas on 6 May 1763. Published on 16 May, price 1*s*., it sold about 4,000 impressions in a few weeks.

41. *Grenville Papers*, ii. 4.

42. Malmesbury MSS, Harris Diary, 9 Dec. 1762. Wilkes had actually attended the usual eve-of-session meeting of ministerial supporters at the Cockpit in

Whitehall on 24 Nov. Edmund Burke heard that 'five were not friends, and one of the five a capital enemy, Wilkes. It was rather impudent of him to appear there' (*Burke Corr.*, i. 158).

43. *Bedford Papers*, iii. 202. For an account of what Wilkes wrote on the peace in the *North Briton* see Nobbe, *North Briton*, 101–20.

44. BL Add. MSS 22131, fos. 24–5. For the copies of the *Monitor*, and legal opinions thereon, see ibid., fos. 4, 7–22. Grenville's lukewarm attitude to the peace terms had led to his demotion to being First Lord of the Admiralty.

45. BL Add. MSS 30878, fo. 22; Howell, *State Trials*, xix. 1029–76.

46. BL Add. MSS 30878, fo. 68.

47. Ibid. 22131, fos. 31–2.

48. Weatherly, *Churchill–Wilkes Letters*, 34–5.

49. BL Add. MSS 22131, fos. 29–30.

50. Ibid. 30878, fo. 18. Wilkes had been sent to see Pitt by Charles Townshend to find out his views on the peace terms. They were, of course, condemnatory (Williams, *Chatham*, ii. 145–6).

51. Malmesbury MSS, photocopies, A91–2, Examination of Richard Balfe on 29 Apr. 1763.

52. Guildhall MSS 2892, printed Nobbe, *North Briton*, 136.

53. For a general survey of this episode see Nobbe, *North Briton*, 130–40.

54. Hamilton, *Essay on Woman*, 223.

55. These letters are reproduced and printed in Hamilton, *Essay on Woman*, 68.

56. Nobbe, *North Briton*, 141–206, surveys the paper from Dec. 1762 to Apr. 1763.

57. BL Add. MSS 32946, fo. 206.

58. Walpole, *Letters* (Toynbee), v. 294. See Almon, *Wilkes*, i. 70–90, for the text of the Dedication.

59. Walpole, *Letters* (Toynbee), v. 298.

60. BL Add. MSS 30878, fos. 25, 28; 35400, fos. 42, 46; *Grenville Papers*, ii. 220; Nobbe, *North Briton*, 202–6.

61. Walpole, *Letters* (Toynbee), v. 315. The story was in wide circulation. James Harris heard the answer was 'he could not say with certainty how far, but that he was now making the experiment'. Malmesbury MSS, photocopies, B. 56–7.

62. Sandwich MSS.

63. BL Add. MSS 30878, fos. 25–8.

64. For a version of this, see Almon, *Wilkes*, i. 176–203. There is a full account of the contest, won by the ministry, in Sutherland, *East India Company*, 83–109. The draft *North Briton* is the source of much of her information, and her testimony to its accuracy, where it can be checked, is a tribute to the care Wilkes displayed as an investigative journalist.

Chapter 3

1. BL Add. MSS 6834, fos. 49–50. The popular riots arising from the impeachment of Dr Sacheverell in 1709–10 had been the last memorable anti-government disturbance.

2. Almon, *Wilkes*, i. 94–5. Pitt's complicity has sometimes been doubted, but the ministry believed in it. Lord Le Despencer, the former Sir Francis Dashwood, told James Harris in a conversation at Grenville's house on 22 May 'that Mr Pitt was certainly an abetter of Lord Temple in Wilkes's affair, and privately suggested, what the others avowed openly'. Malmesbury MSS, Memorandum of 22 May 1763. For the King's Speech see *Commons Journals*, xxix. 665–6.

3. For a manuscript copy see Wilkes MSS (Clements), i, no. 41; and for a modern reprint see Hamilton, *Essay on Woman*, 79–86.

4. *Grenville Papers*, ii. 192: a diary entry for 19 Aug. George III's keen interest in the case is demonstrated by the detailed account of the arrest of Wilkes he sent to Bute on 30 Apr. (*Bute Letters*, 232–3). For evidence of his personal hostility to Wilkes see BL Add. MSS 32949, fo. 191; 32954, fos. 65, 123. Wilkes himself wrote on 9 July: 'I hear from all hands that the King is enraged at my insolence, as he terms it, I regard neither his frowns, nor his smiles. I will ever be his faithful subject, never his servant' (*Grenville Papers*, ii. 73).

5. Guildhall MSS, 214/3, fos. 49–50.

6. BL Add. MSS 32951, fo. 123.

7. The information below on events from 23 April to 9 May has been taken, unless otherwise indicated, from a printed *State of Facts Relative to Mr Wilkes*. Copies have been found in Malmesbury MSS, photocopies, A. 89–107; Guildhall MSS 2892; BL Add. MSS 22132. fos. 4–25, 69–89. Compilations of papers and evidence amassed by the ministry may be found in Guildhall MSS 214, 2892; and BL Add. MSS 22131–2. Events were widely reported in the contemporary press.

8. The written opinion of the two law officers, that the paper was 'a most infamous and seditious libel', is dated 27 Apr. For copies of this correspondence see BL Add. MSS 22132, fos. 26–7, 30–1; Guildhall MSS 2892/1, 3.

9. For copies see BL Add. MSS 22131, fos. 37–8; 22132, fos. 28–9; Guildhall MSS 2892/2.

10. For their accounts of subsequent events see BL Add. MSS 22132, fos. 47–61.

11. 'The whole business had been ill conducted by the Solicitor of the Treasury', he commented on 15 July (BL Add. MSS 35400, fos. 83–6).

12. For transcripts of this examination see Guildhall MSS 2892/5, and BL Add. MSS 22132, fos. 35–6.

13. For the letters from Wilkes to Balfe see BL Add. MSS 22132, fos. 90–102.

14. *Bute Papers*, 232.

15. The best precedent for such an arrest of an MP was that of Lord Egremont's own father, Sir William Wyndham, for suspected treason during the Jacobite Rising of 1715, a point gleefully seized upon by the press, which noted that no suspicion of disloyalty attached to Wilkes (*St. James's Chronicle*, 28 May 1763).

16. It also meant that the date of the warrant preceded the acquisition of evidence against Wilkes, a matter much discussed at a meeting of some twenty leading ministerial MPs on 13 Jan. 1764 (Malmesbury MSS, photocopies, B. 98–9). It was probably Webb who compiled the 151-page 'Justification of the issuing and

execution of the General Warrant' (Guildhall MSS 214/2, fos. 3–78; another copy, fos. 182–314).

17. Nobbe, *North Briton*, 218–19. Churchill was never arrested.

18. The writ was sued for by Arthur Beardmore's clerk David Meredith (Guildhall MSS 2892/19). Lord Temple had sent Beardmore there (Almon, *Wilkes*, iv. 101–4).

19. For copies see BL Add. MSS 22131, fos. 48–9; 22132, fo. 64; Guildhall MSS 2892/20; Almon, *Wilkes*, i. 105–6. The story was current that on arrival at the Tower Wilkes asked 'not to be put in any bed where a Scotch man had laid', only to meet the reply, 'That was impossible'. Malmesbury MSS, photocopies, B. 57.

20. For affidavits as to this search by Wood and others see Guildhall MSS 2892/7–16, 18; Almon, *Wilkes*, i. 141–51. The papers were put into a sealed bag, kept by Lovell Stanhope, law clerk to the Secretaries of State, until handed over to Webb on 18 May (BL Add. MSS 22132, fo. 46). Many or all of these papers were never returned to Wilkes, and remain in the Crown papers (Guildhall MSS 214/1, *passim*). For letters of Temple to Wilkes see ibid., fos. 226–7, 230, 232–3, 234, 338–41. Also there are letters of Wilkes seized from printers; ibid., fos. 88–107.

21. Guildhall MSS 2892, Memorandum by Sir John Cust, 30 Apr. 1763. For a 'Deduction of the Proofs that Mr Wilkes was the author and publisher of North Briton No 45' see BL Add. MSS 22132, fos. 103–13.

22. Guildhall MSS 2892/17.

23. BL Add. MSS 32948, fos. 201–2.

24. Guildhall MSS 2892/21; BL Add. MSS 22131, fos. 61–76; Almon, *Wilkes*, i. 107–9. In case he needed bail sureties Wilkes asked the Duke of Grafton, who refused from fear of 'an insult to the Crown', and Lord Temple, who scornfully wrote to Grafton. 'I think he has been proceeded against in a manner that ought to give a just alarm to every true friend of this Constitution; in that light I hold it an honour to be his bail, and so does the Duke of Bolton, who on the same principle has voluntarily offered himself' (*Grafton Autobiography*, 190, 192; *Grenville Papers*, ii. 53–5; BL Add. MSS 30867, fo. 205).

25. BL Add. MSS 22131, fos. 77–104; Almon, *Wilkes*, i. 109–12.

26. BL Add. MSS 35353, fos. 325–6; 35400, fo. 54. The popular acclaim at the Trial of the Seven Bishops in 1688 had presaged the fall of James II.

27. Almon, *Wilkes*, i. 113–15. On 7 May Temple was then himself dismissed as Lord Lieutenant (*Grenville Papers*, ii. 55). The dismissal of Wilkes was the personal wish of George III, that of Temple the suggestion of Egremont (*Bute Papers*, 233).

28. Almon, *Wilkes*, i. 116–18.

29. BL Add. MSS 22131, fos. 105–15; Howell, *State Trials*, xix. 981–94. Pratt's judgment is also printed in Almon, *Wilkes*, i. 118–22.

30. Malmesbury MSS, photocopies, B. 57; BL Add. MSS 32948, fo. 252.

31. Bleackley, *Wilkes*, 113, famously described this as 'the birthcry of British

Radicalism'. That what became a contemporary catchphrase was coined on this occasion is confirmed by two hostile paragraphs in the *St. James's Chronicle* of 10 May. For the speech by Wilkes see Almon, *Wilkes*, i. 122–3.

32. *Lloyd's Evening Post*, 6 May 1963; *St. James's Chronicle*, 7 May 1763.

33. BL Add. MSS 32948, fos. 234–5.

34. Ibid. 30867, fo. 206; printed in Almon, *Wilkes*, i. 124.

35. *St. James's Chronicle*, 7 May 1763; *London Chronicle*, 7 May 1763.

36. Nobbe, *North Briton*, 232.

37. BL Add. MSS 32948, fo. 252. In fact, the refusal probably came from the sitting magistrate, John Spinnage (*St. James's Chronicle*, 10 May 1763; Almon, *Wilkes*, i. 125–6).

38. Almon, *Wilkes*, i. 126–7. The contempt and scorn of Wilkes for the reply to his 'mere piece of gayety' is recorded by Treasury Lord James Harris (Malmesbury MSS, photocopies, B. 57).

39. BL Add. MSS 30867, fos. 207–8; printed in Almon, *Wilkes*, i. 128–9.

40. BL Add. MSS 22132, fos. 35–6, 39–40, 41–2, 43–6.

41. Ibid. 22131, fos. 116–17.

42. Malmesbury MSS, photocopies, A. 107.

43. BL Add. MSS 22131, fos. 127–8.

44. *Grenville Papers*, ii. 60–4. In 1767 Wilkes informed his brother Heaton that he had received no money from Temple 'till after I was in the *Tower* and the business grew too great for a private gentleman' (Wilkes MSS (Clements), ii, no. 15).

45. BL Add. MSS 32949, fos. 56–63.

46. Ibid., fos. 191–2.

47. Wilkes did not yet engross political discussion, for the Cider Tax and the Peace of Paris were still live issues.

48. Almon, *Wilkes*, i. 139.

49. *Grenville Papers*, ii. 75.

50. Guildhall MSS 214/1, fo. 54, Note by Michael Curry.

51. BL Add. MSS 22131, fos. 171–2, W. Faden to [John Kidgell].

52. Ibid., fos. 133–70; *Chatham Papers*, ii. 230–5.

53. Malmesbury MSS, photocopies, B. 62, 703–5.

54. Almon, *Wilkes*, i. 134, prints an undated Treasury Board minute recording 'His Majesty's pleasure' that all expenses should be met in any of the actions brought against Halifax and others for executing the general warrant.

55. *St. James's Chronicle*, 7 July 1763. Dryden Leach himself was awarded £400 damages on 10 Dec. (Howell, *State Trials*, xix. 1006). A petition of the three Messengers in this case, certified by Nathan Carrington on 16 July 1764, stated that they had actually spent £1,850. 10s. 11d. It is not clear whether this total includes any damages, which would have been £2,900 altogether (BL Add. MSS 22132, fo. 170).

56. *St. James's Chronicle*, 12 July 1763.

57. *Grenville Papers*, ii. 71–2.

58. Almon, *Wilkes*, i. 131–2, 135–6.

59. *Grenville Papers*, ii. 78–9.

60. *St. James's Chronicle*, 12 July 1763.

61. *Grenville Papers*, ii. 72, 74.

62. Ibid. 76–7. Yet on 4 June, when Wilkes gave an entertainment at Aylesbury to mark the King's birthday, loyal toasts had been followed by two others. 'Freedom of speech within doors and freedom of the press without. May no house be safer than a man's own house' (*St. James's Chronicle*, 7 June 1763). Wilkes had written afterwards to Temple, 'If I have the honour of being expelled, the declaration is universal that I shall be re-chosen' (*Grenville Papers*, ii. 59).

63. Ibid. 78.

64. 'What two damned adulterers we are. But so far from the least inclination to repentance I am now planning a deep scheme for Madam Carpentier to fall into my mouth in a week' (BL Add. MSS 30880B, fo. 10).

65. Malmesbury MSS, photocopies, B. 700–1.

66. There were unfounded press rumours that among Pitt's demands was the appointment of Wilkes to the Treasury Board (*London Chronicle*, 3 and 8 Sept. 1763).

67. BL Add. MSS 30818, fos. 32–3.

68. Malmesbury MSS, photocopies, B. 61, 80, 84–8, 599–600.

69. Ibid., B. 702–3.

70. Ibid., quoted, Tomlinson, Thesis, 49.

71. BL Add. MSS 22132, fos. 238–9.

72. For 'Michael Curry's Third Narrative' see ibid., fos. 279–80. The 1768 affidavit is printed in Almon, *Wilkes*, i. 155–63.

73. Much detail can be found in Hamilton, *Essay on Woman*, *passim*, and in 'A genuine account of the proceedings against Mr Wilkes for being the Author, Printer and Publisher of the *Essay on Woman*', apparently compiled by Webb (Guildhall MSS 214/2, fos. 79–181). A fairly accurate account, by printer Thomas Farmer, of how the ministry obtained a copy of the *Essay on Woman* appeared in the *St. James's Chronicle* for 3 Dec. 1763: 'Mr Cury himself once declared to me at the Ben Johnson's Head in Shoe Lane that he was offered a place of one hundred pounds per annum.'

74. BL Add. MSS 22132, fos. 279–80.

75. Ibid. 32951, fo. 220.

76. Hamilton, *Essay on Women*, 101.

77. *Grenville Papers*, ii. 153–5. On 5 Nov. Sandwich visited the Bishop, who later that day wrote to him referring to Wilkes as 'the diabolic monster . . . I thank God I can heartily forgive him; . . . but it is no reason, the public should' (Sandwich MSS, V14).

78. Guildhall MSS 214/1, fos. 220–1, 224–5; reproduced in Hamilton, *Essay on Woman*, 112–13.

79. John Almon recalled that 'Mr Wilkes had not the least expectation of this circumstance' (Almon, *Wilkes*, ii. 9). For details of the country tour of the witnesses, see Hamilton, *Essay on Woman*, 114–15.

80. Nobbe, *North Briton*, 240.
81. *Grenville Papers*, ii. 137.
82. The absence of officials prevented the appointment of a jury for 11 Nov. (*St. James's Chronicle*, 10 Nov. 1763).
83. Malmesbury MSS, photocopies, B. 85.
84. Ibid., B. 91–5; *Grenville Papers*, ii. 151–3.
85. *Corr. of George III*, i. 63. George III replied that 'the continuation of Wilkes's impudence is amazing, when his ruin is so near' (*Grenville Papers*, ii. 161). He had attended also in 1762.
86. BL Add. MSS 32951, fo. 220.
87. Guildhall MSS 2892, Memorandum by Sir John Cust, 9 Nov. 1763. On 15 Nov. Wilkes wrote a letter to Cust, briefly recapitulating the events he thought to be breaches of Parliamentary privilege (Wilkes MSS (Clements), i, no. 53).
88. *Commons Journals*, xxix. 667–8; Malmesbury MSS, Parliamentary Diary of James Harris, 15 Nov. 1763, from which all quotations are taken. For Grenville's report to George III, and lists of speakers, see *Corr. of George III*, i. 53–8. There is little except the complaint by Wilkes in Almon, *Debates*, vi. 230–3, or Almon, *Wilkes*, ii. 1–7.
89. In his *Letter to the Electors of Aylesbury*, published 22 Oct. 1764, Wilkes wrote how 'the most abandoned man of the age' had complained that 'I had published an infamous poem, which no man there had ever seen', blaming Sandwich for the fact that it was now widely read. Versions even more scurrilous than the original were soon in popular circulation, a circumstance that blackened the name of Wilkes even more.
90. *Lords Journals*, xxx. 415–17; Walpole, *Memoirs of George III*, i. 245–9.
91. Ibid. 251–3; Almon, *Wilkes*, ii. 12–17. An account of the duel appeared in the *St. James's Chronicle* for 17 Nov. 1763. There was no suggestion of ministerial involvement, and Martin went to France to escape a murder charge if Wilkes should die.
92. The House of Lords meanwhile on 17 Nov. voted an Address to the King requesting prosecution of the author of the *Essay on Woman*, and received a royal assurance on 22 Nov. (*Lords Journals*, xxx. 420, 422).
93. *Commons Journals*, xxix. 674; Malmesbury MSS, Parliamentary Diary of James Harris, 23 Nov. 1763; Walpole, *Memoirs of George III*, i. 257–9; *Corr. of George III*, i. 61–2, Grenville to the King.
94. That was the wording noted by diarist Harris. Wilkes was incensed at Pitt's hypocrisy, for in his *Letter to the Duke of Grafton* (12 Dec. 1766), where he quoted Pitt's words as 'blasphemer of my God' and 'libeller of my King', he said that Pitt had read with great delight the first, manuscript, version of the *Essay on Woman*. His disgust with Pitt was soon public knowledge, for Horace Walpole informed Lord Hertford on 9 Dec. 1763 that 'Wilkes has already expressed his resentment on being given up by Pitt, who, says Wilkes, ought to be expelled for an Imposter' (Walpole, *Letters* (Toynbee), v. 407). Walpole did not know the deeper reason for Wilkes's anger.

95. *Commons Journals*, xxix. 675; Malmesbury MSS, Parliamentary Diary of James Harris, 24 Nov. 1763, from which the quotations are taken, unless otherwise stated; Walpole, *Memoirs of George III*, i. 259–61; *Corr. of George III*, i. 62–3, Grenville to the King.

96. *Lords Journals*, xxx. 426–9; Walpole, *Memoirs of George III*, i. 261–2; Malmesbury MSS, Parliamentary Diary of James Harris, 29 Nov. 1763.

97. *Lords Journals*, xxx. 430, 432–3; *Commons Journals*, xxix. 677, 685, 689; Almon, *Debates*, vi. 239–44.

98. *St. James's Chronicle*, 3 Dec. 1763; Walpole, *Memoirs of George III*, i. 262–3; Malmesbury MSS, Parliamentary Diary of James Harris, 6–8 Dec. 1763.

99. *Grenville Papers*, i. 234–5.

100. *Commons Journals*, xxix. 696, 698–9; Almon, *Debates*, i. 245–7; Walpole, *Memoirs of George III*, i. 263–4.

101. Ibid. 264; *Grenville Papers*, ii. 237.

102. Walpole, *Letters* (Toynbee), v. 421.

103. *Grenville Papers*, ii. 239.

104. Howell, *State Trials*, xix. 1153–68.

105. Almon, *Wilkes*, ii. 28–9.

106. *Grenville Papers*, ii. 239.

107. BL Add. MSS 38201, fos. 358–9; printed in *Jenkinson Papers*, 242.

108. *St. James's Chronicle*, 8 Dec. 1763.

109. Walpole, *Letters* (Toynbee), v. 409, 413. Sandwich's new-found enmity towards Wilkes had earlier been manifested in his efforts to obtain such proof. On 1 Nov. he had asked Lord Le Despencer if he could use his contacts in Aylesbury to 'find out one or more people there who could prove Mr Wilkes's hand writing, or any one who has heard him own himself the author or manager of the North Briton' (BL Egerton MSS 2136, fo. 85).

110. *St. James's Chronicle*, 27 Dec. 1763.

111. Ibid. 8 Dec. 1763.

112. *Corr. of George III*, i. 60.

113. Almon, *Wilkes*, ii. 28–9.

114. *Commons Journals*, xxix. 689, 696–7, 709–10; Almon, *Debates*, vi. 247–9.

115. For King's Messenger Nathan Carrington's report of 27 Dec. on this flight see BL Add. MSS 22131, fos. 234–5.

116. BL Add. MSS 30867, fos. 245, 248. For descriptions of the sea voyage to Temple and his brother Heaton see *Grenville Papers*, ii. 185–6, and Wilkes MSS (Clements), i, no. 59, printed in the *St. James's Chronicle* of 29 Dec. 1763.

117. Malmesbury MSS, photocopies, B. 94–5.

118. Ibid., B. 96–7. It therefore always was the ministry's intention to avoid a Parliamentary decision on the legality of general warrants, and John Almon (as well as some modern commentators) was wrong to assume that was a tactic adopted on 17 Feb. as the debate that day swung against the administration (Almon, *Debates*, vi. 271–2).

119. Almon, *Wilkes*, ii. 36–40, 75–7; *Grenville Papers*, ii. 250.

120. BL Add. MSS 30868, fos. 1–27; 30885, fos. 100–5.
121. Ibid. 30867, fo. 6.
122. Ibid., fo. 21.
123. Ibid. 30868, fo. 23.
124. Ibid., fo. 24.
125. For the proceedings of this day see *Commons Journals*, xxix. 721–3; Malmesbury MSS, Parliamentary Diary of James Harris, 19 Jan. 1764 (from which all quotations are taken); Almon, *Debates*, vi. 249–55. For the evidence submitted to the House see BL Add. MSS 22131, fos. 239–53.
126. The objection was subsequently met. Two notaries confirmed the signatures, and took an oath to that effect before Lord Hertford on 5 Feb. (Almon, *Wilkes*, ii. 45–6).
127. The Wilkite claim that Curry had been bribed to give evidence was met by the explanation in his 1768 affidavit. He had been paid one and a half guinea's subsistence for 26 weeks, and for this and persuading some printers to compromise their legal actions he received £233. 6s. 8d. (Almon, *Wilkes*, i. 162–3). In a letter to Webb on 8 June 1765 Curry complained that no one in the printing trade would employ him after his zeal in the Wilkes case (BL Add. MSS 22132, fos. 287–8).
128. Kearsley had been examined on oath by Lovell Stanhope on 9 May 1763 to confirm that these letters were in Wilkes's writing (BL Add. MSS 22131, fos. 118–19).
129. Ibid. 32954, fo. 123.
130. *Commons Journals*, xxix. 723, 729, 834; Malmesbury MSS, Parliamentary Diary of James Harris, 20 and 23 Jan. 1764.
131. *Lords Journals*, xxx. 457–9; Walpole, *Memoirs of George III*, i. 282.
132. *Commons Journals*, xxix. 786, 792; Malmesbury MSS, Parliamentary Diary of James Harris, 3 and 6 Feb. 1764.
133. *Commons Journals*, xxix. 838–9; Malmesbury MSS, Parliamentary Diary of James Harris, 13 Feb. 1764.
134. For a list of warrants from 1662 to 1689 see BL Add. MSS 22132, fos. 313–23.
135. *Commons Journals*, xxix. 842–3; Malmesbury MSS, Parliamentary Diary of James Harris, 14 Feb. 1764; Walpole, *Memoirs of George III*, i. 287–92; *Grenville Papers*, ii. 261–4, Grenville to the King. For the evidence of this day see BL Add. MSS 22131, fos. 274–304.
136. He did so, on 21 Feb., after consulting Grenville, but the measure was so coldly received that he withdrew it (Malmesbury MSS, Parliamentary Diary of James Harris, 21 Feb. 1764).
137. A famous description of the scene by Horace Walpole to Lord Hertford was more light-hearted. 'You would have almost laughed to see the spectres produced by both sides; one would have thought that they had sent a search-warrant for Members of Parliament into every hospital. Votes were brought down in flannels and blankets, till the floor of the House looked like the pool of Bethesda' (Walpole, *Letters* (Toynbee), vi. 10–11).

138. *Commons Journals*, xxix. 846; Malmesbury MSS, Parliamentary Diary of James Harris, 17 Feb. 1764; Walpole, *Memoirs of George III*, i. 293–302; Almon, *Debates*, vi. 269–76, including a minority list.

139. *Grenville Papers*, ii. 258–9.

140. Ibid. 491–2, Mrs Grenville's diary.

141. Elliot, *Border Elliots*, 391–2.

142. So noted James Harris, relieved that the trial was not by 'a London jury, where the Crown is known to have no chance for justice' (Malmesbury MSS, photocopies, B. 100).

143. Howell, *State Trials*, xix. 1075–7; BL Add. MSS 22132, fos. 120–43. Curry had turned King's evidence, Balfe was given a free pardon, and Kearsley a promise of immunity which he claimed in 1765 (Rea, *Press in Politics*, 82–4).

144. Almon, *Wilkes*, ii. 70–3. 'The prosecution for the *Essay on Woman* is unjust, mean and base', he wrote to Heaton on 16 Mar. (Wilkes MSS (Clements), i, no. 63).

145. BL Add. MSS 22132, fos. 245–6.

146. Almon, *Wilkes*, ii. 86.

147. Howell, *State Trials*, xix. 1001–28.

148. The Entick versus Carrington judgment, also delivered by Pratt as Lord Camden, on 27 Nov. 1765, confirmed and strengthened his earlier ruling (Rea, *Press in Politics*, 66–7).

149. *Commons Journals*, xxx. 70; *Ryder Diary*, 239–53; BL Add. MSS 32965, fos. 320–2.

150. *Commons Journals*, xxx. 753–4; Malmesbury MSS, Parliamentary Diary of James Harris, 22 Apr. 1766.

151. *Commons Journals*, xxx. 771–2; Malmesbury MSS, Parliamentary Diary of James Harris, 25 Apr. 1766. In 1775 Norton recalled that at first Yorke had favoured the legality of general warrants, whereas he had not, and had persuaded his colleague to change his opinion (Malmesbury MSS, photocopies, B. 807).

152. *Commons Journals*, xxx. 780, 822; Malmesbury MSS, Parliamentary Diary of James Harris, 29 Apr., 9 and 14 May 1766.

Chapter 4

1. Walpole, *Letters* (Toynbee), v. 435–6.

2. BL Add. MSS 30868, fos. 24–5; printed Almon, *Wilkes*, ii. 48–55.

3. BL Add. MSS 30868, fos. 40–1; printed Almon, *Wilkes*, ii. 56–7.

4. *Grenville Papers*, ii. 267–9.

5. Almon, *Wilkes*, ii. 52, 81.

6. Ibid. 39, 53, 65, 69, 78–9.

7. Ibid. 59.

8. That was the price Cotes stated in 1767, but in a letter of 20 July 1764 he had told Wilkes it was £4,800 (Wilkes MSS (Clements), ii, no. 14).

9. Almon, *Wilkes*, ii. 62, 66; *Grenville Papers*, iv. 16; Bleackley, *Wilkes*, 152–3.

10. BL Add. MSS 30868, fos. 108–9.

11. Ibid., fos. 110–1.

12. *Grenville Papers*, iv. 3.
13. Wilkes MSS (Clements), iii, no. 26.
14. Almon, *Wilkes*, ii. 63.
15. Bleackley, *Wilkes*, 155–65.
16. The pamphlet is reprinted in Almon, *Wilkes*, iii. 85–121. For a holograph copy see Guildhall MSS 3332, fos. 125–36.
17. Wilkes MSS (Clements), i, no. 79.
18. BL Add. MSS 30868, fos. 144, 149, 160; Almon, *Wilkes*, ii. 90, 91, 97.
19. Wilkes MSS (Clements), i, no. 83; Almon, *Wilkes*, ii. 100; *Grenville Papers*, ii. 454–6.
20. BL Add. MSS 30868, fo. 149; Almon, *Wilkes*, ii. 101. For this history Wilkes hoped to use such new sources as a diary of James II, and letters sent home by French ambassadors in London (*Grenville Papers*, ii. 455–6).
21. Wilkes MSS (Clements), i, no. 81.
22. Almon, *Wilkes*, ii. 93, 100–3.
23. *John Wilkes Patriot: An Unfinished Autobiography*, 52.
24. Wilkes MSS (Clements), i, no. 87. His travels are vividly recounted in letters to his daughter, though without mention of Gertrude Corradini! (Almon, *Wilkes*, ii. 107–89). Other accounts by Wilkes are in letters to Cotes, ibid., ii. 190–205; and in his *Autobiography*, 30–61. See also Bleackley, *Wilkes*, 163–73.
25. His elder brother Israel thereby lost a minor post he held under the Grenville ministry. 'It was imprudent in him to accept a place to disgust personally all the Whigs and affront the Duke of Newcastle', John wrote to Heaton on 26 Aug. (Wilkes MSS (Clements), i, no. 88).
26. Almon, *Wilkes*, ii. 219.
27. Ibid. 207, 209.
28. Walpole, *Letters* (Toynbee), vi. 326–7.
29. Ibid. 346.
30. Ibid. 316.
31. Wilkes MSS (Clements), i, no. 88. For the letter to Cotes see Almon, *Wilkes*, ii. 210.
32. Ibid., v. 240–2.
33. BL Add. MSS 30868, fo. 199.
34. Wilkes MSS (Clements), i, no. 89.
35. BL Add. MSS 30868, fos. 201–2.
36. Wilkes MSS (Clements), i, no. 91a; printed in Treloar, *Wilkes and the City*, 43–5.
37. Wilkes MSS (Clements), i, no. 91b. News of the offer evidently leaked beyond ministerial circles, for on 18 Dec. 1765 James Harris, then in opposition with Grenville, noted a rumour that Wilkes had been given a pension of £1,000 a year (Malmesbury MSS, Harris Diary).
38. BL Add. MSS 30868, fo. 209; printed in Treloar, *Wilkes and the City*, 46.
39. Printed ibid. 47.
40. *Burke Corr.*, i. 231.
41. BL Add. MSS 30869, fos. 2–3.

42. Ibid., fos. 6–7.
43. Ibid., fo. 10.
44. Ibid. 30868, fos. 207–8; printed Almon, *Wilkes*, ii. 216–21.
45. BL Add. MSS 30869, fo. 1.
46. Ibid., fos. 22–3; printed Almon, *Wilkes*, ii. 225. In 1771 the then hostile John Horne claimed that Wilkes asked Walpole to obtain for him an Irish pension of £1,000 for thirty years and a pardon (*Horne Tooke Memoirs*, i. 384).
47. Ibid. 383–4. These amounts add up to £1,120. Contemporary estimates of what Wilkes actually received varied from £630 to well over £1,000 (Langford, *Rockingham Administration*, 218). The *Gazetteer* on 1 Apr. 1768 asserted that 'ever since his exile' Wilkes had enjoyed £1,200 a year, 'a private subscription of a very few of his friends', including some of the current ministry.
48. BL Add. MSS 30868, fos. 207–8.
49. Ibid. 42084, fo. 26.
50. Ibid. 30869, fo. 33; 42085, fo. 4; *Grenville Papers*, iv. 3.
51. Almon, *Anecdotes of Pitt*, ii. 10–16; Bleackley, *Wilkes*, 176–7.
52. *Horne Tooke Memoirs*, i. 384–5.
53. BL Add. MSS 30869, fo. 42.
54. *Burke Corr.*, i. 257.
55. BL Add. MSS 30877, fos. 56–7; printed *Burke Corr.*, i. 259.
56. Almon, *Wilkes*, ii. 231. Grafton's brother, Colonel Charles Fitzroy, assured Wilkes in Paris that the Duke was 'my real friend' (BL Add. MSS 42085, fo. 3).
57. *Horne Tooke Memoirs*, i. 207, 214.
58. *Grafton Autobiography*, 192–3.
59. Almon, *Wilkes*, iii. 178–81; Wilkes MSS (Clements), i, no. 97.
60. Ibid.
61. Almon, *Wilkes*, iii. 184–218. For another copy see Guildhall MSS 3332, fos. 138–55. It so happened that by an unfortunate coincidence a Colonel John Hale had the temerity to write to Chatham on 7 Dec. 'It is the wish of Town and Country, it is the wish of the people, that his Majesty's mercy may be extended to poor Wilkes.' On 12 Jan. 1767 he apologized for this unsolicited advice, a letter 'as ill-judged as it was well meant' (PRO 30/8/39, fos. 26–7).
62. BL Add. MSS 30869, fo. 111.
63. Wilkes MSS (Clements), ii, no. 14.
64. BL Add. MSS 30869, fo. 121.
65. Wilkes MSS (Clements), i, no. 95; ii, nos. 2, 10, 12.
66. BL Add. MSS 30869, fo. 111.
67. Wilkes MSS (Clements), i, no. 97; *Grenville Papers*, iv. 2.
68. Wilkes MSS (Clements), ii, no. 2.
69. Ibid., no. 7.
70. Ibid., no. 12.
71. BL Add. MSS 42085, fos. 21–2, printed *Grenville Papers*, iv. 15–17. In this letter Wilkes claimed to be a reformed character. 'Time has cured me of a thousand follies, which too gay a nature had soured my youth with.'

72. Wilkes MSS (Clements), ii, no. 22.

73. Ibid., no. 15.

74. Ibid., nos. 10, 12, 13, 20; BL Add. MSS 42085, fos. 21–2.

75. Wilkes MSS (Clements), ii, no. 22.

76. Ibid., no. 24.

77. Ibid., no. 27.

78. Almon, *Wilkes*, iii. 136, 144–5, 148–50, 160–3; Wilkes MSS (Clements), ii, nos. 25, 27.

79. John Almon published it in 1768 as *The History of England from the Revolution to the Accession of the Brunswick Line. Volume I*. It was reprinted in Almon, *Wilkes*, v. 160–205.

80. Bleackley, *Wilkes*, 181–5.

81. Walpole, *Last Journals*, i. 379 n.

82. Wilkes MSS (Clements), ii, no. 25.

83. *Gazetteer*, 22 Feb. 1768.

84. BL Add. MSS 30869, fos. 159–60. A temporary tiff with Lord Temple destroyed any chance that he would give Wilkes a seat (ibid., fo. 139; BL Add. MSS 42085, fos. 176–7, printed *Grenville Papers*, iv. 188–90).

85. BL Add. MSS 30869, fos. 148–9.

86. Ibid., fos. 155–6.

87. Ibid., fos. 159–60; *Public Advertiser*, 26 Aug. 1767; *St. James's Chronicle*, 6 Oct. 1767.

88. Wilkes MSS (Clements), ii, nos. 35, 36.

89. Malmesbury MSS, photocopies, B. 908, 25 Nov. 1768.

90. Bleackley, *Wilkes*, 184–5.

91. Wilkes MSS (Clements), ii, no. 44; Almon, *Wilkes*, iii. 222–37.

92. Wilkes MSS (Clements), ii, nos. 46, 47.

Chapter 5

1. Almon, *Wilkes*, iii. 263–5. It was widely if erroneously believed that Wilkes had bargained for a pardon by not embarrassing the King by contesting the Westminster constituency on his doorstep (*Gazetteer*, 12 Mar. 1768).

2. Guildhall MSS 3332(1), 233. This might have been a response to an exchequer writ, stating his property to be forfeit as an outlaw, served on Wilkes by Nuttall on 19 Mar. (Almon, *Wilkes*, iii. 166). But another source attributes that incident to 10 Apr. (Guildhall MSS 3332(1), 159–60).

3. *Gazetteer*, 10 Feb., 10, 12, 16, 17, 18 Mar. 1768.

4. For these political developments see Brooke, *Chatham Administration*, 248–333; and Thomas, *Townshend Duties Crisis*, 36–50.

5. The ministry did consider the arrest of Wilkes, but believed 'that step would have secured his election'; whether for London or Middlesex is unclear (*Grafton Autobiography*, 194, 199–201; *Grenville Papers*, iv. 271; Almon, *Wilkes*, iii. 265–6; Hamer, Thesis, 37–8).

6. *Gazetteer*, 20 Feb., 10, 12, 14, 16 Mar. 1768.

7. Guildhall MSS 3332(1), 156–7.

8. Sir William was retiring from Parliament, and concerned only to obtain a safe borough seat for his son William (BL Add. MSS 32989, fos. 232–3).

9. *Gazetteer*, 10, 12, 14, 15, 16 Mar. 1768.

10. Ibid. 17 Mar. 1768.

11. Guildhall MSS 3332(1), 157–8. A typical story current about Wilkes was that he was asked on 18 Mar. 'whether he was not tired with standing?', and answered, 'Not in the least, Sir! I am determined to stand to the last, and then I shall get a seat' (*Gazetteer*, 24 Mar. 1768).

12. Guildhall MSS 3332(1), 159–60. Lord Temple gave Wilkes a qualifying freehold, as he had presumably already done with respect to London (Bleackley, *Wilkes*, 189). Landed estates of £600 and £300 per annum were necessary respectively for county and borough MPs.

13. *Gazetteer*, 25, 26 Mar. 1768.

14. Malmesbury MSS, photocopies, A. 465.

15. *Gazetteer*, 26 Mar. 1768.

16. *Horne Tooke Memoirs*, i. 218–21.

17. *Gazetteer*, 26, 30, 31 Mar. 1768.

18. The following account has been put together from a dozen or so reports in the *Gazetteer* for 29 and 30 Mar., *Lloyd's Evening Post* for 28 and 30 Mar., and the *St. James's Chronicle* for 29 and 31 Mar. Some reports wrongly state that the poll lasted two days, and Horace Walpole also made that mistake (Walpole, *Memoirs of George III*, iii. 128–9). For confirmation that voting took place only on the Monday see Guildhall MSS 3332(1), 161; and a report sent to the Duke of Newcastle (BL Add. MSS 32989, fos. 268–9).

19. So stated correspondent 'Stentor' in the *St. James's Chronicle* of 11 Dec. 1768 when condemning violence used on behalf of Proctor in a recent Middlesex by-election. Only one brief contemporary press report supports this account, stating that several gentlemen were prevented from polling (*Lloyd's Evening Post*, 28 Mar. 1768).

20. There is a conflict of evidence as to whether Cooke himself attended, or whether a relative deputized for him, as stated by Walpole, *Memoirs of George III*, iii. 128–9. Several newspaper reports refer to him as present but ill.

21. This occasion, as the only poll Wilkes attended apart from 1784, is the probable setting for the apocryphal story that at a contested election Wilkes commented to an opponent, 'I wonder whether there are more fools or knaves down there', pointing to the voters. 'I will tell them what you say, and put an end to you', answered his opponent. 'It is yourself who would be put an end to', replied Wilkes, 'for I shall tell them it was a falsehood' (Bleackley, *Wilkes*, 190–1).

22. Wilkes MSS (Clements), ii, no. 52.

23. *The Gazetteer*, 2 Apr. 1768; Walpole, *Memoirs of George III*, iii. 129.

24. *Grafton Autobiography*, 194, 199.

25. Rudé, *Wilkes and Liberty*, 74–81.

26. Ibid. 82–9.

27. *Gazetteer*, 29, 30 Mar., 2, 9 Apr. 1768; *Lloyd's Evening Post*, 30 Mar. 1768.

28. *Grenville Papers*, iv. 268.
29. Guildhall MSS 3332(1), 162–3.
30. There he was ostracized by most polite society and cut dead by Lord Camden (*Grafton Autobiography*, 199; *Grenville Papers*, iv. 267; *Gazetteer*, 30, 31 Mar., 1 Apr. 1768).
31. *Gazetteer*, 16 Apr. 1768; Walpole, *Memoirs of George III*, iii. 129–31.
32. *Grenville Papers*, iv. 264.
33. *Corr. of George III*, ii. 14–17.
34. Malmesbury MSS, photocopies, A. 469.
35. *Corr. of George III*, ii. 18.
36. BL Add. MSS 32989, fos. 355–6. For copies of Weymouth's letter see Guildhall MSS 3332(1), 230–1. Weymouth, more hotheaded than his cabinet colleagues, as the Falkland Islands Crisis of 1770 was to show, may have taken this step on his own initiative.
37. *Corr. of George III*, ii. 17.
38. *Grafton Autobiography*, 199–200.
39. BL Add. MSS 32989, fos. 329–30; *Corr. of George III*, ii. 18, 19; *Grafton Autobiography*, 200.
40. BL Add. MSS 32989, fos. 329–30, 375–6. Believing the ministry would not wish to appear 'precipitate' by bringing the Wilkes case before the brief May session of Parliament, Rockingham and Newcastle decided not to summon their supporters to attend then (BL Add. MSS 32990, fos. 1–4, 11–12).
41. Ibid. 32989, fos. 252, 268–9, and *passim*.
42. Ibid., fos. 294–5.
43. Ibid., fos. 299–300.
44. Ibid., fos. 319–20.
45. *Gazetteer*, 23 Apr. 1768.
46. BL Add. MSS 32989, fos. 353–4.
47. *Grafton Autobiography*, 199.
48. *Grenville Papers*, iv. 271.
49. For these proceedings see Howell, *State Trials*, xix. 1077–85; and BL Add. MSS 30883, fos. 49–62; 32989, fos. 363–6; 35867, fos. 97–103; 36204, fos. 270–3. For Wilkes's speech see Guildhall MSS 3332(1), 234–6.
50. BL Add. MSS 32989, fos. 367–8. At a meeting with the Crown's law officers on 16 Apr. Sir Fletcher Norton had asked why such a warrant had not been issued (*Grenville Papers*, iv. 270–1).
51. *Grafton Autobiography*, 200–1.
52. *Corr. of George III*, ii. 20–1.
53. Ibid. 21. George III was here displaying a double standard of morality, for on 16 Apr. Prime Minister Grafton had outraged polite society by publicly escorting his mistress Nancy Parsons to the Opera House when his own wife had been present there (*Grenville Papers*, iv. 275–7).
54. Hamer, Thesis, 40–1.
55. *Grenville Papers*, iv. 284.

56. Ibid. 293.

57. *Corr. of George III*, ii. 22.

58. *Grafton Autobiography*, 201.

59. Howell, *State Trials*, xix. 1085–92.

60. Guildhall MSS 3332(1), 164–5. Something of the drama is conveyed in two letters from James West to Newcastle, written before the return of Wilkes to prison was known. In the first he commented, 'God knows what next is to happen. *This* surely must not be suffered'; and, later, 'No one can yet tell what is become of him' (BL Add. MSS 32989, fos. 396–7, 402–3).

61. SP 44/142, 143–6, quoted in Rudé, *Wilkes and Liberty*, 48. Lord Temple wrote to congratulate Wilkes on 'your sober and discreet conduct of yesterday manifested in a dutiful submission to the law' (BL Add. MSS 42086, fo. 22).

62. Guildhall MSS 3332(1), 166–7.

63. Almon, *Wilkes*, iii. 287 n.

64. Much information about the 'Massacre' can be found in Guildhall MSS 3332(1), 169–88; in BL Add. MSS 30884, fos. 65–76 (trial evidence); and in the contemporary press. For an eyewitness account by a ministerial supporter see Thomas, *London Journal*, 4 (1978), 221–6. For various accounts see Almon, *Wilkes*, iii. 273–80; Rudé, *Wilkes and Liberty*, 49–55; and Davies, Thesis, 55–69.

65. Bamber Gascoyne, a past and future MP who was a ministerial supporter, witnessed the affair. He denied that the magistrates gave any order to fire, and blamed the soldiers, who 'fired in my opinion very willingly and very rashly' (Thomas, *London Journal*, 4 (1978), 224).

66. The trial was at the Surrey Assizes at Guildford on 8 and 9 Aug. Two of the three were discharged, and the third was found not guilty, because of a conflict of evidence. The defence was that the murder had been by another soldier, who had conveniently disappeared (Almon, *Wilkes*, iii. 280; BL Add. MSS 30884, fos. 65–76). Wilkes went to give evidence but was not called (Guildhall MSS 3332(1), 195–202).

67. Ibid. 401.

68. BL Add. MSS 32990, fo. 37; Rudé, *Wilkes and Liberty*, 53.

69. Guildhall MSS 3332(1), 184. Barrington was to tell the House of Commons on 23 Nov. that this was on his advice and that he wrote the letter (BL Egerton MSS 215, fos. 220–1).

70. It is printed in *Cavendish Debates*, i. 5–6.

71. BL Egerton MSS 215, fos. 19–49.

72. Ibid., fos. 50–60.

73. *Corr. of George III*, ii. 24.

74. BL Add. MSS 32990, fo. 71; Walpole, *Memoirs of George III*, iii. 141–3.

75. BL Add. MSS 32990, fos. 87–8.

76. BL Egerton MSS 215, fos. 78–82.

77. BL Add. MSS 32990, fos. 107–8. Westminster Hall was the venue of the main lawcourts.

78. Ibid., fos. 39, 53.

79. The matter was also to be twice raised in the House of Commons. On 8 Mar. 1769 Edmund Burke moved for a Committee to inquire into the incident, and on 25 Apr. 1771 John Glynn presented a request for an inquiry from William Allen's father. Only 41 and 35 MPs respectively supported these motions. For reports of these debates see Thomas, *Sources for Debates of the House of Commons 1768–1774*, 11, 41.

80. *Grenville Papers*, iv. 279–80.

81. BL Add. MSS 32989, fos. 377–8, James West to Newcastle, 24 Apr. 1768.

82. Howell, *State Trials*, xix. 1092–8; Guildhall MSS 3332(1), 168; BL Add. MSS 32990, fos. 25–6; 35867, fos. 105–14, 116–7; 36204, fos. 273–5; *Grenville Papers*, iv. 290–3. The absence of Solicitor-General John Dunning from this and subsequent legal occasions was probably deliberate. He was a Chathamite, and a friend of Wilkes, having advised him on this very subject.

83. *Grafton Autobiography*, 210.

84. Ibid. 202–3.

85. For these see Malmesbury MSS, photocopies, A. 560–6. There had been a late rumour that the outlawry would be confirmed (BL Add. MSS 32990, fos. 180–1).

86. Howell, *State Trials*, xix. 1098–116; Walpole, *Memoirs of George III*, iii. 151–2.

87. BL Add. MSS 32990, fos. 186–7. Hayes was the home of Chatham. Newcastle wrote on 10 June to congratulate Mansfield on his 'most able and judicious conduct' (ibid., fos. 190–1).

88. Guildhall MSS 3332(1), 189–90.

89. Ibid. 165–6, 190.

90. Malmesbury MSS, photocopies, A. 342–5; Howell, *State Trials*, xix. 1076, 1169, 1406; Guildhall MSS 3332(1), 166.

91. BL Add. MSS 30870, fo. 229, Stratford Canning to Wilkes.

92. Howell, *State Trials*, xix. 1117–24; Guildhall MSS 3332(1), 191; *Corr. of George III*, ii. 30; BL Add. MSS 35867, fos. 120–1; 36204, fos. 275–81.

93. Guildhall MSS 3332(1), 192–4. Wilkes appealed to the House of Lords, in its judicial capacity, against sentence. His appeal was rejected on 16 Jan. 1769 (ibid. 242; Walpole, *Memoirs of George III*, iii. 198, 201). For this proceeding see *Lords Journals*, xxxii. 200–23 (*passim*); BL Add. MSS 36174, fos. 57–62; 38206, fo. 59.

94. Thomas, *Townshend Duties Crisis*, 80–93.

95. *Gazetteer*, 10 June 1768.

96. Guildhall MSS 3332(1), 209–11.

97. BL Add. MSS 32990, fos. 204–5.

98. Convicted at the Old Bailey on 9 Jan. 1769, they later had their death sentences respited (BL Add. MSS 35608, fo. 352). For the events of the day see Guildhall MSS 3332(1), 211–17, and Rudé, *Wilkes and Liberty*, 59–61.

99. BL Egerton MSS 215, fos. 336–59.

100. Guildhall MSS 3332(1), 217–25.

101. Rudé, *Wilkes and Liberty*, 80.

102. Malmesbury MSS, photocopies, B. 911.

Chapter 6

1. For fuller details on the change of ministry see Brooke, *Chatham Administration*, 375–84, and Hamer, Thesis, 14–24. Chatham's successor as Lord Privy Seal, Lord Bristol, did not rate cabinet status.
2. Almon, *Wilkes*, iii. 292–3.
3. Guildhall MSS 3332 (1), 207–9.
4. Almon, *Wilkes*, iii. 293–6. Wilkes did later take up the idea of an approach to the King, Sir Joseph Mawbey presenting a petition dated 28 Nov. on his behalf. No answer was made to this appeal for 'royal clemency', and since Wilkes claimed that 'the unfair methods to convict your petitioner have been palpable and manifest' this may merely have been an attempt to annoy George III, or his ministers (ibid., iii. 296–7). For another copy see Guildhall MSS 3332(1), 443.
5. Evidence had been collected during the summer to substantiate the complaints, notably an affidavit sworn by Curry on 3 Aug. before Lord Mayor Harley, and one of 16 June by George Kearsley that letters from Wilkes to him had been seized under the general warrant (Guildhall MSS 3332(1), 202–7, 446–7).
6. BL Egerton MSS 215, fos. 140–51.
7. Hughes, *EHR*, 72 (1947), 219.
8. BL Egerton MSS 215, fos. 196–225.
9. Ibid., fos. 240–7.
10. Ibid., fos. 253–5.
11. *Commons Journals*, xxxii. 68, 74, 79. The brief prepared on behalf of Wilkes shows exactly why each witness was summoned (BL Add. MSS 30884, fos. 2–25). That Wilkes genuinely intended to call them is confirmed by a later complaint of the 'enormous expense' of keeping the witnesses in attendance from 24 Nov. 1768 to 27 Jan. 1769 (Guildhall MSS 3332(1), 247).
12. BL Egerton MSS 215, fos. 255–60.
13. Ibid., fos. 260–81, 327–36, 359–65; *Commons Journals*, xxxii. 87, 89, 94–5, 99.
14. That was the version in the newspaper: see also BL Egerton MSS 216, fo. 23; Add. MSS 30883, fo. 69; and Guildhall MSS 3332(1), 232. But Almon, *Wilkes*, iii. 273 n., later published it in a milder version: 'how long the design had been planned before it was carried into execution.'
15. *Commons Journals*, xxxii. 108–9; BL Egerton MSS 216, fos. 23–48. North complained to Grafton about Dunning, whose behaviour was defended by Lord Chancellor Camden (*Grafton Autobiography*, 227–8).
16. *Lords Journals*, xxxii. 191–2, 198; *Commons Journals*, xxxii. 113; BL Egerton MSS 216, fos. 48–73.
17. A Grenvillite meeting on 16 Dec. wrongly assumed that 'the cabinet has now agreed to expel Wilkes' (Malmesbury MSS, photocopies, B. 914).
18. BL Add. MSS 35867, fos. 122–3.
19. *Grafton Autobiography*, 201.
20. *Corr. of George III*, ii. 73.

21. PRO/30/8/62, fos. 145–6.

22. Ibid., fo. 147.

23. BL Egerton MSS 216, fos. 73–93; *Commons Journals*, xxxii. 129–30.

24. *Corr. of George III*, ii. 74–5. This was probably a cabinet, but may have been a meeting of Commons supporters.

25. BL Egerton MSS 216, fos. 179–217; *Commons Journals*, xxxii. 156–7. The expensive Wilkes array of witnesses was thereby rendered virtually superfluous (Guildhall MSS 3332(1), 247).

26. BL Add. MSS 30870, fo. 105.

27. Howell, *State Trials*, xix. 175–7.

28. BL Egerton MSS 216, fos. 219–306; 217, fos. 3–55; *Commons Journals*, xxxii. 169–72.

29. BL Egerton MSS 217, fos. 55–116; *Commons Journals*, xxxii. 175–6.

30. *Chatham Papers*, iii. 349.

31. *Grenville Papers*, iv. 480. Almon, however, gives the full pamphlet title as *A Letter to the Right Hon. George Grenville, occasioned by his Publication of the Speech he made in the House of Commons* (Almon, *Wilkes*, iii. 300).

32. Wilkes MSS (Clements), iii, no. 25. For further information on Grenville's speech, including discussion of its authenticity and motivation, see Thomas, *Parliamentary History*, 12 (1993), 238 n.

33. BL Add. MSS 30870, fo. 107.

34. Walpole, *Memoirs of George III*, iii. 219.

35. BL Egerton MSS 217, fos. 124–246; *Commons Journals*, xxxii. 178–9.

36. Guildhall MSS 3332(1), 289–95; *Gazetteer*, 15, 16, 17 Feb. 1769; *St. James's Chronicle*, 16 Feb. 1769.

37. BL Egerton MSS 217, fos. 338–90; *Commons Journals*, xxxii. 228–9.

38. Guildhall MSS 3332(1), 296–303; *Gazetteer*, 18, 20, 23, 24 Feb. 1769; *St. James's Chronicle*, 18, 23 Feb. 1769. For a printed copy of the election Address of 22 Feb. see Malmesbury MSS, photocopies, B. 919.

39. PRO/30/8/63, fos. 247–8.

40. Guildhall MSS 3332(1), 303–6; *Gazetteer*, 16, 17, 18 Mar. 1769; *St. James's Chronicle*, 16, 18 Mar. 1769; *Chatham Papers*, iii. 352 n.

41. BL Egerton MSS 219, fos. 107–38; *Commons Journals*, xxxii. 324–5.

42. Guildhall MSS 3332(1), 309–13; *Gazetteer*, 29, 31 Mar., 3 Apr. 1769; *St. James's Chronicle*, 30 Mar. 1769.

43. Roche had previously visited Wilkes in prison. His idea was to give up the seat to Wilkes when he was a free man (BL Add. MSS 30870, fo. 134). For further evidence of Roche's attempt to involve himself with Wilkes see BL Add. MSS 30876, fos. 22–3, 27.

44. Guildhall MSS 3332(1), 314–20; *Gazetteer*, 5, 10, 12 Apr. 1769; *St. James's Chronicle*, 13 Apr. 1769.

45. BL Egerton MSS 219, fos. 201–20; *Commons Journals*, xxxii. 385.

46. Malmesbury MSS, photocopies, B. 941.

47. BL Egerton MSS 219, fos. 220–88; *Commons Journals*, xxxii. 386–7.

48. Walpole, *Memoirs of George III*, iii. 237.

49. A list for 3 Feb. was printed in the *North Briton* for 15 Apr., perhaps to influence voting for that day, with some corrections in the *North Briton* for 22 Apr. A list for 15 Apr. appeared in the *London Magazine* for 1769 at pp. 270–1.
50. BL Egerton MSS 219, fos. 322–4; Walpole, *Memoirs of George III*, iii. 240–1; *Commons Journals*, xxxii. 447.
51. BL Egerton MSS 219, fos. 329–433.
52. A division list was published in the *North Briton* for 27 May 1769. For an analysis of the Commons voting in 1769 on the Middlesex Elections case see Thomas, *Parliamentary History*, 12 (1993), 244–5.
53. *Chatham Papers*, iii. 361. Altogether 215 MPs had voted with the opposition.
54. For lists of those present and of the toasts see *Chatham Papers*, iii. 359–61. Another Thatched House dinner took place on 8 Jan. 1770, the eve of the next session, with eighty MPs present (ibid., iii. 390). But it did not become a regular event.
55. For the role of Bill of Rights Society members see Chapter 7.
56. *Burke Corr.*, ii. 70, 96.
57. For the petitioning campaign see Rudé, *Wilkes and Liberty*, 105–34; and Sutherland, *The City of London and the Opposition to Government 1768–1774*, 24–32.
58. Thomas, *Townshend Duties Crisis*, 143–5.
59. BL Egerton MSS 3711, fos. 1–61; *Commons Journals*, xxxii. 456–7. There is a minority voting list in Almon, *Debates*, viii. 175–7.
60. Thomas, *House of Commons*, 184, 275–6.
61. BL Egerton MSS 3711, fos. 165–238.
62. Almon, *Debates*, viii. 190–2.
63. BL Egerton MSS 3711, fos. 165–238; Almon, *Debates*, viii. 223–4.
64. Thomas, *Lord North*, 35–7.
65. *Cavendish Debates*, ii. 245–56; Almon, *Debates*, ix. 109–11.
66. Ibid. 346–7.
67. BL Egerton MSS 245, fos. 296–9.
68. On this see Chapter 8.
69. BL Egerton MSS 245, fos. 299–318. The *Middlesex Journal* of 5 June 1773 published a division list.
70. *Corr. of George III*, iii. 66.
71. *Diary of Sylas Neville*, 61–2.
72. Wilkes MSS (Clements), iii, no. 23.

Chapter 7

1. Wilkes MSS (Clements), iii, no. 30.
2. Ibid., no. 23, Wilkes to Suard, 20 June 1769.
3. Ibid., no. 25.
4. Ibid., no. 32.
5. Ibid., no. 34.
6. *Horne Tooke Memoirs*, i. 274–5. Information on the finances of Wilkes is incomplete, complex, and contradictory, and no precise computations are attempted in this study. Sums have been rounded off to the nearest pound sterling.

7. *London Chronicle*, 23 Feb. 1769; *London Evening Post*, 18 June 1771. John Horne later gave the total as £3,023, a figure repeated by Almon (*Horne Tooke Memoirs*, i. 275; Almon, *Wilkes*, iv. 8).

8. *Horne Tooke Memoirs*, i. 276. For the advertisement see the *London Chronicle*, 28 Feb. 1769.

9. BL Add. MSS 30871, fo. 25; Wilkes MSS (Clements), vi, no. 29.

10. On his death in 1802 William Tooke left Horne Tooke only £500 (*Horne Tooke Memoirs*, i. 163, 422–30; ii. 44, 271).

11. Davies, Thesis, 103.

12. *Horne Tooke Memoirs*, i. 30–96, 278–9.

13. Davies, Thesis, 94–6, 326–32.

14. Ibid. 93–9. See ibid. 333–6 for a list of known meetings and Chairmen.

15. Guildhall MSS 3332(1), 431–2.

16. Ibid. 431–4. Horne confirms the £300 on 7 Mar., but not the £600 on 11 Apr., stating instead that £300 was also voted on 6 June (*Horne Tooke Memoirs*, i. 276–7).

17. *London Chronicle*, 13 May 1769.

18. Guildhall MSS 3332(1), 435–6.

19. *Horne Tooke Memoirs*, i. 276–7. This is repeated by Almon, *Wilkes*, iv. 9.

20. Guildhall MSS 3332(1), 435–7; *London Chronicle*, 13 May 1769.

21. Guildhall MSS 3332(1), 449–54; *London Chronicle*, 10 June 1769.

22. *Burke Corr.*, ii. 534.

23. Walpole, *Memoirs of George III*, iii. 240.

24. Davies, Thesis, 111–22.

25. *Horne Tooke Memoirs*, i. 280–1, 283, 304. It is not altogether clear whether or not Wilkes included the £1,200 in this £2,000.

26. *London Evening Post*, 25 Jan. 1770.

27. Guildhall MSS 3332(1), 438–41, 470.

28. BL Add. MSS 35369, fo. 135.

29. Ibid. 30871, fo. 27.

30. Guildhall MSS 3332(1), 470–1; *London Evening Post*, 12 Apr. 1770.

31. Ibid. 5 May 1770. In 1771 the then hostile John Horne published some different totals, allegedly from the Society's accounts. He stated the discharged debts of Wilkes at £12,000; his paid election expenses as £2,973; and the unpaid debt as £6,822 (*Horne Tooke Memoirs*, i. 282). Almon, *Wilkes*, iv. 10, again drawing on Horne, repeated this last total but added that it was compounded by the Society in the summer of 1770.

32. *Gazetteer*, 6 Apr. 1768.

33. Treloar, *Wilkes and the City*, 69–72.

34. Guildhall MSS 3332(1), 237–9; *Gazetteer*, 2, 3, 4 Jan. 1769.

35. Guildhall MSS 3332(1), 241–4.

36. Davies, Thesis, 126–8; Sharpe, *London and the Kingdom*, iii. 84–5.

37. Guildhall MSS 3332(1), 292–3; Sharpe, *London and the Kingdom*, iii. 88–9.

38. *London Chronicle*, 7, 12 Oct. 1769.

39. Wilkes MSS (Clements), iii, no. 25.

40. *London Chronicle*, 7, 9 Dec. 1769; *Grenville Papers*, iv. 494.

41. For lists of those present see *Lloyd's Evening Post*, 23, 26 Mar. 1770; Maccoby, *English Radicalism*, 137.

42. Guildhall MSS 3332(1), 454–9; Treloar, *Wilkes and the City*, 86–92; Sharpe, *London and the Kingdom*, iii. 91–8; Maccoby, *English Radicalism*, 139–43.

43. Guildhall MSS 3332(1), 459–62; *Cavendish Debates*, i. 535–45.

44. *London Evening Post*, 27, 31 Mar., 10 Apr. 1770.

45. Guildhall MSS 3332(1), 479–83; *London Evening Post*, 24 May 1770. Chatham commended Beckford warmly, 'The spirit of Old England spoke', and Beckford's speech was engraved on his statue erected in Guildhall (*Chatham Papers*, iii. 458–64).

46. Almon, *Wilkes*, iv. 20–3.

47. Guildhall MSS 3332(1), 475–9. Wilkes told his daughter that eighteen Aldermen were present at the Guildhall (Almon, *Wilkes*, iv. 25).

48. Ibid. 56–7.

49. Guildhall MSS 3332(1), 472–5; printed, Almon, *Wilkes*, iv. 14–19.

50. Guildhall MSS 3332(1), 471.

51. Walpole, *Letters* (Toynbee), vii. 375.

52. *Horne Tooke Memoirs*, i. 282–5, 304–5; Almon, *Wilkes*, iv. 13, 36–7.

53. *Horne Tooke Memoirs*, i. 284–7.

54. Treloar, *Wilkes and the City*, 261.

55. Wilkes MSS (Clements), iii, no. 34.

56. Walpole, *Letters* (Toynbee), vii. 377–8. The letters Wilkes wrote to his daughter, then in Paris, emphasize his quiet, respectable life (Almon, *Wilkes*, iv. 30–77).

57. *Horne Tooke Memoirs*, i. 305.

58. Guildhall MSS 3332(1), 414–15.

59. Walpole, *Letters* (Toynbee), vii. 375–6.

60. *Burke Corr.*, ii. 131–2.

61. *Corr. of George III*, ii. 141.

62. *London Evening Post*, 3 May 1770.

63. Ibid. 30 June 1770; Almon, *Wilkes*, iv. 56–7, 59–60, 64.

64. *London Evening Post*, 26 June 1770.

65. Ibid. 28, 30 June, 5, 12 July 1770; Almon, *Wilkes*, iv. 64, 66.

66. The letter describes Wilkes as 'that victim to a woman's wrath'. This is presumably a reference to the Princess Dowager of Wales, mother of George III and reputed lover of Lord Bute, who was popularly supposed to be a malign influence on her son.

67. *Middlesex Journal*, 11, 15, 20 Sept., 2 Oct. 1770; *London Evening Post*, 8 Nov. 1770; PRO 30/8/25, fo. 46.

68. BL Add. MSS 30871, fos. 42–3.

69. *London Evening Post*, 13, 16 Oct. 1770.

70. Ibid. 30 Oct., 1, 3 Nov. 1770. Trecothick's behaviour did not save him from a pamphlet attack by Wilkes, *Annals of the Mayorality of the Right Hon. Barlow*

Trecothick, Esq., published on 8 Nov. This satirized his lack of hospitality; criticized a manifesto of 5 Oct. declaring that 'he was a party man', describing him as a 'tool' of 'the Rockingham faction'; and alleged that on 24 Oct. 'he admitted into the City whole bands of ruffians, under the name of press-gangs, . . . and let them loose against the laws, the peace, the liberties, and franchises of London' (*Horne Tooke Memoirs*, i. 191–3).

71. *Chatham Papers*, iii. 480, 483.
72. *London Evening Post*, 17 Nov. 1770.
73. On 22 Jan. 1771 the Wilkites nevertheless passed a resolution, reaffirmed in Mar., for the prosecution of those Aldermen who had backed the press warrants (*Middlesex Journal*, 24 Jan., 16 Mar. 1771).
74. *London Chronicle*, 29 Apr., 16, 18 May 1769.
75. *London Evening Post*, 6 Sept. 1770.
76. Ibid. 29 Nov. 1770.
77. *Horne Tooke Memoirs*, i. 288–91.
78. Guildhall MSS 3332(1), 489–93; *London Evening Post*, 1, 3 Nov. 1770; Walpole, *Memoirs of George III*, iv. 121–2.
79. *Middlesex Journal*, 1 Jan. 1771. For this controversy see *Horne Tooke Memoirs*, i. 179–96.
80. For a fuller account of this development see Davies, Thesis, 197–215.
81. BL Add. MSS 30871, fo. 52.
82. *London Evening Post*, 29 Jan. 1771. The whole Macleane episode was, as Wilkes suspected, a move to discredit him. It culminated in a Macleane challenge to a duel for a newspaper libel, which Wilkes declined, denying authorship. Macleane, *Reward is Secondary*, 258–73, has a long account. See also BL 30871, fos. 56, 57, 60–1; *London Evening Post*, 29 Jan. 1771; *London Chronicle*, 26 Jan. 1771.
83. *Middlesex Journal*, 23 Feb. 1771; *Horne Tooke Memoirs*, i. 297–9.
84. *London Evening Post*, 9 Mar. 1771.
85. Guildhall MSS 3332(2), 9–10; *London Evening Post*, 23 Mar. 1771.
86. Ibid. 11 Apr. 1771.

Chapter 8

1. This chapter incorporates much of my paper in the *BIHR* 32 (1960), 86–98. Another account appeared simultaneously in Haig, *The Gazetteer*, 102–18. For other descriptions see Davies, Thesis, 173–96; Treloar, *Wilkes and the City*, 115–22; and Sharpe, *London and the Kingdom*, iii. 107–19. John Horne's version is in *Horne Tooke Memoirs*, i. 329–51.
2. Ibid. 344. This view of the House of Commons as the centre-piece of the constitution underlay Fox's clash with George III in 1782–4, and was reflected in Edmund Burke's famous declaration to his Bristol electors that he was their representative, not their delegate.
3. Thomas, *EHR* 74 (1959), 623–4, and sources therein cited.
4. Ibid. 624–5.
5. Cannon, *Junius Letters*, 455–6.

6. So wrote diarist Wraxall in 1781, when examining the question by comparing Junius with the known writings of Wilkes: 'It must be owned that Wilkes possessed a Classic Pen, keen, rapid, cutting. . . . But the difference between the two productions cannot be mistaken by any man who allows his reason fair play' (Wraxall, *Hist. Memoirs*, ii. 92–3).

7. *Grenville Papers*, iv. 495.

8. Cannon, *Junius Letters*, 163, 172.

9. There can no longer be any reasonable doubt but that Francis was Junius. See the discussion on this point ibid. 539–72.

10. Almon, *Memoirs*, 119. That was published in 1790. In 1805 Almon, *Wilkes*, v. 52, stated that 'on the meeting of the new Parliament in the year 1769, some occasional sketches of the proceedings of the House of Commons were printed in the *London Evening Post*'.

11. Thomas, *EHR* 74 (1959), 625–9.

12. *Horne Tooke Memoirs*, i. 314–15.

13. Malmesbury MSS, Memo. of 4 Apr. 1772.

14. BL Egerton MSS 224, fos. 81–7; *Commons Journals*, xxxiii. 149.

15. This account, reprinted in the *Gazetteer* on 26 Oct., may have been part of the ongoing Wilkes–Horne feud, with Horne seeking to gain credit for a Radical coup ascribed to Wilkes.

16. BL Egerton MSS 225, fos. 15–25, 80–4, 89–94; *Commons Journals*, xxxiii. 154, 162, 183–4, 194, 208.

17. *Corr. of George III*, ii. 220–1.

18. *Middlesex Journal*, 24 Oct. 1771.

19. Almon, *Memoirs*, 120; Almon, *Wilkes*, v. 57–60.

20. *Chatham Papers*, iv. 95–6, 102, 105, 116.

21. *Corr. of George III*, ii. 219–20.

22. BL Egerton MSS 225, fos. 146–7; *Commons Journals*, xxxiii. 224.

23. Walpole, *Memoirs of George III*, iv. 190; *Corr. of George III*, ii. 229. There are many references in later debates to ministerial support of the campaign against Parliamentary reporting.

24. BL Egerton MSS 226, fos. 2–43; *Commons Journals*, xxxiii. 249–51.

25. The sheriffs, William Baker and Joseph Martin, were both Rockinghamite MPs. There is no evidence that they took any part in the scheme.

26. BL Add. MSS 30871, fo. 69. After the visit of Morris, Thompson wrote to inform Wilkes, 'agreeable to his desire . . . that not the least objection is at present seen to the adoption of the plan proposed' (ibid., fo. 70).

27. In a public letter to the Speaker on that day, however, Evans announced his refusal to attend until 'it is known whether a British subject has, or has not, a right to be tried by a jury' (Guildhall MSS 3332(2), 3–4; *London Evening Post*, 21 Mar. 1771). The House of Commons did not read the order for his appearance that day, and never considered his case again.

28. BL Egerton MSS 226, fos. 45–70; *Commons Journals*, xxxiii. 258–9.

29. *London Evening Post*, 16 Mar. 1771; Guildhall MSS. 3332(2), 10–13.

30. In a Commons speech of 20 Mar. Solicitor-General Wedderburn denounced this arrest as 'a plain and manifest collusion' (BL Egerton MSS 226, fos. 354–5). See also Almon, *Wilkes*, v. 54.

31. BL Add. MSS 30871, fo. 71; Guildhall MSS 3332(2), 1–3. Despite four applications to the Treasury Carpenter never received the reward (*Middlesex Journal*, 19, 23 Mar. 1771; Haig, *Gazetteer*, 112).

32. The following account is based on the reports given to the House of Commons on 18 Mar. (*Commons Journals*, xxxiii. 263–4; BL Egerton MSS 226, fos. 70–81; Cobbett, *Parl. Hist.*, xvii. 96–102).

33. Almon, *Memoirs*, 120.

34. On 19 Mar. the *Middlesex Journal* reported that Morris, 'whose pride is to be thought one of the lower class of the people', had been given a general retainer by the City.

35. Guildhall MSS 3332(2), 9; *Gazetteer*, 16 Mar. 1771. Unlike Carpenter he was not identified, not charged with assault, and made no application for the reward (Haig, *Gazetteer*, 113–14).

36. *Corr. of George III*, ii. 232–3.

37. *London Evening Post*, 21 and 23 Mar. 1771; Walpole, *Memoirs*, iv. 191–2; *Chatham Papers*, iv. 121–2.

38. BL Egerton MSS 226, fos. 70–141; *Commons Journals*, xxxiii. 263–4.

39. *Chatham Papers*, iv. 116, 118.

40. Ibid., 121.

41. BL Egerton MSS 226, fo. 142.

42. *Corr. of George III*, ii. 235.

43. Guildhall MSS 3332(2), 13–17; *London Evening Post*, 23 Mar. 1771.

44. BL Egerton MSS 226, fos. 346–65.

45. *Corr. of George III*, ii. 235–6.

46. *Chatham Papers*, iv. 122–3.

47. BL Egerton MSS 227, fos. 68–9; *Commons Journals*, xxxiii. 280–6.

48. When Crosby and Oliver went to the House of Commons on 20 Mar., Wilkes followed in another coach to Westminster, but then prudently returned to the City (Guildhall MSS 3332(2), 19).

49. BL Egerton MSS 226, fos. 141–368; 227, fos. 2–62; *Commons Journals*, xxxiii. 265–80.

50. BL Egerton MSS 226, fos. 365–8.

51. John Yorke, MP, to Lord Hardwicke (BL Add. MSS 35375, fos. 37–8).

52. *Cavendish Debates*, ii. 443 n.

53. Walpole, *Memoirs of George III*, iv. 195–6.

54. Guildhall MSS 3332(2), 17–18; *Middlesex Journal*, 21 Mar. 1771.

55. *London Evening Post*, 21 Mar. 1771. There was soon a rumour that Kirkman would be elected a sheriff in recognition of his 'support of liberty' (*Middlesex Journal*, 28 Mar. 1771).

56. *London Evening Post*, 26 Mar. 1771; *Middlesex Journal*, 26 Mar. 1771.

57. *Chatham Papers*, iv. 123, 126.

58. *Middlesex Journal*, 28 Mar. 1771.
59. For the proceedings of the day see BL Egerton MSS 227, fos. 62–226; *Chatham Papers*, iv. 125–7, 131–6; and *Commons Journals*, xxxiii. 283–6.
60. *Middlesex Journal*, 28 Mar. 1771.
61. *London Evening Post*, 30 Mar. 1771; *Middlesex Journal*, 30 Mar. 1771.
62. BL Egerton MSS 228, fos. 6–135; *Chatham Papers*, iv. 138–40; *Commons Journals*, xxxiii. 289–90.
63. Walpole, *Memoirs of George III*, iv. 201–2, 205.
64. The report is printed in Cobbett, *Parl. Hist.*, xvii. 187–212.
65. Almon, *Debates*, ix. 305–7.
66. Guildhall MSS 3332(2), 25–8, 36–8.
67. *Gentleman's Magazine*, 41 (1771), 141; *Rockingham Memoirs*, ii. 207–9.
68. *London Evening Post*, 6 and 23 Apr. 1771; *General Evening Post*, 2 May 1771; *Chatham Papers*, iv. 171. Newspapers reported that the ministry was also trying to put an end to the situation, by arranging for an MP unconnected with the administration to move for the discharge of the prisoners (*St. James's Chronicle*, 13 Apr. 1771; *London Evening Post*, 18 Apr. 1771). Certainly an approach, through the Speaker, was made to Chathamite MP John Calcraft (*Chatham Papers*, iv. 152–3).
69. *London Evening Post*, 9 May 1771; Walpole, *Memoirs of George III*, iv. 125.
70. *Middlesex Journal*, 9 Apr. 1771.
71. *London Evening Post*, 14 May 1771.
72. Guildhall MSS 3332(2), 41–2.
73. Ibid. 149–50.
74. No copies have been found of the *Whitehall Evening Post*, or of the other two papers prosecuted, the *Morning Chronicle* and the *London Packet*.
75. Thomas, *EHR* 74 (1959), 629–30.
76. Cannon, *Junius Letters*, 437.
77. Almon, *Wilkes*, v. 62–3.
78. Cannon, *Junius Letters*, 416, 420–1, 437; *Grenville Papers*, iv. 536. Bill of Rights Society member Edmund Dayrell reported the scheme to Lord Temple, saying that Wilkes 'wishes to repose in the faithful bosom of his Mentor, who never deserted him in his greatest difficulties, and in whom *alone* he will confide' (ibid., iv. 537). Yet this letter was written long after the breach between Temple and Wilkes.
79. *Middlesex Journal*, 14 Feb. 1775; Walpole, *Last Journals*, i. 432. On this episode see Lowe, *Parliamentary History*, 7 (1988), 248–56.

Chapter 9

1. *Gazetteer*, 30 May 1771. The letter is printed in Ross, *Radical Adventurer*, 20–1.
2. Wilkes did reply, and consulted Secretary of State Lord Rochford (BL Add. MSS 30871, fos. 135, 142, 144). For the subsequent lively career of Morris see Ross, *Radical Adventurer*, 23–45. His diary from 15 May 1772 to 20 Feb. 1774 is printed, ibid. 51–210.
3. *Middlesex Journal*, 30 Apr. 1771.

4. Davies, Thesis, 326–32, details exactly how the Bill of Rights Society members split.

5. Guildhall MSS 3332(2), 42–3; *London Evening Post*, 18 Apr. 1771; *Middlesex Journal*, 18 and 20 Apr. 1771.

6. *London Evening Post*, 2 May 1771; Davies, Thesis, 235–6.

7. *Horne Tooke Memoirs*, i. 197–318. For a summary of this press controversy see Davies, Thesis, 216–24.

8. *London Evening Post*, 27 and 30 Apr. 1771; *Middlesex Journal*, 18 May 1771. For more detail see Davies, Thesis, 244–6.

9. *London Evening Post*, 20 Apr. 1771.

10. Ibid. 15 June 1771; Davies, Thesis, 239–40.

11. Cannon, *Junius Letters*, 416–17.

12. Guildhall MSS 3332(2), 137–45. The document is reproduced in Davies, Thesis, 320–4.

13. Cannon, *Junius Letters*, 406–13, 417–19.

14. BL Add. MSS 30871, fo. 74. Both letters were published in the *Middlesex Journal* for 16 Apr. 1771.

15. At the end of 1771 Luttrell, dissatisfied with his rewards from government, did threaten to resign, an event that 'might occasion some noise', George III commented to Lord North (*Corr. of George III*, ii. 308). He was evidently dissuaded from doing so.

16. *Middlesex Journal*, 13 Apr. 1771. The expenses were to be £1,800 (Bleackley, *Wilkes*, 290).

17. Sharpe, *London and the Kingdom*, iii. 121.

18. *Corr. of George III*, ii. 255–6.

19. Guildhall MSS 3332(2), 123–37.

20. *Corr. of George III*, ii. 256–7.

21. Walpole, *Letters* (Toynbee), viii. 55–6.

22. Cannon, *Junius Letters*, 250–82.

23. Ibid. 258.

24. Ibid. 398–403, 416.

25. Ibid. 414–16, 420.

26. *Grenville Papers*, iv. 535–6. The *London Evening Post* of 1 Oct. 1771 stated that this request, or a repetition of it, was made after the first day's poll revealed that Townsend had no chance.

27. *Corr. of George III*, ii. 285.

28. *Grenville Papers*, iv. 536.

29. Cannon, *Junius Letters*, 427; *London Evening Post*, 17 Oct. 1771.

30. Ibid. 30 June, 2, 4, 9 July 1772.

31. Almon, *Wilkes*, iv. 134.

32. Fitzmaurice, *Shelburne*, ii. 287.

33. Guildhall MSS 3332(2), 162–4.

34. *London Evening Post*, 24 Oct. 1772.

35. Ibid. 7 Apr. 1772; Davies, Thesis, 262.

36. *Public Advertiser*, 25 Sept. 1771.
37. Treloar, *Wilkes and the City*, 124–5.
38. Maccoby, *English Radicalism*, 174–5; for other evidence of Wilkes's concern over the treatment of prisoners see Bleackley, *Wilkes*, 273.
39. Guildhall MSS 3332(2), 157–61. This last case had evidently aroused strong feeling, for City Chamberlain Sir Stephen Janssen, when polling for Wilkes and Townsend on 2 Oct., gave sheriff Watkin Lewes a paper: 'I never will give my poll on the side espoused by Ministers, who have dared to advise his majesty to pardon murders and buggery' (Guildhall MSS 3332(2), 165).
40. *Corr. of George III*, ii. 397–401.
41. Guildhall MSS 3332(2), 172–6, 182–3.
42. *London Evening Post*, 2 Nov. 1771.
43. Ibid. 24 and 29 Oct. 1772. The majority included Sawbridge.
44. Walpole, *Last Journals*, i. 157–8. Wilkes, widely held responsible for these riots, welcomed an inquiry by the Court of Common Council, and it proved unsuccessful (*London Evening Post*, 17 Nov. 1772).
45. Guildhall MSS 3332(2), 182–3. On 7 Dec. 1772 Wilkes obtained a sworn deposition that James Townsend had whipped two 6-year-old children for picking up sticks on his land (BL Add. MSS 30871, fo. 158). But he is not known to have used this to blacken Townsend's reputation.
46. Bleackley, *Wilkes*, 277–9.
47. Almon, *Debates*, x. 188–91.
48. Walpole, *Last Journals*, i. 180.
49. Ibid. 182–5; Guildhall MSS 3332(2), 184–8.
50. *London Evening Post*, 19 and 22 Dec. 1772.
51. Guildhall MSS 3332(2), 189–200; Walpole, *Last Journals*, i. 189, 193–6. Wilkes again tried to claim his seat on 15 Feb. 1774 after a similar summons, a challenge the House of Commons preferred to ignore (Guildhall MSS 3332(2), 224–5, 227–8; Walpole, *Last Journals*, i. 297). On 12 Apr., however, Henry Luttrell put the ministry in a dilemma by moving that the Middlesex sheriffs be summoned to answer his complaint. The ministry preferred the ignominy of rejecting this motion to another quarrel with the Wilkites (Walpole, *Last Journals*, i. 330–1).
52. *London Evening Post*, 24, 29 June, 3 July 1773; 25 and 28 June 1774.
53. *Public Advertiser*, 24 Sept. 1773.
54. Guildhall MSS 3332(2), 203–7.
55. Ibid. 216–24.
56. Walpole, *Last Journals*, i. 250.
57. *Corr. of George III*, iii. 20, 27, 29, 31, 33–4.
58. Ibid. 35, 37; *London Evening Post*, 4 Dec. 1773.
59. Sharpe, *London and the Kingdom*, iii. 141.
60. *Middlesex Journal*, 13 and 27 Mar. 1773.
61. *London Evening Post*, 25, 28, 30 June 1774. Grieve was so little known that this Wilkite newspaper named him as 'John Greive'.

62. Guildhall MSS 3332(2), 228.

63. Ibid. 229–36.

64. BL MS Facs 340(1), 12. The existence of this list suggests that the ministry had still hoped to prevent the election of Wilkes.

65. Walpole, *Last Journals*, i. 397–8.

66. Guildhall MSS 3332(2), 242–4.

67. *Corr. of George III*, iii. 133–4.

68. BL Add. MSS 38733, fos. 3–4; Sandwich MSS F41/69; *Corr. of George III*, iii. 136, 141–3. When warned that the Duke of Northumberland might retaliate in Middlesex for Wilkite opposition to his son Lord Percy in Westminster, Wilkes said 'he laughed at the idea of an opposition' (BL Add. MSS 30875, fos. 82–3).

69. Walpole, *Last Journals*, i. 404.

70. Guildhall MSS 3332(2), 246–9.

71. *Corr. of George III*, iii. 137.

72. Ibid. 137–41, 144–5; BL Add. MSS 37833, fo. 3; Walpole, *Last Journals*, i. 398–9.

73. Ibid. 404.

74. Bleackley, *Wilkes*, 293–4.

75. PRO 30/8/46, fos. 94–5, 97–8.

76. Walpole, *Last Journals*, i. 399–401, 405; *Corr. of George III*, iii. 142, 144–5, 148–50.

77. There were other Radical candidates, some successful, unconnected with Wilkes (Davies, Thesis, 277–90; Christie, *Guildhall Miscellany*, 2/4 (1962), 155–64).

78. Treloar, *Wilkes and the City*, 139, 142.

79. Guildhall MSS 3332(2), 236–7.

80. Ibid. 239–42; Treloar, *Wilkes and the City*, 144–7; Bleackley, *Wilkes*, 283–5.

81. Guildhall MSS 3332(2), 287–8.

82. *London Evening Post*, 20 June 1776.

83. Bleackley, *Wilkes*, 288–9.

84. The actions of Wilkes as Mayor concerning America are discussed in the next chapter.

85. BL Add. MSS 30871, fo. 258.

86. Ibid. 30872, fos. 3–4.

87. *London Evening Post*, 13 and 20 Feb. 1776.

88. *Public Advertiser*, 21 Feb. 1776; *London Evening Post*, 24 Feb. 1776.

89. *Gazetteer*, 30 May 1771.

90. BL Add. MSS 30872, fos. 10–11.

91. *London Evening Post*, 24 Feb. 1776.

92. *Public Advertiser*, 21 Feb. 1776.

93. *London Evening Post*, 20, 22, 24, 27 Feb. 1776.

94. Treloar, *Wilkes and the City*, 194–5.

95. *London Evening Post*, 20, 22, 25 June, 2 July 1776.

96. BL Add. MSS 30895, fo. 97.

97. An odd consequence of these Hopkins–Wilkes contests was that the Lord Chamberlain, Lord Hertford, refused to license R. B. Sheridan's play 'The

School for Scandal', because one character, Moses, was widely held to resemble Hopkins. The playwright made a personal plea before the play opened on 8 May 1777 (Treloar, *Wilkes and the City*, 197–8).

98. *London Evening Post*, 1 July 1777.
99. Ibid. 2 July 1778.
100. For the election of Wilkes as City Chamberlain see Chapter 11, below.

Chapter 10

1. Maier, *WMQ* 20 (1963), 373–95.
2. Thomas, *Townshend Duties Crisis*, 113–14, 120–1.
3. Sainsbury, *Disaffected Patriots*, 7–13.
4. Quoted in Davies, Thesis, 291.
5. *Horne Tooke Memoirs*, i. 178.
6. Wilkes MSS (Clements), i, no. 91.
7. Davies, Thesis, 293.
8. Individual colonists had already written to Wilkes (Almon, *Wilkes*, v. 261–5). In 1770 a Bostonian wrote to say that he had named his son Wilkes in 1766 (BL Add. MSS 30871, fo. 34).
9. BL Add. MSS 30870, fo. 45.
10. Ibid., fo. 46.
11. Ibid., fos. 75–6.
12. Ibid., fos. 222–3; Almon, *Wilkes*, v. 252–6, 265–9; Ford, *Mass. Hist. Soc. Procs.*, 47 (1914), 194–212. For the background see Thomas, *Townshend Duties Crisis*, 82–3, 86–8.
13. BL Add. MSS 30870, fos. 135–6.
14. For evidence that this confrontation might have been contrived by Boston resistance leaders see sources cited in Thomas, *Townshend Duties Crisis*, 180–1.
15. BL Add. MSS 30871, fos. 18–22; Almon, *Wilkes*, v. 265–9.
16. Ibid. 256–7; *St. James's Chronicle*, 10 Feb. 1770. The Virginia tobacco may not have been sent (Greene, *JSH* 29 (1963), 6 n.).
17. BL Add. MSS 30870, fo. 237; Almon, *Wilkes*, v. 402–3.
18. BL Add. MSS 30871, fo. 7.
19. Both the Governor of South Carolina and the British government were indignant at what they deemed misuse of public funds (Greene, *JSH* 29 (1963), 21–4).
20. BL Add. MSS 30871, fo. 50. The hint is in Latin.
21. *London Evening Post*, 12 July 1770; Davies, Thesis, 294. Oliver's reference was to the colonial trade boycott, then on the point of collapse.
22. PRO 30/8/25, fos. 59–60.
23. *Horne Tooke Memoirs*, i. 191–3.
24. Ibid. 233.
25. *Franklin Papers*, xvii. 257.
26. *London Evening Post*, 25 July 1771.
27. Simmons and Thomas, *Proceedings and Debates*, iv. 65–6, 76, 80.
28. Ibid. 104–5, 107, 118, 130–1, 134–5, 137, 142, 144.

29. Ibid. 260, 261, 284, 309, 311, 394, 397, 400–1, 409.

30. *London Evening Post*, 10 May 1774.

31. Simmons and Thomas, *Proceedings and Debates*, iv. 400.

32. Ibid. 463, 470, 474.

33. *London Evening Post*, 4 June 1774.

34. *Commons Journals*, xxxiv. 803.

35. Simmons and Thomas, *Proceedings and Debates*, v. 185–93, 211–12. A minority list of 32 names on a jury clause included Oliver and Townsend, but not Sawbridge, Bull, or even Glynn (*London Evening Post*, 30 June 1774).

36. Simmons and Thomas, *Proceedings and Debates*, iv. 473; v. 13, 485.

37. *London Evening Post*, 23 June 1774.

38. Ibid.

39. Ibid. 24 Sept. 1774.

40. *Franklin Papers*, xxi. 155.

41. *London Evening Post*, 4 and 23 June 1774.

42. This version was reprinted in Almon, *Parl. Reg.*, i. 141–6, and in Simmons and Thomas, *Proceedings and Debates*, v. 365–8. It was evidently the practice of Wilkes to send copies of his Parliamentary speeches to the press; and, while they may not have been authentic accounts of what he had actually said, they can be presumed to constitute his opinions, and are so treated in this study.

43. Simmons and Thomas, *Proceedings and Debates*, vi. 8–9.

44. Walpole, *Last Journals*, i. 450.

45. Simmons and Thomas, *Proceedings and Debates*, v. 287–99. For the background see Thomas, *Tea Party to Independence*, 182–4.

46. *London Evening Post*, 11 Feb. 1775.

47. Ibid. 23 Feb. 1775.

48. *Gazetteer*, 15 Mar. 1775.

49. For the official version of the Remonstrance see Guildhall MSS 3332(2), 289–92; printed in the *London Evening Post* for 11 Apr. The version published in that paper for 6 Apr. is garbled, and inaccurate in quotation.

50. *Corr. of George III*, iii. 199–200.

51. *London Evening Post*, 11 Apr. 1775.

52. Walpole, *Last Journals*, i. 456.

53. Guildhall MSS 3332(2), 298–9.

54. *Lloyd's Evening Post*, 7 July 1775; *London Evening Post*, 24 June 1775; Guildhall MSS 3332(2), 304–13; *Corr. of George III*, iii. 231–2. See also Bradley, *Popular Politics*, 44–7.

55. Guildhall MSS 3332(2), 284–5; *London Evening Post*, 9 Feb., 16 and 25 Mar. 1775.

56. Ibid. 8 June 1775.

57. Thomas, *Tea Party to Independence*, 273.

58. Davies, Thesis, 336. I have found no press reports of this meeting. The presumption must be that the Society simply collapsed rather than was formally discontinued. In a sense its successor was the London Association, a specifically pro-American society that existed between 1775 and 1777. For an account of it see Sainsbury, *Disaffected Patriots*, 106–13. There is no evidence that Wilkes was

directly involved, but secretary Thomas Joel apparently kept him informed (BL Add. MSS 30871, fos. 231, 261).

59. *London Evening Post*, 28 Sept. 1775.

60. *Morning Chronicle*, 7 July 1775.

61. *Corr. of George III*, iii. 233.

62. *Morning Chronicle*, 8 July 1775.

63. *Corr. of George III*, iii. 233–4; Guildhall MSS 3332(2), 313–15.

64. Walpole, *Last Journals*, i. 473.

65. Guildhall MSS 3332(2), 322–4; Sharpe, *London and the Kingdom*, iii. 158–60; Walpole, *Last Journals*, i. 476.

66. Guildhall MSS 3332(2), 324–6.

67. Sharpe, *London and the Kingdom*, iii. 160, 165–6.

68. *London Evening Post*, 26 Sept. 1775.

69. Thomas, *Tea Party to Independence*, 275.

70. *London Evening Post*, 24 Feb. 1776. For this episode see above, Chapter 9.

71. Identical reports of his speech appeared in the *London Chronicle* and *London Evening Post* for 28 Oct. 1775. For the text see Simmons and Thomas, *Proceedings and Debates*, vi. 97–8.

72. BL Add. MSS 30871, fos. 249–50.

73. Simmons and Thomas, *Proceedings and Debates*, vi. 290–302. Reports of the speech by Wilkes were published on 30 Nov. in the *London Chronicle* and *London Evening Post*.

74. *HMC Carlisle*, 314–15.

75. *Peter Oliver's Origin and Progress of the American Revolution*, 78.

76. BL Add. MSS 20733, fo. 103.

77. *London Evening Post*, 2 and 5 Nov. 1776. The speech was reprinted in Almon, *Parl. Reg.*, vi. 12–18.

78. Malmesbury MSS, Memo of 15 May 1777.

79. *London Evening Post*, 2 Dec. 1777. The speech was reprinted in Almon, *Parl. Reg.*, viii. 5–14.

80. PRO 30/8/56, fos. 200–1, Shelburne to Chatham, undated.

81. *London Evening Post*, 11 Dec. 1777; Almon, *Parl. Reg.*, viii. 130–56.

82. *Hutchinson Diary*, ii. 171.

83. For the text of these Bills see Almon, *Parl. Reg.*, viii. 404–8.

84. Ibid. 421–31.

85. Ibid., ix. 216–41.

86. Ibid., xi. 18–30.

87. BL Add. MSS 30872, fos. 101–4.

88. Wraxall, *Historical Memoirs*, i. 380.

89. Debrett, *Parl. Reg.*, i. 167–74.

Chapter 11

1. Rumours of his ill health in 1774 contributed to the idea that Wilkes was a spent force (*Gibbon Letters*, ii. 247; *Hutchinson Diary*, i. 291).

2. Wraxall, *Historical Memoirs*, ii. 296.

3. Malmesbury MSS, Memo. of 15 May 1777.

4. Wraxall, *Historical Memoirs*, ii. 296–7.

5. Bleackley, *Wilkes*, 301.

6. Before the opening of the new Parliament in Nov. 1774 Wilkes spread the rumour that he intended to propose for Speaker an MP who had been a coffee-house waiter, Robert Mackreth. The scandalized King commented to North that 'this would appear impossible to be true if the author's character was not known to be so void of decency' and urged him to get Mackreth to vacate his seat (*Corr. of George III*, iii. 154). It was, of course, a joke.

7. Almon, *Parl. Reg.*, i. 116. James Harris noted Wilkes as saying that he kept the day 'not as a fast, but a feast' (BL Add. MSS 35612, fo. 170).

8. Almon, *Parl. Reg.*, i. 129–30.

9. Walpole, *Last Journals*, i. 437–8.

10. *Gibbon Letters*, ii. 61.

11. Almon, *Parl. Reg.*, i. 214–30. For a minority list see ibid. 230–3.

12. *Corr. of George III*, iii. 179–81.

13. Almon, *Parl. Reg.*, iii. 495–500; Guildhall MSS 3332(2), 331–8.

14. Almon, *Parl. Reg.*, vii. 131–6; ix. 35; xi. 249. The voting on these occasions was 140–84, 88–36, and 202–122.

15. *London Evening Post*, 16 Mar. 1780.

16. Debrett, *Parl. Reg.*, iii. 140–2.

17. Cobbett, *Parl. Hist.*, xxii. 1407–11.

18. Walpole, *Last Journals*, i. 450.

19. Almon, *Parl. Reg.*, iii. 432–42.

20. BL Add. MSS 30872, fo. 168.

21. Almon, *Parl. Reg.*, vii. 143–9.

22. Walpole, *Last Journals*, ii. 8; Almon, *Parl. Reg.*, vi. 241–8.

23. On this generally see Sainsbury, *Disaffected Patriots*, 134–40.

24. Almon, *Parl. Reg.*, vi. 12.

25. Guildhall MSS 3332(2), 342–3.

26. *Corr. of George III*, iv. 20.

27. Walpole, *Last Journals*, ii. 21. He was nevertheless credited with this character-istic *bon mot* on the subject: 'Some one was asking Wilkes what he thought about paying the Civil List Debt? I shall never, replies he, be against helping any one to pay his debts' (Malmesbury MSS, Memo. of 22 Mar. 1777).

28. Almon, *Parl. Reg.*, vii. 67–82.

29. Ibid. 168.

30. Ibid., ix. 138–47; Walpole, *Last Journals*, ii. 162–3.

31. Almon, *Parl. Reg.*, ix. 98–112.

32. Ibid., xvi. 67–8.

33. Bleackley, *Wilkes*, 54–5.

34. On this episode see Ditchfield, *Parliamentary History*, 7 (1988), 61–5.

35. Almon, *Parl. Reg.*, xii. 100–6.

36. For this debate see ibid. 309–18.
37. Malmesbury MSS, Memo. of 24 Mar. 1779.
38. BL Add. MSS 30872, fo. 100.
39. Hibbert, *King Mob*, 16–19.
40. Almon, *Parl. Reg.*, ix. 197–9, 268; x. 406–8; Walpole, *Last Journals*, ii. 174–5.
41. Almon, *Parl. Reg.*, xii. 141–2.
42. On 31 May the Court of Aldermen resolved to ask the City MPs to seek repeal of the Catholic Relief Act. The note of this by Wilkes does not indicate his own attitude or even whether he was present (BL Add. MSS 30866, fo. 238).
43. Hibbert, *King Mob*, 48–90.
44. BL Add. MSS 30866, fos. 240–1.
45. The evidence of his diary is not positive enough to justify any assumption that Wilkes himself shot any rioters (ibid., fo. 241; printed, Hibbert, *King Mob*, 102).
46. Walpole, *Last Journals*, ii. 320.
47. Malmesbury MSS, photocopies, A. 368.
48. BL Add. MSS 30866, fos. 241–8.
49. Wraxall, *Historical Memoirs*, i. 359–60.
50. BL Add. MSS 38307, fos. 183–4.
51. Almon, *Parl. Reg.*, xvii. 724, 754.
52. Ibid. 724–37.
53. BL Add. MSS 30872, fos. 196, 199–200.
54. *Morning Post*, 17 Nov. 1779.
55. *Morning Chronicle*, 12 Nov. 1779. At a Livery meeting on 15 Nov. Cranke secured a nomination by about 250 voters (*London Evening Post*, 18 Nov. 1779).
56. Ibid. 20 and 23 Nov. 1779.
57. *Morning Post*, 18 Nov. 1779.
58. *Morning Chronicle*, 12 Nov. 1779.
59. *London Evening Post*, 13 and 16 Nov. 1779; Treloar, *Wilkes and the City*, 202.
60. Guildhall MSS 3332(2), 354–9; *London Evening Post*, 23 and 25 Nov. 1779; Treloar, *Wilkes and the City*, 201.
61. *Corr. of George III*, iv. 451–2, 459.
62. BL Add. MSS 30872, fos. 123, 136–7; 30875, fo. 123.
63. *London Evening Post*, 13 Nov. 1779.
64. Almon, *Parl. Reg.*, xvi. 169–72.
65. Ibid. 172–4.
66. Ibid., xvii. 54–6, 70–1.
67. Wilkes MSS (Clements), iii, no. 53.
68. BL Add. MSS 30876, fo. 139. This is a draft newspaper paragraph in Wilkes's hand.
69. Walpole, *Last Journals*, ii. 268; BL Add. MSS 38593, fos. 1–45. He attended only four of thirty-five meetings from Nov. 1780 to Nov. 1782 (ibid. 38594, fos. 1–44). Nor did Wilkes join the reformist Society for Promoting Constitutional Information, founded in 1780 (T. 11/1133). I owe this reference to Dr Martin Fitzpatrick.

70. BL Add. MSS 30877, fo. 90.
71. Guildhall MSS 3332(2), 367.
72. BL Add. MSS 30872, fos. 190, 222–4.
73. Cobbett, *Parl. Hist.*, xxii. 1407–10.
74. Wraxall, *Historical Memoirs*, ii. 298–9.
75. *Morning Herald*, 10 Aug. 1782.
76. Ibid. 13 Nov. 1782.
77. Ibid. 28 Jan. 1783.
78. Ibid. 27 Feb. and 15 Mar. 1783.
79. Ibid. 6 Mar. and 8 Apr. 1783.
80. Debrett, *Parl. Reg.*, xii. 356–66. In 1773 Wilkes in the Court of Common Council had attacked North's milder India Regulating Bill with similar vehemence (*London Evening Post*, 29 May 1773); cited and quoted in Bowen, *Revenue and Reform*, 176.
81. Wraxall, *Historical Memoirs*, iv. 575–8.
82. *Morning Post*, 27 Jan. 1784.
83. Wraxall, *Historical Memoirs*, iv. 815.
84. [BL] *Catalogue of Political and Personal Satires*, iv, no. 6568.
85. BL Add. MSS 30872, fo. 241.
86. *Morning Herald*, 23 Apr. 1784.
87. Namier and Brooke, *House of Commons 1754–1790*, i. 331. Variant contemporary totals were Mainwaring 2,118, Wilkes 1,825, and Byng 1,751 in the *Morning Herald*, 24 Apr. 1784; and Mainwaring 2,117, Wilkes 1,858, and Byng 1,787 in the *Public Advertiser*, 24 Apr. 1784.
88. *Morning Herald*, 26 Apr. 1784.
89. *Public Advertiser*, 27 Apr. 1784.
90. Wilkes MSS (Clements), iv (unnumbered): 5 Oct. 1784, Wilkes to [the Earl of Buchan].
91. BL Add. MSS 30872, fo. 261.
92. Debrett, *Parl. Reg.*, xviii. 85.
93. BL Add. MSS 30874, fo. 8.
94. Stockdale, *Debates*, i, Appendix, 8; xii. 49.
95. Laprade, *Parliamentary Papers of John Robinson 1774–1784*, 68.
96. Wilkes voted for the ministry in the famous 1786 tie over the Duke of Richmond's naval dockyard scheme, but was absent during the Regency Bill Crisis of 1788–9 (Debrett, *Parl. Reg.*, xix. 228–30; xxv. 296).
97. For evidence of this friendship see BL Add. MSS 30866, fo. 197; 30874, fos. 219–20; 30877, fo. 104; Almon, *Wilkes*, v. 1–4.
98. For this episode see Stockdale, *Debates*, xii. 35–50; and Wraxall, *Posthumous Memoirs*, ii. 326–8.
99. BL Add. MSS 30873, fo. 209.
100. *The World*, 20 Mar. and 17 June 1790; *Gazetteer*, 29 June 1790.
101. *The World*, 18 June 1790; BL Add. MSS 30877, fo. 98.
102. *The World*, 17 and 18 June 1790.

103. BL Add. MSS 30873, fo. 209. For the confidence of a supporter 'that you may continue member so many more years as you have already been' see ibid. 30874, fo. 26.
104. *Public Advertiser*, 24 June 1790.
105. *Gazetteer*, 29 June 1790.
106. *Public Advertiser*, 26 and 29 June 1790.
107. *The World*, 8 July 1790.
108. Ibid. 4 Dec. 1790.
109. Almon, *Wilkes*, v. 161–205.
110. Ibid. 156–9.
111. *Morning Post*, 19 Apr. 1794.
112. Ibid. 13 June 1794.
113. Ibid. 24 June 1794.

Chapter 12

1. Treloar, *Wilkes and the City*, 175–8, 182–3, 188.
2. Ibid. 198–9. I have found no press reports of any relevant debates.
3. *Rockingham Memoirs*, ii. 235–7.
4. Almon, *Wilkes*, v. 82–5.
5. BL Add. MSS 30872, fo. 91.
6. Ibid., fos. 92–3.
7. Almon, *Wilkes*, v. 85.
8. Ibid. 37.
9. Ibid.
10. Treloar, *Wilkes and the City*, 219.
11. Masters, *Chamberlain*, 61–2.
12. Treloar, *Wilkes and the City*, 219–20; *Morning Post*, 4 Mar. 1791. That cash balance, Treloar estimated, would produce an average income at 5% of £1,100, yet just earlier he judged the same profits to vary from £1,200 to £2,000, the figure stated in this text.
13. *Morning Post*, 11 June 1791.
14. Masters, *Chamberlain*, 64.
15. BL Add. MSS 30895, fos. 96–7.
16. Ibid., fos. 98–100; *Morning Post*, 27 June 1791.
17. BL Add. MSS 30895, fo. 98.
18. *Annual Register*, 39 (1797), 377.
19. *Morning Herald*, 30 Dec. 1797; *Gentleman's Magazine*, 68 (1798), 76.
20. BL Add. MSS 30872, fo. 22.
21. The *London Calendars* for 1785 and 1795 both name one principal clerk and four assistant clerks in the Inner Office, and one Clerk of the Chamber and a Yeoman of the Chamber in the Outer Office.
22. Masters, *Chamberlain*, 34–64, *passim*.
23. Almon, *Wilkes*, iv. 200–1; Treloar, *Wilkes and the City*, 205.
24. *Morning Post*, 1 and 10 Mar. 1784.

25. For this oration see Almon, *Wilkes*, iv. 201–4. Some others are printed ibid. 204–16.

26. Ibid. 200; v. 87.

27. BL Add. MSS 30876, fo. 139.

28. *Annual Register*, 39 (1797), 377.

29. *Gentleman's Magazine*, 67 (1797), 1077.

30. Almon, *Wilkes*, v. 147–9; BL Add. MSS 30874, fo. 33; Bleackley, *Wilkes*, 366.

31. BL Add. MSS 30871, fo. 212.

32. Wilkes MSS (Clements), ii, no. 67.

33. Almon, *Wilkes*, v. 152–5.

34. Wilkes MSS (Clements), iii, no. 23; Almon, *Wilkes*, v. 117.

35. BL Add. MSS 30874, fo. 112. During his French exile Wilkes had asked Cotes to make financial provision for her (ibid. 30868, fo. 40; Almon, *Wilkes*, ii. 60–1). And he may have continued to do so himself.

36. Almon, *Wilkes*, v. 118–22; Bleackley, *Wilkes*, 281.

37. Wilkes MSS (Clements), iii, no. 24.

38. BL Add. MSS 30872, fos. 276–9; 30873, fo. 134; Almon, *Wilkes*, v. 123–39; Bleackley, *Wilkes*, 394. In his will Wilkes left him only £100 (Almon, *Wilkes*, v. 90–1).

39. For more detail see Bleackley, *Wilkes*, 339–59.

40. BL Add. MSS 30880 B, fo. 71.

41. Almon, *Wilkes*, v. 140.

42. Wilkes MSS (Clements), ii, no. 115.

43. Almon, *Wilkes*, v. 86.

44. BL Add. MSS 30866, fos. 194–215.

45. Quoted in Bleackley, *Wilkes*, 396–7.

46. BL Add. MSS 32566, fo. 153.

47. Ibid. 32568, fo. 24.

48. *Gentleman's Magazine*, 68 (1798), 81.

49. BL Add. MSS 30866; partly printed, Treloar, *Wilkes and the City*, 259–89. He had been elected to a number of societies, including the Freemasons in 1769 (ibid. 73).

50. Wraxall, *Historical Memoirs*, ii. 297.

51. Hill and Powell, *Boswell's Life of Johnson*, iii. 64–79. They met again on 8 May 1781, but Johnson had prior engagements for a third encounter Boswell planned at Wilkes's own house (ibid., iv. 101–7, 224).

52. Wilkes was only told of this compliment after Mansfield's death ten years later (BL Add. MSS 30874, fo. 92).

53. *Annual Register*, 39 (1797), 370.

54. Deane, *Sales Catalogues*, 89–123.

55. Wilkes MSS (Clements), iii, no. 26.

56. Ibid., nos. 2, 9a, 11.

57. Deane, *Sales Catalogues*, 117–78.

58. Almon, *Parl. Reg.*, xi. 30.

59. Ibid., vii. 127–30. James Harris, himself a champion of the British Museum,

noted that ''Twas not ill said by Wilkes speaking on the Museum Bill in April 1777 that the three great enemies to literature and the fine arts, were stupidity, ignorance and superstition' (Malmesbury MSS, undated memo).

60. Williamson, *Wilkes*, 187.
61. Almon, *Parl. Reg.*, vii. 130–1.
62. Ibid. 141–2.
63. *Gentleman's Magazine*, 68 (1798), 77.
64. Almon, *Wilkes*, iv. 218–21.
65. BL Add. MSS 30873, fo. 114.
66. Ibid., fos. 193–4, 202, 206, 207–8; 30874, fos. 6, 9, 12; Almon, *Wilkes*, iv. 226.
67. BL Add. MSS 30874, fo. 38; Almon, *Wilkes*, iv. 231–5. Almon, ibid. 230, stated that it was the Austrian ambassador Count Revicsky who persuaded Wilkes to publish the two classical works.
68. *Gentleman's Magazine*, 60 (1790), 1013. For contemporary and modern criticism of Wilkes as a classical scholar see Bleackley, *Wilkes*, 385–6.
69. BL Add. MSS 30874, fos. 192–3.
70. *Gentleman's Magazine*, 68 (1798), 81.
71. Almon, *Wilkes*, v. 105–16; Bleackley, *Wilkes*, 390.
72. *Gentleman's Magazine*, 54 (1784), 517.
73. Bleackley, *Wilkes*, 368–9.
74. BL Add. MSS 30874, fos. 103, 107.
75. Treloar, *Wilkes and the City*, 214; Trench, *Portrait of a Patriot*, 31–2.
76. *Annual Register*, 39 (1797), 377. For a cartoon of him in precisely that attire, dated 1797, see Bleackley, *Wilkes*, 396. The same report prefaced that statement with the comment that 'notwithstanding the defects of his person, Mr Wilkes at one time actually set the fashions, and introduced blue hair powder on his return from France'. But it concluded with this remark: 'Like most of the old school, he never descended from the dignity of a cocked hat, and it is but of late that he abjured the long-exploded fashion of wearing a gold button and loop.'
77. Bleackley, *Wilkes*, 380–1, 390.
78. Almon, *Wilkes*, iv. 225, 331–3; v. 77–9; Bleackley, *Wilkes*, 379–80; Treloar, *Wilkes and the City*, 210–13.
79. Wilkes MSS (Clements), iv (unnumbered).
80. Fitzgerald, *Wilkes*, ii. 297; Almon, *Wilkes*, v. 152.
81. Ibid. 87. I have measured the distance on an 18th-cent. map of London.
82. *Annual Register*, 39 (1797), 376–7.
83. Almon, *Wilkes*, v. 90–3.
84. Ibid. 94–7.
85. Ibid. 105–16.

Chapter 13

1. *Gentleman's Magazine*, 68 (1798), 81.
2. Ibid. 67 (1797), 1077.
3. *Annual Register*, 39 (1797), 377–8.

4. Bleackley, *Wilkes*, 403–5.

5. Wilkes MSS (Clements), iii, no. 23. The word 'gout' may be an Anglo-French pun.

6. Bleackley, *Wilkes*, 426.

7. Ibid. 358. This line of argument is echoed by Trench, *Portrait of a Patriot*, 31.

8. Walpole, *Last Journals*, i. 438.

9. Bleackley, *Wilkes*, 376.

10. Twiss, *Life of Eldon*, ii. 356. I owe the exact quotation to David Wilkinson. There is a problem about this piece of evidence. It is partly given in the present tense; yet Wilkes did not frequent the King's levees until 1782, whereas Glynn died in 1779.

11. *Burke Corr.*, i. 352.

12. Bleackley, *Wilkes*, 413.

Index